Contents

	Page
Acknowledgements	2
About this manual	2
Introduction to the Metro	2
General dimensions, weights and capacities	7
Buying spare parts and vehicle identification numbers	8
Tools and working facilities	9
Jacking and Towing	11
Recommended lubricants and fluids	13
Safety first!	14
Routine maintenance	15
Fault diagnosis	18
Chapter 1 Engine	22
Chapter 2 Cooling system	43
Chapter 3 Fuel and exhaust systems	50
Chapter 4 Ignition system	62
Chapter 5 Clutch	71
Chapter 6 Manual gearbox and automatic transmission	78
Chapter 7 Final drive	101
Chapter 8 Driveshafts	106
Chapter 9 Braking system	111
Chapter 10 Electrical system	123
Chapter 11 Suspension and steering	145
Chapter 12 Bodywork and fittings	158
Chapter 13 Supplement: revisions and information on later models	174
General repair procedures	252
Conversion factors	253
Index	254

Austin mini Metro 1.0 L

Austin Metro City

Austin mini Metro 1.3 HLS

Austin mini Metro 1.3 HLS

MG Metro 1300 with optional sunroof

MG Metro Turbo

General dimensions, weights and capacities

Dimensions
Turning circle (between kerbs)	33 ft 6 in (10.21 m)
Wheelbase	7 ft 4.625 in (2.251 m)
Overall length:	
All models except Vans	11 ft 2.05 in (3.405 m)
Vans	11 ft 2.00 in (3.403 m)
Overall width (excluding mirrors):	
Pre-1983 models	5 ft 0.875 in (1.546 m)
1983-on models (except Turbo)	5 ft 1.18 in (1.554 m)
Turbo	5 ft 1.5 in (1.563 m)
Overall height (approx):	
All 1.0 models, all Vans and MG Turbo	4 ft 5.5 in (1.360 m)
All 1.3 models except Vans and MG Turbo	4 ft 5.875 in (1.368 m)
Ground clearance (approx):	
Manual transmission (early models)	4.375 in (112 mm)
Manual transmission (later models)	5.906 in (150 mm)
Automatic transmission	5.750 in (146 mm)
Vans	5.315 in (135 mm) minimum

Weights
Kerb weights (approx, with full fuel tank):	
Metro City 3-door	1594 lb (723 kg)
Metro 1.3 HLE	1814 lb (823 kg)
Metro	1620 lb (735 kg)
Metro Van	1632 lb (740 kg)
Metro L	1638 lb (743 kg)
Metro 1.0 HLE	1646 lb (747 kg)
Metro City 5-door	1798 lb (816 kg)
Metro 1.3 HL and 1.3S	1662 lb (754 kg)
Metro 1.3L and 1.3 HLS 3-door	1695 lb (769 kg)
Metro 1.3L 5-door	1816 lb (824 kg)
MG1300	1711 lb (776 kg)
MG Turbo	1852 lb (840 kg)
Metro Vanden Plas	1731 lb (785 kg)
Metro Automatic	1773 lb (804 kg)
Maximum braked trailer weight (subject to local legislation):	
Metro 1.0 HLE	1433 lb (650 kg)
Metro 1.0 Van	1896 lb (860 kg)
All other 1.0 models	1874 lb (850 kg)
Metro 1.3 Van	1929 lb (875 kg)
Metro Automatic	1433 lb (650 kg)
All other 1.3 models	2095 lb (950 kg)
Maximum vehicle loading:	
Passenger vehicles	705 lb (320 kg)
Metro 1.0 Van	794 lb (360 kg)
Metro 1.3 Van	882 lb (400 kg)
Maximum roof rack load	106 lb (48 kg)

Capacities (approx)
Engine/manual gearbox oil (without filter)	8.5 pints (4.8 litres)
Oil filter (manual gearbox)	0.6 pint (0.3 litre)
Engine/automatic transmission oil (without filter)	8.8 pints (5.0 litres)
Oil filter (automatic transmission)	1.0 pint (0.6 litre)
Cooling system (including heater)	8.5 pints (4.8 litres)
Fuel tank	6.6 gallons (30 litres)

Buying spare parts
and vehicle identification numbers

Buying spare parts

Spare parts are available from many sources, for example: BL garages, other garages and accessory shops, and motor factors. Our advice regarding spare parts is as follows:

Officially appointed BL garages – This is the best source of parts which are peculiar to your car and are otherwise generally not available (eg complete cylinder heads, internal gearbox components, badges, interior trim etc). It is also the only place at which you should buy parts if your car is still under warranty; non-BL parts may invalidate the warranty. To be sure of obtaining the correct parts it will always be necessary to give the storeman your car's engine number and chassis number, and if possible, to take the old part along for positive identification. Many parts are available under a factory exchange scheme – any parts returned should always be clean! It obviously makes good sense to go to the specialists on your car for this type of part as they are best equipped to supply you.

Other garages and accessory shops – These are often very good places to buy material and components needed for the maintenance of your car (eg oil filters, spark plugs, bulbs, drivebelts, oil and grease, touch-up paint, filler paste etc). They also sell general accessories, usually have convenient opening hours, charge lower prices and can often be found not far from home.

Motor factors – Good factors will stock all the more important components which wear out relatively quickly (eg clutch components, pistons, valves, exhaust systems, brake pipes/seals and pads, etc). Motor factors will often provide new or reconditioned components on a part exchange basis – this can save a considerable amount of money.

Vehicle identification numbers

Modifications are a continuing and unpublicised process in vehicle manufacture quite apart from major model changes. Spare parts manuals and lists are compiled upon a numerical basis, the individual vehicle numbers being essential to correct identification of the component required.

When ordering spare parts, always give as much information as possible. Quote the car model, year of manufacture, body and engine numbers as appropriate.

The vehicle identification number is stamped on a plate on the left-hand side of the bonnet lock crossmember (photo).

The engine number is stamped on a plate attached to the front of the cylinder block by the alternator upper mounting.

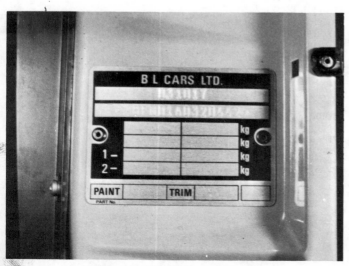

Vehicle identification number plate

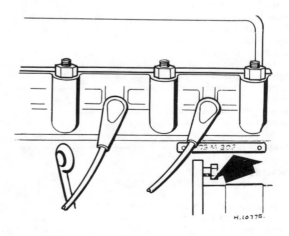

Engine number location (arrowed)

Tools and working facilities

Introduction

A selection of good tools is a fundamental requirement for anyone contemplating the maintenance and repair of a motor vehicle. For the owner who does not possess any, their purchase will prove a considerable expense, offsetting some of the savings made by doing-it-yourself. However, provided that the tools purchased are of good quality, they will last for many years and prove an extremely worthwhile investment.

To help the average owner to decide which tools are needed to carry out the various tasks detailed in this manual, we have compiled three lists of tools under the following headings: *Maintenance and minor repair, Repair and overhaul,* and *Special.* The newcomer to practical mechanics should start off with the *Maintenance and minor repair* tool kit and confine himself to the simpler jobs around the vehicle. Then, as his confidence and experience grow, he can undertake more difficult tasks, buying extra tools as, and when, they are needed. In this way, a *Maintenance and minor repair* tool kit can be built-up into a *Repair and overhaul* tool kit over a considerable period of time without any major cash outlays. The experienced do-it-yourselfer will have a tool kit good enough for most repair and overhaul procedures and will add tools from the *Special* category when he feels the expense is justified by the amount of use these tools will be put to.

It is obviously not possible to cover the subject of tools fully here. For those who wish to learn more about tools and their use there is a book entitled *How to Choose and Use Car Tools* available from the publishers of this manual.

Maintenance and minor repair tool kit

The tools given in this list should be considered as a minimum requirement if routine maintenance, servicing and minor repair operations are to be undertaken. We recommend the purchase of combination spanners (ring one end, open-ended the other); although more expensive than open-ended ones, they do give the advantages of both types of spanner.

Combination spanners - 10, 11, 12, 13, 14 & 17 mm
Combination spanners — $\frac{7}{16}$, $\frac{1}{2}$, $\frac{9}{16}$, $\frac{5}{8}$, $\frac{3}{4}$, $\frac{13}{16}$, $\frac{7}{8}$ and $\frac{15}{16}$ in AF
Adjustable spanner - 9 inch
Spark plug spanner (with rubber insert)
Spark plug gap adjustment tool
Set of feeler gauges
Brake adjuster spanner
Brake bleed nipple spanner
Screwdriver - 4 in long x $\frac{1}{4}$ in dia (flat blade)
Screwdriver - 4 in long x $\frac{1}{4}$ in dia (cross blade)
Combination pliers - 6 inch
Hacksaw (junior)

Tyre pump
Tyre pressure gauge
Grease gun
Oil can
Fine emery cloth (1 sheet)
Wire brush (small)
Funnel (medium size)

Repair and overhaul tool kit

These tools are virtually essential for anyone undertaking any major repairs to a motor vehicle, and are additional to those given in the *Maintenance and minor repair* list. Included in this list is a comprehensive set of sockets. Although these are expensive they will be found invaluable as they are so versatile - particularly if various drives are included in the set. We recommend the $\frac{1}{2}$ in square-drive type, as this can be used with most proprietary torque spanners. If you cannot afford a socket set, even bought piecemeal, then inexpensive tubular box wrenches are a useful alternative.

The tools in this list will occasionally need to be supplemented by tools from the *Special* list.

Sockets (or box spanners) to cover range in previous list
Reversible ratchet drive (for use with sockets)
Extension piece, 10 inch (for use with sockets)
Universal joint (for use with sockets)
Torque wrench (for use with sockets)
Mole wrench - 8 inch
Ball pein hammer
Soft-faced hammer, plastic or rubber
Screwdriver - 6 in long x $\frac{5}{16}$ in dia (flat blade)
Screwdriver - 2 in long x $\frac{5}{16}$ in square (flat blade)
Screwdriver - 1$\frac{1}{2}$ in long x $\frac{1}{4}$ in dia (cross blade)
Screwdriver - 3 in long x $\frac{1}{8}$ in dia (electricians)
Pliers - electricians side cutters
Pliers - needle nosed
Pliers - circlip (internal and external)
Cold chisel - $\frac{1}{2}$ inch
Scriber
Scraper
Centre punch
Pin punch
Hacksaw
Valve grinding tool
Steel rule/straight-edge
Allen keys
Selection of files
Wire brush (large)
Axle-stands
Jack (strong scissor or hydraulic type)

Special tools

The tools in this list are those which are not used regularly, are expensive to buy, or which need to be used in accordance with their manufacturers' instructions. Unless relatively difficult mechanical jobs are undertaken frequently. it will not be economic to buy many of these tools. Where this is the case, you could consider clubbing together with friends (or joining a motorists' club) to make a joint purchase, or borrowing the tools against a deposit from a local garage or tool hire specialist.

The following list contains only those tools and instruments freely available to the public, and not those special tools produced by the vehicle manufacturer specifically for its dealer network. You will find occasional references to these manufacturers' special tools in the text of this manual. Generally, an alternative method of doing the job without the vehicle manufacturers' special tool is given. However, sometimes, there is no alternative to using them. Where this is the case and the relevant tool cannot be bought or borrowed you will have to entrust the work to a franchised garage.

Valve spring compressor
Piston ring compressor
Balljoint separator
Universal hub/bearing puller
Impact screwdriver
Micrometer and/or vernier gauge
Dial gauge
Stroboscopic timing light
Dwell angle meter/tachometer
Universal electrical multi-meter
Cylinder compression gauge
Lifting tackle
Trolley jack
Light with extension lead

Buying tools

For practically all tools, a tool dealer is the best source since he will have a very comprehensive range compared with the average garage or accessory shop. Having said that, accessory shops often offer excellent quality tools at discount prices, so it pays to shop around.

Remember, you don't have to buy the most expensive items on the shelf, but it is always advisable to steer clear of the very cheap tools. There are plenty of good tools around at reasonable prices, so ask the proprietor or manager of the shop for advice before making a purchase.

Care and maintenance of tools

Having purchased a reasonable tool kit, it is necessary to keep the tools in a clean serviceable condition. After use, always wipe off any dirt, grease and metal particles using a clean, dry cloth, before putting the tools away. Never leave them lying around after they have been used. A simple tool rack on the garage or workshop wall, for items such as screwdrivers and pliers is a good idea. Store all normal spanners and sockets in a metal box. Any measuring instruments, gauges, meters, etc, must be carefully stored where they cannot be damaged or become rusty.

Take a little care when tools are used. Hammer heads inevitably become marked and screwdrivers lose the keen edge on their blades from time to time. A little timely attention with emery cloth or a file will soon restore items like this to a good serviceable finish.

Working facilities

Not to be forgotten when discussing tools, is the workshop itself. If anything more than routine maintenance is to be carried out, some form of suitable working area becomes essential.

It is appreciated that many an owner mechanic is forced by circumstances to remove an engine or similar item, without the benefit of a garage or workshop. Having done this, any repairs should always be done under the cover of a roof.

Wherever possible, any dismantling should be done on a clean flat workbench or table at a suitable working height.

Any workbench needs a vice: one with a jaw opening of 4 in (100 mm) is suitable for most jobs. As mentioned previously, some clean dry storage space is also required for tools, as well as the lubricants, cleaning fluids, touch-up paints and so on which become necessary.

Another item which may be required, and which has a much more general usage, is an electric drill with a chuck capacity of at least $\frac{5}{16}$ in (8 mm). This, together with a good range of twist drills, is virtually essential for fitting accessories such as wing mirrors and reversing lights.

Last, but not least, always keep a supply of old newspapers and clean, lint-free rags available, and try to keep any working area as clean as possible.

Jaw gap (in)	Spanner size
0.250	$\frac{1}{4}$ in AF
0.276	7 mm
0.313	$\frac{5}{16}$ in AF
0.315	8 mm
0.344	$\frac{11}{32}$ in AF; $\frac{1}{8}$ in Whitworth
0.354	9 mm
0.375	$\frac{3}{8}$ in AF
0.394	10 mm
0.433	11 mm
0.438	$\frac{7}{16}$ in AF
0.445	$\frac{3}{16}$ in Whitworth; $\frac{1}{4}$ in BSF
0.472	12 mm
0.500	$\frac{1}{2}$ in AF
0.512	13 mm
0.525	$\frac{1}{4}$ in Whitworth; $\frac{5}{16}$ in BSF
0.551	14 mm
0.563	$\frac{9}{16}$ in AF
0.591	15 mm
0.600	$\frac{5}{16}$ in Whitworth; $\frac{3}{8}$ in BSF
0.625	$\frac{5}{8}$ in AF
0.630	16 mm
0.669	17 mm
0.686	$\frac{11}{16}$ in AF
0.709	18 mm
0.710	$\frac{3}{8}$ in Whitworth, $\frac{7}{16}$ in BSF
0.748	19 mm
0.750	$\frac{3}{4}$ in AF
0.813	$\frac{13}{16}$ in AF
0.820	$\frac{7}{16}$ in Whitworth; $\frac{1}{2}$ in BSF
0.866	22 mm
0.875	$\frac{7}{8}$ in AF
0.920	$\frac{1}{2}$ in Whitworth; $\frac{9}{16}$ in BSF
0.938	$\frac{15}{16}$ in AF
0.945	24 mm
1.000	1 in AF
1.010	$\frac{9}{16}$ in Whitworth; $\frac{5}{8}$ in BSF
1.024	26 mm
1.063	$1\frac{1}{16}$ in AF; 27 mm
1.100	$\frac{5}{8}$ in Whitworth; $\frac{11}{16}$ in BSF
1.125	$1\frac{1}{8}$ in AF
1.181	30 mm
1.200	$\frac{11}{16}$ in Whitworth; $\frac{3}{4}$ in BSF
1.250	$1\frac{1}{4}$ in AF
1.260	32 mm
1.300	$\frac{3}{4}$ in Whitworth; $\frac{7}{8}$ in BSF
1.313	$1\frac{5}{16}$ in AF
1.390	$\frac{13}{16}$ in Whitworth; $\frac{15}{16}$ in BSF
1.417	36 mm
1.438	$1\frac{7}{16}$ in AF
1.480	$\frac{7}{8}$ in Whitworth; 1 in BSF
1.500	$1\frac{1}{2}$ in AF
1.575	40 mm; $\frac{15}{16}$ in Whitworth
1.614	41 mm
1.625	$1\frac{5}{8}$ in AF
1.670	1 in Whitworth; $1\frac{1}{8}$ in BSF
1.688	$1\frac{11}{16}$ in AF
1.811	46 mm
1.813	$1\frac{13}{16}$ in AF
1.860	$1\frac{1}{8}$ in Whitworth; $1\frac{1}{4}$ in BSF
1.875	$1\frac{7}{8}$ in AF
1.969	50 mm
2.000	2 in AF
2.050	$1\frac{1}{4}$ in Whitworth; $1\frac{3}{8}$ in BSF
2.165	55 mm
2.362	60 mm

Jacking and towing

To change a roadwheel, remove the spare wheel and tool kit from the well in the rear compartment (photo). Apply the handbrake and chock the wheel diagonally opposite the one to be changed. Make sure that the car is located on firm level ground. Lever off the hub cover (photo) and slightly loosen the wheel nuts with the spanner provided. Raise the jack and insert the peg in the nearest jacking point to the wheel being removed (photo). Using the handle provided, raise the jack until the wheel is free of the ground (photo). Unscrew the wheel nuts and remove the wheel, then remove the wheel finisher if fitted.

Fit the finisher to the spare wheel and fit the wheel on the studs. Fit and tighten the wheel nuts with their tapered ends towards the wheel. Lower the jack, then finally tighten the wheel nuts and refit the hub cover. Remove the chock, and refit the wheel and tool kit to the rear compartment.

Spare wheel compartment

Levering off the hub cover

Body jacking point

Jacking the car

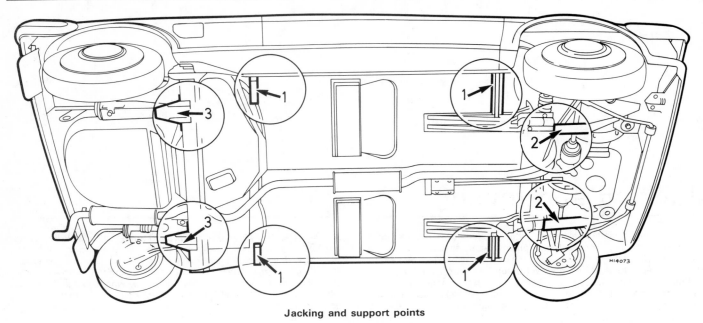

Jacking and support points

1   Jacking brackets   *2   Front jacking points (servicing)*   *3   Rear jacking points (servicing)*

Rear lashing eye – not to be used for towing

When jacking up the car with a trolley jack, lift under the widest points of the subframe (2 and 3 in the illustration). To raise both wheels at the same time use a 36 in (914 mm) length of square steel tubing placed beneath the subframes with a central spigot to fit the jack. *Never* jack up the car beneath the suspension arms. To support the car, place axle stands under the jacking points beneath the sills or under the widest points of the subframe.

Provided a fault has not developed in the gearbox or final drive, the car may be towed on its four wheels using either lashing eye located on the front subframe. The lashing eye located beneath the left-hand rear underbody is intended for use on a transporter only, and should not be used for towing another vehicle (photo).

On automatic transmission models always check that the engine oil level is correct before towing the car, and do not tow the car at speeds greater than 30 mph (50 km/h) or for a distance of more than 30 miles (50 km). If these conditions cannot be met, or if transmission damage is suspected, the car must be towed with the front wheels clear of the ground.

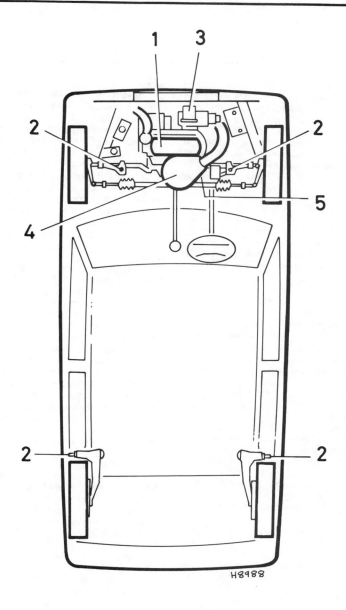

H8988

Recommended lubricants and fluids

Component or system	Lubricant type/specification	Duckhams recommendation
1 Engine/transmission*	Multigrade engine oil, viscosity SAE 15W/50 (pre August 1983) or 10W/40 (August 1983 on)	Duckhams QXR, Hypergrade, or 10W/40 Motor Oil
2 Suspension grease points	Multi-purpose lithium based grease	Duckhams LB 10
3 Distributor	Multigrade engine oil, viscosity SAE 15W/50 or 10W/40	Duckhams QXR, Hypergrade, or 10W/40 Motor Oil
4 Carburettor piston damper	Multigrade engine oil, viscosity SAE 15W/50 or 10W/40	Duckhams QXR, Hypergrade or 10W/40 Motor Oil
5 Brake and clutch fluid reservoirs	Hydraulic fluid to FMVSS 116 DOT 3 or SAE J1703C	Duckhams Universal Brake and Clutch Fluid

*Note: Austin Rover specify a 10W/40 oil to meet warranty requirements for models produced after August 1983. Duckhams QXR and 10W/40 Motor Oil are available to meet these requirements

Safety first!

Professional motor mechanics are trained in safe working procedures. However enthusiastic you may be about getting on with the job in hand, do take the time to ensure that your safety is not put at risk. A moment's lack of attention can result in an accident, as can failure to observe certain elementary precautions.

There will always be new ways of having accidents, and the following points do not pretend to be a comprehensive list of all dangers; they are intended rather to make you aware of the risks and to encourage a safety-conscious approach to all work you carry out on your vehicle.

Essential DOs and DON'Ts

DON'T rely on a single jack when working underneath the vehicle. Always use reliable additional means of support, such as axle stands, securely placed under a part of the vehicle that you know will not give way.

DON'T attempt to loosen or tighten high-torque nuts (e.g. wheel hub nuts) while the vehicle is on a jack; it may be pulled off.

DON'T start the engine without first ascertaining that the transmission is in neutral (or 'Park' where applicable) and the parking brake applied.

DON'T suddenly remove the filler cap from a hot cooling system – cover it with a cloth and release the pressure gradually first, or you may get scalded by escaping coolant.

DON'T attempt to drain oil until you are sure it has cooled sufficiently to avoid scalding you.

DON'T grasp any part of the engine, exhaust or catalytic converter without first ascertaining that it is sufficiently cool to avoid burning you.

DON'T allow brake fluid or antifreeze to contact vehicle paintwork.

DON'T syphon toxic liquids such as fuel, brake fluid or antifreeze by mouth, or allow them to remain on your skin.

DON'T inhale dust – it may be injurious to health (see *Asbestos* below).

DON'T allow any spilt oil or grease to remain on the floor – wipe it up straight away, before someone slips on it.

DON'T use ill-fitting spanners or other tools which may slip and cause injury.

DON'T attempt to lift a heavy component which may be beyond your capability – get assistance.

DON'T rush to finish a job, or take unverified short cuts.

DON'T allow children or animals in or around an unattended vehicle.

DO wear eye protection when using power tools such as drill, sander, bench grinder etc, and when working under the vehicle.

DO use a barrier cream on your hands prior to undertaking dirty jobs – it will protect your skin from infection as well as making the dirt easier to remove afterwards; but make sure your hands aren't left slippery.

DO keep loose clothing (cuffs, tie etc) and long hair well out of the way of moving mechanical parts.

DO remove rings, wristwatch etc, before working on the vehicle – especially the electrical system.

DO ensure that any lifting tackle used has a safe working load rating adequate for the job.

DO keep your work area tidy – it is only too easy to fall over articles left lying around.

DO get someone to check periodically that all is well, when working alone on the vehicle.

DO carry out work in a logical sequence and check that everything is correctly assembled and tightened afterwards.

DO remember that your vehicle's safety affects that of yourself and others. If in doubt on any point, get specialist advice.

IF, in spite of following these precautions, you are unfortunate enough to injure yourself, seek medical attention as soon as possible.

Asbestos

Certain friction, insulating, sealing, and other products – such as brake linings, brake bands, clutch linings, torque converters, gaskets, etc – contain asbestos. *Extreme care must be taken to avoid inhalation of dust from such products since it is hazardous to health.* If in doubt, assume that they *do* contain asbestos.

Fire

Remember at all times that petrol (gasoline) is highly flammable. Never smoke, or have any kind of naked flame around, when working on the vehicle. But the risk does not end there – a spark caused by an electrical short-circuit, by two metal surfaces contacting each other, by careless use of tools, or even by static electricity built up in your body under certain conditions, can ignite petrol vapour, which in a confined space is highly explosive.

Always disconnect the battery earth (ground) terminal before working on any part of the fuel or electrical system, and never risk spilling fuel on to a hot engine or exhaust.

It is recommended that a fire extinguisher of a type suitable for fuel and electrical fires is kept handy in the garage or workplace at all times. Never try to extinguish a fuel or electrical fire with water.

Fumes

Certain fumes are highly toxic and can quickly cause unconsciousness and even death if inhaled to any extent. Petrol (gasoline) vapour comes into this category, as do the vapours from certain solvents such as trichloroethylene. Any draining or pouring of such volatile fluids should be done in a well ventilated area.

When using cleaning fluids and solvents, read the instructions carefully. Never use materials from unmarked containers – they may give off poisonous vapours.

Never run the engine of a motor vehicle in an enclosed space such as a garage. Exhaust fumes contain carbon monoxide which is extremely poisonous; if you need to run the engine, always do so in the open air or at least have the rear of the vehicle outside the workplace.

If you are fortunate enough to have the use of an inspection pit, never drain or pour petrol, and never run the engine, while the vehicle is standing over it; the fumes, being heavier than air, will concentrate in the pit with possibly lethal results.

The battery

Never cause a spark, or allow a naked light, near the vehicle's battery. It will normally be giving off a certain amount of hydrogen gas, which is highly explosive.

Always disconnect the battery earth (ground) terminal before working on the fuel or electrical systems.

If possible, loosen the filler plugs or cover when charging the battery from an external source. Do not charge at an excessive rate or the battery may burst.

Take care when topping up and when carrying the battery. The acid electrolyte, even when diluted, is very corrosive and should not be allowed to contact the eyes or skin.

If you ever need to prepare electrolyte yourself, always add the acid slowly to the water, and never the other way round. Protect against splashes by wearing rubber gloves and goggles.

When jump starting a car using a booster battery, for negative earth (ground) vehicles, connect the jump leads in the following sequence: First connect one jump lead between the positive (+) terminals of the two batteries. Then connect the other jump lead first to the negative (–) terminal of the booster battery, and then to a good earthing (ground) point on the vehicle to be started, at least 18 in (45 cm) from the battery if possible. Ensure that hands and jump leads are clear of any moving parts, and that the two vehicles do not touch. Disconnect the leads in the reverse order.

Mains electricity

When using an electric power tool, inspection light etc, which works from the mains, always ensure that the appliance is correctly connected to its plug and that, where necessary, it is properly earthed (grounded). Do not use such appliances in damp conditions and, again, beware of creating a spark or applying excessive heat in the vicinity of fuel or fuel vapour.

Ignition HT voltage

A severe electric shock can result from touching certain parts of the ignition system, such as the HT leads, when the engine is running or being cranked, particularly if components are damp or the insulation is defective. Where an electronic ignition system is fitted, the HT voltage is much higher and could prove fatal.

Routine maintenance

Maintenance is essential for ensuring safety and desirable for the purpose of getting the best in terms of performance and economy from your car. Over the years the need for periodic lubrication has been greatly reduced if not totally eliminated. This has unfortunately tended to lead some owners to think that because no such action is required, the items either no longer exist, or will last forever. This is certainly not the case; it is essential to carry out regular visual examination as comprehensively as possible in order to spot any possible defects at an early stage before they develop into major expensive repairs.

Every 250 miles (400 km) or weekly – whichever comes first

Engine/gearbox
Check the level of the oil and top up if necessary (photos)
Check the coolant level and top-up if necessary (photo)
Check the level of electrolyte in the battery and top-up as necessary (photo)
Check the level of fluid in the clutch master cylinder reservoir, and top-up as necessary (photo)

Oil dipstick markings

Topping up the engine oil level

Topping up the coolant level

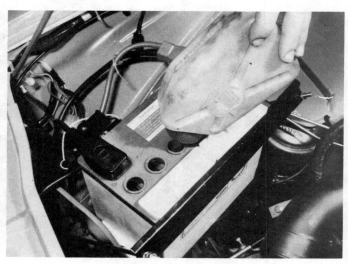

Topping up the battery electrolyte level

Checking the tyre pressure

Windscreen washer fluid reservoir

Tailgate washer fluid reservoir

Topping up brake fluid level

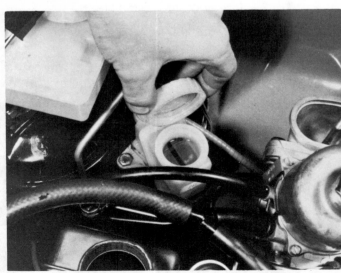

Clutch fluid reservoir

Topping up the carburettor piston damper

Tyres

Check the tyre pressures (photo)
Visually examine the tyres for wear and damage

Lights and wipers

Check that all the lights work
Clean the headlamps
Check the windscreen/tailgate washer fluid levels and top-up if necessary (photos)

Brakes

Check the level of fluid in the brake master cylinder reservoir, and top-up as necessary (photo)

Every 6000 miles (10 000 km) or 6 months – whichever comes first. Automatic transmission and Turbo models only

Engine/gearbox

Change the engine oil, clean the magnetic drain plug and renew the filter
Top-up the carburettor piston damper
Check the operation of the transmission parking pawl (not Turbo)

Every 12 000 miles (20 000 km) or 12 months – whichever comes first

Engine/gearbox

Renew the air cleaner element
Top-up the carburettor piston damper (photo)
Check and adjust the valve clearances
Check and adjust the engine idle speed and carburettor mixture
Change the engine oil, clean the magnetic drain plug and renew the filter
Check the alternator and water pump drivebelt; renew and retension if necessary
Check and lubricate the throttle and choke controls
Check the fuel supply system for damage, deterioration, and leaks
Renew fuel line filter (Turbo only)
Check the cooling system and hoses for leaks
Check, and adjust if necessary, the clutch return stop clearance
Check the clutch hydraulic pipes for leaks
Check the exhaust system for leaks and security
Renew the spark plugs
Check and adjust the distributor contact points (when applicable)
Lubricate the distributor
Check, and if necessary adjust, the ignition timing
Clean the distributor cap and coil
Check the driveshaft gaiters for splits and leakage

Electrical

Check the battery condition. Clean and grease the terminals
Check, and if necessary adjust, the headlamp alignment

Brakes

Visually check the hydraulic circuit for damage, deterioration and leaks
Check the operation of the brake pad wear warning indicators
Check the front brake pads and discs for wear
Check the rear brake linings and drums for wear
Lubricate the handbrake linkages and cables
Adjust the rear brakes
Check the handbrake operation and adjust if necessary
Check the brake servo hose for condition and security

Steering and suspension

Grease the front and rear suspension pivots
Check the Hydragas units and lines for leaks
Check the rack-and-pinion unit for security and damage
Check the steering joints and arms for wear and damage
Check the steering gaiters for splits and leakage
Check, and if necessary adjust, the front wheel alignment
Check the suspension joints and mountings for wear and damage

Body

Lubricate the door locks and hinges
Lubricate the foot pedal pivots
Check the door locks and bonnet lock for operation
Clear any debris from the heater air intake and drain
Check the windows for operation

Seat belts

Check the seat belts for security and condition

Every 18 000 miles (30 000 km) or 18 months – whichever comes first

Brakes

Renew the brake fluid in the brake hydraulic circuit

Every 24 000 miles (40 000 km) or 24 months – whichever comes first

Engine

Drain the cooling system and flush it, then refill with new antifreeze solution
Renew the oil filler cap
Renew the distributor contact points (when applicable)
Renew the alternator drivebelt

Every 36 000 miles (60 000 km) or 3 years – whichever comes first

Brakes

Renew the brake fluid and all the fluid seals and flexible hoses in the brake hydraulic circuit

Fault diagnosis

Introduction

The car owner who does his or her maintenance according to the recommended schedules should not have to use this section of the manual very often. Modern component reliability is such that, provided those items subject to wear or deterioration are inspected or renewed at the specified intervals, sudden failure is comparatively rare. Faults do not usually just happen as a result of sudden failure, but develop over a period of time. Major mechanical failures in particular are usually preceded by characteristic symptoms over hundreds or even thousands of miles. Those components which do occasionally fail without warning are often small and easily carried in the car.

With any fault finding, the first step is to decide where to begin investigations. Sometimes this is obvious, but on other occasions a little detective work will be necessary. The owner who makes half a dozen haphazard adjustments or replacements may be successful in curing a fault (or its symptoms), but he will be none the wiser if the fault recurs and he may well have spent more time and money than was necessary. A calm and logical approach will be found to be more satisfactory in the long run. Always take into account any warning signs or abnormalities that may have been noticed in the period preceding the fault – power loss, high or low gauge readings, unusual noises or smells, etc – and remember that failure of components such as fuses or spark plugs may only be pointers to some underlying fault.

The pages which follow here are intended to help in cases of failure to start or breakdown on the road. There is also a Fault Diagnosis Section at the end of each Chapter which should be consulted if the preliminary checks prove unfruitful. Whatever the fault, certain principles apply. These are as follows:

Verify the fault. This is simply a matter of being sure that you know what the symptoms are before starting work. This is particularly important if you are investigating a fault for someone else who may not have described it very accurately.

Don't overlook the obvious. For example, if the car won't start, is there petrol in the tank? (Don't take anyone else's word on this particular point, and don't trust the fuel gauge either!) If an electrical fault is indicated, look for loose or broken wires before digging out the test gear.

Cure the disease, not the symptom. Substituting a flat battery with a fully charged one will get you off the hard shoulder, but if the underlying cause is not attended to, the new battery will go the same way. Similarly, changing oil-fouled spark plugs for a new set will get you moving again, but remember that the reason for the fouling (if it wasn't simply an incorrect grade of plug) will have to be established and corrected.

Don't take anything for granted. Particularly, don't forget that a 'new' component may itself be defective (especially if it's been rattling around in the boot for months), and don't leave components out of a fault diagnosis sequence just because they are new or recently fitted. When you do finally diagnose a difficult fault, you'll probably realise that all the evidence was there from the start.

Electrical faults

Electrical faults can be more puzzling than straightforward mechanical failures, but they are no less susceptible to logical analysis if the basic principles of operation are understood. Car electrical wiring exists in extremely unfavourable conditions – heat, vibration and chemical attack – and the first things to look for are loose or corroded connections, and broken or chafed wires, especially where the wires pass through holes in the bodywork or are subject to vibration.

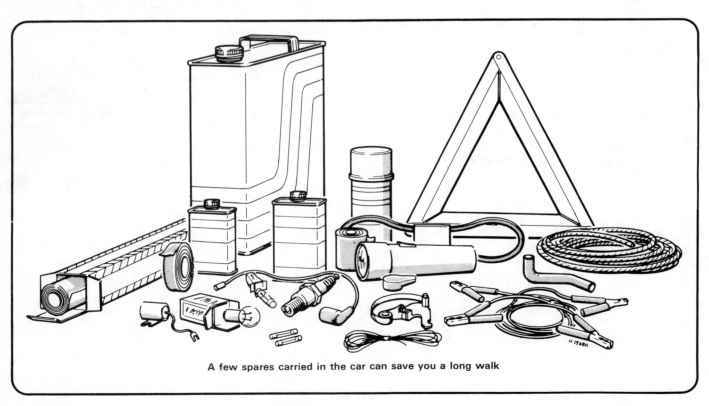

A few spares carried in the car can save you a long walk

All metal-bodies cars in current production have one pole of the battery 'earthed', ie connected to the car bodywork, and in nearly all modern cars it is the negative (–) terminal. The various electrical components – motors, bulb holders etc – are also connected to earth, either by means of a lead or directly by their mountings. Electric current flows through the component and then back to the battery via the car bodywork. If the component mounting is loose or corroded, or if a good path back to the battery is not available, the circuit will be incomplete and malfunction will result. The engine and/or gearbox are also earthed by means of flexible metal straps to the body or subframe; if these straps are loose or missing, starter motor, generator and ignition trouble may result.

Assuming the earth return to be satisfactory, electrical faults will be due either to component malfunction or to defects in the current supply. Individual components are dealt with in Chapter 10. If supply wires are broken or cracked internally this results in an open-circuit, and the easiest way to check for this is to bypass the suspect wire temporarily with a length of wire having a crocodile clip or suitable connector at each end. Alternatively, a 12V test lamp can be used to verify the presence of supply voltage at various points along the wire and the break can thus be isolated.

If a bare portion of a live wire touches the car bodywork or other earthed metal part, the electricity will take the low-resistance path thus formed back to the battery: this is known as a short-circuit. Hopefully a short-circuit will blow a fuse, but otherwise it may cause burning of the insulation (and possibly further short-circuits) or even a fire. This is why it is inadvisable to bypass persistently blowing fuses with silver foil or wire.

Spares and tool kit

Most cars are only supplied with sufficient tools for wheel changing; the *Maintenance and minor repair* tool kit detailed in *Tools and working facilities*, with the addition of a hammer, is probably sufficient for those repairs that most motorists would consider attempting at the roadside. In addition a few items which can be fitted without too much trouble in the event of breakdown should be carried. Experience and available space will modify the list below, but the following may save having to call on professional assistance:

Spark plugs, clean and correctly gapped
HT lead and plug cap – long enough to reach the plug furthest from the distributor
Distributor rotor, condenser and contact breaker points
Drivebelt – emergency type may suffice
Spare fuses
Set of principal light bulbs
Tin of radiator sealer and hose bandage
Exhaust bandage
Roll of insulating tape
Length of soft iron wire
Length of electrical flex
Torch or inspection lamp (can double as test lamp)
Battery jump leads
Tow-rope
Ignition waterproofing aerosol
Litre of engine oil
Sealed can of hydraulic fluid
Emergency windscreen
'Jubilee' (worm drive) hose clips
Tube of filler paste

If spare fuel is carried, a can designed for the purpose should be used to minimise risks of leakage and collision damage. A first aid kit and a warning triangle, whilst not at present compulsory in the UK, are obviously sensible items to carry in addition to the above.

When touring abroad it may be advisable to carry additional spares which, even if you cannot fit them yourself, could save having to wait while parts are obtained. The items below may be worth considering:

Choke and throttle cables
Cylinder head gasket
Alternator brushes
Tyre valve core

One of the motoring organisations will be able to advise on availability of fuel etc in foreign countries.

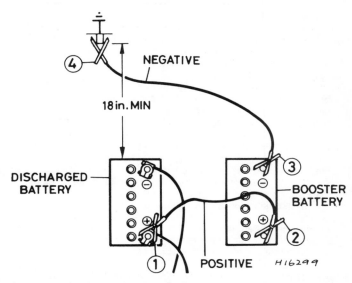

Jump start lead connections for negative earth vehicles – connect leads in the order shown

Checking for a spark while cranking the engine

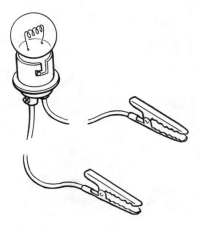

A simple test lamp is useful for tracing electrical faults

Engine will not start

Engine fails to turn when starter operated
Flat battery (recharge, use jump leads, or push start) .
Battery terminals loose or corroded
Battery earth to body defective
Engine earth strap loose or broken
Starter motor (or solenoid) wiring loose or broken
Ignition/starter switch faults
Major mechanical failure (seizure) or long disuse (piston rings rusted to bores)
Starter or solenoid internal fault (see Chapter 10).

Starter motor turns engine slowly
Partially discharged battery (recharge, use jump leads, or push start)
Battery terminals loose or corroded
Battery earth to body defective
Engine earth strap loose
Starter motor (or solenoid) wiring loose
Starter motor internal fault (see Chapter 10)

Starter motor (inertia) spins without turning engine
Flat battery
Starter motor pinion sticking on sleeve
Flywheel gear teeth damaged or worn
Starter motor mounting bolts loose

Engine turns normally but fails to start
Damp or dirty HT leads and distributor cap (crank engine and check for spark) (photo)
Dirty or incorrectly gapped CB points
No fuel in tank (check for delivery at carburettor) (photo)
Excessive choke (hot engine) or insufficient choke (cold engine)
Fouled or incorrectly gapped spark plugs (remove, clean and regap)
Other ignition system fault (See Chapter 4)
Other fuel system fault (see Chapter 3)
Poor compression (See Chapter 1)
Major mechanical failure

Engine fires but will not run
Insufficient choke (cold engine)
Air leaks at carburettor or inlet manifold

Fuel starvation (see Chapter 3)
Ignition fault (see Chapter 4)

Engine cuts out and will not restart

Engine cuts out suddenly – ignition fault
Loose or disconnected LT wires
Wet HT leads or distributor cap (after traversing water splash)
Coil or condenser failure (check for spark)
Other ignition fault (see Chapter 4)

Engine misfires before cutting out – fuel fault
Fuel tank empty
Fuel pump defective or feed blocked (check for delivery)
Fuel tank filler vent blocked (suction will be evident on releasing cap)
Carburettor needle valve sticking
Carburettor jets blocked (fuel contaminated)
Other fuel system fault (See Chapter 3)

Engine cuts out – other causes
Serious overheating
Major mechanical failure

Engine overheats

Ignition (no-charge) warning light illuminated
Slack or broken drivebelt – retension or renew (Chapter 2) (photo)

Ignition warning light not illuminated
Coolant loss due to internal or external leakage (see Chapter 2)
Thermostat defective
Low oil level
Brakes binding
Radiator clogged externally or internally
Electric cooling fan not operating correctly
Engine waterways clogged
Ignition timing incorrect or automatic advance malfunctioning
Mixture too weak

Note: *Do not add cold water to an overheated engine or damage may result.*

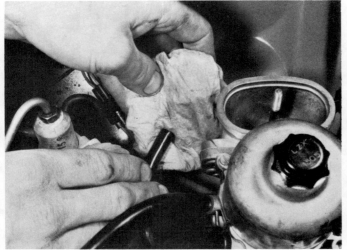

Checking for fuel delivery through the carburettor supply hose while an assistant cranks the engine

Checking the drivebelt tension

Low engine oil pressure

Warning light illuminated with engine running
Oil level low or incorrect grade
Defective sender unit
Wire to sender unit earthed
Engine overheating
Oil filter clogged or bypass valve defective
Oil pressure relief valve defective
Oil pick-up strainer clogged
Oil pump worn or mountings loose
Worn main or big-end bearings

Note: *Low oil pressure in a high-mileage engine at tickover is not necessarily a cause for concern. Sudden pressure loss at speed is far more significant. In any event, check the warning light sender before condemning the engine.*

Engine noises

Pre-ignition (pinking) on acceleration
Incorrect grade of fuel
Ignition timing incorrect
Distributor faulty or worn
Worn or maladjusted carburettor
Excessive carbon build-up in engine

Whistling or wheezing noises
Leaking vacuum hose
Leaking carburettor or manifold gasket
Blowing head gasket

Tapping or rattling
Incorrect valve clearances
Worn valve gear
Worn timing chain
Broken piston ring (ticking noise)

Knocking or thumping
Unintentional mechanical contact
Worn drivebelt
Peripheral component fault (alternator, water pump etc)
Worn big-end bearings (regular heavy knocking, perhaps less under load)
Worn main bearings (rumbling and knocking, perhaps worsening under load)
Piston slap (most noticeable when cold)

Chapter 1 Engine

For modifications and information applicable to later models, see Supplement at end of manual

Contents

Ancillary components – refitting 37
Ancillary components – removal 8
Camshaft – refitting 33
Camshaft – removal 13
Camshaft and tappets – examination and renovation 24
Crankcase ventilation system – description 18
Crankshaft and main bearings – examination and renovation 21
Crankshaft and main bearings – refitting 29
Crankshaft and main bearings – removal 17
Cylinder block and crankcase – examination and renovation 22
Cylinder head – decarbonising, valve grinding, and renovation 27
Cylinder head – dismantling 10
Cylinder head – reassembly and refitting 36
Cylinder head – removal 9
Engine – adjustment after major overhaul 40
Engine – refitting to gearbox 38
Engine – separation from gearbox 6
Engine dismantling – general 7
Engine/gearbox assembly – refitting 39
Engine/gearbox assembly – removal 5
Engine reassembly – general 28
Examination and renovation – general 19

Fault diagnosis – engine 42
Flywheel/torque converter – examination and renovation 26
General description 1
Major operations only possible after removal of the
engine/gearbox from the car 3
Major operations possible with the engine/gearbox in the car 2
Method of engine removal 4
Oil filter – refitting 31
Oil filter – removal 15
Oil pump – examination and renovation 20
Oil pump – refitting 32
Oil pump – removal 14
Pistons and connecting rods – examination and renovation 23
Pistons and connecting rods – refitting 30
Pistons and connecting rods – removal 16
Tappets (998 cc engine) – refitting 34
Tappets (998 cc engine) – removal 12
Timing cover, chain, and gears – examination and renovation 25
Timing cover, chain, and gears – refitting 35
Timing cover, chain, and gears – removal 11
Valve clearances – adjustment 41

Specifications

998 cc engine (Standard, L, and HLE models)

Type .... Four in-line, overhead valve

Bore .... 2.543 in (64. 59 mm)

Stroke .... 3.0 in (76.2 mm)

Capacity .... 998 cc (60.96 cu in)

Firing order .... 1 – 3 – 4 – 2

Compression ratio
Metro Standard (fleet option) .... 8.3 to 1
Metro Standard and L .... 9.6 to 1
Metro HLE .... 10.3 to 1

Crankshaft
Main journal diameter .... 1.7505 to 1.7512 in (44.46 to 44.48 mm)
Main bearing running clearance .... 0.0007 to 0.0029 in (0.018 to 0.074 mm)
Main journal minimum regrind diameter .... 1.7305 in (43.96 mm)
Crankpin journal diameter .... 1.6252 to 1.6259 in (41.28 to 41.298 mm)
Crankpin running clearance .... 0.001 to 0.0027 in (0.025 to 0.069 mm)
Crankpin minimum regrind diameter .... 1.6052 in (40.77 mm)
Endfloat .... 0.002 to 0.003 in (0.051 to 0.076 mm)

Connecting rods
Length between centres .... 5.75 in (146.05 mm)

Pistons
Skirt clearance in cylinder:
    Top .... 0.0021 to 0.0033 in (0.053 to 0.084 mm)
    Bottom .... 0.0004 to 0.0014 in (0.010 to 0.036 mm)
Oversizes available .... 0.010, 0.020, 0.030, and 0.040 in (0.254, 0.508, 0.762, and 1.016 mm)

Piston rings
Clearance in groove:
    Top compression .... 0.002 to 0.0035 in (0.051 to 0.089 mm)
    2nd and 3rd compression .... 0.002 to 0.004 in (0.051 to 0.102 mm)

End gap:
    Compression .... 0.007 to 0.012 in (0.178 to 0.305 mm)
    Oil control rails .... 0.014 to 0.041 in (0.38 to 1.04 mm)

Gudgeon pins
Fit in piston .... Hand push at 20°C (68°F)
Running clearance in connecting rod .... 0.0007 to 0.001 in (0.02 to 0.03 mm)

Camshaft
Journal diameter:
    Front .... 1.6655 to 1.6660 in (42.304 to 42.316 mm)
    Centre .... 1.62275 to 1.62325 in (41.218 to 41.231 mm)
    Rear .... 1.37275 to 1.3735 in (34.868 to 34.887 mm)
Running clearance in bearings .... 0.001 to 0.00225 in (0.025 to 0.057 mm)
Endfloat .... 0.003 to 0.007 in (0.076 to 0.178 mm)
Valve lift:
    Inlet .... 0.318 in (8.08 mm)
    Exhaust .... 0.300 in (7.62 mm)

Valves
Seat angle .... 45°
Head diameter:
    Inlet .... 1.093 to 1.098 in (27.76 to 27.89 mm)
    Exhaust .... 1.000 to 1.005 in (25.40 to 25.53 mm)
Stem diameter:
    Inlet .... 0.2793 to 0.2798 in (7.094 to 7.107 mm)
    Exhaust .... 0.2788 to 0.2793 in (7.082 to 7.094 mm)
Clearance in guide:
    Inlet .... 0.0015 to 0.0025 in (0.038 to 0.064 mm)
    Exhaust .... 0.002 to 0.003 in (0.051 to 0.076 mm)
Valve guides:
    Length .... 1.687 in (42.85 mm)
    Outside diameter .... 0.470 to 0.471 in (11.94 to 11.96 mm)
    Inside diameter .... 0.2813 to 0.2818 in (7.145 to 7.158 mm)
    Fitted height above head .... 0.594 in (15.09 mm)
Valve springs:
    Free length .... 1.95 in (49.53 mm)
Valve timing (at valve clearance of 0.021 in/0.53 mm):
    Inlet opens .... 9° BTDC
    Inlet closes .... 41° ABDC
    Exhaust opens .... 49° BBDC
    Exhaust closes .... 11° ATDC
Valve clearance (cold) .... 0.012 in (0.30 mm)

Lubrication system
Oil pump:
    Type .... Bi-rotor
    Outer rotor endfloat .... 0.005 in (0.127 mm)
    Inner rotor endfloat .... 0.005 in (0.127 mm)
    Outer rotor-to-body clearance .... 0.010 in (0.254 mm)
    Rotor lobe clearance .... 0.006 in (0.152 mm)
System pressure:
    Idling .... 15 lbf/in² (1.05 kgf/cm²)
    Running .... 60 lbf/in² (4.2 kgf/cm²)
Warning light switch operating pressure .... 6 to 10 lbf/in² (0.4 to 0.7 kgf/cm²)
Pressure relief valve operating pressure .... 60 lbf/in² (4.2 kgf/cm²)
Pressure relief valve spring free length .... 2.86 in (72.63 mm)
Oil type/specification* .... Multigrade engine oil, viscosity SAE 15W/50 (pre August 1983) or
10W/40 (August 1983 on) (Duckhams QXR, Hypergrade, or 10W/40
Motor Oil)

*__Note:__ *Austin Rover specify a 10W/40 oil to meet warranty requirements for models produced after August 1983. Duckhams QXR and 10W/40
Motor Oil are available to meet these requirements*

1275 cc engine (L, S and HLS models)
Specifications as 998 cc engine except for the following differences:

Bore .... 2.78 in (70.61 mm)

Stroke .... 3.2 in (81.28 mm)

Capacity .... 1275 cc (77.8 cu in)

Compression ratio .... 9.4 to 1

Crankshaft

Main journal diameter	2.0011 to 2.0017 in (50.83 to 50.84 mm)
Main bearing running clearance	0.0003 to 0.0024 in (0.008 to 0.076 mm)
Main journal minimum regrind diameter	1.9811 in (50.32 mm)
Crankpin journal diameter	1.7497 to 1.7504 in (44.44 to 44.46 mm)
Crankpin running clearance	0.0015 to 0.0032 in (0.0381 to 0.0813 mm)
Crankpin minimum regrind diameter	1.7297 in (43.93 mm)

Pistons

Skirt clearance in cylinder:	
Top	0.0029 to 0.0045 in (0.074 to 0.114 mm)
Bottom	0.0009 to 0.0025 in (0.023 to 0.064 mm)
Oversizes available	0.010 and 0.020 in (0.254 and 0.508 mm)

Piston rings

Clearance in groove:	
Top compression	0.0015 to 0.0035 in (0.038 to 0.089 mm)
2nd compression	0.0015 to 0.0035 in (0.038 to 0.089 mm)
End gap:	
Top compression	0.010 to 0.017 in (0.25 to 0.45 mm)
2nd compression	0.008 to 0.013 in (0.020 to 0.033 mm)
Oil control rails	0.015 to 0.041 in (0.38 to 1.04 mm)

Gudgeon pins

Fit in piston	Drop through to hand push at 20°C (68°F)
Interference fit in connecting rod	0.0008 to 0.0015 in (0.02 to 0.04 mm)

Camshaft

Valve lift:	
Inlet and exhaust	0.318 (8.08 mm)

Valves

Head diameter:	
Inlet	1.307 to 1.312 in (33.20 to 33.32 mm)
Exhaust	1.1515 to 1.1565 in (29.25 to 29.38 mm)
Valve guides:	
Fitted height above head	0.540 in (13.72 mm)
Valve timing (at valve clearance of 0.021 in/0.53 mm):	
Inlet opens	9° BTDC
Inlet closes	41° ABDC
Exhaust opens	55° BBDC
Exhaust closes	17° ATDC

All engines

Torque wrench settings

	lbf ft	kgf m
Brake servo pipe banjo	37	5.1
Camshaft locating plate	8	1.1
Camshaft nut	65	8.9
Connecting rod big-end – bolts	37	5.1
Connecting rod big-end – nuts	33	4.6
Crankshaft pulley bolt	75	10.3
Cylinder head nuts	50	6.9
Cylinder block side cover (998 cc only)	3.5	0.5
Front plate to bearing cap	5	0.7
Front plate to crankcase	16	2.2
Main bearing bolts	63	8.7
Manifold to cylinder head	16	2.2
Oil filter head nuts	16	2.2
Oil pipe banjo	57	7.8
Oil pressure switch	18	2.5
Oil pump bolts	8	1.1
Pressure relief valve nut	45	6.2
Oil separator to flywheel housing	15	2.0
Cylinder head bypass plug	12	1.7
Water jacket drain plug	27	3.7
Rocker cover	3.5	0.5
Rocker shaft pedestal	24	3.2
Valve clearance adjusting nut	16	2.2
Timing cover to front plate:		
$\frac{1}{4}$ in diameter	5	0.7
$\frac{5}{16}$ in diameter	12	1.7

1 General description

The engine is of four cylinder, in-line, overhead valve type mounted transversely at the front of the car and fitted over the gearbox. A low compression version is available for fleet use.

The crankshaft is of three bearing type, and the centre main bearing incorporates thrust washers to control crankshaft endfloat. A torsional damper is fitted.

The camshaft is chain driven from the crankshaft and is supported in three bearings. The timing chain tensioner is of spring plate and bonded rubber type. The valves are operated from the camshaft by pushrod and rocker arm.

The oil pump is driven from the rear (flywheel) end of the camshaft, and a skew gear on the camshaft drives the distributor via a driveshaft.

The main design differences between the 998 cc and 1275 cc engines are as follows:

(a) The 998 cc engine has side covers which can be removed to remove the tappets, whereas the 1275 cc engine has no side covers; the tappets can only be removed from the crankcase

(b) The 998 cc engine has diagonally split big-end bearings and fully floating gudgeon pins, whereas the 1275 cc engine has cross split big-end bearings and gudgeon pins which are an interference fit in the connecting rods

The engine has been designated the 'A Plus' since it is an improved version of the 'A-Series' engine fitted to BL Mini models. The improvements include a toughened crankshaft, a crankshaft torsional damper, and hard wearing exhaust valves and seatings. A fully closed crankcase ventilation system is employed, and piston blow-by gases are drawn into the inlet manifold via oil separators and a port on the carburettor.

2 Major operations possible with the engine/gearbox in the car

The following operations can be carried out without having to remove the engine/gearbox from the car:

(a) Removal and servicing of the cylinder head
(b) Removal of the timing cover, chain, and gears
(c) Removal of the tappets (cam followers) on the 998 cc engine only
(d) Removal of the flywheel and clutch (Chapter 5) or torque converter (Chapter 6)
(e) Renewal of the engine mountings

3 Major operations only possible after removal of the engine/gearbox from the car

The following operations can only be carried out after removal of the engine/gearbox from the car:

(a) Removal of the camshaft
(b) Removal of the oil pump
(c) Removal of the piston/connecting rod assemblies
(d) Renewal of the crankshaft main bearings and big-end bearings
(e) Removal of the tappets (cam followers) on the 1275 cc engine only

4 Method of engine removal

The engine and gearbox assembly must be lifted from the car as a complete unit, then the engine separated from the gearbox on the bench.

5 Engine/gearbox assembly – removal

1 Support the bonnet fully open.
2 Disconnect the battery negative then positive leads, and remove the battery as described in Chapter 10.

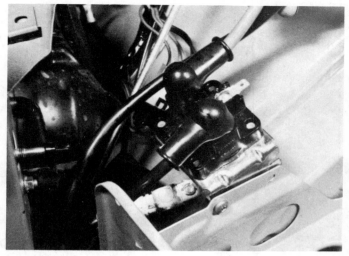
5.3 Removing the solenoid

5.10 Engine earth lead location

3 Remove the solenoid and place it to one side, then unbolt and remove the battery carrier (photo).
4 Drain the cooling system as described in Chapter 2.
5 Unscrew the drain plug and drain the engine/gearbox oil into a suitable container. Refit the drain plug.
6 Remove the radiator as described in Chapter 2.
7 Unbolt and remove the crossmember stay. Disconnect the bonnet lock cable and remove the crossmember.
8 Remove the air cleaner as described in Chapter 3.
9 Disconnect the exhaust system from the manifold with reference to Chapter 3.
10 Unbolt the engine earth lead from the flywheel housing (photo). Disconnect and remove the starter supply lead.
11 Disconnect and remove the hose from the water pump, expansion tank, and heater.
12 Disconnect the expansion tank vent pipe and heater hose from the thermostat housing.
13 Disconnect and plug the fuel supply hose from the fuel pump.
14 Where fitted, disconnect the brake servo vacuum hose from the inlet manifold.
15 Remove the clutch slave cylinder as described in Chapter 5, (manual gearbox models only) but leave it attached to the hydraulic hose.
16 Identify then disconnect the wiring from the coil low tension terminals, alternator, water temperature sender unit, and oil pressure switch.

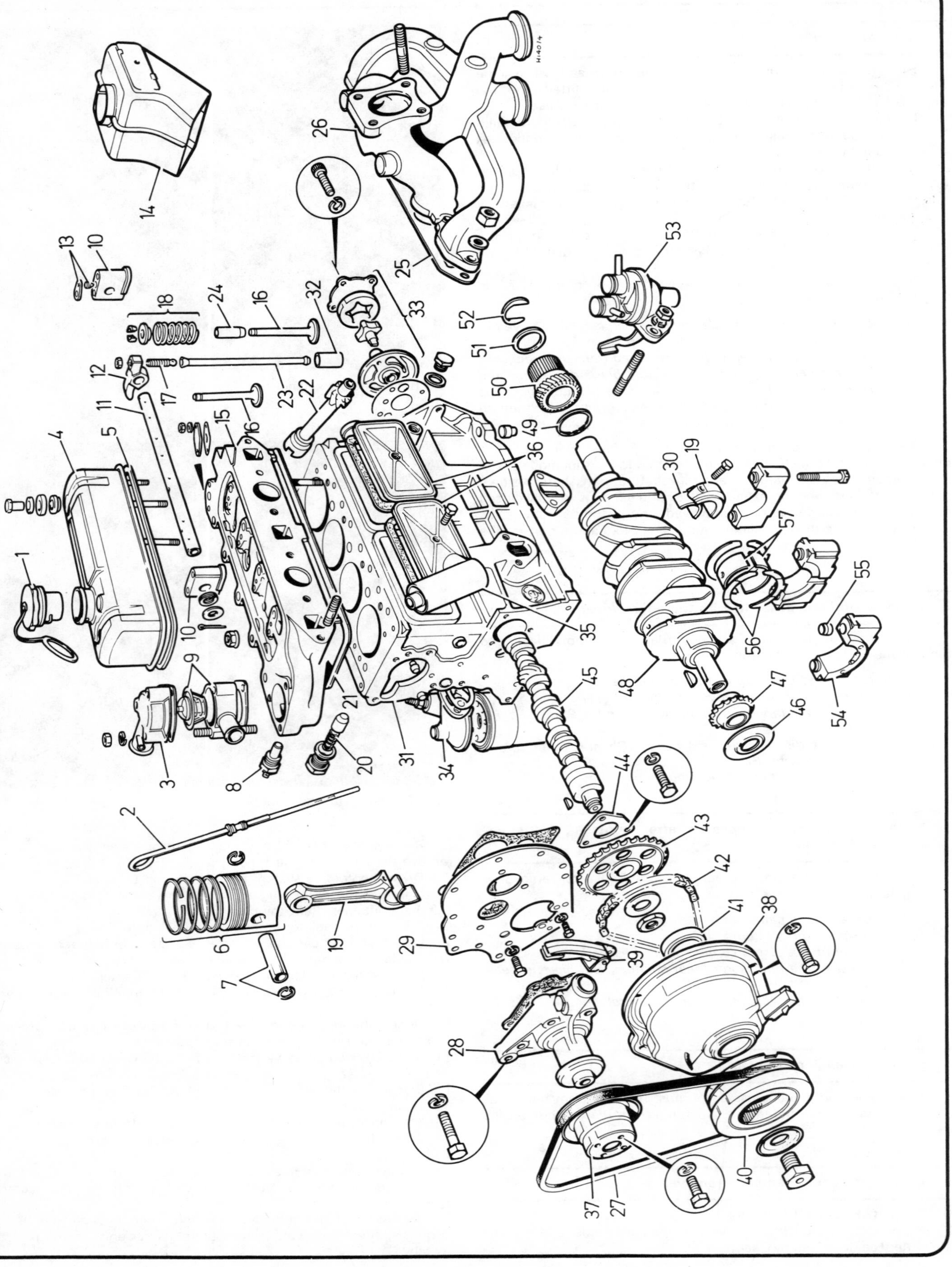
1
2
3
4
5
6
7
8
9
10
11
12
13
14
15
16
17
18
19
20
21
22
23
24
25
26
27
28
29
30
31
32
33
34
35
36
37
38
39
40
41
42
43
44
45
46
47
48
49
50
51
52
53
54
55
56
57

Fig. 1.1 Exploded view of the 998 cc engine (Sec 1)

1 Oil filler cap	13 Lockplate and screw	24 Valve guide	36 Side covers	47 Crankshaft gear
2 Dipstick	14 Hot air stove	25 Manifold gasket	37 Water pump pulley	48 Crankshaft
3 Water outlet elbow	15 Cylinder head	26 Inlet and exhaust manifold	38 Timing cover	49 Thrust washer
4 Valve cover	16 Valve	27 Drivebelt	39 Chain tensioner	50 Primary gear
5 Gasket	17 Rocker adjusting screw	28 Water pump	40 Crankshaft pulley	51 Backing ring
6 Piston and rings	18 Valve spring, cup and collets	29 Front mounting plate	41 Oil seal	52 Thrust washer
7 Gudgeon pin and circlips	19 Connecting rod and cap	30 Big-end bearing shell	42 Timing chain	53 Fuel pump
8 Temperature sender unit	20 Oil pressure relief valve	31 Cylinder block	43 Camshaft gear	54 Main bearing cap
9 Thermostat and housing	21 Cylinder head gasket	32 Tappet	44 Locating plate	55 Dowel
10 Rocker shaft pedestal	22 Distributor driveshaft	33 Oil pump	45 Camshaft	56 Crankshaft thrust washers
11 Rocker shaft	23 Pushrod	34 Oil filter head	46 Oil thrower	57 Main bearing shells
12 Rocker arm		35 Oil separator		

17 Remove the cross-head screws and withdraw the air cleaner elbow from the carburettor. Remove the gasket.

18 Unscrew the speedometer cable from the gearbox and place it to one side.

19 Disconnect the choke and throttle cables from the carburettor with reference to Chapter 3.

20 Turn the steering as necessary to allow access from the front, and remove the rebound buffers from the subframe on both sides. The buffers are located beneath the suspension upper arms and are secured by two cross-head screws.

21 Insert distance pieces such as suitably sized nuts in place of the buffers to retain the suspension in the normal running position.

22 Apply the handbrake, jack up the front of the car, and support it on axle stands.

23 On manual gearbox models, drive out the roll pin and disconnect the gear selector rod from the selector shaft. Unbolt the steady rod from the gearbox.

24 On automatic transmission models, unbolt the bellcrank cover plate from the right-hand side of the gearbox and disconnect the selector cable (refer to Chapter 6 if necessary). Disconnect the pipes from the oil cooler.

25 On all models where fitted, unbolt the exhaust downpipe bracket from the gearbox.

26 The driveshaft inner joints must now be released from the spring rings on the differential side gears. To do this, it is preferable to use tool 18G 1240 (see Chapter 8). However, it may be possible to use two levers but take care not to damage the differential side covers. If difficulty is experienced, rotate the front wheel slightly to a different position. Once released, the inner joints can be prevented from engaging the spring rings again by wrapping a length of thick wire or plastic tubing around the driveshaft.

27 Attach a suitable hoist to the engine/gearbox unit; two brackets fitted to the valve cover nuts may be used for lifting (photo). Take the weight of the unit.

28 Unscrew and remove the engine front mounting bolts, and remove the spacers, noting their location (photos).

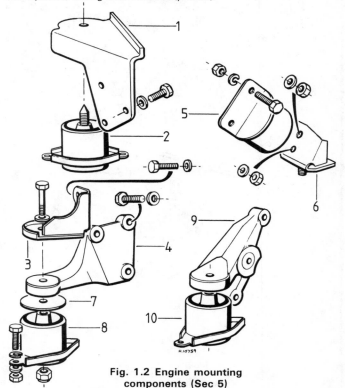

Fig. 1.2 Engine mounting components (Sec 5)

1	Right-hand rear bracket	6	Left-hand rear bracket
2	Right-hand rear mounting	7	Buffer plate
3	Right-hand front bracket stiffener	8	Right-hand front mounting
4	Right-hand front bracket	9	Left-hand front bracket
5	Left-hand rear mounting	10	Left-hand front mounting

H14075

Fig. 1.3 Exploded view of the 1275 cc engine (Sec 1)

1 Oil filler cap
2 Dipstick
3 Water outlet elbow
4 Valve cover
5 Gudgeon pin
6 Piston and rings
7 Temperature transmitter
8 Housing
9 Thermostat
10 Gasket
11 Rocker shaft
12 Rocker arm
13 Lockplate

14 Locating screw
15 Pedestal
16 Hot air stove
17 Connecting rod and cap
18 Oil pressure relief valve
19 Cylinder head gasket
20 Cylinder head
21 Exhaust valve
22 Adjusting screw
23 Valve spring, cup and collets
24 Cylinder block
25 Distributor driveshaft

26 Pushrod
27 Tappet
28 Inlet valve seal
29 Valve guide
30 Inlet valve
31 Manifold gasket
32 Inlet and exhaust manifold
33 Oil filter head
34 Drivebelt
35 Water pump pulley
36 Water pump
37 Chain tensioner
38 Oil filter

39 Oil pump
40 Drain plug
41 Crankshaft pulley
42 Timing cover and oil separator
43 Oil seal
44 Timing chain
45 Camshaft gear
46 Locating plate
47 Camshaft
48 Fuel pump insulator block
49 Oil thrower

50 Crankshaft gear
51 Crankshaft
52 Thrust washer
53 Primary gear
54 Backing ring
55 Thrust washer
56 Crankshaft thrust washers
57 Main bearing shell
58 Big-end shell
59 Fuel pump
60 Main bearing cap
61 Front mounting plate

5.27 Suitable engine lifting bracket

5.28A Left-hand front engine mounting (from above)

5.28B Left-hand front engine mounting (from below)

5.28C Right-hand front engine mounting (from below)

5.29A Right-hand rear engine mounting (from above) – engine removed

5.29B Right-hand rear engine mounting (from below)

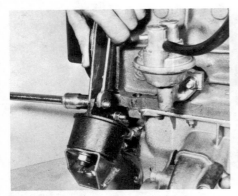

5.29C Left-hand rear engine mounting (from below)

5.30A Removing the engine/gearbox

5.30B Engine compartment with engine/gearbox removed

8.1A Left-hand rear engine mounting

8.1B The oil pressure switch

9.1A Rocker cover washer and seal

9.1B Removing the rocker cover

9.4 Removing the rocker shaft assembly

9.5 Removing a pushrod

29 Unscrew and remove the engine rear mounting nuts, right-hand side from the top and left-hand side from underneath (photos).
30 Raise the engine/gearbox unit from the engine compartment and at the same time lever the driveshaft inner joints from the differential side gears. Make sure that all wires, cables, and hoses have been disconnected, and take care not to damage any component mounted on the bulkhead or engine compartment panels (photos).
31 Lower the units onto a workbench or a large piece of wood placed on the floor.

6 Engine – separation from gearbox

The procedure is identical to that for the removal of the gearbox given in Chapter 6, Section 2 or 14 as applicable.

7 Engine dismantling – general

1 If possible mount the engine on a stand for the dismantling procedure, but failing this, support it in an upright position with blocks of wood placed under each side of the crankcase.
2 Cleanliness is most important, and if the engine is dirty, it should be cleaned with paraffin while keeping it in an upright position.
3 Avoid working with the engine directly on a concrete floor, as grit presents a real source of trouble.
4 As parts are removed, clean them in a paraffin bath. However, do not immerse parts with internal oilways in paraffin as it is difficult to remove, usually requiring a high pressure hose. Clean oilways with nylon pipe cleaners.
5 It is advisable to have suitable containers to hold small items according to their use, as this will help when reassembling the engine and also prevent possible losses.
6 Always obtain complete sets of gaskets when the engine is being dismantled, but retain the old gaskets with a view to using them as a pattern to make a replacement if a new one is not available.
7 When possible, refit nuts, bolts, and washers in their location after being removed, as this helps to protect the threads and will also be helpful when reassembling the engine.
8 Retain unserviceable components in order to compare them with the new parts supplied.

8 Ancillary components – removal

With the engine separated from the gearbox, the externally mounted ancillary components, as given in the following list, can be removed. The removal sequence need not necessarily follow the order given:

Inlet and exhaust manifold and carburettor (Chapter 3)
Fuel pump (Chapter 3)
Alternator (Chapter 10)
HT leads and spark plugs (Chapter 4)
Oil filter cartridge (Section 15 of this Chapter)

Rear engine mountings and brackets (photo)
Distributor (Chapter 4)
Dipstick
Oil pressure switch (photo) and water temperature switch
Water pump (Chapter 2)
Thermostat (Chapter 2)

9 Cylinder head – removal

Note: *If the engine is still in the car, first carry out the following operations:*

(a) *Disconnect the battery negative lead*
(b) *Drain the cooling system*
(c) *Remove the inlet and exhaust manifold complete with carburettor*
(d) *Disconnect the cooling system top hose, heater hose, and expansion tank hose from the thermostat housing*
(e) *Remove the HT leads (and spark plugs if required)*
(f) *Disconnect the lead from the water temperature sender unit*

1 Unscrew the two nuts, remove the washers, and withdraw the rocker cover and gasket (photos).
2 Unscrew the rocker shaft pedestal small nuts and remove the washers. Note the lockwasher fitted to the second pedestal from the front.
3 Unscrew the cylinder head nuts half a turn at a time in the reverse order to that shown in Fig. 1.12. Remove the coil and bracket.
4 Lift the rocker shaft and pedestals from the studs (photo).
5 Shake the pushrods free from the tappets (cam followers), then withdraw them from the cylinder head keeping them in strict order to ensure correct refitting (photo).
6 Lift the cylinder head from the block (photo). If it is stuck, tap it free with a wooden mallet. *Do not insert a lever into the gasket joint – you may damage the mating surfaces.*
7 Remove the cylinder head gasket from the cylinder block (photo).

10 Cylinder head – dismantling

1 Using a valve spring compressor, compress each valve spring in turn until the split collets can be removed (photo). Release the compressor and remove the cup and spring. If the cups are difficult to release, do not continue to tighten the compressor, but gently tap the top of the tool with a hammer. Always make sure that the compressor is held firmly over the cup.
2 On the 1275 cc engine remove the oil seals from the inlet valve guides (photo). A small seal may also be fitted at the bottom of the collet groove on the valve stems.
3 Remove each valve from the combustion chambers keeping them in their order of removal, together with the respective valve springs and cups (photos). Identify each valve according to the cylinder, remembering that No 1 cylinder is at the thermostat end of the cylinder head.

9.6 Removing the cylinder head (1275 cc engine)

9.7 Removing the cylinder head gasket (1275 cc engine)

10.1 Removing the valve split collets

10.2 Removing an inlet valve guide oil seal (1275 cc engine)

10.3A Removing an inlet valve

10.3B Valve components

11.4 Removing the crankshaft pulley and damper (1275 cc engine)

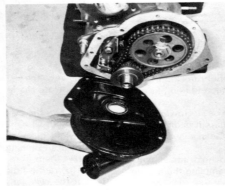
11.5 Removing the timing cover (1275 cc engine)

11.6 Correct location for the crankshaft oil thrower

11.7 Removing the camshaft gear retaining nut

13.5 Removing the distributor driveshaft

13.8 Removing the camshaft locating plate

13.9 Removing the camshaft on the 1275 cc engine (crankshaft removed for clarity)

13.10 Removing the tappets (1275 cc engine)

14.4A Removing the oil pump ...

11 Timing cover, chain, and gears – removal

Note: *If the engine is still in the car, first carry out the following operations:*

    (a) Disconnect the battery negative lead
    (b) Remove the drivebelt and the water pump pulley

1   Using a spanner on the crankshaft pulley bolt, rotate the engine until No 4 piston is at top dead centre on the compression stroke. This will align the timing gear marks.
2   On the 1275 cc engine, disconnect the crankcase ventilation hose from the oil separator on the timing cover.
3   Unlock and unscrew the crankshaft pulley bolt. If the engine is removed, a block of wood placed between a crankshaft web and the crankcase will keep the crankshaft stationary. If the engine is in the car, select top gear and apply the handbrake.
4   Lever the pulley and damper off the front of the crankshaft (photo).
5   Unbolt and remove the timing cover, and remove the gasket (photo).
6   Remove the oil thrower, noting which way round it is fitted (photo).
7   Flatten the lockwasher, then unscrew the camshaft gear retaining nut (photo). Use a screwdriver through one of the gear holes to restrain the gear. Remove the lockwasher.
8   Check that the alignment marks on the timing gears are facing each other, then unbolt and remove the chain tensioner.
9   Using two levers, ease the two gears and chain from the camshaft and crankshaft.
10 Remove the gears from the chain, but identify the outer face of the chain so that it can be refitted in its original position if necessary.

12 Tappets (998 cc engine) – removal

Note: *If the engine is still in the car, first carry out the following operations:*

    (a) Disconnect the battery negative lead
    (b) Remove the inlet and exhaust manifold complete with carburettor
    (c) Remove the rocker cover
    (d) Remove the rocker shaft and pushrods

1   Disconnect the crankcase ventilation hose from the oil separator on the timing-chain-end side cover.
2   Unbolt the side covers from the cylinder block and remove the gaskets. Remove the bolts, cup washers, and seals from the side covers.
3 Lift the tappets from their bores, keeping them in strict order so that they can be refitted in their original positions. Identify them if necessary.

13 Camshaft – removal

1   Remove the engine and gearbox as described in Section 5. It is not necessary to separate the engine from the gearbox, unless the tappets are to be removed on the 1275 cc engine.

2   Remove the rocker cover, rocker shaft, and pushrods.
3   On the 998 cc engine, remove the tappets as described in Section 12.
4   On both the 998 cc and 1275 cc engines, remove the distributor (Chapter 4) and fuel pump (Chapter 3).
5   Using a $\frac{5}{16}$ in bolt, remove the distributor driveshaft from the cylinder block (photo).
6   Remove the timing cover, chain, and gears as described in Section 11.
7   On the 1275 cc engine, invert the engine so that the tappets are clear of the camshaft.
8   Unbolt the crankshaft locating plate from the engine front plate (photo).
9   Withdraw the camshaft from the timing chain end of the cylinder block, taking care not to damage the three camshaft bearings as the lobes of the cams pass through them (photo).
10 If the 1275 cc engine is separated from the gearbox, remove the tappets keeping them identified for location (photo). If the 1275 cc engine is not separated from the gearbox, do not place it upright otherwise the tappets will fall into the gearbox.

14 Oil pump – removal

1   Remove the engine and gearbox as described in Section 5.
2   Remove the flywheel/torque converter housing with reference to Chapter 6.
3   On automatic transmission models only, remove the oil feed pipe from the oil pump.
4   On all models, flatten the lockwashers, then unbolt the oil pump from the cylinder block and remove the gasket (photos).

15 Oil filter – removal

1   On manual gearbox models, using a strap wrench unscrew the oil filter cartridge from the housing and discard it (photos).
2   If required, remove the nuts, washers, and banjo union screw, and withdraw the oil filter head and pipe (photo). Remove the gasket.
3   On automatic transmission models, place a suitable container beneath the oil filter bowl, then unscrew the centre bolt , remove the bowl, and discard the oil filter element. Clean the bowl with paraffin and wipe dry; if necessary the centre bolt may be removed by extracting the circlip.
4   If required, unbolt the oil filter head from the gearbox and remove the gasket.

16 Pistons and connecting rods – removal

1   Remove the engine and gearbox as described in Section 5.
2   Separate the engine from the gearbox as described in Section 6.
3   Remove the cylinder head as described in Section 9.
4   Check the big-end caps for identification marks. If necessary, use a centre punch on the caps and connecting rods to identify them; mark them on the camshaft side to ensure correct refitting.
5   Turn the crankshaft so that No 1 crankpin is at its lowest point.

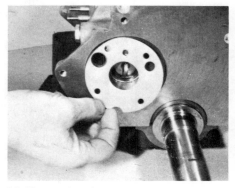

14.4B ... and gasket

15.1A The oil filter cartridge

15.1B Removing the oil filter cartridge

15.2 Removing the oil filter head

16.6 Removing a big-end bearing cap

17.3 Removing the engine front plate

17.5 Checking the crankshaft endfloat with a feeler blade

17.7 Removing the crankshaft

17.8 Removing a main bearing shell

18.1 Showing the location of the crankcase ventilation hoses (1275 cc engine)

20.1 Removing the oil pump cover

20.5A Checking the oil pump inner rotor endfloat ...

20.5B ... outer rotor endfloat ...

20.5C ... outer rotor clearance ...

20.5D ... rotor lobe clearance (central) ...

Using a ½ in AF socket, unscrew the big-end bearing bolts (998 cc) or nuts (1275 cc).

6   Withdraw the cap complete with the bearing shell (photo).

7   Using the handle of a hammer, tap the piston and conecting rod from the bore and withdraw it from the top of the cylinder block.

8   Loosely refit the cap to the connecting rod.

9   Repeat the procedure given in paragraphs 5 to 8 on No 4 piston and connecting rod, then turn the crankshaft through half a turn and repeat the procedure on No 2 and No 3 pistons.

17 Crankshaft and main bearings – removal

1   Follow the procedure for removing the pistons and connecting rods described in Section 16, but it is not necessary to completely remove them from the cylinder blocck.

2   Remove the timing cover, chain, and gears as described in Section 11.

3   Unbolt the front plate from the engine, and remove the gasket (photo). Invert the engine.

4   Check the main bearing caps for identification marks, and if necessary use a centre punch to identify them.

5   Before removing the crankshaft, check that the endfloat is within the specified limits by inserting a feeler blade between the centre crankshaft web and the thrust washers (photo). This will indicate whether new thrust washers are required or not.

6   Unscrew the bolts and remove the main bearing caps complete with bearing shells. Recover the thrust washers from the centre main bearing cap.

7   Lift the crankshaft from the crankcase and remove the remaining centre bearing thrust washers (photo).

8   Extract the bearing shells from the crankcase recesses and the caps, and identify them for location (photo).

18 Crankcase ventilation system – description

The crankcase ventilation system comprises hoses from the crankcase area linked and connected to a port on the carburettor (photo). One hose is attached to an oil separator bolted to the flywheel housing (manual gearbox models only), and the other is attached to an oil separator on the cylinder block side cover (998 cc) or timing cover (1275 cc).

Periodically the hoses should be examined for security and condition. Cleaning them will not normally be necessary except when the engine is well worn and sludge has accumulated.

19 Examination and renovation – general

With the engine completely stripped, clean all the components and examine them for wear. Each part should be checked, and where necessary renewed or renovated as described in the following Sections. Renew main and big-end shell bearings as a matter of course, unless you know that they have had little wear and are in perfect condition.

20 Oil pump – examination and renovation

1   Remove the retaining screw and withdraw the cover from the locating dowels (photo).

2   Lift the two rotors from the pump body.

3   Clean the components with paraffin and wipe dry.

4   Refit the rotors to the pump body, making sure that the chamfer on the outer rotor enters the body first.

5   Using a feeler blade, and where necessary a straight edge, check that the rotor clearances are as given in the Specifications (photos). If any clearance is outside that specified, or if damage is evident on any component, renew the complete oil pump.

6   If the oil pump is serviceable, refit the cover and tighten the retaining screw. Operate the pump in clean engine oil to prime it.

21 Crankshaft and main bearings – examination and renovation

1   Examine the bearing surfaces of the crankshaft for scratches or scoring and, using a micrometer, check each journal and crankpin for ovality. Where this is found to be in excess of 0.001 in (0.0254 mm) the crankshaft will have to be reground and undersize bearings fitted.

2   Crankshaft regrinding should be carried out by a suitable engineering works, who will normally supply the matching undersize main and big-end shell bearings.

3   If the crankshaft endfloat is more than the maximum specified amount, new thrust washers should be fitted to the centre main bearing; these are usually supplied together with the main and big-end bearings on a reground crankshaft.

22 Cylinder block and crankcase – examination and renovation

1   The cylinder bores must be examined for taper, ovality, scoring, and scratches. Start by examining the top of the bores; if these are worn, a slight ridge will be found which marks the top of the piston ring travel. If the wear is excessive, the engine will have had a high oil consumption rate accompanied by blue smoke from the exhaust.

2   If available, use an inside dial gauge to measure the bore diameter just below the ridge and compare it with the diameter at the bottom of the bore, which is not subject to wear. If the difference is more than 0.006 in (0.152 mm), the cylinders will normally require reboring with new oversize pistons fitted.

3   Provided the cylinder bore wear does not exceed 0.008 in (0.203 mm), however, special oil control rings and pistons can be fitted to restore compression and stop the engine burning oil.

4   If new pistons are being fitted to old bores, it is essential to roughen the bore walls slightly with fine glasspaper to enable the new piston rings to bed in properly.

5   Thoroughly examine the crankcase and cylinder block for cracks and damage and use a piece of wire to probe all oilways and waterways to ensure they are unobstructed.

6   Check the tappet bores for wear and scoring; if excessive, they can be reamed and oversize tappets fitted.

7   Unscrew the oil pressure relief valve cap and remove the valve and spring (photo). Check the valve seating for excessive wear and check that the spring free length is as specified. Renew the valve and spring as necessary, and refit them to the cylinder block.

20.5E ... and rotor lobe clearance (off centre)

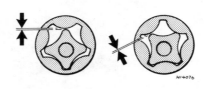

Fig. 1.4 Oil pump rotor lobe clearance checking points (Sec 20)

22.7 Removing the oil pressure relief valve

23 Pistons and connecting rods – examination and renovation

1   Examine the pistons for ovality, scoring, and scratches. Check the connecting rods for wear and damage (photo).
2   If the pistons or connecting rods are to be renewed on the 1275 cc engine, it is recommended that this work is carried out by a BL garage, who will have the necessary tooling to extract the gudgeon pins from the connecting rods.
3   To remove the pistons from the connecting rods on the 998 cc engine, extract the circlips and push out the gudgeon pin. If the ambient temperature is below 20°C (68°F), heat the piston in hot water first.
4   Check the small-end bushes for wear, and if necessary have a BL garage fit and ream new bushes.
5   Lubricate the gudgeon pin and bores with graphited oil, then locate the connecting rod in the piston as shown in Fig. 1.5 and press in the gudgeon pin. Note that the diagonal split on the connecting rod must face the camshaft side of the piston. Fit the circlips.
6   If new rings are to be fitted to the original pistons, expand the old rings over the top of the pistons. The use of two or three old feeler blades will be helpful in preventing the rings dropping into empty grooves. Note that the oil control ring is in three sections.
7   Before fitting the new rings to the piston, insert them into the cylinder bore and use a feeler gauge to check that the end gaps are within the specified limits.
8   After fitting the rings, check the compression rings for groove clearances using a feeler blade (photo). Make sure that the word 'Top', where marked on the compression rings, is towards the top of the piston. Arrange the compression ring gaps at 90 degrees to each other on the camshaft side of the piston.

24 Camshaft and tappets – examination and renovation

1   Examine the camshaft bearing surfaces, cam lobes, and skew gear for wear. If excessive, renew the shaft.
2   Check the locating plate for wear and renew it if necessary.
3   Check the camshaft bearings for wear and if necessary remove them with a suitable diameter length of tubing. Fit the new pre-finished bearings with their oil holes aligned with the oilways in the cylinder block.
4   Examine the tappets for wear and renew them if necessary.

25 Timing cover, chain, and gears – examination and renovation

1   Examine all the teeth on the camshaft and crankshaft sprockets. If these are 'hooked' in appearance, renew the sprockets.
2   Examine the chain tensioner for wear and renew it if necessary.
3   Examine the timing chain for wear. If it has been in operation for a considerable time, or if when held horizontally (rollers vertical) it takes on a deeply bowed appearance, renew it.
4   Check the timing cover for damage and renew it if necessary. It is good practice to renew the timing cover oil seal whenever the timing cover is removed. To do this, drive out the old seal with a suitable drift, and install the new seal using a block of wood to make sure that it enters squarely (photo).

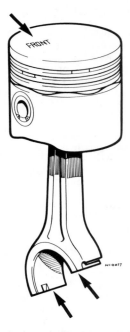

Fig. 1.5 Correct relationship of the piston and connecting rod on the 998 cc engine (Sec 23)

26 Flywheel/torque converter – examination and renovation

1   Examine the clutch driven plate mating surface of the flywheel with reference to Chapter 5.
2   Check the starter ring gear teeth; if they are chipped or worn the ring gear must be renewed. Although the procedure is identical for the flywheel and torque converter, it is recommended that the work on the torque converter is entrusted to a BL garage.
3   Partially drill the ring gear from the side, then carefully split it with a cold chisel and remove it, taking suitable precautions to prevent injury from flying fragments.
4   Heat the new ring to 392°F (200°C) in an electric oven, then quickly fit it to the flywheel/torque converter. Allow the ring to cool naturally without quenching.

27 Cylinder head – decarbonising, valve grinding, and renovation

1   The operation will normally only be required at comparatively high mileages. However, if persistent pinking occurs and performance has deteriorated even though the engine adjustments are correct, de-carbonising and valve grinding may be required.
2   With the cylinder head removed, use a scraper to remove the carbon from the combustion chambers and ports. Remove all traces of gasket from the cylinder head surface, then wash it thoroughly with paraffin.

23.1 Piston and connecting rod components (1275 cc engine)

23.8 Checking the compression ring groove clearance (1275 cc engine)

25.4 Fitting the timing cover oil seal

29.3 Installing the centre main bearing thrust washers

29.4 Installing the centre main bearing cap and thrust washers

29.5 Tightening the main bearing cap bolts

3   Use a straight edge and feeler blade to check that the cylinder head surface is not distorted. If it is, it must be resurfaced by a suitably equipped engineering works.
4   If the engine is still in the car, clean the piston crowns and cylinder bore upper edges, but make sure that no carbon drops between the pistons and bores. To do this, locate two of the pistons at the top of their bores and seal off the remaining bores with paper and masking tape. Press a little grease between the two pistons and their bores to collect any carbon dust; this can be wiped away when the piston is lowered. To prevent carbon build-up, polish the piston crown with metal polish, but remove all traces of the polish afterwards.
5   Examine the heads of the valves for pitting and burning, especially the exhaust valve heads. Renew any valve which is badly burnt. Examine the valve seats at the same time. If the pitting is very slight, it can be removed by grinding the valve heads and seats together with coarse, then fine, grinding paste.
6   Where excessive pitting has occurred, the valve seats must be recut or renewed by a suitably equipped engineering works.
7   Valve grinding is carried out as follows. Place the cylinder head upside down on a bench with a block of wood at each end to give clearance for the valve stems.
8   Smear a trace of coarse carborundum paste on the seat face and press a suction grinding tool onto the valve head. With a semi-rotary action, grind the valve head to its seat, lifting the valve occasionally to redistribute the grinding paste. When a dull matt even surface is produced on both the valve seat and the valve, wipe off the paste and repeat the process with fine carborundum paste as before. A light

spring placed under the valve head will greatly ease this operation. When a smooth unbroken ring of light grey matt finish is produced on both the valve and seat, the grinding operation is complete.
9   Scrape away all carbon from the valve head and stem, and clean away all traces of grinding compound. Clean the valves and seats with a paraffin soaked rag, then wipe with a clean rag.
10   If the valve guides are worn, indicated by a side-to-side motion of the valve, new guides must be fitted. To do this, use a suitable mandrel to press the worn guides downwards and out through the combustion chamber. Press the new guides into the cylinder head in the same direction until they are at the specified fitted height.
11   If the original valve springs have been in use for 20 000 miles (32 000 km) or more. renew them. Where fitted, the inlet valve oil seals should also be renewed whenever the cylinder head is dismantled.
12   Examine the pushrods and rocker shaft assembly for wear and renew them as necessary. Dismantling and reassembly of the rocker components is straightforward if reference is made to Figs. 1.1 and 1.7.

28 Engine reassembly – general

1   To ensure maximum life with minimum trouble from a rebuilt engine, not only must everything be correctly assembled, but it must also be spotlessly clean. All oilways must be clear, and locking washers and spring washers must be fitted where indicated. Oil all bearings and other working surfaces thoroughly with engine oil during assembly.
2   Before assembly begins, renew any bolts or studs with damaged threads.
3   Gather together a torque wrench, oil can, clean rag, and a set of engine gaskets and oil seals, together with a new oil filter cartridge.

29 Crankshaft and main bearings – refitting

1   Clean the backs of the bearing shells and the bearing recesses in both the cylinder block and main bearing caps.
2   Press the main bearing shells into the cylinder block and caps and oil them liberally.
3   Using a little grease, stick the thrust washers to each side of the centre main bearings with their oilways facing away from the bearing (photo). Similarly fit the thrust washers to the centre main bearing cap.
4   Lower the crankshaft into position, then fit the main bearing caps in their previously noted locations (photo).
5   Insert and tighten evenly the main bearing cap bolts to the specified torque (photo). Check that the crankshaft rotates freely, then check that the endfloat is within the specified limits by inserting a feeler blade between the centre crankshaft web and the thrust washers.
6   Smear the front plate gasket with sealing compound and locate it on the front of the cylinder block. Fit the engine front plate and tighten the two lower retaining bolts.
7   With the engine upright, refit the timing cover, chain, and gears as described in Section 35.
8   Refit the pistons and connecting rods as described in Section 30.

Fig. 1.6 Valve guide fitted height dimension 'A' (Sec 27)

Arrow indicates direction of removal and fitting

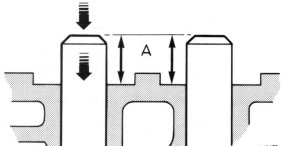

Fig. 1.7 Rocker shaft components (Sec 27)

30.2A Installing a big-end bearing shell

30.2B Lubricating a crankpin

30.3 Installing a piston and connecting rod

30 Pistons and connecting rods – refitting

1   Clean the backs of the bearing shells and the recesses in the connecting rods and big-end caps.

2   Press the big-end bearing shells into the connecting rods and caps in their correct positions and oil them liberally (photos).

3   Fit a ring compressor to No 1 piston, then insert the piston and connecting rod into No 1 cylinder. With No 1 crankpin at its lowest point, drive the piston carefully into the cylinder with the wooden handle of a hammer, and at the same time guide the connecting rod onto the crankpin (photo). Make sure that the 'Front' mark on the piston crown is facing the timing chain end of the engine, and that the connecting rod offset is as shown in Fig. 1.8.

4   Fit the big-end bearing cap in its previously noted position, then tighten the bolts (998 cc) or nuts (1275 cc) evenly to the specified torque.

5   Check that the crankshaft turns freely.

6   Repeat the procedure given in paragraphs 3 to 5 for No 4 piston and connecting rod, then turn the crankshaft through half a turn and repeat the procedure on No 2 and No 3 pistons.

7   Refit the cylinder head as described in Section 36.

8   Refit the engine to the gearbox as described in Section 38.

9   Refit the engine and gearbox as described in Section 39.

31 Oil filter – refitting

1   *On manual gearbox models,* if removed refit the oil filter head and pipe to the cylinder block together with a new gasket. Tighten the retaining nuts and the banjo union screw.

2   Wipe clean the sealing faces of the oil filter cartridge and the filter head. Smear the sealing rubber with engine oil, then fit and tighten the cartridge by hand only.

3   *On automatic transmission models,* if removed refit the oil filter head to the gearbox together with a new gasket. Tighten the bolts evenly.

4   Prise out the old sealing ring, wipe the groove clean, and insert a new sealing ring in the oil filter head groove.

5   Insert the new element in the oil filter bowl, then locate the bowl centrally on the sealing ring and tighten the centre bolt.

32 Oil pump – refitting

1   Make sure that the mating faces of the oil pump and cylinder block are clean, then fit the oil pump together with a new gasket, and tighten the retaining bolts evenly to the specified torque. Make sure that the cut-outs in the gasket are correctly aligned with the pump, and, if the camshaft is already in position, make sure that the pump spindle engages the slot in the camshaft.

2   Bend the lockwashers to lock the bolts.

3   On automatic transmission models only, fit the oil feed pipe together with new O-rings if necessary.

4   If the engine and gearbox were removed purposely to remove the oil pump, refit the flywheel/torque converter housing with reference to Chapter 6, and refit the engine and gearbox as described in Section 39.

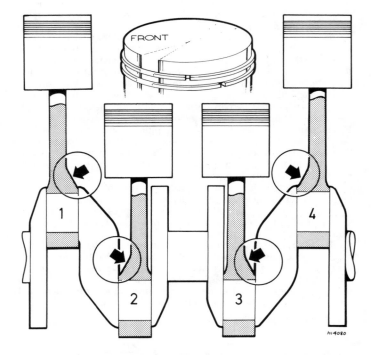

Fig. 1.8 Diagram showing connecting rod offset – arrowed (Sec 30)

33 Camshaft – refitting

1   If the 1275 cc engine is separated from the gearbox, lubricate the tappets with engine oil and insert them in their original locations with the engine inverted.

2   Oil the camshaft bearings and carefully insert the camshaft from the timing chain end of the cylinder block. Make sure that the oil pump spindle engages the slot in the camshaft.

3   Fit the locating plate to the front plate and tighten the bolts evenly.

4   Using a dial gauge, vernier calipers, or feeler blade and bridging piece, check that the camshaft endfloat is within the specified limits. If not, renew the locating plate.

5   With the engine upright, refit the timing cover, chain, and gears as described in Section 35.

6   Turn the engine until No 1 piston is at top dead centre (TDC) on the compression stroke. If the cylinder head is not yet fitted, use two pushrods to determine the point when No 4 cylinder valves are rocking – in this position No 1 piston is at TDC compression.

7   Using the $\frac{5}{16}$ in bolt, insert the distributor driveshaft into the cylinder block with the larger segment uppermost (see Fig. 1.10) and the slot in the 4 o'clock position. As the driveshaft engages the skew

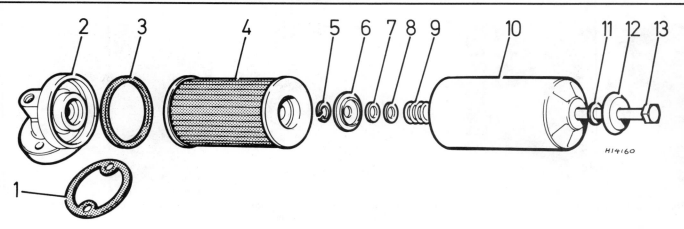

Fig. 1.9 Oil filter components on automatic transmission models (Sec 31)

1 Gasket	5 Circlip	8 Washer	11 Seal
2 Head	6 Pressure plate	9 Spring	12 Collar
3 Sealing ring	7 Seal	10 Bowl	13 Centre bolt
4 Element			

gear on the camshaft, it will turn anticlockwise to the 2 o'clock position. Remove the bolt (photo).

8   Refit the distributor (Chapter 4) and the fuel pump (Chapter 3).

9   On the 998 cc engine refit the tappets as described in Section 34.

10   Refit the pushrods and rocker shaft and adjust the tappets as described in Section 41. Refit the rocker cover.

11   Refit the engine and gearbox as described in Section 39.

34 Tappets (998 cc engine) – refitting

1   Lubricate the tappets with engine oil and insert them in their original locations.

2   Refit the side covers together with new gaskets, and insert the bolts with the seals and cup washers. Tighten the bolts to the specified torque.

3   Reconnect the crankcase ventilation hose to the oil separator.

4   If the engine is in the car, reverse the procedure given in Section 12, but adjust the valve clearances as described in Section 41, and retighten the cylinder head nuts with reference to Section 36.

35 Timing cover, chain, and gears – refitting

1   Locate the timing gears on the crankshaft and camshaft without the chain, and check their alignment using a straight edge and feeler blade as shown (photos).

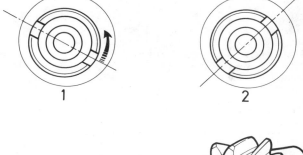

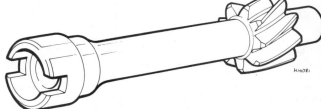

Fig. 1.10 Distributor driveshaft fitting procedure (Sec 33)

1   Initial fitting position   2   Fitted position

33.7 Installed position of distributor driveshaft

35.1A Checking the timing gear alignment by comparing the camshaft gear teeth-to-rule dimension ...

35.1B ... with the crankshaft gear teeth-to-rule dimension

35.2 Crankshaft gear shim location

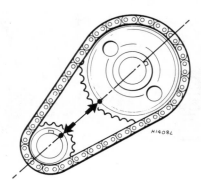

Fig. 1.11 Timing gear alignment marks (arrowed) and centre line (Sec 35)

35.6A Tightening the camshaft gear retaining nut

35.6B Camshaft gear retaining nut locked, and tuning marks aligned

35.7 Fitting the timing chain tensioner

35.11 Tightening the crankshaft pulley bolt

2   Remove the gears, and if necessary extract the Woodruff key and fit shims to the crankshaft to obtain the alignment. Refit the key (photo).
3   Turn the crankshaft so that the Woodruff key is at top dead centre, and turn the camshaft so that the key is at 2 o'clock. In this position No 4 cylinder is at TDC compression.
4   Loop the timing chain over the two gears so that the timing marks are facing each other on the centre line (see Fig. 1.11).
5   Locate the two gears on the crankshaft and camshaft and press them firmly home. Using a straight edge check that the timing marks are still on the centre line.
6   Fit the camshaft gear retaining nut and lockwasher, and tighten the nut while using a screwdriver through one of the gear holes to restrain the gear. Bend the lockwasher to lock the nut (photos).
7   Fit the chain tensioner and tighten the bolts, while keeping firm thumb pressure against the top of the bracket to provide the preload (photo).
8   Locate the oil thrower on the crankshaft with the side marked 'F' facing outwards.
9   Stick the timing cover gasket to the front plate, then fit the timing cover and retain it with two upper bolts inserted loosely.
10   Oil the timing cover oil seal, then temporarily fit the crankshaft pulley to centralize the timing cover. Insert and tighten evenly the upper retaining bolts, then remove the pulley and fit the lower bolts.
11   Fit the crankshaft pulley and damper on the crankshaft followed by the lockwasher and bolt. Tighten the bolt to the specified torque (photo) – if the engine is removed, place a block of wood between a crankshaft web and the crankcase; if the engine is in the car, select top gear and apply the handbrake.
12   Bend the lockwasher to lock the bolt. Remove the block of wood as applicable.
13   On the 1275 cc engine, connect the crankcase ventilation hose to the oil separator on the timing cover.
14   If the engine is in the car, reverse the introductory procedure given in Section 11 with reference to Chapter 2.

36 Cylinder head – reassembly and refitting

1   Fit the valves in their original sequence or, if new valves have been obtained, to the seat to which they have been ground.
2   Oil the valve stems liberally and, on the 1275 cc engine, fit the oil seals to the inlet valve guides and collet grooves where applicable.
3   Working on one valve, fit the spring and cup, then compress the spring with the compressor and insert the split collets. Release the compressor and remove it.
4   Repeat the procedure given in paragraph 3 on the remaining valves. Tap the end of each valve stem with a non-metallic mallet to settle the collets.
5   Make sure that the faces of the cylinder head and block are perfectly clean, then fit the new gasket over the studs with the words 'TOP' and 'FRONT' correctly positioned (photo). Do not use jointing compound.
6   Lower the cylinder head over the studs and onto the gasket.

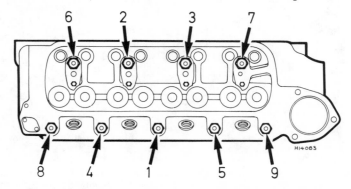

Fig. 1.12 Cylinder head nut tightening sequence (Sec 36)

36.5 Cylinder head gasket 'FRONT' marking

36.9 Tightening the cylinder head nuts

36.10 Tightening the rocker shaft pedestal nuts

7 Insert the pushrods in their original locations, then lower the rocker shaft and pedestals over the studs, at the same time guiding the adjusting screws into the pushrods.
8 Locate the coil and bracket on the stud furthest from the thermostat, and fit the rocker shaft lockwasher to the second pedestal from the front.
9 Fit the cylinder head nuts and tighten them to half the specified torque in the order shown in Fig. 1.12 (photo). After several minutes, tighten the nuts to the final torque, again in the order recommended.
10 Fit the rocker shaft pedestal washers and nuts, and tighten them evenly to the specified torque (photo).
11 Adjust the valve clearances as described in Section 41.
12 Fit the valve cover with a new gasket and tighten the two nuts.
13 If the engine is in the car, reverse the introductory procedure given in Section 9, and refill the cooling system with reference to Chapter 2.
14 Drive the car for five to ten miles, then allow the engine to cool and remove the valve cover. Working in the order shown in Fig. 1.12, loosen half a turn, then immediately tighten, each cylinder head nut to the specified torque. Readjust the valve clearances, then refit the valve cover.

37 Ancillary components – refitting

Refer to Section 8, and refit the listed components with reference to the Chapters indicated, where applicable.

38 Engine – refitting to gearbox

The procedure is identical to that for the refitting of the gearbox given in Chapter 6, Section 2.

39 Engine/gearbox assembly – refitting

Reverse the removal procedure given in Section 5, but note the following additional points:

(a) *Insert the left-hand side driveshaft into the differential unit first, then twist the engine and insert the right-hand side driveshaft*
(b) *Adjust the choke and throttle cables as described in Chapter 3*
(c) *Refill the engine/gearbox with oil*
(d) *Refill the cooling system as described in Chapter 2*
(e) *On automatic transmission models adjust the selector cable as described in Chapter 6*

40 Engine – adjustment after major overhaul

1 With the engine/gearbox refitted to the car, make a final check to ensure that everything has been reconnected and that no rags or tools have been left in the engine compartment.
2 If new pistons or crankshaft bearings have been fitted, turn the carburettor slow running screw in about half a turn to compensate for the initial tightness of the new components.

3 Pull the choke fully out and start the engine. This may take a little longer than usual as the fuel pump and carburettor float chamber may be empty.
4 As soon as the engine starts, push in the choke until the engine runs at a fast tickover. Check that the oil pressure light goes out.
5 Check the oil filter, fuel hoses, and water hoses for leaks.
6 Run the engine until normal operating temperature is reached, then adjust the slow running as described in Chapter 3.
7 Drive the car for five to ten miles, then allow the engine to cool and remove the valve cover. Working in the order shown in Fig. 1.12 loosen half a turn, then immediately tighten, each cylinder head nut to the specified torque. After the engine has completely cooled, readjust the valve clearances as described in Section 41 then refit the valve cover.
8 If new pistons or crankshaft bearings have been fitted, the engine must be run-in for the first 500 miles (800 km). *Do not* exceed 45 mph (72 km/h), operate the engine at full throttle, or allow the engine to labour in any gear.

41 Valve clearances – adjustment

1 The valve clearances must be adjusted with the engine cold.
2 Remove the valve cover and gasket.
3 Turn the engine with a spanner on the crankshaft pulley bolt until No 8 valve (No 4 cylinder exhaust) is fully open. Alternatively, the engine can be turned by engaging 4th gear, releasing the handbrake, and rocking the car backwards and forwards.
4 Insert a feeler blade of the correct thickness between the rocker arm and valve stem of No 1 valve (No 1 cylinder exhaust). If the blade is not a firm sliding fit, loosen the locknut on the rocker arm with a ring spanner and turn the adjusting screw with a screwdriver (photo). Tighten the locknut whilst holding the adjusting screw stationary, then recheck the adjustment.

41.4 Checking the valve clearances

5   Repeat the procedure given in paragraphs 3 and 4 on the remaining valves using the 'rule of nine' method as given below:

Valve open	Adjust valve
8 exhaust	1 exhaust
6 inlet	3 inlet
4 exhaust	5 exhaust
7 inlet	2 inlet
1 exhaust	8 exhaust

3 inlet
5 exhaust
2 inlet

6 inlet
4 exhaust
7 inlet

6   Check the valve cover gasket for damage and renew it if necessary. Refit the valve cover and gasket with the filler cap towards the timing chain end of the engine. Tighten the nuts to the specified torque.

42 Fault diagnosis – engine

Symptom	Reason(s)
Engine fails to start	Discharged battery Loose battery connection Loose or broken ignition leads Moisture on spark plugs, distributor cap, or HT leads Incorrect spark plug or contact points gap Cracked distributor cap or rotor Dirt or water in carburettor Empty fuel tank Faulty fuel pump Faulty starter motor Low cylinder compressions
Engine idles erratically	Intake manifold air leak Leaking cylinder head gasket Worn rocker arms, timing chain, and gears Worn camshaft lobes Faulty fuel pump Incorrect valve clearances Loose crankcase ventilation hoses Carburettor adjustment incorrect Uneven cylinder compressions
Engine misfires	Spark plugs or contact points gap incorrect Faulty coil or condenser Dirt or water in carburettor Carburettor adjustment incorrect Burnt out valve Leaking cylinder head gasket Distributor cap cracked Incorrect valve clearances Uneven cylinder compressions Worn carburettor
Engine stalls	Carburettor adjustment incorrect Intake manifold air leak Ignition timing incorrect
Excessive oil consumption	Worn pistons and cylinder bores Valve guides and valve stem seals worn Oil leaking from valve cover, differential side cover oil seals, timing cover oil seal, or selector shaft oil seal
Engine backfires	Carburettor adjustment incorrect Ignition timing incorrect Incorrect valve clearances Intake manifold air leak Sticking valve

Chapter 2 Cooling system

For modifications and information applicable to later models, see Supplement at end of manual

Contents

Antifreeze mixture	5
Cooling fan assembly – removal, overhaul and refitting	9
Cooling fan thermostatic switch – testing, removal and refitting	10
Cooling system – draining	2
Cooling system – filling	4
Cooling system – flushing	3

Drivebelt – renewal and adjustment	11
Fault diagnosis – cooling system	13
General description	1
Radiator – removal, inspection, cleaning and refitting	6
Temperature gauge transmitter – removal and refitting	12
Thermostat – removal, testing and refitting	7
Water pump – removal and refitting	8

Specifications

System type	Thermo-syphon with belt driven pump, pressurized front mounted radiator and electric cooling fan
Expansion tank cap pressure	15 lbf/in² (1.05 kgf/cm²)
Thermostat opens at	88°C (190°F)
Drivebelt tension	0.16 in (4 mm) deflection between water pump and alternator pulleys under load of 7.5 to 8.2 lbf (3.3 to 3.6 kgf)
Cooling fan motor minimum brush length	0.187 in (4.76 mm)
System capacity (including heater)	8.5 Imp pints (4.9 litres)

Torque wrench settings

	lbf ft	kgf m
Coolant temperature transmitter	14	2.0
Water outlet elbow	8	1.1
Water pump bolts	16	2.2
Water pump pulley	8	1.1
Cooling fan through-bolts	1	0.2

1 General description

The cooling system is of pressurized type and includes a front mounted radiator, belt driven water pump and an electric cooling fan. The thermostat is located in the water outlet at the front of the cylinder head. The radiator is of aluminium construction with plastic end tanks, and is not provided with a drain plug. A drain plug is, however, provided at the rear of the cylinder block.

The system functions as follows. Cold water in the bottom of the radiator circulates through the bottom hose and metal pipe to the water pump, where the pump impeller pushes the water around the cylinder block and head passages. After cooling the cylinder bores, combustion surfaces, and valve seats, the water reaches the underside of the thermostat which is initially closed, and is diverted through the heater inlet hose to the heater. After leaving the heater the water is returned to the water pump inlet hose. When the engine is cold, the thermostat remains closed and the water circulates only through the engine and heater. When the coolant reaches the predetermined temperature (see Specifications), the thermostat opens and the water passes through the top hose to the top of the radiator. As the water circulates down through the radiator, it is cooled by the in-rush of air when the car is in forward motion, supplemented by the action of the electric cooling fan when necessary. Having reached the bottom of the radiator, the water is now cooled and the cycle is repeated.

The electric cooling fan is controlled by a thermostatic switch located in the left-hand side radiator tank. Water temperature is monitored by a sender unit located beneath the thermostat in the cylinder head.

2 Cooling system – draining

1 It is preferable to drain the cooling system when the engine has cooled. If this is not possible, place a cloth over the expansion tank filler cap and turn it slowly in an anti-clockwise direction until the first stop is reached, then wait until all the pressure has been released.
2 Remove the filler cap.
3 Place a suitable container beneath the left-hand side of the radiator.
4 Loosen the clip and ease the bottom hose away fron the radiator outlet. Drain the coolant into the container.
5 Place a second container beneath the cylinder block drain plug located on the rear right-hand side next to the clutch slave cylinder. If necessary, remove the hot air stove from the exhaust manifold (Chapter 3, Section 14) to improve access to the drain plug. Unscrew the plug and drain the coolant.

3 Cooling system – flushing

1 After some time the radiator and engine waterways may become restricted or even blocked with scale or sediment, which reduces the efficiency of the cooling system. When this occurs, the coolant will appear rusty and dark in colour and the system should then be flushed. In severe cases, reverse flushing may be required as described later.

Fig. 2.1 Cooling system components (Sec 1)

1   *Radiator*
2   *Fan motor*
3   *Thermostatic switch*
4   *Water pump*
5   *Cylinder head outlet elbow*
6   *Sandwich plate*
7   *Cylinder block drain plug*
8   *Expansion tank filler cap*

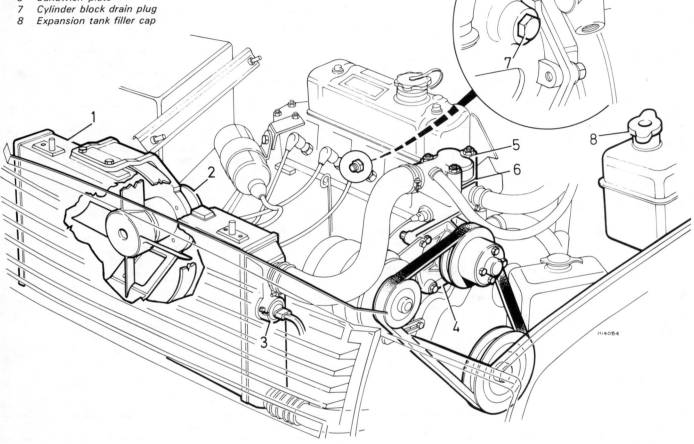

2   Disconnect the top hose from the cylinder head outlet elbow, and the bottom hose from the radiator outlet.
3   Insert a hose in the top hose, and allow water to circulate through the radiator until it runs clear from the outlet.
4   Insert the hose in the expansion tank filler neck and allow water to run out of the cylinder head outlet elbow and bottom hose until clear.
5   Disconnect the heater inlet hose from the front of the cylinder head, insert the hose, and allow water to circulate through the heater and out through the bottom hose until clear.
6   In severe cases of contamination, the system should be reverse flushed. To do this, remove the radiator, invert it, and insert a hose in the outlet. Continue flushing until clear water runs from the inlet.
7   The engine should also be reverse flushed. To do this, remove the thermostat and insert the hose into the cylinder head. Continue flushing until clear water runs from the cylinder block drain plug and bottom hose.
8   The use of chemical cleaners should only be necessary as a last resort, and the regular renewal of antifreeze should prevent the contamination of the system.

4   Cooling system – filling

1   Reconnect the radiator bottom hose and heater hose.
2   Refit the thermostat if removed, and reconnect the top hose to the outlet elbow.
3   Insert and tighten the cylinder block drain plug.
4   Pour coolant into the expansion tank filler neck until it reaches the level mark, then refit the cap.
5   Run the engine at a fast idling speed for three minutes, then stop the engine and check the level in the expansion tank. Top up the level as necessary, being careful to release pressure from the system before removing the filler cap if necessary.

5   Antifreeze mixture

1   The antifreeze mixture should be renewed every two years or 24 000 miles (40 000 km), whichever occurs sooner. This is necessary

not only to maintan the antifreeze properties, but also to prevent corrosion which would otherwise occur as the properties of the inhibitors become progressively less effective.

2 Always use an ethylene glycol based antifreeze suitable for use in a mixed metal cooling system.

3 Before adding antifreeze, the cooling system should be completely drained and flushed, and all hose connections checked for tightness.

4 The quantity of antifreeze and levels of protection are given in the following table, and it is recommended that the antifreeze concentration should never fall below 30% by volume.

Concentration	Quantity	Commences freezing	Frozen solid
33⅓%	3 Imp pints (1.8 litres)	-19°C (-2°F)	-36°C (-33°F)
50%	4.25 Imp pints (2.5 litres)	-36°C (-33°F)	-48°C (-53°F)

5 After filling with antifreeze, a label should be attached to the radiator stating the type of antifreeze and the date installed. Any subsequent topping up should be made with the same type and concentration of antifreeze.

6 Radiator – removal, inspection, cleaning and refitting

1 Disconnect the battery negative lead.

2 Drain the cooling system as described in Section 2.

3 Unscrew the bonnet lock cross panel securing screws and central bolt, and move the headlamp shrouds (if fitted). Remove the screws and lift the grille from its mountings (photo).

4 Position the bonnet lock cross panel to one side leaving the release cable still attached (photo).

5 Loosen the clip and disconnect the top hose from the radiator.

6 Pull the plug connector from the thermostatic switch on the left-hand side of the radiator. Disconnect the plug and socket in the cooling fan motor supply leads.

7 Lift the radiator and fan assembly from the lower location pegs, and remove it from the car (photos).

8 Unbolt the electric cooling fan assembly from the radiator.

9 Release the thermostatic switch and sealing bush from the radiator.

10 Radiator repair is best left to a specialist, but minor leaks may be repaired or sealed using a proprietary coolant additive. Clear the radiator matrix of flies and small leaves with a soft brush or by hosing.

11 Reverse flush the radiator as described in Section 3. Renew the top and bottom hoses and clips if they are damaged or deteriorated.

12 Refitting is a reversal of removal, but always fit a new sealing bush to the thermostatic switch. Fill the cooling system as described in Section 4.

7 Thermostat – removal, testing and refitting

1 Remove the expansion tank filler cap. If the engine is still hot, place a cloth over the cap and turn it slowly anti-clockwise until the first stop is reached, then wait until all the pressure has been released.

2 Place a suitable clean container beneath the radiator outlet, then disconnect the bottom hose and drain approximately 4 pints (2.3 litres) of coolant. Reconnect the bottom hose and tighten the clip.

3 Unscrew the three nuts and lift the outlet elbow from the sandwich plate. Peel off the gasket (photo).

4 Withdraw the thermostat from its seat in the sandwich plate (photo).

5 To test whether the unit is serviceable, suspend it with a piece of string in a container of water. Gradually heat the water and note the

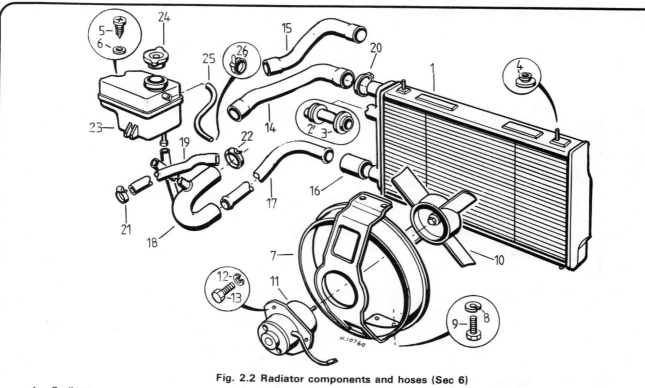

Fig. 2.2 Radiator components and hoses (Sec 6)

1 Radiator	9 Bolt	15 Top hose (1275 cc)	21 Clip
2 Thermostatic switch	10 Fan blades	16 Bottom hose	22 Clip
3 Sealing bush	11 Fan motor	17 Bottom pipe	23 Expansion tank
4 Mounting bush	12 Washer	18 Inlet hose	24 Filler cap
5 Screw	13 Bolt	19 Heater inlet hose	25 Vent pipe
7 Fan motor mounting bracket	14 Top hose (998 cc)	20 Clip	26 Clip
8 Washer			

6.3 Removing the front grille – lower mounting shown

6.4 Bonnet lock cross panel/radiator location pin

6.7A Radiator lower location point (arrowed)

6.7B Radiator and cooling fan assembly

7.3 Removing the thermostat outlet elbow

7.4 Removing the thermostat

temperature at which the thermostat starts to open. Remove the thermostat from the water and check that it is fully closed when cold.

6   Renew the thermostat if the opening temperature is not as specified, or if the unit does not fully close when cold.

7   If the sandwich plate-to-cylinder head gasket has been disturbed, clean up the mating faces and fit a new gasket.

8   Refitting is a reversal of removal, but use a new gasket. Top up the cooling system with reference to Section 4.

8   Water pump – removal and refitting

1   Disconnect the battery negative lead.

2   Remove the drivebelt as described in Section 11.

3   Remove the alternator adjustment nut and pivot bolts. Place the alternator to one side.

4   Remove the windscreen washer bottle and place it to one side. Unscrew the four bolts and remove the pulley from the water pump (photo).

5   Drain the cooling system as described in Section 2.

6   Loosen the clip and disconnect the inlet hose from the water pump.

7   Unscrew and remove the water pump retaining bolts, noting their length and location.

8   Using a soft-faced mallet, tap the water pump from the two locating dowels and remove it from the cylinder block (photo). Remove the gasket.

9   If the water pump is faulty, renew it, as BL do not supply individual components separately.

10   Clean the mating faces of the water pump and cylinder block.

11   Refitting is a reversal of removal, but use a new gasket and tension the drivebelt as described in Section 11. Fill the cooling system as described in Section 4.

9   Cooling fan assembly – removal, overhaul and refitting

1   Follow the initial radiator removal procedure described in Section 6, but do not drain the cooling system or disconnect the top and bottom hoses (paragraphs 2 and 5). Unbolt the cooling fan assembly.

2   Extract the C-clip and withdraw the fan blades from the motor spindle.

3   Remove the securing bolts and withdraw the motor from the mounting bracket.

4   Unscrew the through-bolts and remove the commutator end cover complete with armature from the yoke.

5   Remove the drive pin, circlip, plain washer, wave washer, and plain washer from the armature spindle.

6   Remove the armature from the end cover, and remove the thrust washer and circlip.

7   Remove the three cross-head screws and lift the brush carrier assembly from the end cover.

8   Check the length of the brushes and compare with the minimum length given in the Specifications. Renew the brush carrier assembly if the brushes are worn below the limit.

9   Clean the commutator with a petrol moistened cloth, and if necessary use fine glasspaper to remove carbon deposits. If the commutator is badly burnt or worn, it should be lightly skimmed in a lathe and the copper swarf cleaned from the segments. Do not undercut the segments.

10   Lubricate the armature shaft bearings with oil.

11   Reassemble the cooling fan assembly in reverse order, but make sure that the mating marks on the end cover and yoke are aligned. Check that the armature rotates freely; if necessary, lightly strike the end cover with a soft-faced mallet to centralize the bearing.

12   Refitting is a reversal of removal, with reference to Section 6 as necessary.

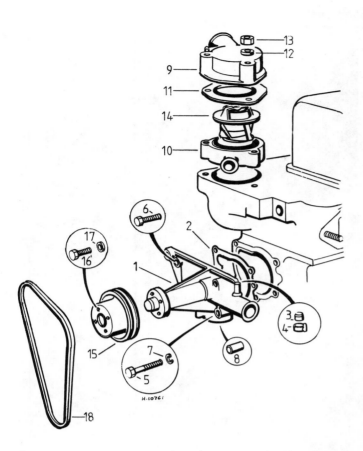

8.4 Removing the water pump pulley

Fig. 2.3 Thermostat and water pump components (Secs 7 and 8)

1	Water pump	10	Sandwich plate
2	Gasket	11	Gasket
3	Plug	12	Washer
4	Clip	13	Nut
5	Bolt (long)	14	Thermostat
6	Bolt (short)	15	Pulley
7	Washer	16	Bolt
8	Dowel	17	Washer
9	Outlet elbow	18	Drivebelt

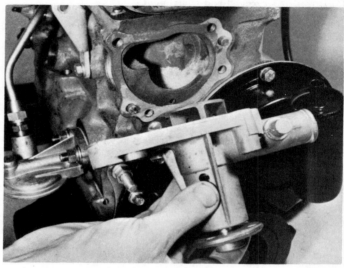

8.8 Removing the water pump

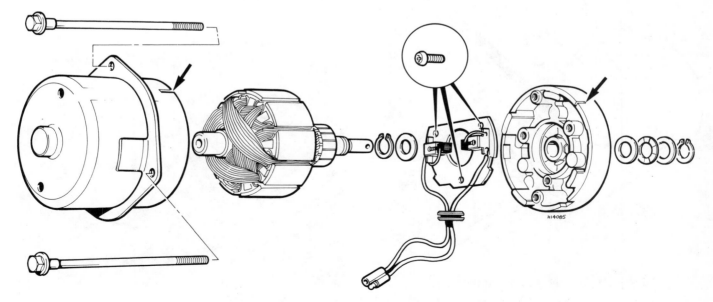

Fig. 2.4 Cooling fan motor components – assembly marks arrowed (Sec 9)

10 Cooling fan thermostatic switch – testing, removal and refitting

1   If the thermostatic switch located on the left-hand side of the radiator develops a fault, it is most likely to fail open-circuited. This will cause the fan motor to remain stationary even though the coolant may reach boiling point (photo).
2   To test for a faulty thermostatic switch, disconnect the plug and connect a length of wire or suitable metal object between the two plug terminals. If the fan operates with the ignition switched on, the thermostatic switch is proved faulty and must be renewed.
3   Disconnect the battery negative lead, and remove the plug from the switch. Remove the expansion tank filler cap.
4   Place a suitable clean container beneath the radiator outlet, then disconnect the bottom hose and drain approximately 4 pints (2.3 litres) of coolant. Reconnect the bottom hose and tighten the clip.
5   Release the retaining plate and withdraw the thermostatic switch and seal from the radiator (photo).
6   Refitting is a reversal of removal, but use a new seal and top up the cooling system with reference to Section 4.

11 Drivebelt – renewal and adjustment

1   The drivebelt should be checked and re-tensioned after 12 months or 12 000 miles (20 000 km) whichever occurs sooner. It should be renewed at 24 months or 24 000 miles (40 000 km) intervals whichever occurs sooner.
2   To remove the drivebelt, loosen the alternator pivot bolts and adjustment nut, and swivel the alternator in towards the cylinder block.
3   Slip the drivebelt from the alternator pulley, water pump pulley, and crankshaft pulley.
4   Fit the new drivebelt over the pulleys, then lever the alternator away from the cylinder block until the specified tension is achieved (photo). The alternator must *only* be levered at the drive end bracket.
5   Tighten the adjustment nut and link pivot bolt, followed by the alternator pivot bolts.
6   Run the engine at 1000 rpm for five minutes, then recheck the tension and adjust if necessary. If preferred, a torque wrench may be used to check the drivebelt tension (photo). The clockwise torque on the alternator nut to produce slip must be between 11 and 11.5 lbf ft (1.5 and 1.6 kgf m).

10.1 Cooling fan thermostatic switch location

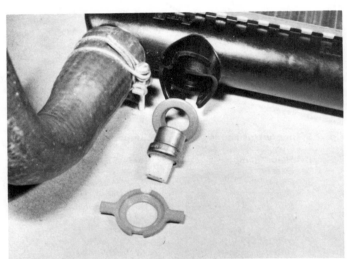

10.5 Thermostatic switch components

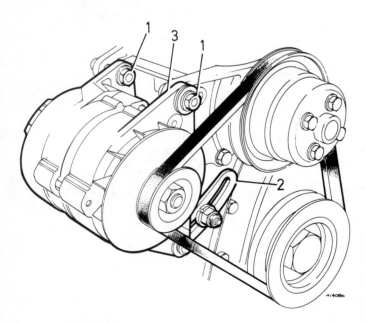

Fig. 2.5 Drivebelt adjustment (Sec 11)

1   Alternator pivot bolts
2   Adjusting link
3   Alternator drive end bracket

11.4 Checking the drivebelt for tension

11.6 Checking the drivebelt tension with a torque wrench

12.3 Temperature gauge transmitter location

12 Temperature gauge transmitter – removal and refitting

1   Remove the expansion tank filler cap. If the engine is hot, place a cloth over the cap, and unscrew it slowly to the first stop to allow all pressure to be released, before removing the cap.

2   Place a suitable clean container beneath the radiator outlet, then loosen the clip and disconnect the bottom hose. Drain approximately

4 pints (2.3 litres) of coolant, then reconnect the bottom hose and tighten the clip.

3   Disconnect the supply lead, and unscrew the transmitter from the front of the cylinder head (photo).

4   Refitting is a reversal of removal, but tighten the transmitter to the specified torque wrench setting. Top up the cooling system with reference to Section 4.

13 Fault diagnosis – cooling system

Symptom	Reason(s)
Overheating	Low coolant level
	Faulty expansion tank pressure cap
	Thermostat sticking shut
	Drivebelt slipping
	Open circuit thermostatic switch
	Faulty cooling fan motor
	Clogged radiator matrix
	Retarded ignition timing
Slow warm-up	Thermostat sticking open
	Incorrect temperature thermostat
Coolant loss	Damaged or deteriorated hose
	Leaking water pump or cylinder head outlet elbow joint
	Blown cylinder head gasket
	Leaking radiator

Chapter 3 Fuel and exhaust systems

For modifications and information applicable to later models, see Supplement at end of manual

Contents

Accelerator cable – removal and refitting	7
Accelerator pedal – removal and refitting	8
Air cleaner and element – removal and refitting	2
Carburettor – dismantling, overhaul and reassembly	13
Carburettor – general description	9
Carburettor – idle and fast idle adjustment	10
Carburettor – removal and refitting	12
Carburettor – throttle damper adjustment	11
Choke control cable – removal and refitting	6
Exhaust system – checking, removal and refitting	15
Fault diagnosis – fuel and exhaust systems	16
Fuel gauge sender unit – removal and refitting	5
Fuel pump – testing, removal and refitting	3
Fuel tank – removal, servicing and refitting	4
General description	1
Inlet and exhaust manifold – description, removal and refitting	14

Specifications

Air cleaner .... Automatic air temperature control type, with renewable paper element

Fuel pump
Type .... Mechanical, diaphragm, operated by eccentric on camshaft
Fuel pump pressure (minimum) .... 6 lbf/in^2 (0.4 kgf/cm^2)

Carburettor

	998 cc	1275 cc
Type	SU HIF 38	SU HIF44
Specification number:		
Metro low compression	FZX 1298	–
Metro and Metro L	FZX 1278	–
Metro HLE	FZX 1376 or FZX 1380	–
Metro L, S and HLS (manual)	–	FZX 1280
Metro L, S and HLS (automatic)	–	FZX 1281
Piston spring colour	Red	Red
Jet size	0.090 in	0.100 in
Needle identification:		
Metro low compression	ADU	–
Metro and Metro L	ADP	–
Metro HLE	ADX or ADZ	–
Metro L, S and HLS	–	BEJ
Idling speed	750 rpm	750 rpm
Fast idle speed	1300 rpm	1100 rpm
Exhaust gas content at idling	2.5 ± 1%	2.5 ± 1%
Piston damper oil type/specification	Multigrade engine oil, viscosity SAE 15W/50 or 10W/40 (Duckhams QXR, Hypergrade, or 10W/40 Motor Oil)	

Fuel tank capacity .... 6.6 Imp gals (30 litres)

Fuel octane rating
Metro low compression .... 91 RON (2 star)
All other models .... 97 RON (4 star)

Torque wrench settings

	lbf ft	kgf m
Carburettor nuts	16	2.2
Fuel pump nuts	16	2.2
Throttle damper	8	1.1

1 General description

The fuel system comprises a rear mounted fuel tank, a camshaft operated fuel pump, and an SU HIF (Horizontal, Integral Floatchamber) carburettor.

The air cleaner is of automatic air temperature control type and incorporates a disposable paper element.

The exhaust system is in two sections; the front section incorporates the downpipe(s) and front silencer, and the rear section incorporates the rear silencer and tailpipe. The exhaust system is suspended on rubber mountings although the front downpipe is attached rigidly to the right-hand side differential unit side cover. Twin downpipes are incorporated on all models except the low compression version.

2 Air cleaner and element – removal and refitting

1 Unscrew and remove the two wing nuts on the top of the air cleaner.

2   Withdraw the air cleaner, at the same time disconnecting it from the hot air shroud tube.

3   The air cleaner element should be renewed every 12 000 miles (20 000 km) or 12 months, whichever occurs first. To remove it, use a wide-bladed screwdriver to separate the lid from the body, then lift out the element and discard it (photos).

4   Clean the interior of the air cleaner with a fuel-moistened cloth, and wipe dry. The air temperature control flap should be in the open position when cold, in order to admit warm air from the heating stove. By heating the bimetallic strap with a hair dryer, the flap should close the warm air aperture (photo). If the operation of the temperature control is in doubt, renew the air cleaner body complete.

5   Install the new element and snap the cover onto the body.

6   Check that the seal is in good condition, then refit the air cleaner and connect it to the hot air shroud tube. Insert and tighten the two wing nuts.

3   Fuel pump – testing, removal and refitting

1   The fuel pump is located on the rear left-hand side of the cylinder block and is of sealed construction. In the event of faulty operation, the pump should be renewed complete.

2   To test the operation of the fuel pump, remove the air cleaner as described in Section 2, then disconnect the fuel pipe from the carburettor. Disconnect the HT lead from the coil, and spin the engine on the starter while holding a wad of rag near the fuel pipe. Well defined spurts of fuel should be ejected from the pipe if the fuel pump is operating correctly, provided there is fuel in the fuel tank.

3   To remove the fuel pump, disconnect the battery negative lead, and remove the air cleaner if not already removed.

4   Disconnect and plug the fuel feed pipe. Disconnect the fuel outlet pipe (photos).

5   Unscrew and remove the two retaining nuts and spring washers, and withdraw the fuel pump from the studs (photo).

6   Remove the insulator block and gasket (photo).

7   Clean all traces of gasket from the crankcase, insulator block, and fuel pump flange.

8   Refitting is a reversal of removal, but fit new gaskets either side of the insulator. Locate the rocker arm on top of the camshaft eccentric,

then push the pump onto the studs. Tighten the nuts to the specified torque.

4   Fuel tank – removal, servicing and refitting

Note: *For safety reasons the fuel tank must always be removed in a well ventilated area, never over a pit.*

1   Disconnect the battery negative lead. Remove the tank filler cap (photo).

2   Siphon or pump all the fuel from the fuel tank (there is no drain plug).

3   Jack up the rear of the car and support it on axle stands, but position the right-hand stand to allow for the removal of the tank and lowering the subframe. Chock the front wheels.

4   Detach the retaining strap from the right-hand rear Hydragas suspension unit. Unbolt the right-hand side of the rear subframe and lower the subframe sufficiently to remove the fuel tank.

5   Loosen the clip and disconnect the short hose from the fuel tank gauge sender unit (photo).

6   Disconnect the supply lead from the gauge sender unit and unclip it from the fuel tank flange.

7   *Loosen* the two rear fuel tank retaining bolts (photo). Unscrew and remove the two front retaining bolts.

8   Lower the fuel tank and disconnect the vent tube. Withdraw the fuel tank from under the car.

9   If the tank is contaminated with sediment or water, remove the gauge sender unit as described in Section 5 and swill the tank out with clean fuel. If the tank is damaged or leaks, it should be repaired by specialists, or alternatively renewed. *Do not under any circumstances solder or weld a fuel tank.*

10 Refitting is a reverse of removal. Access to the vent tube is gained by removing the right-hand plastic pocket (photo).

5   Fuel gauge sender unit – removal and refitting

Note: *For safety reasons the fuel gauge sender unit must always be removed in a well ventilated area, never over a pit.*

2.3A Removing the air cleaner lid

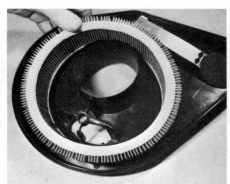

2.3B Lifting out the air cleaner element

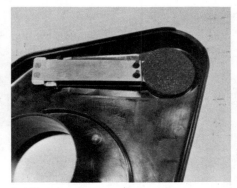

2.4 The air temperature control flap

3.4A Disconnecting the feed pipe from the fuel pump

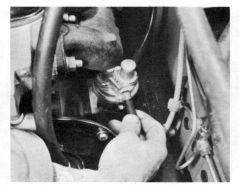

3.4B Disconnecting the outlet pipe from the fuel pump

3.5 Removing the fuel pump

3.6 Fuel pump insulator block and gaskets

4.1 Fuel tank filler cap

4.5 Fuel tank gauge sender unit location

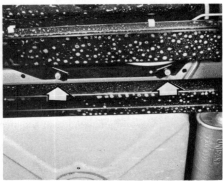

4.7 Fuel tank rear retaining bolt locations

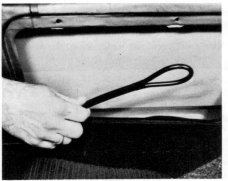

4.10 Fuel tank vent tube

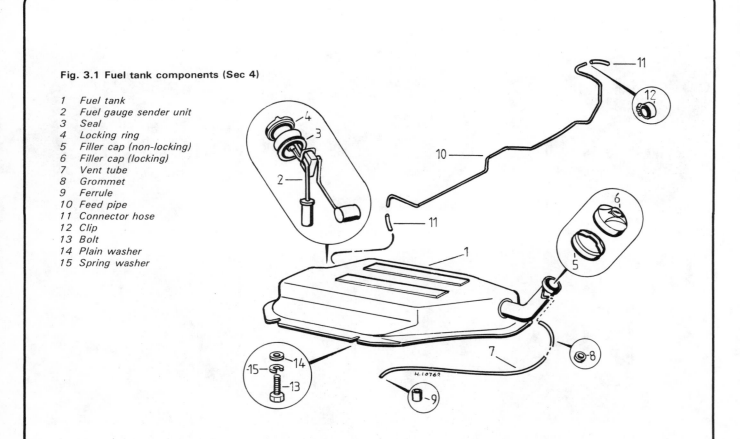

Fig. 3.1 Fuel tank components (Sec 4)

1   Fuel tank
2   Fuel gauge sender unit
3   Seal
4   Locking ring
5   Filler cap (non-locking)
6   Filler cap (locking)
7   Vent tube
8   Grommet
9   Ferrule
10 Feed pipe
11 Connector hose
12 Clip
13 Bolt
14 Plain washer
15 Spring washer

H.10762

1   Follow the procedure given in paragraphs 1 to 5 of Section 4.
2   Using two crossed screwdrivers, turn the locking ring to release it from the tank.
3   Withdraw the locking ring, seal, and sender unit.
4   Refitting is a reversal of removal, but always fit a new seal.

6   Choke control cable – removal and refitting

1   Disconnect the battery negative lead.
2   Remove the air cleaner and, with the choke now fully in, loosen the screw to release the inner cable from the carburettor lever (photo). Remove the small clamp.
3   Release the outer cable at the carburettor end, by removing the clip (photo).
4   Remove the screws retaining the steering column cowls to the outer column bracket.
5   Separate the cowls and withdraw the right-hand cowl.
6   Disconnect the lighting switch multi-plug and withdraw the left-hand cowl over the direction indicator switch.
7   Unclip the choke warning switch, remove the nut, and withdraw the choke cable through the bulkhead and cowl (photo).
8   Refitting is a reversal of removal, but before tightening the clamping pin, adjust the position of the inner cable to provide 0.08 in (2 mm) free movement.

7   Accelerator cable – removal and refitting

1   Disconnect the battery negative lead.
2   Remove the air cleaner, and loosen the screw to release the inner cable from the throttle lever.
3   Slide the outer cable from th carburettor bracket (photo).
4   Working inside the car, prise the retaining clip from the top of the accelerator pedal, and disconnect the inner cable (photo).
5   Prise the plastic bush from the bulkhead (engine side), and

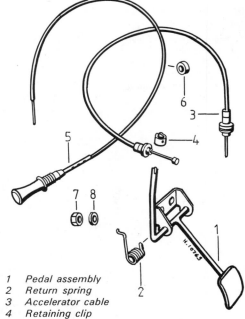
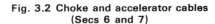

1   Pedal assembly
2   Return spring
3   Accelerator cable
4   Retaining clip
5   Choke cable
6   Grommet
7   Locknut
8   Washer

Fig. 3.2 Choke and accelerator cables (Secs 6 and 7)

6.2 Choke cable – inner cable and clamp pin

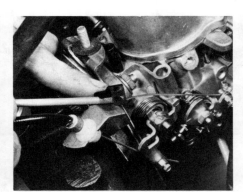
6.3 Removing the choke outer cable

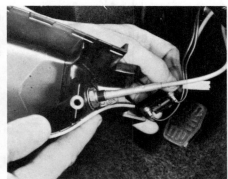
6.7 Choke warning switch and cable connection to steering column cowl

7.3 Removing the accelerator outer cable

7.4 Accelerator cable-to-pedal connection

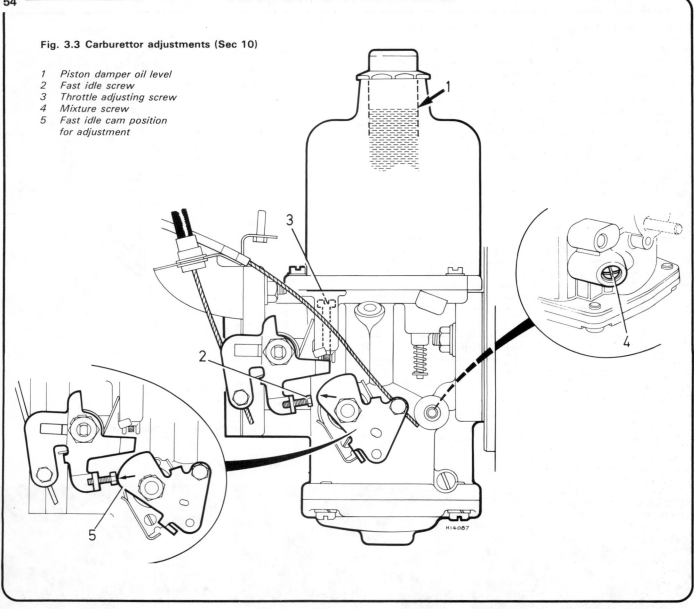

Fig. 3.3 Carburettor adjustments (Sec 10)

1 Piston damper oil level
2 Fast idle screw
3 Throttle adjusting screw
4 Mixture screw
5 Fast idle cam position
  for adjustment

H14087

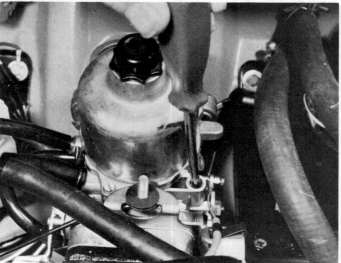

10.7 Adjusting the idling speed

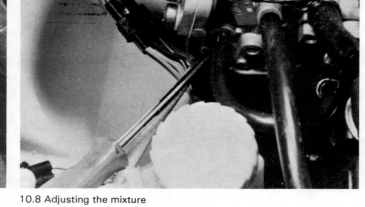

10.8 Adjusting the mixture

withdraw the complete accelerator cable from the engine compartment.

6   Refitting is a reversal of removal, but before tightening the clamping pin, adjust the position of the inner cable to provide 0.16 in (4 mm) free movement. Check that with the accelerator pedal fully depressed, the throttle lever is fully open, and with the pedal fully released the lever is in the closed position.

8   Accelerator pedal – removal and refitting

1   Working inside the car, prise the retaining clip from the top of the accelerator pedal and pull the inner cable out of the slot.
2   Unbolt and remove the accelerator pedal.
3   Refitting is the reverse of the removal procedure.

9   Carburettor – general description

The SU HIF carburettor is of variable choke, constant depression type, incorporating a sliding piston which automatically controls the mixture of air and fuel supplied to the engine in relation to the throttle valve position and engine speed.

The carburettor functions as follows. With the engine stationary, the sliding piston remains in its lowest position due to its weight and the pressure of the piston spring. When the engine is started and is allowed to idle, the throttle valve passes a small amount of air. Because the piston is in a low position, it offers a large restriction, and the resultant pressure reduction draws fuel from the jet, and atomisation occurs to provide a combustible mixture. Since the inside section of the tapered needle is across the mouth of the jet, a relatively small amount of fuel is passed.

When the throttle valve is opened, the amount of air passing through the carburettor is increased, which causes a greater depression beneath the sliding piston. An internal passageway connects this depression with the suction chamber above the piston, which now rises. The piston now offers less of a restriction and the depression is reduced, with the result that a point is reached where the forces of depression, gravity, and spring tension balance out. The tapered needle has now been raised, and more fuel passes from the jet.

The overall effect of this type of carburettor is that the depression remains relatively constant, and the fuel/air mixture is controlled to a fine degree over the complete throttle valve movement.

Fuel enrichment for cold starting is provided by a choke cable-operated valve, which admits more fuel into the airstream passing through the carburettor.

The jet adjusting (mixture) screw mechanism incorporates a bi-metal strip, which alters the position of the jet to compensate for varying fuel densities resulting from varying fuel temperatures.

A throttle damper is fitted to certain models in order to retard the action of the throttle lever as it returns to the idling position. This prevents an overweak mixture during deceleration and reduces the emission of certain harmful gases from the exhaust system.

10   Carburettor – idle and fast idle adjustment

Note: *Accurate adjustment of the carburettor is only possible after adjustment of the ignition timing, contact breaker gap, and spark plug gaps. Incorrect valve clearances can also affect carburettor adjustment.*

1   Connect a tachometer to the engine in accordance with the manufacturer's instructions. Remove the air cleaner.
2   Unscrew the piston damper and check that the oil level is level with the top of the hollow piston rod. If not, top up with clean engine oil. Refit the piston damper.
3   Check that the choke control cable has 0.08 in (2 mm) free play.
4   If available, connect an exhaust gas analyser to the engine in accordance with the manufacturer's instructions.
5   Run the engine at a fast idling speed until it reaches its normal operating temperature, indicated by the electric cooling fan operating. Continue to run the engine for a further five minutes.
6   Increase the engine speed to 2500 rpm for 30 seconds and repeat this at three-minute intervals during the adjustment procedure. This will ensure that any excess fuel is cleared from the intake manifold.
7   Allow the engine to idle and check the idling speed against that given in Specifications. If necessary, turn the throttle adjustment screw on top of the carburettor clockwise to increase the speed or anti-clockwise to decrease the speed (photo).
8   To adjust the idling mixture, slowly turn the mixture screw, located on the right-hand side of the carburettor, clockwise (to enrich) or anti-clockwise (to weaken), until a point is reached where the engine speed is fastest (photo).
9   Slowly turn the mixture screw anti-clockwise until the engine speed just commences to drop.
10   Turn the throttle adjustment screw to regain the specified idling speed.
11   If an exhaust gas analyser is being used, adjust the mixture screw to obtain the specified idling exhaust gas content, then readjust the throttle screw.
12   Pull out the choke control knob until the arrow on the fast idle cam is aligned with the fast idle adjusting screw, then check that the fast idle speed is as given in Specifications. If not, turn the fast idle adjusting screw as necessary.
13   Return the choke control knob, and switch off the engine
14   Disconnect the tachometer and exhaust gas analyser as necessary.
15   Refit the air cleaner with reference to Section 2.

11   Carburettor – throttle damper adjustment

1   Remove the air cleaner as described in Section 2.
2   Locate the throttle damper on the right-hand side of the carburettor (photo). Loosen the nut and bolt securing the clamp to the throttle spindle.
3   Locate a 0.12 in (3 mm) thick feeler gauge between the clamp lever and the damper plunger.
4   Depress the clamp lever until the plunger is fully compressed, then tighten the nut and bolt.
5   Release the clamp lever, and remove the feeler gauge.
6   Refit the air cleaner with reference to Section 2.

12   Carburettor – removal and refitting

1   Disconnect the battery negative lead.
2   Remove the air cleaner as described in Section 2.
3   Loosen the screws securing the choke and accelerator inner cables to their respective levers. Disconnect the outer cables and withdraw them from the carburettor.
4   Note the locations, then disconnect the vent tube and crankcase ventilation tube from the carburettor.
5   Disconnect and plug the fuel inlet pipe.
6   Disconnect the distributor vacuum pipe from the carburettor.

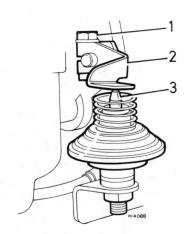

Fig. 3.4 The throttle damper (Sec 11)

1   *Clamp bolt*   2   *Lever*   3   *Plunger*

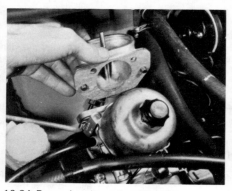

11.2 Throttle damper location

12.9A Removing the carburettor elbow

12.9B Removing the carburettor

7   Unscrew and remove the carburettor mounting nuts and washers.
8   Disconnect the carburettor heater wires (where fitted to cold country models).
9   Withdraw the carburettor from the inlet manifold studs, and, if necessary, remove the air cleaner elbow and gasket by unscrewing the two cross-head screws (photos).
10 Withdraw the gasket, control bracket complete with throttle damper, gasket, distance piece or heater (cold countries), and final gasket. If necessary, remove the throttle damper from the control bracket.
11 Refitting is a reversal of removal, but tighten the mounting nuts to the specified torque in diagonal sequence (where applicable), and always fit new gaskets. Make sure that the mating faces of each component are clean. Connect the choke and accelerator cables with reference to Sections 6 and 7. Adjust the throttle damper as described in Section 11. Adjust the idle and fast idle speeds as described in Section 10.

13 Carburettor – dismantling, overhaul and reassembly

1   Wash the exterior of the carburettor with paraffin and wipe dry.
2   Mark the float chamber cover in relation to the carburettor body. Remove the screws and withdraw the cover and sealing ring.
3   Unscrew and remove the mixture screw and withdraw the seal.
4   Unscrew the jet retaining screw and remove the spring.
5   Withdraw the jet and bi-metal lever assembly. Disengage the lever from the jet.
6   Unscrew and remove the float pivot and seal.
7   Withdraw the float and the needle valve.
8   Unscrew and remove the needle valve seat.
9   Unscrew and remove the piston damper and drain the oil.
10 Mark the suction chamber in relation to the carburettor body. Remove the screws and withdraw the suction chamber.
11 Remove the piston spring, and carefully lift the piston and needle assembly from the main body.
12 Unscrew the needle retaining grub screw. Remove the needle, guide, and spring from the piston.
13 From beneath the main body, unscrew the jet bearing nut and withdraw the bearing.
14 Note how the spring is attached to the fast idle cam lever. Bend back the locktabs, then unscrew the nut and remove the washer.
15 Hold the return spring against the main body, and use a screwdriver to prise the cam lever from the end of the cold start spindle. Remove the spring.
16 Remove the end cover and spindle seat.
17 Remove the two screws and withdraw the retaining plate, cold start body, and gasket.
18 Remove the O-ring from the end of the cold start spindle, and withdraw the spindle from the main body. Remove the cold start seal.
19 Dismantling of the throttle spindle is not recommended unless the components are damaged or excessively worn. If they are, first note how the return spring is attached to the throttle lever.
20 Mark the throttle valve in relation to the spindle and main body.
21 Remove the throttle valve screws while supporting the spindle with a block of wood if necessary.
22 Open the throttle and withdraw the valve disc.

23 Remove any burrs from the spindle screw holes with a fine file.
24 Bend back the locktabs and unscrew the spindle nut. Remove the lockwasher, plain washer, throttle lever, and return spring.
25 From the opposite end of the spindle, loosen the nut and bolt and remove the throttle damper lever.
26 Check the threaded end of the spindle and the main body in relation to each other, then withdraw the spindle. Remove the two seals.
27 Clean all the components in fuel and allow to dry. Thoroughly examine the components for damage and excessive wear. In particular check the throttle spindle and bearings for wear; if excessive, renewal of the spindle may be sufficient, but if the bearings are worn it may be necessary to renew the complete carburettor, as new bearings are not always available. Check the needle valve and seating for excessive ridging. Examine the main body for cracks and for security of the brass fittings and piston key. Check the tapered needle, jet, and jet bearing for wear. Shake the float and listen for any trapped fuel which may have entered through a small crack or fracture. Renew the components as necessary and obtain a complete set of gaskets and seals, and two new throttle valve screws if necessary.
28 Clean the inside of the suction chamber and the periphery of the piston with methylated spirit. *Do not use any form of abrasive.* Lubricate the piston rod with engine oil and insert it into the suction chamber. Hold the two components horizontal and spin the piston in several positions; the piston must spin freely without touching the suction chamber.
29 Commence reassembly by fitting the throttle spindle and two seals to the main body. The seals must be slightly recessed in their housings.
30 Locate the return spring and throttle lever on the end of the spindle, and fit the plain washer, lockwasher, and nut. Tighten the nut while holding the lever, and bend over the locktabs to lock.
31 Engage the return spring with the throttle lever and main body, and tension the spring.
32 Fit the throttle valve disc to the spindle in its original position, and insert the new screws, tightening them loosely (coat the threads with a liquid locking agent).
33 Open and close the throttle several times to settle the disc, then tighten the screws while supporting the spindle on a block of wood. Using a small chisel, spread the ends of the screws to lock them.
34 Locate the throttle damper lever loosely on the end of the spindle.
35 Locate the cold start seal in the main body with the cut-out uppermost.
36 Insert the cold start spindle (hole uppermost), and fit the O-ring.
37 Fit the cold start body with the cut-out uppermost, and the retaining plate with the slotted flange facing the throttle spindle. Use a new gasket, then insert and tighten the retaining screws.
38 Fit the spindle seat and end cover, followed by the spring, cam lever, lockwasher, and nut. Make sure that the spring is correctly engaged, then tighten the nut and bend over the locktabs to lock.
39 Insert the jet bearing and nut, and tighten the nut.
40 Connect the bi-metal lever with the fuel jet, making sure that the jet head moves freely in the cut-out.
41 Insert the mixture screw and seal into the main body. Fit the jet to the bearing, and at the same time engage the slot in the bi-metal lever with the small diameter of the mixture screw.
42 Insert the jet retaining screw with the spring, and tighten the screw.

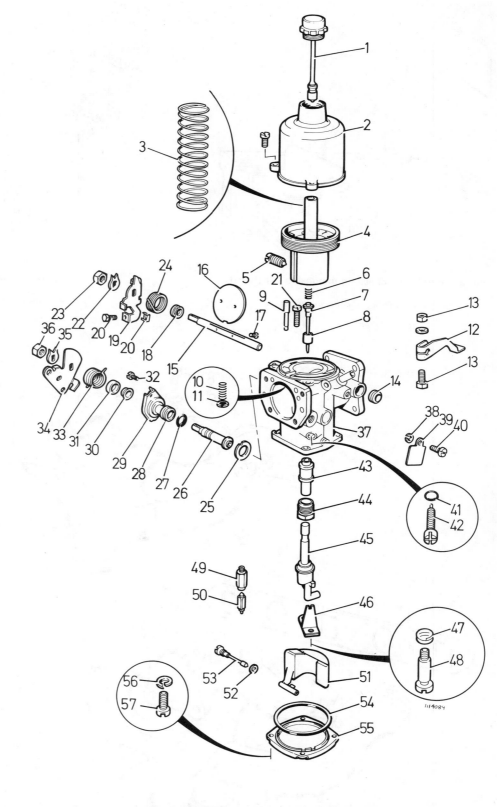

1 Piston damper
2 Suction chamber
3 Spring
4 Piston
5 Grub screw
6 Spring
7 Needle
8 Guide
9 Lifting pin
10 Spring
11 Circlip
12 Throttle damper lever
13 Clamp bolt and nut
14 Seal
15 Throttle spindle
16 Throttle valve disc
17 Screw
18 Seal
19 Throttle lever
20 Fast idle adjustment
    screw
21 Idle adjustment screw
22 Lockwasher
23 Nut
24 Return spring
25 Cold start seal
26 Cold start spindle
27 O-ring
28 Cold start body
29 Retaining plate
30 Seat
31 End cover
32 Screw
33 Return spring
34 Fast idle cam
35 Lockwasher
36 Nut
37 Main body
38 Spring washer
39 Identification tab
40 Screw
41 Seal
42 Mixture screw
43 Jet bearing
44 Jet bearing nut
45 Jet assembly
46 Bi-metal lever
47 Spring
48 Screw
49 Needle valve seat
50 Needle valve
51 Float
52 Seal
53 Pivot
54 Seal
55 Float chamber cover
56 Spring washer
57 Screw

Fig. 3.5 Exploded view of the carburettor (Sec 13)

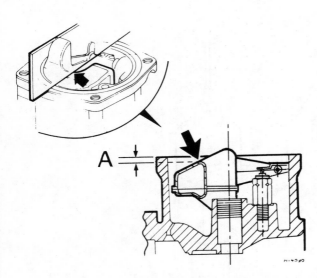

Fig. 3.6 Float level checking dimension (A) (Sec 13)

Arrows indicate checking point

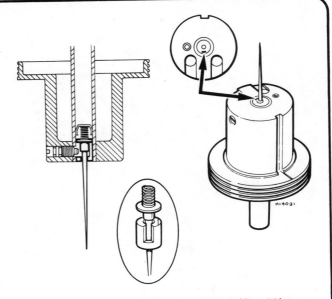

Fig. 3.7 Tapered needle installation (Sec 13)

Arrows indicate etch mark location

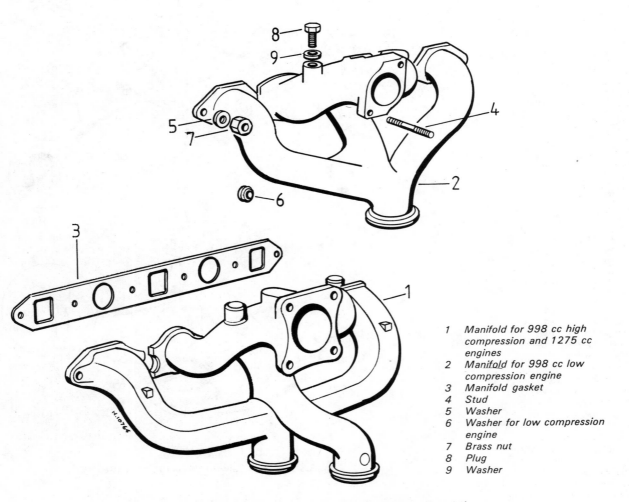

1 Manifold for 998 cc high
   compression and 1275 cc
   engines
2 Manifold for 998 cc low
   compression engine
3 Manifold gasket
4 Stud
5 Washer
6 Washer for low compression
   engine
7 Brass nut
8 Plug
9 Washer

Fig. 3.8 The combined inlet and exhaust manifolds (Sec 14)

43 Adjust the mixture screw so that the top of the jet is flush with the venturi bridge.

44 Insert and tighten the needle valve seat, and with the carburettor inserted, insert the needle valve.

45 Position the float, then insert the pivot and seal through the body and float and tighten.

46 To check the float level adjustment, hold the carburetter inverted, with the float keeping the needle valve shut. Refer to Fig. 3.6 and, using a straight edge and feeler blade, check that the centre portion of the float is between 0.020 and 0.040 in (0.5 and 1.0 mm) below the surface of the float chamber face. If not, bend the brass tab which contacts the needle valve as necessary.

47 Fit the float chamber cover in its original position together with a new sealing ring. Tighten the screws in diagonal sequence.

48 Insert the spring, needle, and guide into the piston with the guide etch marks facing the suction transfer holes, and with the bottom face of the guide flush with the bottom face of the piston.

49 Insert and tighten the guide retaining grub screw.

50 Lower the piston and needle assembly into the main body, at the same time engaging the slot with the piston key.

51 Locate the spring over the piston rod.

52 Hold the suction chamber directly over the piston with its location mark aligned with the mark on the body, then lower it over the spring and piston rod. It is important not to tension the spring by twisting the suction chamber.

53 Insert and tighten the suction chamber retaining screws. Lift the piston with the finger, then release it and check that it returns to the venturi bridge without any assistance. If not, it may be necessary to loosen the retaining screws and slightly reposition the suction chamber.

54 Pour clean engine oil into the top of the suction chamber until the level is 0.5 in (13 mm) above the top of the hollow piston rod. Refit and tighten the piston damper.

14 Inlet and exhaust manifold – description, removal and refitting

1   The inlet and exhaust manifolds are manufactured as one integral casting. On 998 cc low compression models the exhaust manifold passageways converge into a single downpipe, but on all other models, the central siamesed exhaust manifold passageway is connected to a separate downpipe. In the latter case, the two downpipes converge just in front of the front silencer.

2   To remove the manifold, first remove the carburettor as described in Section 12.

3   Remove the clamp(s) securing the downpipe(s) to the manifold.

4   Twist the plate on the heat stove, unscrew the nuts, and withdraw the stove (photos).

5   Unscrew the remaining nuts, remove the washers where fitted, and withdraw the manifold from the cylinder head (photo).

6   Remove the gasket. Clean the mating faces of the manifold, cylinder head, and exhaust system downpipe.

7   Refitting is a reversal of removal, but use a new gasket, and make sure that the downpipe is correctly located on the manifold before fitting the clamp. A little sealing paste will prevent the downpipe joint(s) from leaking.

15 Exhaust system – checking, removal and refitting

1   The exhaust system should be examined for leaks, damage, and security every 12 000 miles (20 000 km) or 12 months, whichever occurs first. To do this, apply the handbrake and allow the engine to idle. Lie down on each side of the car in turn, and check the full length of the exhaust system for leaks while an assistant temporarily places a wad of cloth over the tailpipe. If a leak is evident, stop the engine and use a proprietary repair kit to seal it. If the leak is excessive or damage is evident, renew the section. Check the rubber mountings for deterioration, and renew them if necessary.

2   To remove the exhaust system, jack up the front and rear of the car and support it on axle stands. Alternatively, locate the front wheels on car ramps and jack up the rear and support with axle stands.

3   Lift the spare wheel cover in the luggage compartment and unscrew the rear exhaust mounting nut. Remove the lockwasher and plain washer (photo).

14.4A Remove the retaining nuts ...

14.4B ... and withdraw the heat stove

14.5 Removing the manifold (1.3 HLS)

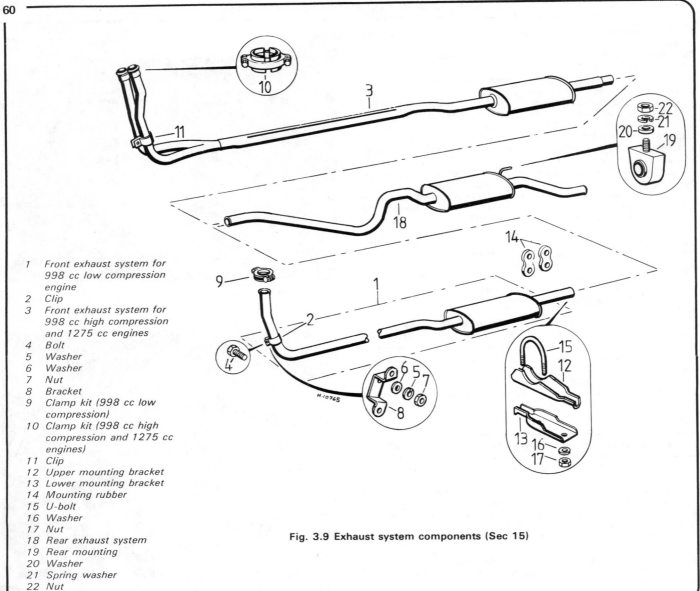

1 Front exhaust system for 998 cc low compression engine
2 Clip
3 Front exhaust system for 998 cc high compression and 1275 cc engines
4 Bolt
5 Washer
6 Washer
7 Nut
8 Bracket
9 Clamp kit (998 cc low compression)
10 Clamp kit (998 cc high compression and 1275 cc engines)
11 Clip
12 Upper mounting bracket
13 Lower mounting bracket
14 Mounting rubber
15 U-bolt
16 Washer
17 Nut
18 Rear exhaust system
19 Rear mounting
20 Washer
21 Spring washer
22 Nut

Fig. 3.9 Exhaust system components (Sec 15)

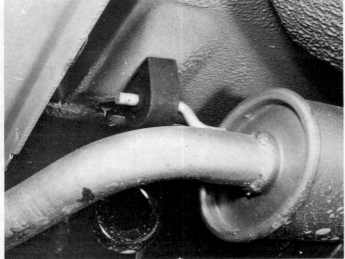

15.3 Exhaust system rear mounting

15.4 Exhaust system intermediate mounting

15.6A Exhaust system front downpipe clamp

15.6B Exhaust system front mounting clamp (1.3 HLS)

15.8 Exhaust system front downpipes (1.3 HLS)

4 Working under the car, disconnect the intermediate rubber mountings (photo), lower the rear section, and remove the rear mounting.
5 Unscrew the nuts and remove the two mounting plates and U-bolt. Tap around the joint with a hammer, and twist the rear section from the front section, removing it from the rear of the car. If necessary, carefully heat the joint with a blowlamp to assist removal, *but shield the fuel tank, fuel lines, and underbody adequately from heat.*

6 Remove the front downpipe clamp(s), and remove the bolt from the front mounting clamp (photos).
7 Lower the front exhaust section from the car.
8 Refitting is a reversal of removal, but fit the downpipe(s) to the manifold before finally positioning the rear section to the rear mounting and tightening the intermediate clamp (photo). Use a little sealing paste at the manifold joint(s) to prevent leakage. Run the engine and check for leaks as described in paragraph 1.

16 Fault diagnosis – fuel and exhaust systems

Symptom	Reason(s)
Excessive fuel consumption	Air cleaner element choked
	Leaks in fuel tank, carburettor, or fuel lines
	Float level incorrect
	Mixture adjustment incorrect
	Valve clearances incorrect
	Brakes binding
	Tyres underinflated
Insufficient fuel supply or weak mixture	Sticking needle valve
	Faulty fuel pump
	Leaking fuel pipe unions
	Leaking manifold gasket
	Leaking carburettor mounting gasket
	Mixture adjustment incorrect

Chapter 4 Ignition system

For modifications and information applicable to later models, see Supplement at end of manual

Contents

Coil – description and testing 8
Condenser – testing, removal and refitting 4
Contact breaker points – checking and adjustment 2
Contact breaker points – renewal 3
Distributor – dismantling, overhaul and reassembly 7

Distributor – removal and refitting 5
Fault diagnosis – ignition system 10
General description 1
Ignition timing – adjustment 6
Spark plugs and HT leads – general 9

Specifications

System type .... 12 volt battery, coil, and distributor with self-cleaning contact breaker points

Coil
Type .... Lucas 45D4, Lucas 59D4 or Ducellier
Ballast resistance .... 1.3 to 1.5 ohms

Distributor
Type .... Lucas 45D4 or Ducellier
Rotor rotation .... Anti-clockwise
Dwell angle:
    Lucas .... 54° ± 5°
    Ducellier .... 57° ± 2.5°
Contact breaker gap:
    Lucas .... 0.014 to 0.016 in (0.35 to 0.40 mm)
    Ducellier (initial) .... 0.015 in (0.38 mm)
Condenser capacity .... 0.18 to 0.25 mfd
Centrifugal advance (decelerating):
    998 cc .... 22° to 26° at 4800 rpm
                                   14° to 18° at 2800 rpm
                                       10° to 14° at 1500 rpm
                                       0° to 2° at 600 rpm
    1275 cc .... 24° to 28° at 5200 rpm
                                       23° to 27° at 2800 rpm
                                       16° to 20° at 2500 rpm
                                       8° to 12° at 1600 rpm
                                       0° to 4° at 700 rpm
Vacuum advance (maximum):
    998 cc (except HLE) .... 12° to 16° at 11 in (279 mm) Hg
    998 cc (HLE) .... 14° to 16° at 9 in (229 mm) Hg
    1275 cc .... 14° to 18° at 8 in (203 mm) Hg
Lubricant type/specification .... Multigrade engine oil, viscosity SAE 15W/50 or 10W/40 (Duckhams QXR, Hypergrade, or 10W/40 Motor Oil)

Firing order 1-3-4-2

Ignition timing at 1500 rpm (with vacuum disconnected)
998 cc (except HLE) .... 15 ° BTDC
998 cc (HLE) .... 8 ± 2° BTDC
1275 cc .... 11° BTDC

Spark plugs
Type .... Unipart GSP 263
Gap .... 0.025 in (0.64 mm)

Torque wrench settings

	lbf ft	kgf m
Spark plugs	18	2.5
Distributor clamp	16	2.2

1 General description

A conventional ignition system is fitted, comprising the battery, coil, distributor, and spark plugs. The distributor is driven by a driveshaft in mesh with the camshaft.

In order that the engine can run correctly, it is necessary for an electrical spark to ignite the fuel/air mixture in the combustion chamber at exactly the right moment in relation to engine speed and load. The ignition system is based on feeding low tension voltage from the battery to the coil, where it is converted to high tension voltage. The high tension voltage is powerful enough to jump the spark plug gap in the cylinders many times a second under high compression, providing that the system is in good condition and that all adjustments are correct.

The ignition system is divided into two circuits, the low tension circuit and the high tension circuit. The low tension (sometimes known as the primary) circuit consists of the battery, lead to the ignition switch, lead from the ignition switch to the low tension or primary coil windings (terminal +), and the lead from the low tension coil windings (coil terminal -) to the contact breaker points and condenser in the distributor. The high tension circuit consists of the high tension or secondary coil windings, the heavy ignition lead from the coil to the distributor cap, the rotor arm, and the spark plug leads and spark plugs.

The system functions in the following manner. Low tension voltage is changed in the coil into high tension voltage by the opening and closing of the contact breaker points in the low tension circuit. High tension voltage is then fed via the carbon brush in the centre of the distributor cap to the rotor arm of the distributor, and each time it comes in line with one of the four metal segments in the cap, which are connected to the spark plug leads, the opening and closing of the contact breaker points causes the high tension voltage to build up, jump the gap from the rotor arm to the appropriate metal segment, and so via the spark plug lead to the spark plug, where it finally jumps the spark plug gap before going to earth. The ignition is advanced and retarded automatically, to ensure that the spark occurs at just the right instant for the particular load at the prevailing engine speed.

The ignition advance is controlled both mechanically and by a vacuum operated system. The mechanical governor mechanism comprises two weights, which move out from the distributor shaft as the engine speed rises due to centrifugal force. As they move outwards they rotate the cam relative to the distributor shaft, and so advance the spark. The weights are held in position by two light springs and it is the tension of the springs which is largely responsible for correct spark advancement.

The vacuum control consists of a diaphragm, one side of which is connected via a small bore tube to the carburettor, and the other side to the contact breaker plate. Depression in the inlet manifold and carburettor, which varies with engine speed and throttle opening, causes the diaphragm to move, so moving the contact breaker plate, and advancing or retarding the spark. A fine degree of control is achieved by a spring in the vacuum assembly.

The ignition system incorporates a resistive wire which is in circuit all the time that the engine is running. When the starter is operated, the resistance is bypassed to provide increased voltage at the spark plugs.

2 Contact breaker points – checking and adjustment

1   Every 12 000 miles (20 000 km) or 12 months the contact breaker points should be checked and adjusted and the distributor lubricated. Due to its location, it is recommended that the distributor is removed to carry out this work (refer to Section 5).

2   Clamp the distributor lightly in a vice and remove the rotor arm.
3   Open the points and examine the condition of their faces. If they are blackened or pitted, remove them as described in Section 3 and dress them using emery tape or a grindstone. On the Ducellier distributor, take care to maintain the contour of the points. If the points are worn excessively, renew them.
4   If the contact points do not show any excessive pitting, turn the drive dog until the heel of the movable contact is on the high point of one of the cam lobes.
5   Using a feeler blade, check that the gap between the two points is as given in the Specifications. If not, loosen the fixed contact screw and reposition the fixed contact until the feeler blade is a firm sliding fit between the two points. Use a screwdriver in the special notch to make a fine adjustment, and when correct, tighten the fixed contact screw (photos).
6   Apply one drop of engine oil to the felt pad in the cam recess, then refit the rotor arm.
7   Wipe clean the ignition coil tower and the distributor cap, and make sure that the carbon brush moves freely against the tension of the spring. Clean the metal segments in the distributor cap, but do not scrape away any metal otherwise the HT spark at the spark plugs will be reduced.
8   Refit the distributor as described in Section 5 and use a dwell meter to check the dwell angle of the points. If this is not as given in the Specifications, reduce the contact points gap in order to increase the dwell angle, or increase the points gap to reduce the dwell angle. On the Ducellier distributor, tool number 18G 1308 may be used to adjust the gap.
9   Check and if necessary adjust the ignition timing as described in Section 6.

3 Contact breaker points – renewal

1   The contact breaker points should be renewed every 24 000 miles (40 000 km) or 24 months whichever is sooner.
2   Remove the distributor as described in Section 5, and clamp it slightly in a vice. Remove the rotor arm (photo).

Lucas distributors
3   Press the moving contact spring from the insulator post and slide out the low tension connector (photos).
4   Unscrew the fixed contact retaining screw and remove the contact breaker set from the baseplate and pin (photo).

Ducellier distributors
5   Remove the spring clip from the two pivot posts.
6   Remove the fibre washer and lift the moving contact from the pivot post. Slide the LT wire retaining block from the distributor body and disconnect the condenser lead.

2.5A Adjusting the contact breaker points gap (Lucas)

2.5B Loosening the fixed contact retaining screw (Lucas)

3.2 Removing the rotor arm (Lucas)

3.3A Disconnecting the contact spring from the insulator (Lucas)

3.3B Disconnecting the low tension connector (Lucas)

3.4 Removing the contact breaker set (Lucas)

3.8 Engaging the nylon plate with the pin – arrowed (Lucas)

4.8 Removing the condenser (Lucas)

5.5 Removing the distributor cap

5.8A Unscrewing the distributor base clamp bolt (engine removed)

5.8B Unscrewing the distributor base clamp bolt (engine in car)

5.9A Installing the distributor (engine removed)

5.9B Installing the distributor (engine in car)

7   Remove the screw and washer and withdraw the fixed contact from the baseplate.

All distributors

8   Refitting is a reversal of removal. Adjust the points gap as described in Section 2. On the Lucas version, make sure that the nylon plate engages the pin (photo).

4   Condenser – testing, removal and refitting

1   The condenser is fitted in parallel with the contact points, and its purpose is to reduce arcing between the points, and also to accelerate the collapse of the coil low tension magnetic field. A faulty condenser can cause the complete failure of the ignition system, as the points will be prevented from interrupting the low tension circuit.
2   To test the condenser, remove the distributor cap and rotate the engine until the contact points are closed. Switch on the ignition and separate the points. If this is accompanied by a *strong* blue flash, the condenser is faulty (a *weak* spark is normal).
3   A further test can be made, for short circuiting, by removing the condenser and using a test lamp and leads connected to the supply lead and body. If the test lamp lights, the condenser is faulty.
4   The most infallible test is to substitute a new unit and check whether the fault persists.
5   To remove the condenser, first remove the distributor as described in Section 5 and clamp it lightly in a vice.

Lucas type

6   Remove the rotor arm, and push the low tension lead and grommet in through the hole in the body.
7   Press the moving contact spring from the insulator post, and slide out the low tension lead connector.
8   Remove the retaining screw and earth lead and withdraw the condenser (photo).

Ducellier type

9   Pull the supply lead from the block on the side of the distributor.
10 Remove the retaining screw and withdraw the condenser.

All types

11 Refitting is a reversal of the removal procedure.

5   Distributor – removal and refitting

1   Disconnect the battery negative terminal lead.
2   Remove the No. 1 spark plug (crankshaft pulley end) and place the thumb over the aperture.
3   Turn the engine in the normal running direction (clockwise from crankshaft pulley end) until pressure is felt in No 1 cylinder, indicating that the piston is commencing its compression stroke. Use a spanner on the crankshaft pulley bolt, or engage top gear and pull the car forwards.
4   Continue turning the engine until the V-notch in the crankshaft pulley is exactly in line with the timing cover pointer TDC mark. Note that the large pointer indicates top dead centre (TDC), and the remaining pointer peaks are in increments of 4° BTDC.
5   Make a mark on the distributor body in line with the No 1 spark plug HT lead terminal in the distributor cap. Remove the cap and check that the rotor arm is pointing to the mark (photo).
6   Make a further mark on the cylinder block in line with the previous mark.
7   Disconnect the low tension lead and the vacuum advance pipe.
8   Remove the single base clamp bolt and withdraw the distributor from the cylinder block. Remove the clamp plate (photos).
9   To refit the distributor, slide it into the cylinder block and engage the offset drive dog with the driveshaft (photos).
10 Turn the body to align the previously made marks on the body and cylinder block. Provided that the engine has not been turned, the rotor arm should also point towards the mark on the body.
11 Fit the clamp and tighten the securing bolt, then refit the distributor cap and reconnect the low tension lead.
12 Refit the No 1 spark plug and HT lead. Reconnect the battery negative lead.

13 Check and, if necessary, adjust the ignition timing as described in Section 6, then refit the vacuum advance pipe.

6   Ignition timing – adjustment

Note: *For the home mechanic, there is only one suitable method which may be used to time the ignition – the stroboscopic timing light method. However; for initial setting-up purposes (ie after a major overhaul, or if the timing has been otherwise completely lost), a basic static timing method should be used to get the engine started. This involves the use of a test bulb. Once the engine is running, the timing should then be correctly set using the stroboscopic timing light method. A further method, employing the light emitting diode (LED) sensor bracket and timing disc located on the bottom of the timing cover, may be used, but the equipment for use with this system will not normally be available to the home mechanic.*

Test bulb method

1   Remove the No 1 spark plug (crankshaft pulley end) and place the thumb over the aperture.
2   Turn the engine in the normal running direction (clockwise from crankshaft pulley end) until pressure is felt in No 1 cylinder, indicating that the piston is commencing its compression stroke. Use a spanner on the crankshaft pulley bolt, or engage top gear and pull the car forwards on manual gearbox models.
3   Continue turning the engine until the V-notch in the crankshaft pulley is exactly in line with the timing cover pointer representing 4° BTDC. Note that the large pointer indicates top dead centre (TDC) and the remaining pointer peaks are in increments of 4° BTDC.
4   Remove the distributor cap and check that the rotor arm is pointing in the direction of the No 1 terminal of the cap.
5   Connect a 12 volt test bulb between the end of the moving contact spring and a suitable earthing point on the engine.
6   Loosen the distributor clamp plate bolt.
7   Switch on the ignition. If the bulb is already lit, turn the distributor body slightly anti-clockwise until the bulb goes out.
8   Turn the distributor body clockwise until the bulb *just* lights up, indicating that the points have just opened. Tighten the clamp bolt.
9   Switch off the ignition and remove the test bulb.
10 Refit the distributor cap and No 1 spark plug and HT lead. Once the engine has been started, check the timing stroboscopically as follows and adjust as necessary.

Stroboscopic timing light method

11 Disconnect and plug the vacuum pipe at the distributor.
12 Wipe clean the crankshaft pulley notch and timing cover pointers. If necessary, use white paint or chalk to highlight the marks.
13 Connect the timing light to the engine in accordance with the manufacturer's instructions (usually between No 1 spark plug and HT lead).
14 Connect a tachometer to the engine in accordance with the manufacturer's instructions.
15 Start the engine and run it at the speed given in the Specifications for stroboscopic timing.
16 Point the timing light at the timing marks and they should appear to be stationary with the crank pulley notch in alignment with the appropriate mark; refer to the Specifications for the ignition timing applicable to the engine being worked on. Note that the large pointer indicates top dead centre (TDC) and the remaining pointer peaks are in increments of 4° BTDC.
17 If adjustment is necessary (ie the pulley notch does not line up with the appropriate mark), loosen the distributor clamp plate bolt and turn the body clockwise to advance and anti-clockwise to retard the ignition timing. Tighten the bolt when the setting is correct.
18 Gradually increase the engine speed while still pointing the timing light at the timing marks. The pulley notch should appear to move anti-clockwise proving that the centrifugal weights are operating correctly. If the ignition advance is not in accordance with the information given in the Specifications, the distributor should be overhauled as described in Section 7 and a check made of the centrifugal mechanism.
19 Switch off the engine and remove the timing light and tachometer.
20 Reconnect the vacuum pipe to the distributor. Disconnect the pipe from the carburettor and remove the distributor cap. Suck on the end of the pipe and check that the baseplate (Lucas) or pivot link (Ducellier) move to advance the points. If not, the vacuum unit may be faulty.
21 Refit the distributor cap and vacuum pipe.

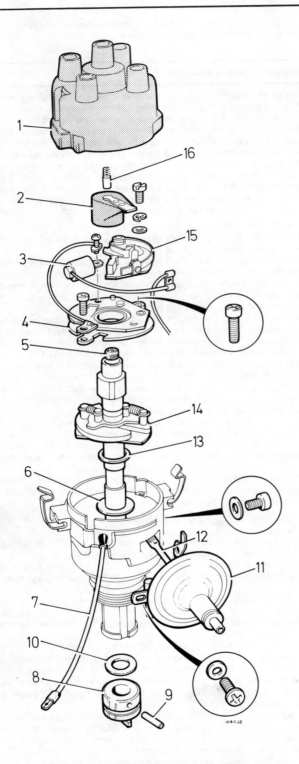

Fig. 4.1 Exploded view of the Lucas distributor (Sec 7)

1	Distributor cap	10	Thrust washer
2	Rotor arm	11	Vacuum unit
3	Condenser	12	Arm
4	Baseplate assembly	13	Spacer
5	Felt pad	14	Centrifugal advance
6	Steel washer		mechanism
7	LT lead	15	Contact set
8	Drive dog	16	Pick-up brush
9	Roll pin		

7   Distributor – dismantling, overhaul and reassembly

Note: *The distributor is designed to operate over very high mileages, and when wear eventually takes place, particularly between the shaft and body, the complete distributor should be renewed. However, if wear between these components is not excessive, the distributor can be overhauled provided that spares are available.*

Lucas distributor

1   Remove the contact breaker points as described in Section 3, and the condenser as described in Section 4.
2   Extract the felt pad from the cam recess.
3   Remove the baseplate securing screws and the earth lead. Withdraw the baseplate.
4   Remove the securing screws and washers and withdraw the vacuum advance unit.
5   Note the relationship between the offset drive dog and the rotor arm location notch. Locate the drive dog on a V-block or vice, and drive out the roll pin with a suitable drift.
6   Remove the drive dog and thrust washer, and withdraw the shaft, steel shim, and nylon spacer.
7   Note the position of the springs, then remove them from the centrifugal mechanism. Further dismantling of the distributor is not recommended.
8   Clean all components with paraffin and wipe dry. Examine each part for damage and deterioration. If the shaft-to-body wear is excessive, renew the complete distributor. If the centrifugal weight and cam mechanism is worn, renew the shaft. Renew the advance springs if they are weak. Check that the baseplate halves move freely and that the spring is not damaged. Clean any carbon from the rotor arm and distributor cap and check them for tracking. Renew the distributor shank O-ring seal if necessary.
9   Commence reassembly by lubricating the shaft with a molybdenum-based grease. Fit the nylon spacer followed by the steel shim, then insert the shaft into the body.
10   Fit the thrust washer and drive dog. Align the drive dog as shown in Fig. 4.2 and secure with a new roll pin. If a new driveshaft is being fitted, hold the shaft and drive dog firmly against each other while drilling to avoid excessive endplay.
11   Fit the vacuum advance unit and secure with the two screws.
12   Lower the baseplate into the distributor, and engage the pin with the vacuum advance unit arm.

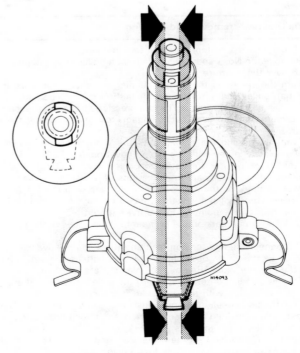

Fig. 4.2 Drive dog-to-rotor arm relationship on the Lucas distributor (Sec 7)

Measuring plug gap. A feeler gauge of the correct size (see ignition system specifications) should have a slight 'drag' when slid between the electrodes. Adjust gap if necessary

Adjusting plug gap. The plug gap is adjusted by bending the earth electrode inwards, or outwards, as necessary until the correct clearance is obtained. Note the use of the correct tool

Normal. Grey-brown deposits, lightly coated core nose. Gap increasing by around 0.001 in (0.025 mm) per 1000 miles (1600 km). Plugs ideally suited to engine, and engine in good condition

Carbon fouling. Dry, black, sooty deposits. Will cause weak spark and eventually misfire. Fault: over-rich fuel mixture. Check: carburettor mixture settings, float level and jet sizes; choke operation and cleanliness of air filter. Plugs can be re-used after cleaning

Oil fouling. Wet, oily deposits. Will cause weak spark and eventually misfire. Fault: worn bores/piston rings or valve guides; sometimes occurs (temporarily) during running-in period. Plugs can be re-used after thorough cleaning

Overheating. Electrodes have glazed appearance, core nose very white — few deposits. Fault: plug overheating. Check: plug value, ignition timing, fuel octane rating (too low) and fuel mixture (too weak). Discard plugs and cure fault immediately

Electrode damage. Electrodes burned away; core nose has burned, glazed appearance. Fault: pre-ignition. Check: as for 'Overheating' but may be more severe. Discard plugs and remedy fault before piston or valve damage occurs

Split core nose (may appear initially as a crack). Damage is self-evident, but cracks will only show after cleaning. Fault: pre-ignition or wrong gap-setting technique. Check: ignition timing, cooling system, fuel octane rating (too low) and fuel mixture (too weak). Discard plugs, rectify fault immediately

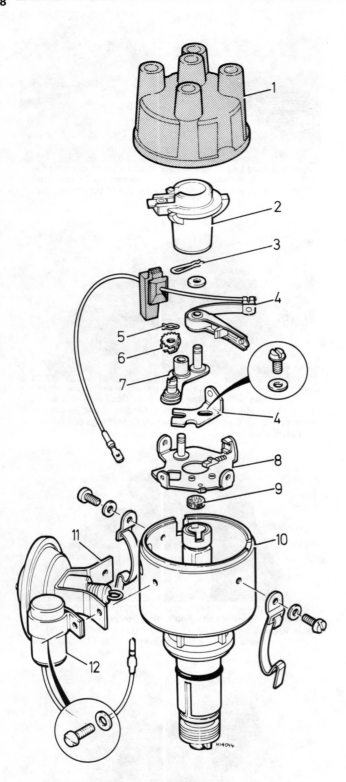

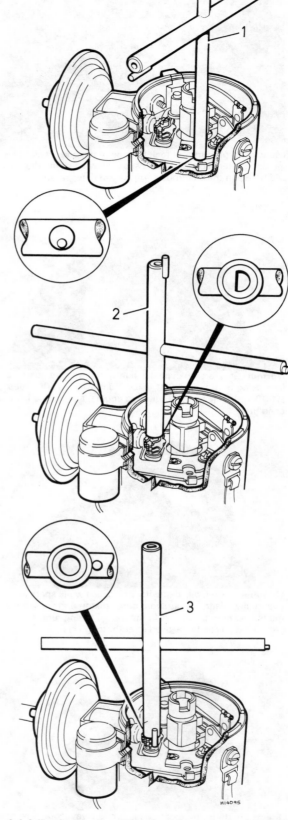

Fig. 4.3 Exploded view of the Ducellier distributor (Sec 7)

1	Distributor cap	7	Eccentric D-post
2	Rotor arm	8	Baseplate
3	Clip	9	Felt pad
4	Contact set	10	Body
5	Clip	11	Vacuum unit
6	Serrated cam	12	Condenser

Fig. 4.4 Adjusting the Ducellier distributor using tool 18G1308 (Sec 7)

1	Dwell angle adjustment	3	Vacuum advance point adjustment
2	Dwell variation adjustment		

13 Fit the earth lead and tighten the two baseplate screws.
14 Fit the condenser and contact breaker points with reference to Sections 4 and 3 respectively.
15 Locate the felt pad in the cam recess, and lubricate it with one drop of engine oil.

Ducellier distributor

16 Remove the contact breaker points as described in Section 3, and the condenser as described in Section 4.
17 Extract the felt pad from the cam recess.
18 Remove the remaining vacuum unit screw and clip.
19 Note the location of the vacuum unit seat in the serrated cam. Extract the clip, disengage the serrated cam and link from the D-post, and withdraw the vacuum unit.
20 Remove the remaining baseplate retaining screw and clip, and withdraw the baseplate complete with nylon pressure pad and spring.
21 Clean all components with paraffin and wipe dry. Examine each part for damage and deterioration. Note that the drive dog is a loose fit on the driveshaft to ensure correct alignment. If the shaft-to-body wear is excessive, or if the advance mechanism is worn renew the complete distributor. Clean any carbon from the rotor arm and distributor cap, and check them both for tracking. Renew the distributor shank O-ring seal if necessary.
22 Commence reassembly by lubricating the centrifugal weight pivot posts, the cam, pressure pad, and contact pivot post with multi-purpose grease.
23 Assemble the spring and pressure pad to the baseplate, and locate the baseplate in the distributor body. Secure the baseplate with one screw and washer inserted through the spring clip.
24 Insert the vacuum unit and locate the link into the serrated cam and over the D-post. Make sure that the vacuum unit seat is correctly mated with the serrated cam. Fit the retaining clip.
25 Secure the vacuum unit with one screw and washer inserted through the remaining spring clip.
26 Locate the felt pad in the cam recess and lubricate it with one drop of engine oil.
27 Fit the condenser and contact breaker points with reference to Sections 4 and 3 respectively.
28 Ideally the vacuum unit setting should be checked after dismantling and reassembling the distributor. To do this, first check and adjust the dwell angle as described in Section 2 at idle speed with the vacuum advance pipe disconnected from the distributor and plugged.
29 Increase the engine speed to 2000 rpm and check that the dwell angle is still within the specified tolerance. If not, the moving contact may be partially seized on the pivot post.
30 Reconnect the vacuum pipe and check the dwell variation while increasing the engine speed to 2000 rpm and then releasing the throttle. To make an adjustment for minimum variation, use tool number 18G1308 on the eccentric D-post. After making a dwell variation adjustment, recheck the basic idle dwell setting and adjust if necessary; also recheck the ignition timing.
31 The serrated cam position determines the point at which vacuum advance commences, but this can only be checked by using a vacuum pump and gauge.

8 Coil – description and testing

1 The coil is bolted to the front of the engine, and it should be periodically wiped down to prevent high tension (HT) voltage loss through possible arcing.
2 To ensure the correct HT polarity at the spark plugs, the LT coil leads must always be connected correctly. The LT lead from the distributor should be connected to the negative (-) terminal on the coil. Incorrect connections can cause bad starting, misfiring, and short spark plug life.
3 Accurate testing of the coil requires special equipment, and for the home mechanic the easiest test is by substitution of a new unit.

9 Spark plugs and HT leads – general

1 The correct functioning of the spark plugs is vital for the correct running and efficiency of the engine. The spark plugs should be renewed every 12 000 miles (20 000 km). However, if misfiring or bad starting is experienced in the service period, they must be removed, cleaned, and regapped. Note that it is advisable, though not essential, to remove the air cleaner for access to No 4 spark plug (refer to Chapter 3).
2 The condition of the spark plugs will also tell much about the overall condition of the engine.
3 If the insulator nose of the spark plug is clean and white, with no deposits, this is indicative of a weak mixture, or too hot a plug. (A hot plug transfers heat away from the electrode slowly – a cold plug transfers it away quickly).
4 If the tip and insulator nose is covered wth hard black-looking deposits, then this is indicative that the mixture is too rich. Should the plug be black and oily, then it is likely that the engine is fairly worn, as well as the mixture being too rich.
5 If the insulator nose is covered with light tan to greyish brown deposits, then the mixture is correct and it is likely that the engine is in good condition.
6 If there are any traces of long brown tapering stains on the outside of the white portion of the plug, then the plug will have to be renewed, as this shows that there is a faulty joint between the plug body and the insulator, and compression is being lost.
7 Plugs should be cleaned by a sand blasting machine, which will free them from carbon more thoroughly than cleaning by hand. The machine will also test the condition of the plugs under compression. Any plug that fails to spark at the recommended pressure should be renewed.
8 The spark plug gap is of considerable importance, as, if it is too large or too small, the size of the spark and its efficiency will be seriously impaired. The spark plug gap should be set to the figure given in the Specifications at the beginning of this Chapter.
9 To set it, measure the gap with a feeler gauge, and then bend open, or close, the *outer* plug electrode until the correct gap is achieved. The centre electrode should *never* be bent as this may crack the insulation and cause plug failure, if nothing worse.
10 Always tighten the spark plugs to the specified torque.
11 Periodically the spark plug leads should be wiped clean and checked for security to the spark plugs.

10 Fault diagnosis – ignition system

By far the majority of breakdown and running troubles are caused by faults in the ignition system, either in the low tension or high tension circuit. There are two main symptoms indicating ignition faults. Either the engine will not start or fire, or the engine is difficult to start and misfires. If it is a regular misfire, ie the engine is only running or two or three cylinders, the fault is almost sure to be in the secondary, or high tension, circuit. If the misfiring is intermittent, the fault could be in either the high or low tension circuits. If the car stops suddenly, or will not start at all, it is likely that the fault is in the low tension circuit. Loss of power and overheating, apart from faulty carburation settings, are normally due to faults in the distributor or incorrect ignition timing.

Engine fails to start

1 If the engine fails to start and the car was running normally when it was last used, first check there is fuel in the petrol tank. If the engine turns over normally on the starter motor and the battery is evidently well charged, then the fault may be in either the high or low tension circuits. First check the HT circuit. If the battery is known to be fully charged, the ignition light comes on, and the starter motor fails to turn the engine, check the tightness of the leads on the battery terminals and the security of the earth lead to its connection to the body. It is quite common for the leads to have worked loose, even if they look and feel secure. If one of the battery terminal posts gets very hot when trying to work the starter motor, this is a sure indication of a faulty connection to that terminal.
2 One of the most common reasons for bad starting is wet or damp spark plug leads and distributor. Remove the distributor cap. If condensation is visible internally dry the cap with a rag and wipe over the leads. Refit the cap.
3 If the engine still fails to start, check that current is reaching the plugs, by disconnecting each plug lead in turn at the spark plug end, and holding the end of the cable about $\frac{3}{16}$ inch (5 mm) away from the cylinder block. Spin the engine on the starter motor.

4   Sparking between the end of the cable and the block should be fairly strong with a regular blue spark. (Hold the lead with rubber to avoid electric shocks). If current is reaching the plugs, then remove them and clean and regap them. The engine should now start.

5   If there is no spark at the plug leads, take off the HT lead from the centre of the distributor cap and hold it to the block as before. Spin the engine on the starter once more. A rapid succession of blue sparks between the end of the lead and the block indicate that the coil is in order and that the distributor cap is cracked, the rotor arm faulty or the carbon brush in the top of the distributor cap is not making good contact with the rotor arm. Or possibly the points are in bad condition; clean and reset them.

6   If there are no sparks from the end of the lead from the coil, check the connections at the coil end of the lead. If it is in order start checking the low tension circuit.

7   Use a 12 volt voltmeter, or a 12 volt bulb and two lengths of wire. With the ignition switch on and the points open test between the low tension wire to the coil (it is marked +) and earth. No reading indicates a break in the supply from the ignition switch. Check the connections at the switch to see if any are loose. Refit them and the engine should run. A reading shows a faulty coil or condenser or broken lead between the coil and the distributor.

8   Remove the condenser from the baseplate on Lucas versions, or disconnect the condenser lead on the Ducellier version. With the points open, test between the moving point and earth. If there now is a reading, then the fault is in the condenser. Fit a new one and the fault is cleared.

9   With no reading from the moving point to earth, take a reading between earth and the negative (-) terminal of the coil. A reading here indicates a broken wire which must be renewed between the coil and distributor. No reading confirms that the coil has failed and must be renewed. For these tests it is sufficient to separate the contact breaker points with a piece of paper.

10   If the engine starts when the starter motor is operated, but stops as soon as the ignition key is returned to the normal running position, the resistive wire may have an open circuit. Connect a temporary lead between the coil positive (+) terminal and the battery positive (+) terminal. If the engine now runs correctly, renew the resistive wire. Note that the resistive wire must not be permanently bypassed, otherwise the coil will overheat and be irrepairably damaged.

Engine misfires

11   If the engine misfires regularly, run it at a fast idling speed. Pull off each of the plug caps in turn and listen to the note of the engine. Hold the plug cap in a dry cloth or with a rubber glove as additional protection against a shock from the HT supply.

12   No difference in engine running will be noticed when the lead from the defective circuit is removed. Removing the lead from one of the good cylinders will accentuate the misfire.

13   Remove the plug lead from the end of the defective plug and hold it about $\frac{3}{16}$ inch (5 mm) away from the block. Restart the engine. If the sparking is fairly strong and regular, the fault must lie in the spark plug.

14   The plug may be loose, the insulation may be cracked, or the points may have burnt away, giving too wide a gap for the spark to jump. Worse still, one of the points may have broken off. Either renew the plug, or clean it, reset the gap, and then test it.

15   If there is no spark at the end of the plug lead, or if it is weak and intermittent, check the ignition lead from the distributor to the plug. If the insulation is cracked or perished, renew the lead. Check the connections at the distributor cap.

16   If there is still no spark, examine the distributor cap carefully for tracking. This can be recognised by a very thin black line running between two or more electrodes, or between an electrode and some other part of the distributor. These lines are paths which now conduct electricity across the cap, thus letting it run to earth. The only answer in this case is a new distributor cap.

17   Apart from the ignition timing being incorrect, other causes of misfiring have already been dealt with under the section dealing with the failure of the engine to start. To recap, these are that:

(a)   *The coil may be faulty giving an intermittent misfire*
(b)   *There may be a damaged wire or loose connection in the low tension circuit*
(c)   *The condenser may be short circuiting*
(d)   *There may be a mechanical fault in the distributor (broken driving spindle or contact breaker spring)*

18   If the ignition timing is too far retarded it should be noted that the engine will tend to overheat, and there will be a quite noticeable drop in power. If the engine is overheating and the power is down, and the ignition timing is correct, then the carburettor should be checked, as it is likely that this is where the fault lies.

Chapter 5 Clutch

For modifications and information applicable to later models, see Supplement at end of manual

Contents

Clutch – adjustment and maintenance	2	Clutch pedal – removal and refitting	6
Clutch – inspection	8	Clutch release bearing – removal and refitting	10
Clutch – refitting	9	Clutch slave cylinder – removal, overhaul and refitting	4
Clutch – removal	7	Fault diagnosis – clutch	11
Clutch hydraulic system – bleeding	5	General description	1
Clutch master cylinder – removal, overhaul and refitting	3		

Specifications

Clutch type ....

Single dry plate and pressure plate located on inner face of flywheel; diaphragm spring and cover located on outer face of flywheel; hydraulic actuation

Clutch plate diameter ....

7.125 in (180.98 mm)

Diaphragm spring colour
Metro standard, Metro L and Metro HLE ....

Brown

Metro 1.3 S and Metro 1.3 HLS ....

Dark blue

Release lever clearance (where applicable) ....

0.040 in (1.016 mm)

Clutch fluid type/specification ....

Hydraulic fluid to FMVSS 116 DOT 3 or SAE J1703C (Duckhams Universal Brake and Clutch Fluid)

Torque wrench settings

	lbf ft	kgf m
Flywheel centre bolt	112	15.5
Driving strap to flywheel	19	2.6
Diaphragm spring cover to pressure plate	16	2.2

1 General description

The clutch is of single dry plate type with a diaphgram spring. Actuation is by hydraulic master cylinder and slave cylinder. The driven plate and pressure plate are located on the inner face of the flywheel, and the diaphragm spring and cover are located on the outer face. The pressure plate protrudes through three apertures in the flywheel and is bolted to the diaphragm spring cover.

The driven plate is free to slide along the splined primary gear, which runs on the crankshaft extension and transmits drive via the idler gear to the gearbox. Drive is transmitted from the flywheel to the pressure plate by six metal driving straps in groups of two. Friction lining material is riveted to the clutch driven plate on each side.

When the clutch pedal is depressed, the slave cylinder is actuated by hydraulic pressure, and the release lever moves the plunger and release bearing against the diaphragm spring cover. The diaphragm spring flexes against the outer face of the flywheel, and the pressure plate is pushed away from the driven plate. Drive then ceases to be transmitted to the gearbox.

When the clutch pedal is released, the diaphragm spring, acting against the outer face of the flywheel, pulls the pressure plate into contact with the friction linings on the driven plate. The driven plate is also moved fractionally along the primary gear splines and into contact with the flywheel inner face. The driven plate is now firmly sandwiched between the pressure plate and flywheel, and so the drive is taken up.

As the friction linings wear, the pressure plate moves closer to the flywheel, and periodic adjustment of the release lever return stop clearance is therefore necessary where a return stop is fitted.

2 Clutch – adjustment and maintenance

1 Every 12 months of 12 000 miles (20 000 km) the clutch return stop clearance should be checked (if applicable), and adjusted if necessary. It is only necessary to adjust the throw-out stop after fitting new clutch parts or a release bearing housing assembly.
2 *To adjust the return stop*, pull the release lever out against the tension of the slave cylinder return spring until all the free movement is taken up.
3 Using a feeler blade, check that the clearance between the return stop and the release lever is as given in the Specifications (photo). If not, loosen the locknut and reposition the return stop screw as necessary, then tighten the locknut. Make sure that the lever is held against the spring tension during the adjustment.
4 *To adjust the throw-out stop*, unscrew the locknut on the end of the release plunger to the limit of the thread, then unscrew the throw-out stop to the locknut.
5 Have an assistant fully depress the clutch pedal and keep it depressed. Screw in the throw out stop until it contacts the housing.
6 With the clutch pedal released, screw in the stop one further flat (60 degrees), and tighten the locknut while holding the stop stationary.

3 Clutch master cylinder – removal, overhaul and refitting

1 Disconnect the battery negative lead.
2 Remove the air cleaner with reference to Chapter 3.
3 Unscrew and plug the hydraulic pipe from the top of the master

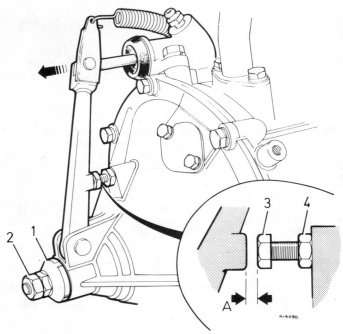

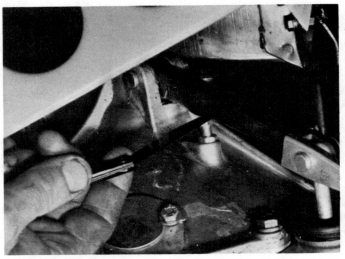

2.3 Checking the clutch return stop clearance

Fig. 5.1 Clutch adjustments (Sec 2)

1   Throw-out stop   3   Return stop
2   Locknut   4   Locknut
                         'A' Indicates return stop clearance

cylinder. Take care not to spill any hydraulic fluid on the surrounding
paintwork as it acts as an effective paint stripper. If any is spilt, wash
off immediately with copious amounts of cold water.
4   Working inside the car, remove the demister elbow, then extract
the split pin and clevis pin, and disconnect the master cylinder pushrod
from the clutch pedal.
5   Have an assistant hold the mounting bolts, then unscrew the nuts
and remove the spring washers from under the bulkhead.
6   Withdraw the master cylinder and gasket from the bulkhead,
taking care to keep it upright to prevent spilling of the hydraulic fluid.
7   Unscrew the filler cap and discard the hydraulic fluid.
8   Prise the boot from the mouth of the master cylinder. Extract the
circlip and withdraw the pushrod assembly.
9   Tap the cylinder on the workbench to remove the piston assembly
and spring. Note the location of the component parts.
10 Using the fingers only, remove the outer seal from the piston.
Remove the spring seat, seal and washer.
11 Clean all the components with methylated spirit and allow to dry.
Make a thorough examination for wear and deterioration. In particular
check the master cylinder bore for scoring and corrosion. If evident,
renew the complete master cylinder. If the bore is good, obtain a repair
kit of seals.
12 Dip the outer seal in clean hydraulic fluid and manipulate it onto
the piston using the fingers only. Dip the inner seal in clean hydraulic
fluid, then fit the washer, seal, and spring seat to the end of the piston.
The seal lips must face the spring end of the piston.
13 Lubricate the cylinder bore with clean hydraulic fluid, then locate
the spring on the spring seat and insert the assembly into the master
cylinder. Take care not to damage the seal lips as they enter the bore.
14 Insert the pushrod assembly and fit the circlip into the groove.
15 Smear the inner sealing surface of the rubber boot with rubber
lubricant, then locate it over the mouth of the cylinder.
16 Refitting is a reversal of removal, but fit a new mounting gasket
and bleed the system as described in Section 5 before refitting the air
cleaner.

---

4   Clutch slave cylinder – removal, overhaul and refitting

1   Unhook the clutch release lever return spring and remove it
(photo).

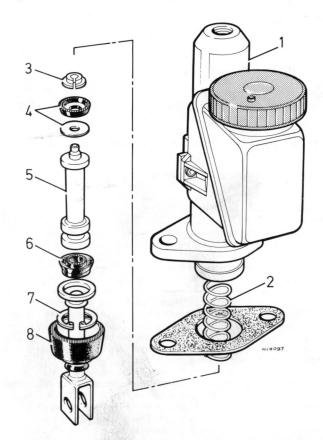

Fig. 5.2 Exploded view of the clutch master cylinder (Sec 3)

1   Master cylinder body   5   Piston
2   Spring   6   Seal
3   Spring seat   7   Circlip
4   Seal and washer   8   Rubber boot

2   Unscrew the clutch master cylinder filler cap, and tighten it down
onto a piece of thin polythene sheeting. This will reduce hydraulic fluid
loss in the subsequent procedure.
3   Loosen only the slave cylinder hose connection.
4   Unbolt the slave cylinder from the flywheel housing and withdraw
it from the pushrod (photos).
5   Unscrew and remove the slave cylinder from the hose.

4.1 Clutch slave cylinder return spring location   4.4A Removing the clutch slave cylinder bolts   4.4B Withdrawing the clutch slave cylinder

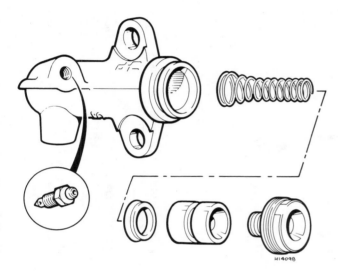

Fig. 5.3 Exploded view of the clutch slave cylinder (Sec 4)

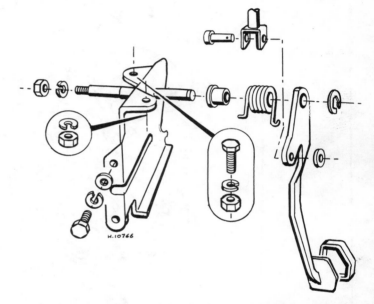

Fig. 5.4 Exploded view of the clutch pedal components (Sec 6)

6   Prise the boot from the mouth of the cylinder, and tap out the piston and spring. Remove the bleed screw. Prise the seal from the piston using the fingers only.

7   Clean all the components with methylated spirit and allow to dry. Examine each part for wear and deterioration. If the slave cylinder bore is scored or corroded, renew the complete unit. If it is in good condition obtain a repair kit.

8   Dip the seal in clean hydraulic fluid and manipulate it onto the piston using the fingers only. The seal lip must face into the cylinder when fitted.

9   Lubricate the cylinder bore with clean hydraulic fluid, then locate the spring (large diameter first) into the bore, followed by the piston. Make sure that the spring locates centrally in the piston and that the seal lip is not damaged as it enters the bore.

10   Smear the inner sealing surfaces of the rubber boot with rubber lubricant, then locate it over the mouth of the cylinder.

11   Insert and tighten the bleed screw.

12   Refitting is a reversal of removal, but bleed the system as described in Section 5. Do *not* leave the polythene sheeting under the filler cap.

5   Clutch hydraulic system – bleeding

Note: *hydraulic fluid is both poisonous and acts as an effective paint stripper if spilt on the car paintwork. If spilt, wash off immediately with copious amounts of cold water. Hydraulic fluid for use in the hydraulic system must have been left unshaken for the previous 24 hours.*

1   Remove the air cleaner as described in Chapter 3.

2   Unscrew the filler cap and top up the clutch master cylinder to the bottom of the filler neck with hydraulic fluid.

3   Connect a bleed tube to the bleed screw on the slave cylinder and place the free end in a jar.

4   Open the bleed screw three-quarters of a turn and have an assistant fully depress the clutch pedal slowly.

5   Tighten the bleed screw, then allow the clutch pedal to return to its stop. Pause for a moment, then repeat the procedure twice more. Top up the master cylinder reservoir, and continue bleeding the system until the fluid entering the jar is free of air bubbles. The fluid must never drop more than half way down the reservoir.

6   Check the tightness of the bleed screw, and fit the filler cap after topping up the reservoir to the bottom of the filler neck.

7   Refit the air cleaner with reference to Chapter 3.

6   Clutch pedal – removal and refitting

1   Disconnect the battery negative lead.

2   Working inside the car, remove the demister elbow, then extract the split pin and clevis pin and disconnect the master cylinder pushrod from the clutch pedal. Retain the clevis pin washer.

3   Extract the circlip from the pedal point, and withdraw the pedal, return spring, and bush.

4   Examine the clutch pedal, bush, and footpad rubber for wear and renew them as necessary.

5   Refitting is a reversal of removal, but make sure that the return spring is correctly located over the pedal and bracket with the hooked end over the pedal.

74

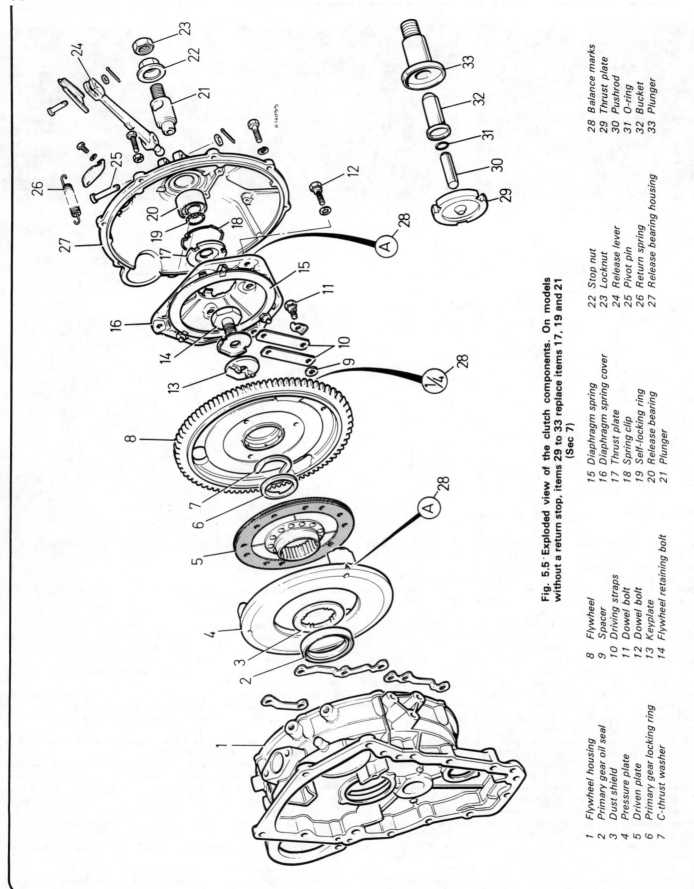

Fig. 5.5 · Exploded view of the clutch components. On models without a return stop, items 29 to 33 replace items 17, 19 and 21 (Sec 7)

1 Flywheel housing
2 Primary gear oil seal
3 Dust shield
4 Pressure plate
5 Driven plate
6 Primary gear locking ring
7 C-thrust washer

8 Flywheel
9 Spacer
10 Driving straps
11 Dowel bolt
12 Dowel bolt
13 Keyplate
14 Flywheel retaining bolt

15 Diaphragm spring
16 Diaphragm spring cover
17 Thrust plate
18 Spring clip
19 Self-locking ring
20 Release bearing
21 Plunger

22 Stop nut
23 Locknut
24 Release lever
25 Pivot pin
26 Return spring
27 Release bearing housing

28 Balance marks
29 Thrust plate
30 Pushrod
31 O-ring
32 Bucket
33 Plunger

7 Clutch – removal

Note: *Before starting work, it is essential to obtain tools 18G304 and 18G304N in order to release the flywheel from the crankshaft taper. A 1½ inch AF socket will also be required to unscrew the flywheel retaining bolt, or tool 18G587 may be used. The tools should be obtained from a tool hire agent. If the engine/gearbox unit is in the car, follow paragraphs 1 to 5*

1 Remove the battery as described in Chapter 10, and remove the battery carrier.

2 Unhook the clutch release lever return spring.

3 Jack up the front of the car and support it with axle stands positioned beneath the rear edges of the front subframe.

4 Support the engine/gearbox unit with a trolley jack and block of wood located beneath the transmission casing.

5 Unscrew the nut and remove the through-bolt and washer from the right-hand front engine mounting. Remove the buffer washer from the mounting.

6 Remove the starter motor as described in Chapter 10.

7 Unbolt the clutch release bearing housing from the flywheel housing, and remove it complete with the mounting bracket. Note the fuel vent pipe bracket and engine mounting bracket locations (photos).

8 Mark the diaphragm spring cover and flywheel in relation to each other.

9 Progressively unscrew the three diaphragm spring cover-to-pressure plate dowel bolts to release the diaphragm spring. Withdraw the cover (photo).

10 Turn the crankshaft with a spanner on the pulley centre bolt, until the slots in the flywheel and crankshaft are horizontal. This will prevent the primary gear C-washer falling out when the flywheel is removed.

11 Insert a wide-bladed screwdriver between the starter ring gear and the flywheel housing, then unscrew the flywheel retaining bolt. Make sure that the socket is fully engaged with the bolt as it is *very* tight.

12 Remove the keyplate and locking washer.

13 Using tools 18G304 and 18G304N, pull the flywheel from the crankshaft taper. It will be necessary to hold the flywheel stationary while tightening the puller centre bolt; strike the centre bolt with a hammer to help release the taper.

14 Withdraw the flywheel, clutch driven plate, and pressure plate.

8 Clutch – inspection

1 Examine the surfaces of the pressure plate and flywheel for scoring. If this is only light, the parts may be re-used, but if excessive, the pressure plate must be renewed and the flywheel friction face ground flat, provided the amount of metal being removed is minimal. If any doubt exists, renew the flywheel.

2 Renew the driven plate if the linings are worn down to or near to the rivets. If the linings appear oil stained, the cause of the oil leak must first be put right; this is most likely to be a failed primary gear oil seal (refer to Chapter 6). Check the driven plate centre splines; if they are worn, renew the driven plate.

3 Examine the diaphragm spring and cover for wear, and the driving holes for elongation. Check the dowel bolts for ridging, and the driving straps for elongated holes. Check the thrust plate for wear. Renew the components as necessary, renewing the dowel bolts and driving straps in complete sets.

4 Spin the release bearing and check it for roughness. Hold the outer race, and attempt to move it laterally against the inner race. If any excessive movement or roughness is evident, renew the release bearing as described in Section 10.

9 Clutch – refitting

1 Refer to Chapter 6 and check that the crankshaft primary gear endfloat is within the specified limits.

2 If removed, fit the driving straps, spacer, and locking plates to the flywheel, but only tighten the bolts finger tight at this stage.

3 Position the pressure plate in the flywheel housing, noting the location of the 'A' mark on its periphery (photo).

7.7A Vent pipe location on the clutch release bearing housing

7.7B Engine mounting bracket location on the clutch release bearing housing

7.7C Removing the clutch release bearing housing

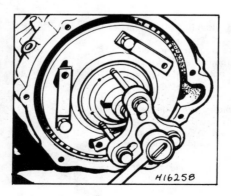

7.9 Removing the clutch diaphragm spring cover

Fig. 5.6 Using a puller to remove the flywheel (Sec 7)

Fig. 5.7 Withdrawing the flywheel (Sec 7)

H16260

Fig. 5.8 Withdrawing the clutch driven
plate (Sec 7)

9.3 Fitting the pressure plate, showing location
of 'A' mark (arrowed)

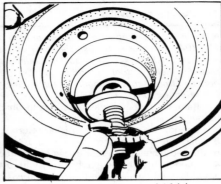

H16261

Fig. 5.9 Fitting the flywheel retaining
bolt (Sec 9)

9.10 Fitting the diaphragm spring cover,
showing the 'A' mark (arrowed)

9.11 Tightening clutch cover driving strap bolts

4   Slide the driven plate, hub side first, onto the primary gear splines, at the same time locating it centrally within the pressure plate.
5   With the crankshaft slot still horizontal, fit the flywheel onto the crankshaft with the 1/4 timing mark aligned with the 'A' mark on the pressure plate.
6   Temporarily fit the three dowel bolts through the driving straps and into the pressure plate.
7   Turn the flywheel to align the keyplate slots, then fit the keyplate, locking washer, and flywheel retaining bolt. If the original bolt was of an encapsulated type, or secured with thread locking compound, the bolt hole threads should be thoroughly cleaned. Use a new bolt with a suitable thread locking compound.
8   Have an assistant insert a wide-bladed screwdriver between the starter ring gear and the flywheel housing, then tighten the flywheel retaining bolt to the specified torque.
9   Bend the locking washer over one flat of the retaining bolt and tap it flat.
10 Remove the three dowel bolts. Locate the diaphragm spring cover on the outer face of the flywheel with the 'A' mark aligned with the flywheel 1/4 timing mark (photo). Insert, but do not tighten, the three dowel bolts.
11 Hold the flywheel stationary, and tighten the driving strap bolts to the specified torque (photo). Bend the locking plates over one flat of each bolt and tap them flat.
12 Tighten the dowel bolts a few turns at a time making sure that they do not foul the driving straps. Finally tighten them to the specified torque.
13 On models with a return stop type release arm, check that the release bearing self-locking ring is correctly and securely positioned on the plunger (photo). Unscrew the return stop to position the shoulder of the plunger 0.188 in (5 mm) from the inner face of the housing ('A' in Fig. 5.10). This will ensure that the release bearing centralizes on

the clutch thrust plate.
14 On all models, check that the thrust plate is secured to the diaphragm spring cover by the spring clip (photo).
15 Locate the release bearing housing on the flywheel housing, at the same time engaging the pushrod into the slave cylinder. Insert and tighten the securing bolts evenly in diagonal sequence, and refit the fuel vent pipe and engine mounting brackets.

9.13 Clutch release bearing

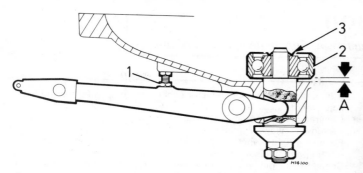

Fig. 5.10 Cross sectional view of release bearing and lever showing setting 'A' before fitting cover (Sec 9)

1   Return stop   3   Self-locking ring
2   Release bearing

16 Fit the starter motor with reference to Chapter 10.
17 If the engine/gearbox unit is in the car, carry out the procedure in the remaining paragraphs.
18 Fit the buffer washer between the right-hand front engine mounting and the bracket. Insert the through-bolt and washer and, with the weight of the engine/gearbox unit on the mounting, tighten the nut.
19 Lower the car to the ground. Refit the clutch release lever return spring and screw in the return stop.
20 Adjust the return stop and throw-out stop as described in Section 2.
21 Refit the battery carrier and battery as described in Chapter 10.

10 Clutch release bearing – removal and refitting

1   Remove the clutch release bearing housing from the flywheel housing by following the procedure given in Section 7, paragraphs 1 to 7. However, do not remove the starter (ie omit paragraph 6). No special tools are required.
2   On models with a return stop type release arm, prise off the release bearing self-locking ring using a screwdriver. Pull the release bearing off the plunger.
3   On models without a return stop type release arm, extract the split pin and remove the washer, pivot pin and release arm. Unscrew the locknut and plunger stop, and withdraw the release bearing assembly from the housing. Using a drift through the holes provided, drive the

9.14 Fitting the clutch cover thrust plate

release bearing and bucket from the plunger then remove the pushrod and O-ring and press the bucket from the bearing.
4   On all models, spin the bearing and check it for roughness. Attempt to move the outer race laterally against the inner race. If any excessive wear or roughness is evident, renew the bearing.
5   To refit the bearing on models with a return stop type release arm, press the release bearing onto the plunger, making sure that it abuts the shoulder.
6   Using a suitable length of tubing, press a new self-locking ring onto the plunger to secure the release bearing. Do not drive the ring on, but use hand pressure only, making sure that the ring is installed squarely and abuts the inner race. Do not overcompress the ring otherwise its locking action will be reduced.
7   To refit the remaining components, refer to Section 9, paragraphs 13 to 21, omitting paragraph 16.
8   To refit the bearing on models without a return stop type release arm, press the bucket into the bearing and insert the pushrod and O-ring with the O-ring 0.625 in (16.0 mm) below the face of the bucket. Press the bearing and bucket into the plunger, locate the assembly in he housing and fit the release arm, plunger stop, and locknut.
9   To refit the remaining components, refer to Section 9, paragraphs 14 to 21, omitting paragraph 16.

11 Fault diagnosis – clutch

Symptom	Reason(s)
Judder when taking up drive	Loose or worn engine/gearbox mountings Worn driven plate friction surfaces or contamination with oil Worn splines on primary gear or driven plate
Clutch drag (failure to disengage)	Incorrect adjustment Driven plate sticking or primary gear splines Damaged diaphragm spring or cover Air in hydraulic system
Clutch slip	Incorrect adjustment Worn driven plate friction surfaces or contamination with oil Weak diaphragm spring
Noise evident on depressing clutch pedal	Dry or worn release bearing

Chapter 6 Manual gearbox and automatic transmission

For modifications and information applicable to later models, see Supplement at end of manual

Contents

Part A: Manual gearbox

First motion shaft – servicing 4
Flywheel housing oil seal – renewal 11
Gearbox – dismantling into major assemblies 3
Gearbox – reassembly 9
Gearbox – removal and refitting 2
Gearchange remote control – removal, overhaul and refitting 10
General description 1
Laygear, reverse idler gear, and shafts – servicing 5
Selector components and gearbox housings – servicing 8
Selector shaft oil seal – renewal 12
Third motion shaft – servicing 6
Transfer gears – servicing 7

Part B: Automatic transmission

Automatic transmission – removal and refitting 14

Automatic transmission selector cable – removal, refitting and adjustment 17
General description 13
Kickdown linkage – adjustment 18
Reversing light switch (automatic transmission) – removal, refitting and adjustment 20
Speedometer pinion and drivegear (automatic transmission) – removal and refitting 21
Starter inhibitor switch – removal, refitting and adjustment 19
Torque converter and oil seal – removal and refitting 15
Torque converter housing and transfer gears – removal, servicing and refitting 16

Part C: Fault diagnosis

Fault diagnosis – manual gearbox and automatic transmission 22

Specifications

Manual gearbox

Type .... Four forward speeds and reverse; synchromesh on all forward speeds

Ratios

	Early models	Later models
1st	3.53 : 1	3.647 : 1
2nd	2.22 : 1	2.185 : 1
3rd	1.43 : 1	1.425 : 1
Top	1.00 : 1	1.00 : 1
Reverse	3.54 : 1	3.667 : 1

Primary gear

Endflot .... 0.0035 to 0.0065 in (0.089 to 0.165 mm)
Thrust washers available .... 0.112 to 0.114 in (2.84 to 2.89 mm) 0.114 to 0.116 in (2.89 to 2.94 mm) 0.116 to 0.118 in (2.94 to 2.99 mm) 0.118 to 0.120 in (2.99 to 3.04 mm)

Idler gear

Endflot .... 0.004 to 0.007 in (0.102 to 0.178 mm)
Thrust washers available .... 0.132 to 0.133 in (3.35 to 3.37 mm), 0.134 to 0.135 in (3.40 to 3.42 mm), 0.136 to 0.137 in (3.45 to 3.47 mm), 0.138 to 0.139 in (3.50 to 3.53 mm)

Laygear

Endflot .... 0.002 to 0.006 in (0.05 to 0.15 mm)
Thrust washers available .... 0.123 to 0.124 in (3.12 to 3.14 mm) 0.125 to 0.126 in (3.17 to 3.20 mm) 0.127 to 0.128 in (3.22 to 3.25 mm) 0.130 to 0.131 in (3.30 to 3.32 mm)

Third motion shaft bearing endflot .... 0 ± 0.001 in (0 ± .025 mm)

Oil capacity (as for engine) .... 8.5 pints (4.8 litres)

Torque wrench settings

	lbf ft	kgf m
Speedometer gear housing bolts	6	0.8
Speedometer gear housing nuts	18	2.5
Drain plug	30	4.1
First motion shaft nut	150	20.7
Gearbox case studs:		
$\frac{3}{8}$ in diameter	8	1.1
$\frac{5}{16}$ in diameter	6	0.8
Gearbox case stud nuts:		
$\frac{3}{8}$ in diameter	25	3.5
$\frac{5}{16}$ in diameter	18	2.5
Gearbox case to crankcase	6	0.8
Bellcrank lever pivot pin nut	21	2.9
Third motion shaft bearing retaining screws	13	1.8
Final drive pinion nut	150	20.7
Flywheel housing nuts and bolts	18	2.5

Automatic transmission

Type .... AP four-speed with manual hold/change facility. Three element torque converter input with oil cooler on front of engine

Ratios
1st	2.690 : 1
2nd	1.845 : 1
3rd	1.460 : 1
4th	1.000 : 1
Reverse	2.690 : 1

Primary gear (torque converter output gear)
Endfloat and thrust washers .... As in manual gearbox

Idler gear
Endfloat .... 0.004 to 0.010 in (0.10 to 0.25 mm)

Input gear
Preload .... 0.001 to 0.003 in (0.02 to 0.07 mm)
Shims available .... 0.003 in (0.07 mm), 0.012 in (0.30 mm)

Oil capacity (as for engine) .... 8.5 pints (4.8 litres)

Torque wrench settings

	lbf ft	kgf m
Transmission case studs and nuts	As in manual gearbox	
Converter centre bolt	112	15.5
Converter bolts	21	2.9
Converter housing nuts and bolts	18	2.5
Input shaft nut	70	9.7
Transmission case to crankcase	12	1.7
Drain plug	28	3.9

PART A: MANUAL GEARBOX

1   General description

The manual gearbox incorporates four forward speeds and one reverse speed, with synchromesh engagement on all forward gears. Gearshift is by means of a floor mounted lever, connected by a remote control housing and extension rod to a selector shaft located in the bottom of the gearbox casing. The selector shaft incorporates an interlock spool, and a stub on the end of the shaft is in contact with a bellcrank lever assembly, which in turn moves the selector forks and the reverse idler gear to select the required gear.

The final drive (differential) unit is attached to the rear of the gearbox casing, and the final drive gear is in mesh with a splined pinion on the end of the third motion shaft.

A drain plug incorporating a magnetic swarf collector is screwed into the right-hand side of the gearbox casing.

When overhauling the gearbox, due consideration should be given to the costs involved, since it is often more economical to obtain a service exchange or good secondhand gearbox rather than fit new parts to the existing gearbox.

2   Gearbox – removal and refitting

1   Remove the engine/gearbox assembly as described in Chapter 1 and drain the oil.

2   Remove the clutch and flywheel as described in Chapter 5.
3   Unbolt the oil separator from the top of flywheel housing, and remove the gasket (photo).
4   Unscrew and remove the outer nuts and bolts from the flywheel housing. Remove the primary gear dust shield.
5   Flatten the locktabs, then unscrew and remove the inner nuts and bolts from the housing. Remove the lockwashers.
6   Wrap adhesive tape around the primary gear splines or use tool 18G1043, then carefully tap the flywheel housing free and withdraw it with the gasket (photo). The idler gear will probably remain with the housing so take care not to drop it.
7   Remove the idler gear and thrust washers (photo).

Fig. 6.1 Tool 18G1043 for fitting flywheel housing oil seal (Sec 2)

2.3 Removing the oil separator

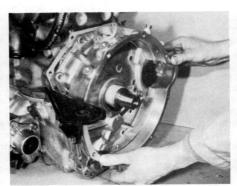

2.6 Removing the flywheel housing

2.7 Removing the idler gear

2.8 Separating the engine from the gearbox

2.9A Removing the gearbox-to-engine gaskets

2.9B Gearbox-to-main bearing cap oil seal

2.9C Oil transfer hole O-ring

2.10A Fitting the flywheel housing gasket

2.10B Adhesive tape used for protecting the flywheel housing oil seal

2.10C Locking a flywheel housing retaining nut

2.13 Checking the idler gear endfloat (gearbox separated from engine)

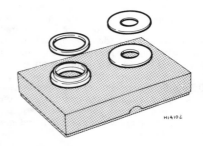

Fig. 6.2 Tool 18G1089 for calculating idler gear thrust washer thickness (Sec 2)

8   Unscrew the gearbox casing to crankcase nuts and bolts, and lift the engine from the gearbox (photo).
9   Remove the two gaskets, main bearing cap oil seal, and the oil transfer hole O-ring (photos).
10   Refitting is a reversal of removal, but fit a new oil transfer hole O-ring, gearbox casing-to-crankcase gaskets, and flywheel housing gasket (photo). Lubricate the new main bearing cap oil seal with engine oil before locating it on the timing chain end main bearing cap. If the flywheel housing is refitted with the primary gear in position, protect the oil seal by wrapping adhesive tape around the primary gear splines (photo) or by using tool 18G1043. Tighten all nuts and bolts to the specified torque, and where applicable, bend the locktabs over one flat of the nuts and bolts to lock them (photo). If either the idler gear, idler gear thrust washers, flywheel housing, or gearbox casing have been renewed, one of the two methods given in paragraphs 11 to 20 must be followed in order to determine the idler gear thrust washer thickness. With either procedure, a selection of thrust washers and an extra flywheel housing gasket should be obtained before starting work.

Method 1 – gearbox separated from engine

11   Fit the idler gear to the gearbox casing needle roller bearing, together with a medium size thrust washer. Locate a small size thrust washer on the outside of the idler gear.
12   Fit the flywheel housing with a new gasket to the gearbox casing, and tighten the nuts and bolts to the specified torque.
13   Using a feeler blade behind the flywheel housing, check the idler gear endfloat with the feeler blade between the inner thrust washer and idler gear (photo). If the endfloat is not as specified, select a different outer thrust washer of a thickness which will correct the endfloat.
14   Remove the flywheel housing and discard the gasket. Fit the correct outer thrust washer, then fit the gearbox using a reversal of the removal procedure and using the remaining new gasket.

Method 2 – gearbox attached to engine

15   Fit the idler gear to the gearbox casing needle roller bearing together with a medium size thrust washer.

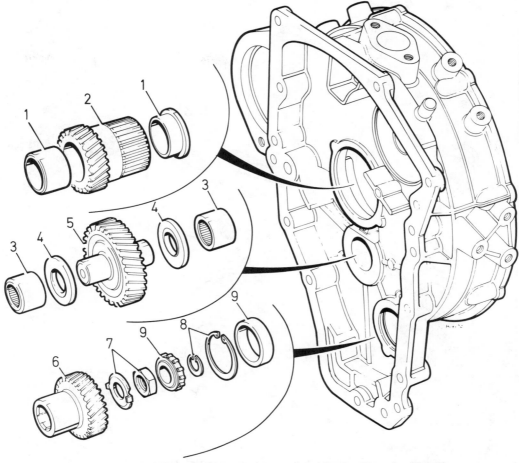

Fig. 6.3 Exploded view of the transfer gears and flywheel housing (Sec 2)

1	Primary gear bushes	4	Thrust washer
2	Primary gear	5	Idler gear
3	Needle roller bearing		

6	First motion shaft gear	8	Circlip
7	Nut and lockwasher	9	Spigot bearing

16 Fit a thin washer followed by a wax washer and a further thin washer from tool 18G1089 to the flywheel side of the idler gear.

17 Fit the flywheel housing with a new gasket and tighten the nuts and bolts to the specified torque.

18 Unscrew the nuts and bolts and remove the flywheel housing and gasket.

19 Remove the thin washers and wax washer, and measure their thickness carefully with a micrometer. Subtract the specified endfloat, and fit a thrust washer of the resulting thickness to the flywheel side of the idler gear.

20 Discard the gasket just used, then fit the flywheel housing with the remaining new gasket.

3   Gearbox – dismantling into major assemblies

1 Remove the final drive (differential) unit as described in Chapter 7.

2 Remove the final drive pinion as described in Chapter 7.

3 Extract the circlip from the end of the first motion shaft (photo).

4 Flatten the locktab then, with first and top gear selected, loosen the first motion shaft nut and unscrew it to the end of the thread to push off the spigot bearing. Screw in the nut and use a spanner to tap the bearing off the shaft.

5 Unscrew and remove the nut and lockwasher, then slide the gear from the first motion shaft (photos).

3.3 Extracting the spigot bearing circlip

3.5A Removing the nut ...

3.5B ... and first motion shaft gear

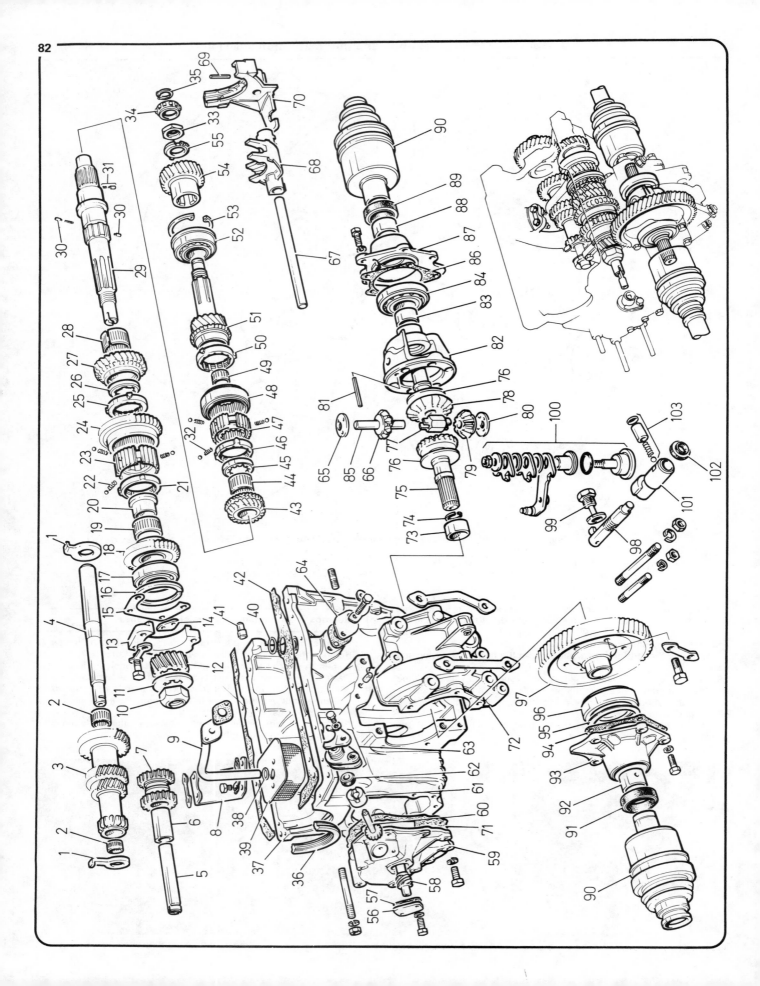

Fig. 6.4 Exploded and phantom views of the gearbox (Sec 3)

1 Laygear thrust washers
2 Needle roller bearing(s) (1 or 2 off large)
3 Laygear
4 Layshaft
5 Reverse idler gear shaft
6 Bush
7 Reverse idler gear
8 Bracket
9 Oil pick-up pipe
10 Final drive pinion nut
11 Lockwasher
12 Final drive pinion
13 Bearing retainer
14 Shaft locking plate
15 Shim
16 Circlip
17 Bearing
18 1st speed gear
19 Needle roller bearing
20 Journal
21 Baulk ring
22 Synchro unit spring
23 1st/2nd synchro hub
24 1st/2nd synchro sleeve and reverse gear
25 Baulk ring
26 Thrust washer
27 2nd speed gear
28 Split needle roller bearing
29 Third motion shaft
30 Locking plungers
31 Locking plunger and spring
32 Synchro unit spring
33 Nut
34 Spigot bearing
35 Circlip
36 Main bearing cap oil seal
37 Gearbox casing
38 O-ring
39 Oil strainer
40 O-ring
41 Dowel
42 Gasket
43 3rd speed gear
44 Split needle roller bearing
45 Thrust washer
46 Baulk ring
47 3rd/top synchro hub
48 3rd/top synchro sleeve
49 Needle roller bearing
50 Baulk ring
51 First motion shaft
52 Bearing
53 Circlip
54 First motion shaft gear
55 Lockwasher
56 Endplate
57 Gasket
58 Speedometer drivegear
59 Speedometer drive housing
60 Speedometer drive pinion
61 Bush
62 Seal
63 Clamp and bearing
64 Blanking plate
65 Thrust washer
66 Differential pinion
67 Selector shaft
68 1st/2nd speed selector fork
69 Roll pin
70 3rd/top speed selector fork
71 Gasket
72 Differential housing
73 Bush
74 Spring ring
75 Differential gear
76 Thrust washer
77 Thrust block
78 Differential gear
79 Differential pinion
80 Thrust washer
81 Roll pin
82 Differential cage
83 Bush
84 Bearing
85 Pinion pin
86 Gasket
87 Side cover
88 Bush
89 Oil seal
90 Inner CV joint
91 Oil seal
92 Bush
93 Side cover
94 Gasket
95 Shim
96 Bearing
97 Final drive gear
98 Selector shaft
99 Drain plug
100 Bellcrank lever assembly
101 Interlock spool
102 Oil seal
103 Detent ball, spring, sleeve and O-ring

3.8A Location of the reverse shaft/layshaft locking plate

3.8B Third motion shaft bearing retainer shim

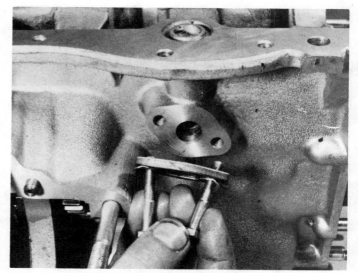

3.9A Removing the blanking plate ...

3.9B ... and oil pick-up pipe

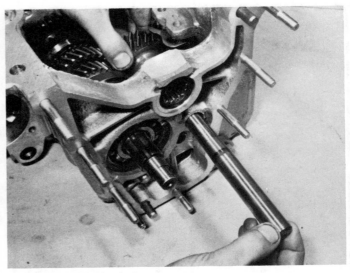

3.10 Removing the layshaft

3.11 Removing the oil strainer bracket bolts

3.12 Removing the laygear

3.13 Extracting the first motion shaft bearing circlip

3.16A Using a spanner ...

3.16B ... and drift to remove the third motion shaft bearing

3.17A Removing the third motion shaft ...

Fig. 6.5 Tool 18G1127 for removing the
third motion shaft bearing (Sec 3)

3.17B ... and oil strainer

6   Move the selector forks to select neutral.
7   Flatten the locktabs then unbolt the third motion shaft bearing retainer.
8   Remove the reverse shaft/layshaft locking plate and the bearing adjustment shims (photos).
9   Flatten the locktabs and unscrew the oil pick-up pipe retaining bolts. Remove the blanking plate and gaskets and withdraw the oil pick-up pipe (photos).
10 Push the layshaft out and withdraw it from the transfer gear end of the gearbox (photo).
11 Flatten the locktabs and unscrew the oil strainer bracket retaining bolts (photo).
12 Remove the small thrust washer, then withdraw the laygear and large thrust washer from the gearbox (photo).
13 Extract the large circlip from the first motion shaft bearing groove (photo).
14 Refit the first motion shaft nut and use a puller or slide hammer to remove the first motion shaft complete with bearing.
15 Using a soft metal drift, drive the third motion shaft towards the clutch end of the gearbox, but do not disengage the 3rd/4th synchro sleeve from its hub, otherwise the synchro balls and springs will be ejected.
16 Insert open-ended spanners over the third motion shaft between the 1st speed gear and the bearing, then tap the end of the third motion shaft to partially remove the bearing. Fully remove the bearing with a suitable drift, or alternatively obtain tool 18G1127 (photos).
17 Withdraw the third motion shaft from the gearbox, and also remove the oil strainer (photos).

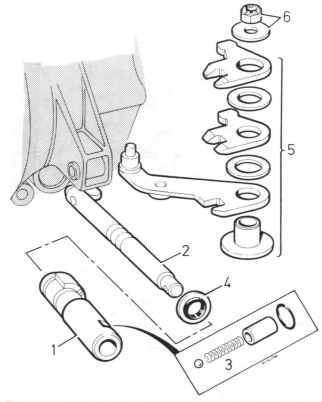

Fig. 6.6 Selector bellcrank lever and shaft components (Sec 3)

1   Interlock spool
2   Selector shaft
3   Detent ball, spring,
    sleeve and O-ring
4   Oil seal
5   Bellcrank levers and pivot
    sleeve assembly
6   Pivot post nut and washer

3.18 Removing the reverse idler shaft and gear

3.19 Removing the 3rd/4th selector fork roll pin

3.20 Removing the selector shaft and forks

3.21A Removing the selector bellcrank lever pivot post nut

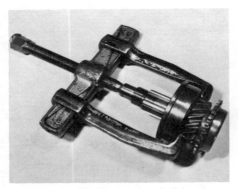

3.21B Removing the bellcrank levers

3.22 Removing the interlock spool and selector shaft

4.3 Removing the first motion shaft bearing

5.1 Laygear, shaft and bearings

18   Remove the reverse idler shaft and gear (photo).
19   Drive the roll pin from the 3rd/4th selector fork and selector shaft (photo).
20   Remove the selector shaft and withdraw the selector forks (photo).
21   Unscrew the selector bellcrank lever pivot post nut, and withdraw the washer, bellcrank levers, intermediate washers, and pivot sleeve. Note the lever positions on the sleeve (photos).
22   Remove the interlock spool and selector shaft from inside the gearbox casing (photo).

4   First motion shaft – servicing

1   Examine the gear teeth for wear and chipping and the dog teeth for wear. Check the gear and shaft splines for wear by refitting the gear and attempting to move the gear within the splines.
2   Check the spigot needle roller bearing for wear; also check the bearing surfaces of the first and third motion shafts.

3   Spin the ball-bearing by hand and check it for roughness. To remove the bearing, position the outer race over an open vice and drive the first motion shaft out of the inner race. Alternatively use a suitable puller (photo).
4   Renew the components as necessary. Fit the new ball-bearing by resting the coned end of the shaft on a block of wood, and, using a suitable length of tube against the inner race, drive it fully onto the shaft. Make sure that the bearing flanged end is towards the splined end of the shaft.

5   Laygear, reverse idler gear, and shafts – servicing

1   Examine the gear teeth for wear and chipping, particularly the spur teeth. Remove the needle roller bearings from the laygear and check them for wear. Check the bearing surfaces of the laygear, reverse idler gear, and the corresponding shafts for wear and pitting (photo).

2   Renew the laygear thrust washers if the laygear endfloat is greater than the maximum given in the Specifications.
3   Renew the laygear and reverse idler gear components as necessary.

6   Third motion shaft – servicing

1   Remove the top baulk ring from the end of the shaft, and press off the 3rd/top synchro unit. Remove the third baulk ring (photos).
2   Depress the locking plunger with a screwdriver, then turn the thrust washer until its splines are aligned with those on the shaft. Remove the thrust washer, plunger, and spring (photos).
3   Remove the 3rd gear and split needle roller bearing (photos).

Fig. 6.7 Tool 18G572 for installing synchro unit balls and springs (Sec 6)

6.1A Removing the top baulk ring ...

6.1B ... 3rd/top synchro unit ...

6.1C ... and 3rd baulk ring

6.2A Depress the locking plunger ...

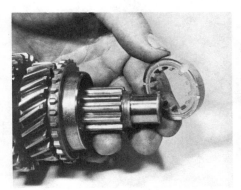

6.2B ... remove the thrust washer ...

6.2C ... plunger and spring from the third motion shaft

6.3A Removing the 3rd gear ...

6.3B ... and split needle roller bearing

6.4A Removing the 1st gear ...

6.4B ... needle roller bearing ...

6.4C ... and bush

6.5A Removing 1st baulk ring ...

6.5B ... 1st/2nd synchro unit ...

6.5C ... and 2nd baulk ring

6.6A Align the holes in the 2nd gear ...

6.6B ... and depress the locking plungers

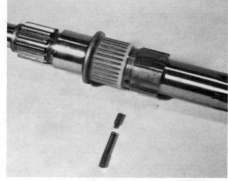
6.7A Removing the plungers and spring ...

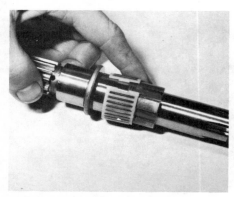
6.7B ... and split needle roller bearing

6.9 Synchro unit ball and spring

6.13A Assemble the synchro unit ...

4   Remove the 1st gear from the speedometer drive end of the shaft, followed by the needle roller bearing and bush (photos).

5   Remove the 1st baulk ring and press off the 1st/2nd synchro unit. Remove the 2nd baulk ring (photos).

6   Turn the 2nd gear to align the holes, then depress the two locking plungers and turn the thrust washer until its splines are aligned with those on the shaft (photos).

7   Remove the thrust washer and 2nd gear together, then remove the plungers and spring followed by the split needle roller bearing (photos).

8   Mark the hub and sleeve of each synchro unit in relation to each other. Identify each baulk ring for position to ensure correct reassembly.

9   To dismantle the synchro units, wrap them each in cloth and push the hubs from the sleeves. Keep the balls and springs separate with each synchro unit (photo).

10   Examine all the gear teeth for wear and chipping. Check the bearing surfaces on all components for excessive wear or pitting. Check the needle roller bearings for wear and damage to the cages. Check the splines on the third motion shaft, synchro hubs and final drive pinion for wear by refitting the components and attempting to move them within the splines. Check the thrust washers, plungers and springs for wear and damage.

11   Check the synchro unit hub and sleeve splines for wear. Check the synchro unit springs and balls for wear. Fit each baulk ring on its respective gear cone, and check that it locks onto the taper before contacting the edge of the gear. If not, the complete synchro unit and baulk rings should be renewed.

12   Renew all components as necessary. During reassembly lubricate all bearing surfaces liberally with gear oil.

13   First assemble the synchro units, preferably using tool 18G572, although a jubilee clip may be used instead. Locate the springs and balls in the hub and hold them depressed using the tool or clip (photos).

14   With the sleeve on a flat surface, insert the hub into the splines with the previous marks and the cut-outs aligned. Using a block of wood, give the hub a sharp tap to force it into the sleeve together with the balls.

15   Repeat the procedure on the remaining synchro unit.

16   Grip the third motion shaft vertically in a soft-jawed vice with the speedometer drive end uppermost (photo).

17   Locate the split needle roller bearing onto the shaft, and insert the spring and two plungers (photo).

18   Depress the plungers and fit the 2nd gear with the cone facing upwards (photo). The plungers will be released after the gear has passed over them, but they cannot escape as the gear cone prevents this.

19   Locate the thrust washer, machined grooves first, on the splines, then depress both plungers and push the thrust washer over them (photo). Turn the thrust washer the width of one spline so that the plungers are released and the washer locked.

20   Fit the baulk ring to the 2nd gear. Press the complete 1st/2nd synchro unit onto the shaft splines, reverse gear teeth end first, at the same time engaging the 2nd baulk ring with the hub.

21   Locate the 1st baulk ring in the synchro hub cut-outs.

22   Locate the 1st gear bush on the shaft, flanged end first, followed by the needle roller bearing and 1st gear, raised cone end first.

23   Hold the gears in position, then invert the assembly in the vice.

24   Locate the 3rd gear needle roller bearing on the shaft, followed by the 3rd gear, gear end first.

25   Insert the spring and plunger into the hole in the shaft. Locate the thrust washer, machined grooves first, on the splines.

26   Depress the plunger and push the thrust washer over it (photo). Turn the thrust washer the width of one spline so that the plunger is released and the washer locked.

27   Locate the 3rd baulk ring to the 3rd gear. Press the complete 3rd/top synchro unit onto the shaft splines, at the same time engaging the 3rd baulk ring with the hub. The raised section of the synchro sleeve must be towards the gear.

28   Locate the top baulk ring in the synchro hub cut-outs.

6.13B ... and use a jubilee clip to depress the balls

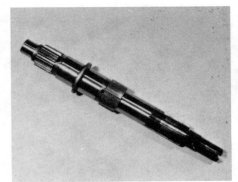
6.16 The dismantled third motion shaft

6.17 Split needle roller bearing and spring and plungers assembled to the third motion shaft

6.18 Fitting the 2nd gear

6.19 Installing the 2nd gear thrust washer

6.26 Fitting the 3rd gear thrust washer

7   Transfer gears – servicing

1   Remove the C-shaped thrust washer from the end of the crankshaft, and withdraw the backing ring, primary gear, and the notched thrust washer (photos).
2   Remove the idler gear and thrust washers from the flywheel housing or gearbox casing; identify the thrust washers side for side (photo).
3   Examine the gear teeth for wear and chipping. Check the primary gear splines and inner bushes for wear; also check the idler gear thrust washers.
4   Check the idler gear needle roller bearings in the flywheel housing and gearbox casing, and the bearing surfaces of the idler gear for wear. To remove the needle roller bearings, use tool 18G1288 or a similar puller.
5   Check the first motion shaft spigot bearing and race for damage. To remove the outer race from the flywheel housing, extract the circlip, and use tool 18G617C.

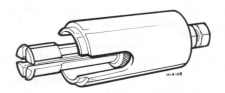

Fig. 6.8 Tool 18G1288 for removing idler gear bearings (Sec 7)

6   Drive the primary gear oil seal from the flywheel housing using a metal tube of suitable diameter.
7   Renew all components as necessary.
8   Using a block of wood, drive the new primary gear oil seal into the flywheel housing with the seal lip facing inwards (photo).

7.1A Removing the thrust washer ...

7.1B ... backing ring ...

7.1C ... primary gear ...

7.1D ... and notched thrust washer from the crankshaft

7.2 Removing the idler gear

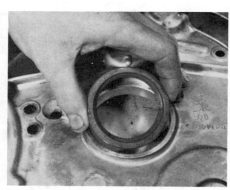

7.8 Installing the primary gear oil seal

7.9 First motion shaft spigot and idler gear bearings in the flywheel housing

7.12 Checking the primary gear endfloat

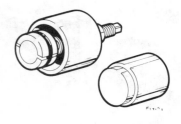

Fig. 6.9 Tool 18G617C for removing first motion shaft spigot bearing outer race (Sec 7)

Fig. 6.10 Tool 18G1289 for fitting idler gear
bearings (Sec 7)

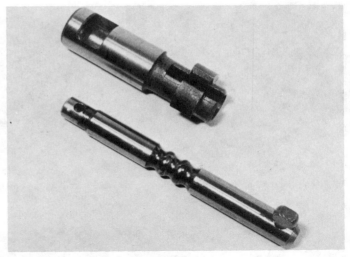

8.1 Interlock spool and selector shaft

9   Using a length of metal tube, drive the first motion shaft spigot
bearing outer race squarely into the flywheel housing. If available use
tool 18G617C. Fit the retaining circlip in its groove (photo).
10   Using a length of metal tube, drive the idler gear needle roller
bearings squarely into the flywheel housing and gearbox casing until
just recessed below the housing/casing surface. Use tool 18G1289 if
available. The chamfered end of the bearings should be inserted first.
11   Locate the notched thrust washer (chamfered side first) onto the
end of the crankshaft, followed by the primary gear (gear end first),
backing ring and C-shaped thrust washer.
12   Using a feeler blade between the backing ring and gear, check that
the primary gear endfloat is as given in the Specifications (photo). If
not, note the measured endfloat, then remove the notched thrust
washer and measure its thickness. An alternative thrust washer must
now be selected and fitted to correct the endfloat.

8   Selector components and gearbox housings – servicing

1   Examine the bellcrank lever components, the selector forks and
the selector shaft for wear and damage, and renew them as necessary
(photo).
2   If the bellcrank lever pivot post is worn, drive it out of the gearbox
casing using a length of metal tubing, while supporting the casing with
blocks of wood.
3   Renew and lubricate the O-ring seal, and drive the new pivot post
into the gearbox casing.
4   Unbolt the endplate and gasket from the speedometer drive
housing and withdraw the speedometer gear.
5   Wash the gearbox casing, flywheel housing and speedometer
drive housing with paraffin and wipe dry with lint-free cloth.
Thoroughly examine the housings for cracks and damage and renew
them as necessary.
6   Check the speedometer drivegear for wear and chipping; also
check the pinion. Renew them as necessary.
7   Fit the drivegear into the housing, and fit the endplate with a new
gasket. Tighten the bolts.

9.3 Inserting the selector shaft through the forks

9   Gearbox – reassembly

Note: *Before reassembly, all components must be clean. During
reassembly, all bearings and bearing surfaces should be lubricated
with gear oil.*
1   Insert the selector shaft into the interlock spool, then locate them
in the gearbox casing from inside with the stub facing away from the
pivot post.
2   Fit the pivot sleeve, bellcrank levers, and intermediate washers
onto the pivot post, then fit the washer and tighten the self-locking nut
to the specified torque.
3   Locate the selector forks in the casing in their correct order, then
insert the selector shaft through the casing and forks (photo).
4   Align the hole in the selector shaft with the hole in the 3rd/4th
selector fork. Drive in the roll pin with a punch until it is flush with the
surface of the fork.
5   Engage the reverse idler gear groove with the reverse bellcrank
lever, with the groove towards the transfer gear end of the gearbox.
Insert the shaft through the casing and idler gear with the slotted end
towards the speedometer drive end of the gearbox.
6   Position the oil strainer loosely in the casing (photo).

9.6 Oil strainer location

9.8 Fitting the third motion shaft bearing

9.9 Installing the needle roller bearing in the first motion shaft

9.10 Installing the first motion shaft

9.11 Checking the first motion shaft bearing circlip groove width

9.13 Laygear needle roller bearing

9.14A A laygear thrust washer (arrowed)

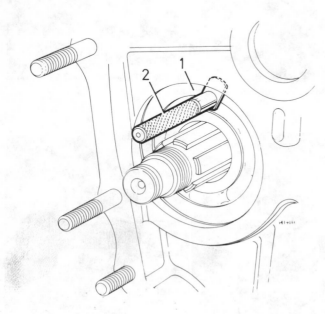

Fig. 6.11 Using tool 18G569 to determine the thickness of the first motion shaft bearing circlip (Sec 9)

1   Bearing   2   Tool

7   Install the third motion shaft assembly into the gearbox, at the same time engaging the two selector forks with their corresponding synchro units.

8   Locate the ball-bearing over the third motion shaft with the circlip towards the speedometer drive end of the gearbox (photo). Hold a block of wood against the inner end of the third motion shaft, then drive the bearing into the centre web of the casing using a length of tubing on the bearing outer track.

9   Locate the needle roller bearing into the end of the first motion shaft (photo).

10 Using a length of tubing on the ball-bearing outer track, drive the first motion shaft and bearing into the casing, making sure that it engages the third motion shaft spigot (photo).

11 Using feeler blades or tool 18G569, determine the width of the first motion shaft bearing circlip groove (photo). If it is between 0.096 and 0.098 in (2.44 and 2.49 mm) the circlip part number 2A3710 should be used; if it is between 0.098 and 0.100 in (2.49 and 2.54 mm) circlip part number 2A3711 should be used. If the original bearing is being re-used, the original circlip can be fitted.

12 Fit the circlip in the groove to secure the first motion shaft bearing.

13 Insert the needle roller bearings into the laygear (photo).

14 Using grease, stick the laygear thrust washers in position on the casing and lower the laygear between them. Insert the layshaft from the transfer gear end of the gearbox. Check that the endfloat is as given in the Specifications (photos).

15 Turn the ends of the layshaft and reverse idler shaft until the slots are parallel to and facing each other, then insert the locking plate.

16 Install the third motion shaft bearing retainer without any shims, and tighten the bolts evenly and firmly. Using feeler blades, determine the gap (if any) between the retainer and the casing (photo). Deduct the specified bearing endfloat from the result to give the thickness of shims to fit.

17 Remove the retainer, then fit the selected shims beneath the reverse shaft/layshaft locking plate to give the specified third motion shaft bearing endfloat.

18 Refit the retainer and tighten the bolts evenly and in diagonal sequence to the specified torque.

19 Engage 1st and top gear to lock the gears.

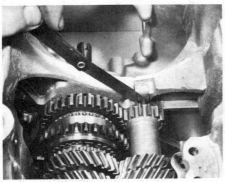

9.14B Checking the laygear endfloat

9.16 Checking for third motion shaft bearing endfloat

9.23 Tightening the first motion shaft nut

9.24 Fitting the first motion shaft spigot bearing

10.3 Removing the steady rod bolt

10.7A Gearchange remote control mountings

10.7B Gearchange remote control assembly

20 Fit the final drive pinion with reference to Chapter 7.
21 Check the third motion shaft endfloat and, if as specified, bend the locktabs onto one flat of each bolt to lock them.
22 Fit the speedometer drive housing with reference to Chapter 7.
23 Slide the first motion shaft gear (flanged end first) onto the first motion shaft splines. Fit the lockwasher and nut, and tighten the nut to the specified torque (photo). Bend the locktab to lock the nut.
24 Drive the spigot bearing, flange end first, onto the end of the first motion shaft and fit the circlip into the groove (photo).
25 Move the selector forks to select neutral, then rotate the selector shaft and spool clockwise into engagement with the bellcrank levers.
26 Insert the oil pick-up pipe into the strainer.
27 Locate new gaskets either side of the casing with the blanking plate on the outside. Fit the lockwasher and bolts, and tighten the bolts. Bend the locktabs to lock the bolts.
28 Fit the oil strainer bracket bolts and lockwasher, and tighten them. Bend the locktabs to lock the bolts.
29 Fit the final drive (differential) unit as described in Chapter 7.
30 Lubricate the gears and bearings liberally with gear oil.

10 Gearchange remote control – removal, overhaul and refitting

1 Jack up the front of the car and support it on axle stands. Apply the handbrake.
2 Using a punch, drive out the roll pin securing the remote control extension rod to the selector shaft at the differential housing.
3 Unscrew and remove the bolt securing the steady rod to the rear of the differential housing (photo).
4 Working inside the car, pull back the rear of the front carpet and disconnect the reversing light switch wiring.
5 Unscrew and remove the nuts securing the remote control bracket to the floor.
6 Working inside the car, twist the gear lever retaining dome anti-clockwise and release it from the housing.
7 Lower the remote control assembly and remove it from under the car (photos).
8 If the assembly is to be overhauled, remove the upper and lower brackets and the bottom cover. Drive out the roll pins and remove the

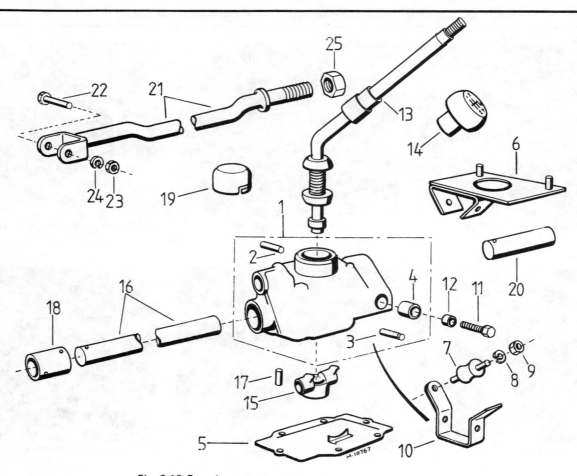

Fig. 6.12 Gearchange remote control components (Sec 10)

1	Housing assembly	8	Spring washer	14	Knob	20 Support rod
2	Long pin	9	Nut	15	Eye	21 Steady rod
3	Short pin	10	Lower mounting bracket	16	Extension rod	22 Bolt
4	Lower bush	11	Bolt	17	Roll pin	23 Nut
5	Bottom cover	12	Nut	18	Coupling	24 Washer
6	Upper mounting bracket	13	Gear lever	19	Retainer	25 Nut
7	Mounting					

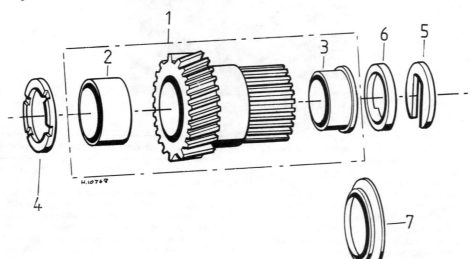

Fig. 6.13 Primary gear components (Sec 11)

1	Primary gear assembly	3	Outer bush	5	C-shaped thrust washer
2	Inner bush	4	Notched thrust washer (selective)	6	Backing ring
				7	Dust shield

extension rod, eye and support rod. Drive the bushes from the housing.
9   Wash the components in paraffin and wipe them dry. Examine them for wear and damage, and check the bushes for deterioration. Renew all components as necessary.
10 Refitting is a reversal of removal, but lubricate the bearing surfaces with multi-purpose grease. Make sure that the gear lever is correctly located before fitting the retaining dome.

11 Flywheel housing oil seal – renewal

1   Remove the clutch and flywheel as described in Chapter 5.
2   Slide the dust shield from the primary gear, noting which way round it is fitted (photo).
3   Remove the C-shaped thrust washer and backing ring from the end of the crankshaft.
4   Using tool 18G1068B, pull the primary gear from the crankshaft; the oil seal will also be pulled from the flywheel housing (photo).
5   Make sure that the notched thrust washer is located correctly on the crankshaft with its chamfer innermost (photo).
6   Wrap adhesive tape over the primary gear splines, or alternatively use tool 18G1043. Lubricate the new oil seal with engine oil and

locate it on the primary gear oil seal surface with the sealing lip facing the gear end (photos).
7   Slide the primary gear onto the end of the crankshaft until the oil seal contacts the housing.
8   Using tool 18G1068B or a suitable length of tubing, drive in the oil seal until it is flush with the flywheel housing (photo).
9   Remove the tool or adhesive tape if fitted, then fit the backing ring and C-shaped thrust washer.
10 Slide the dust shield onto the primary gear splines (inner flange side first). The outer stepped face is marked 'FLYWHEEL SIDE' and must face the splined end of the primary gear. Use the clutch plate to push the shield fully home.
11 Fit the clutch and flywheel as described in Chapter 5.

12 Selector shaft oil seal – renewal

1   Jack up the front of the car and support it on axle stands. Apply the handbrake.
2   Using a punch, drive out the roll pin securing the remote control extension rod to the selector shaft at the differential housing.
3   Separate the extension rod from the selector shaft and remove the rubber bellows (photos).

11.2 Removing the dust shield

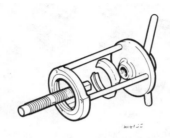

Fig. 6.14 Tool 18G1068B for removing and refitting primary gear oil seal (Sec 11)

11.4 Removing the primary gear and oil seal

11.5 Correct fitting of the notched thrust washer

11.6A Adhesive tape to protect the flywheel housing oil seal

11.6B Locating the oil seal on the primary gear

11.8 Installing the flywheel housing oil seal

12.3A Removing the extension rod ...

12.3B ... and rubber bellows

12.5 Extracting the selector shaft oil seal

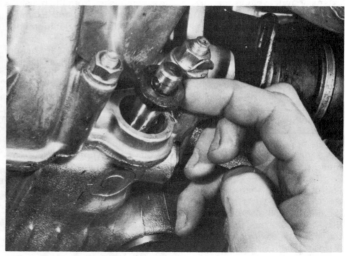

12.7 Fitting the new seal

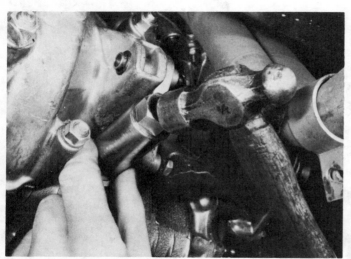

12.8 Using a socket to install the selector shaft oil seal

12.10 Installing the roll pin

4   Unscrew the drain plug and drain the engine oil into a clean container. Refit the drain plug.
5   Using a small screwdriver, hook the selector shaft oil seal from the differential housing (photo).
6   Clean the shaft and housing and wrap some adhesive tape around the shaft shoulder.
7   Smear clean engine oil on the inner lip of the new oil seal and slide it over the tape onto the shaft (photo). Remove the tape.
8   Using a suitably-sized socket, tap the seal into the differential housing until flush with the outer surface (photo).
9   Refit the rubber bellows and locate the extension rod on the selector shaft.
10   Align the holes and drive in the roll pin (photo).
11   Lower the car to the ground, and refill the engine with oil.

PART B: AUTOMATIC TRANSMISSION

13   General description

The automatic transmission incorporates four forward speeds and one reverse speed; speeds 1, 2, and 3 may be selected and held independently of the automatic function. A three-element torque converter transmits drive from the engine to the transmission.

The transmission oil, which also circulates through the engine lubrication system, is cooled by an oil cooler mounted on the front of the engine. Oil pressure is provided by the engine oil pump driven by the camshaft.

Due to the complexity of the automatic transmission, work by the home mechanic should be limited to the procedures given in the following Sections. If the unit is faulty, do not remove the automatic transmission until the fault has been diagnosed by a BL garage.

14   Automatic transmission – removal and refitting

1   Remove the engine/gearbox assembly as described in Chapter 1, and drain the oil.
2   Remove the torque converter and housing as described in Sections 15 and 16.
3   Unscrew the union nut and disconnect the oil feed pipe from the gearbox adaptor.
4   Lever the main oil feed pipe from the oil pump and gearbox casing.
5   Unscrew the bolts and lift the engine from the gearbox.
6   Remove the two gaskets, the main bearing cap oil seal, and the O-ring from the top of the oil pick-up pipe.
7   Refitting is a reversal of removal, but fit a new O-ring and casing-to-crankcase gaskets. Lubricate the new main bearing cap oil seal with

engine oil before locating it on the timing chain end main bearing cap. Tighten all nuts and bolts to the specified torque. Refer to Sections 15 and 16 when refitting the torque converter and housing, and to Chapter 1 when refitting the engine/gearbox assembly.

15 Torque converter and oil seal – removal and refitting

Note: *Before starting work it is essential to obtain tool 18G 1086 in order to release the torque converter from the crankshaft taper, and tools 18G 1068A and 18G 1068B in order to refit the oil seal. A 1½ inch AF socket will also be required to unscrew the torque converter retaining bolt, or tool 18G 587 may be used.*

If the engine/gearbox unit is in the car, follow paragraphs 1 to 6.
1 Drain the engine/gearbox oil into a suitable container, then refit the drain plug.
2 Remove the battery as described in Chapter 10 and remove the battery carrier.
3 Jack up the front of the car and support it with axle stands positioned beneath the rear edges of the front subframe.
4 Take the weight of the engine/gearbox unit with a hoist.
5 Unscrew the nut and remove the through-bolt and washer from the right-hand front engine mounting. Unscrew and remove the nut and washer from the right-hand rear engine mounting.
6 Unscrew the bonnet lock cross panel securing screws and central bolt, and move the headlamp shrouds (if fitted). Remove the screws and withdraw the grille, then position the bonnet lock cross panel and radiator carefully to one side.
7 Remove the starter motor (Chapter 10) and the oil filter assembly (Chapter 1).
8 Unbolt and remove the torque converter cover. If the engine is in the car, it will be necessary to move the carburettor drain pipe and earth cable to one side.
9 Turn the crankshaft with a spanner on the pulley centre bolt, until the slots in the torque converter and crankshaft are horizontal. This will prevent the output gear C-washer subsequently falling out.
10 Insert a wide-bladed screwdriver between the starter ring gear and the torque converter housing, then unscrew the torque converter retaining bolt. Make sure that the socket is fully engaged with the bolt as it is very tight.
11 Remove the keyplate and locking washer, then flatten the locktabs and unscrew three equally spaced bolts from the centre of the torque converter.
12 Using tool 18G 1086, pull the torque converter from the crankshaft taper. It will be necessary to hold the torque converter stationary whilst tightening the puller centre bolt; strike the centre bolt with a hammer to help release the taper. Note that the torque converter will still retain some oil.
13 Using a hooked instrument or alternatively tool 18G 1087, extract the oil seal from the torque converter housing.
14 Commence refitting by using a micrometer or vernier calipers to measure the distance from the housing face to the end of the stator bush in the oil seal bore. If this dimension is less than 0.375 in (9.5 mm), deduct it from 0.375 in (9.5 mm) to obtain the oil seal protrusion from the housing face. If the dimension is equal to, or greater than, 0.375 in (9.5 mm), the oil seal must be fitted flush with the housing face.
15 Using tools 18G 1068A and 18G 1068B or a suitable length of tubing, install the oil seal into the housing to its correct positon. Note that if the oil seal is not positioned correctly it may cover an important drain hole in the housing.
16 Fit new locking plates to the centre of the torque converter by removing and refitting the remaining bolts one at a time. *Do not remove all the bolts at the same time.* Insert and tighten all the bolts to the specified torque, then bend the locktabs onto one flat of each bolt.
17 With the crankshaft slot still horizontal, fit the torque converter onto the crankshaft and align the keyplate slots. Fit the keyplate, locking washer and retaining bolt.
18 Have an assistant insert a wide-bladed screwdriver between the ring gear and the housing, then tighten the torque converter retaining bolt to the specified torque. Bend the locking washer over one flat of the retaining bolt.
19 The remaining refitting procedure is a reversal of the removal procedure given in paragraphs 1 to 8. Fill the engine/gearbox with the correct quantity of the specified oil.

Fig. 6.15 Tool 18G1087 for removing the torque converter oil seal (Sec 15)

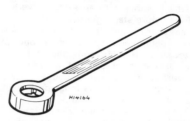

Fig. 6.16 Tool 18G 1088 for use when removing the gearbox input gear nut (Sec 16)

16 Torque converter housing and transfer gears – removal, servicing and refitting

Note: *Before starting work it is esssential to obtain tool 18G 1088 in order to unscrew the gearbox input gear nut. The tool should be obtained from a tool hire agent.*
1 Remove the torque converter as described in Section 15 – it is not necessary to remove the oil seal.
2 Unbolt the low pressure valve from the converter housing and remove the gasket.
3 Fit tool 18G 1088 to the converter output gear, hold the gear stationary, and unscrew the gearbox input gear nut. Remove the washer.
4 Disconnect the selector cable and unscrew the bellcrank pivot pins, then withdraw the bellcrank lever.
5 If the engine is still in the car, remove the right-hand front engine mounting.
6 Wrap adhesive tape around the converter output gear splines or use tool 18G 1098. Unscrew the retaining nuts and bolts, and tap the torque converter housing free; withdraw the housing sufficiently to disconnect the oil feed pipe, then fully withdraw the housing. The idler gear may remain with the housing so take care not to drop it.
7 Remove the idler gear and thrust washers, and the input gear and shims. Keep the shims and washers identified for correct assembly.
8 Remove the C-shaped thrust washer from the end of the crankshaft, and withdraw the backing ring, output gear, and the thrust washer.
9 Examine the housing, transfer gears and bearing for wear and damage and renew them as necessary. If necessary remove the idler gear needle roller bearing using tool 18G 1288 or a similar puller. The input bearing in the converter housing can be removed with a soft metal drift after removing the circlip.
10 Using a length of metal tube, drive the idler gear needle roller bearings squarely into the torque converter housing and gearbox casing until just recessed below the housing/casing surface. Use tool 18G 1289 if available. The chamfered end of the bearings should be inserted first.
11 Locate the thrust washer (chamfered side first) on to the end of the crankshaft, followed by the output gear (gear end first), backing ring, and C-shaped thrust washer.
12 Using a feeler blade between the backing ring and gear, check that the output gear endfloat is as given in the Specifications. If not, note the measured endfloat, then remove the thrust washer and measure its thickness. An alternative thrust washer must now be selected and fitted to correct the endfloat.
13 If either the idler gear, idler gear thrust washers, torque converter housing, input gear, input bearing, or transmission and casing have been renewed, the thickness of the idler gear and input gear washers and shims must be determined as follows. A selection of thrust

Fig. 6.17 Tool 18G 1089A for checking input gear endfloat (Sec 16)

washers and shims together with an extra converter bearing gasket should be obtained before starting work.

14 If only the idler gear components have been renewed, the washer thickness can be determined using either one of the methods described in Section 2. If more components have been renewed, method 2 in Section 2 must be use, but in addition tool 18G 1089A together with a wax washer sandwiched between two metal washers (18G 1089/1) must be fitted to the input gear shaft instead of the input gear. Do not fit the input gear nut.

15 To calculate the input gear shims, determine the extra length of tool 18G 1089A plus the washers compared with the length of the input gear. This dimension plus 0.001 to 0.003 in (0.025 to 0.07 mm) represents the shim thickness to be fitted in order to obtain the required bearing preload.

16 Once the shim and washer thicknesses have been determined, refitting of the transfer gears and torque converter housing is a reversal of the removal procedure. Always fit new gaskets to the converter housing and low pressure valve, and tighten all nuts and bolts to the specified torque.

Fig. 6.18 Exploded view of the selector components (Secs 17 and 20)

1 Selector lever	20 Lockwasher
2 Knob	21 Connector
3 Gate and side plate	22 Olive
4 Bias spring	23 Nut
5 Bolt	24 Gaiter
6 Nyloc nut	25 Gaiter
7 Washer	26 Cable clip
8 Barrel	27 Reversing light switch
9 Pivot pin	28 Bracket
10 Pin retainers	29 Plug
11 Mounting plate	30 Stiffener plate
12 Gasket	31 Seal
13 Screw	32 Nut
14 Washer	33 Washer
15 Selector housing	34 Housing
16 Selector plunger	35 Light unit
17 Selector cable	36 Slide
18 Locknut	37 Light bulb
19 Locknut	

17 Automatic transmission selector cable – removal, refitting and adjustment

1 Jack up the front of the car and support it with axle stands positioned beneath the rear edges of the front subframe. Apply the handbrake.

2 Unbolt the bellcrank cover plate from the gearbox and unclip the selector cable from the subframe.

3 Extract one circlip, remove the pivot pin, and disconnect the cable clevis from the bellcrank lever.

4 Remove the locknut and washer, and withdraw the clevis from the cable.

5 Pull back the rubber covers, unscrew the outer cable locknut and remove the cable from the gearbox.

6 Working beneath the selector housing, unscrew the cable retaining nut, then unscrew the adaptor.

7 Using a split box spanner (if available), loosen the locknut securing the cable to the plunger. Fit the fork and locknut to the inner cable and remove the inner cable from the plunger. Remove the fork and locknut

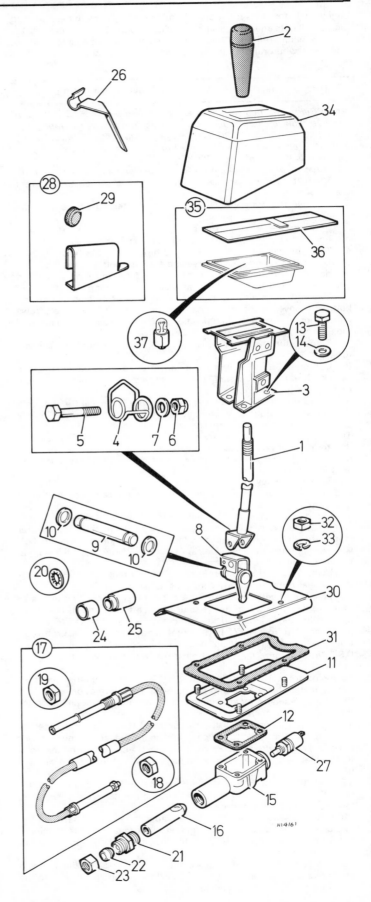

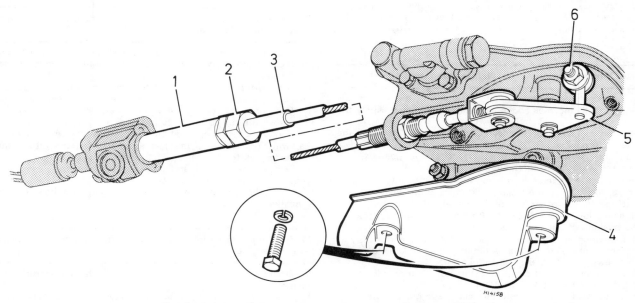

Fig. 6.19 Selector cable components and bellcrank lever (Sec 17)

1	Selector housing	3	Outer cable	5	Bellcrank
2	Nut	4	Cover	6	Transverse selector rod

together with the adaptor olive and outer cable securing nut. Withdraw the cable.

8   Refitting is a reversal of removal, but adjust the cable as follows.

9   With the bellcrank cover removed and the front of the car still supported on axle stands, loosen the large nut on the outer cable beneath the selector housing.

10   At the gearbox end of the cable, turn the bellcrank lever fully anti-clockwise (from below) so that the transverse selector rod is in the 'Park' position.

11   Have an assistant move the selector lever to the 'P' position, making sure that the lever is in the notch at the left-hand side of the gate. If the notch cannot be felt, remove the selector lever nacelle and position the selector lever 0.035 in (0.9 mm) from the end of the gate slot.

12   With the bellcrank lever held stationary, pull the outer cable from the selector housing, then tighten the securing nut.

13   Refit the bellcrank cover and lower the car to the ground. To check the adjustment, select 'N' and start the engine. Move the lever to 'R' and check that reverse is engaged, then slowly move the lever back to 'N' — the gear should disengage when the lever reaches the 'N' position, or slightly before. Repeat the check but this time select '1'. Adjust the inhibitor switch if necessary as described in Section 19.

18 Kickdown linkage – adjustment

1   Run the engine to normal operating temperature and adjust the idling speed as described in Chapter 3.

2   Prise off the starlock washer and extract the clevis pin from the top of the kickdown control rod on the throttle lever.

3   Locate the kickdown bellcrank lever on the rear of the gearbox beneath the manifolds. Insert a 6 mm (0.25 in) diameter rod through the hole in the lever and into the special hole in the gearbox casing.

4   Check that the clevis pin can be inserted without removing the throttle lever. If not, loosen the locknut and turn the control rod as necessary.

5   Tighten the locknut, refit the clevis pin with a new starlock washer, and remove the dowel rod from the gearbox casing.

6   Test drive the car and check that with the accelerator pedal fully depressed the gear changes occur in accordance with the following table:

1 to 2 .... 29 to 37 mph (46 to 59 km/h)
2 to 3 .... 43 to 51 mph (69 to 82 km/h)
3 to 4 .... 61 to 69 mph (98 to 111 km/h)

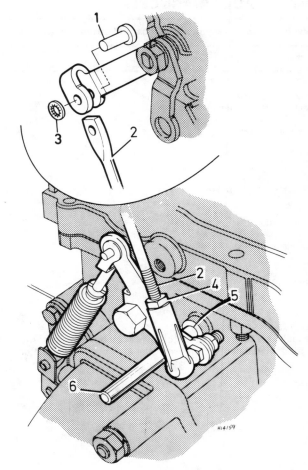

Fig. 6.20 Kickdown linkage components (Sec 18)

1	Clevis pin	4	Locknut
2	Control rod	5	Casing hole
3	Starlock washer	6	Dowel rod for checking

7   If the changes occur at a lower speed, shorten the kickdown control rod by two complete turns and road test the car again. If the changes occur at a higher speed, lengthen the rod by two complete turns.

19 Starter inhibitor switch – removal, refitting, and adjustment

1   Jack up the front of the car and support it with axle stands positioned beneath the rear edges of the front subframe. Apply the handbrake.
2   Adjust the selector cable as described in Section 17. Move the selector lever to position 'D'.
3   Unbolt the guard plate from the front of the gearbox, and disconnect the wiring from the inhibitor switch.
4   Either drain the engine/transmission oil or have ready a suitable tapered plug, then loosen the locknut and unscrew the switch.
5   Refitting is a reversal of removal, but top up the engine/transmission oil as necessary. Before tightening the locknut, adjust the position of the switch as follows.
6   With the wiring disconnected, connect a test lamp and battery to the switch terminals. Screw in the switch until the test lamp just goes out, then screw it in a further three to four flats.
7   Tighten the locknut and check that the test lamp only lights up with the selector lever in positions 'P' or 'N'.
8   Remove the test lamp and refit the wiring and guard plate.
9   Lower the car to the ground and check that the engine will only start with the selector lever in positions 'P' or 'N'.

20 Reversing light switch (automatic transmission) – removal, refitting and adjustment

1   Jack up the front of the car and support it with axle stands positioned beneath the rear edges of the front subframe. Apply the handbrake.
2   Disconnect the wiring from the switch terminals, loosen the locknut, and unscrew the switch from the selector lever housing.
3   Refitting is a reversal of removal, but adjust the switch as follows. First move the selector lever to position 'R'.
4   Connect a test lamp and battery to the switch terminals. Screw in the switch until the test lamp just lights up, then screw it in a further one and a half to three flats.
5   Tighten the locknut and remove the testlamp. Reconnect the wiring and lower the car to the ground.
6   Check that the reversing lights operate only with the selector lever in postion 'R'.

21 Speedometer pinion and drivegear (automatic transmission) – removal and refitting

1   Disconnect the speedometer cable from the left-hand side of the gearbox.
2   Unscrew the clamp bolt and withdraw the pinion assembly.
3   Unbolt the drive housing and withdraw the gasket and drivegear.
4   Refitting is a reversal of removal, but always fit a new gasket.

PART C: FAULT DIAGNOSIS

22 Fault diagnosis – manual gearbox and automatic transmission

Symptom	Reason(s)
Manual gearbox	
Ineffective synchromesh	Worn baulk rings
Jumps out of gear	Weak or broken detent spring Worn selector forks, bellcrank levers, selector shafts, or interlock spool Weak or broken synchro hub springs Worn gears and/or synchro sleeves
Noisy operation (all gears)	Worn bearings Worn gears
Noisy operation (except top gear)	Worn third motion shaft spigot needle roller bearing
Chattering noise from flywheel housing during idling	Worn transfer gears Incorrect idler gear endfloat
Difficult engagement of gears	Worn selector components Clutch fault

Automatic transmission
Most faults are the result of low oil level or incorrect adjustment of the selector cable or kickdown control rod. Internal faults should be diagnosed by a BL garage before the transmission is removed from the car.

Chapter 7 Final drive

For modifications and information applicable to later models, see Supplement at end of manual

Contents

Differential unit – removal, overhaul and refitting 2
Fault diagnosis – final drive 4
Final drive pinion (manual gearbox models) – removal and refitting 3
General description 1

Specifications

Ratio

Metro standard and Metro L	3.647 : 1
Metro HLE, Metro 1.3L, Metro 1.3S, and Metro 1.3HLS	3.444 : 1
Metro Automatic	2.760 : 1

Final drive gear and pinion teeth

Metro standard and Metro L	17/62
Metro HLE, Metro 1.3L, Metro 1.3S, and Metro 1.3 HLS	18/62
Metro Automatic	25/69

Differential bearing preload

....	0.004 in (0.102 mm)

Torque wrench settings

	lbf ft	kgf m
Differential housing nuts – $\frac{5}{16}$ in	18	2.5
Differential housing nuts – $\frac{3}{8}$ in	25	3.5
Side cover bolts	18	2.5
Final drive gear	48	6.6
Speedometer drivegear housing nuts	18	2.5
Final drive pinion nut	150	20.7
Speedometer drivegear housing bolts	6	0.8

1 General description

The final drive unit is located on the rear of the gearbox casing. The final drive gear is driven by a pinion which is splined to the gearbox third motion shaft on manual gearbox models, or to the top and reverse clutch hub on automatic transmission models.

The differential unit incorporates two pinions mounted on a single pin.

2 Differential unit – removal, overhaul and refitting

Note: *Before starting work obtain tool 18G1236, if possible, for protecting the selector shaft oil seal on manual gearboxes. A two-legged puller will be required to remove the differential side bearings as necessary.*

1 Remove the engine/gearbox assembly as described in Chapter 1, and place it on a workbench.

2 Unbolt and remove the left-hand side cover and gasket, and remove the adjustment shim(s). Place the shim(s) in a safe place, as they determine the differential bearing preload.

3 Unbolt and remove the right-hand side cover and gasket; note the exhaust bracket location.

4 On manual gearbox models, extract the selector shaft detent sleeve, O-ring, spring and ball from the gearbox casing on the right-hand side of the differential (photos).

5 Position tool 18G1236 over the end of the selector shaft. Alternatively wrap adhesive tape over the selector shaft hole.

6 On all models, bend back the ends of the locktabs, then unscrew evenly in a diagonal sequence the differential housing securing nuts. Remove the locktabs and washers.

2.4A Removing the selector shaft detent spring and ball

2.4B Removing the selector shaft detent sleeve

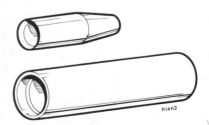

Fig. 7.1 Tool 18G1236 for protecting and fitting selector shaft oil seal (Sec 2)

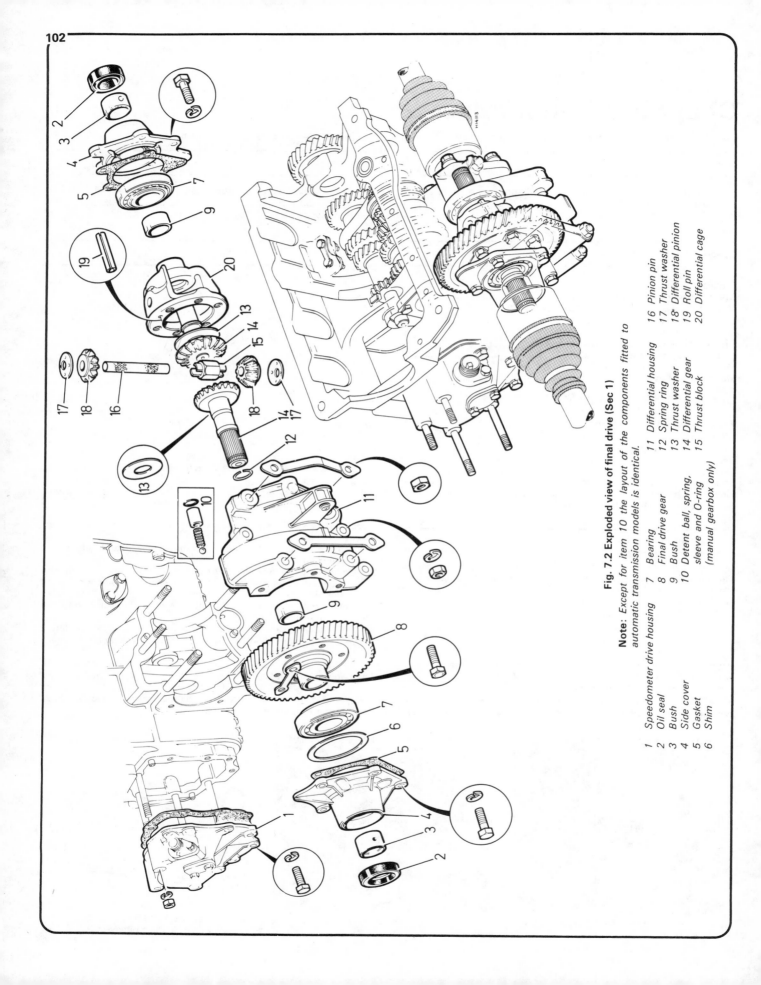

Fig. 7.2 Exploded view of final drive (Sec 1)

Note: Except for item 10 the layout of the components fitted to automatic transmission models is identical.

1 Speedometer drive housing	7 Bearing	11 Differential housing
2 Oil seal	8 Final drive gear	12 Spring ring
3 Bush	9 Bush	13 Thrust washer
4 Side cover	10 Detent ball, spring,	14 Differential gear
5 Gasket	sleeve and O-ring	15 Thrust block
6 Shim	(manual gearbox only)	

16 Pinion pin
17 Thrust washer
18 Differential pinion
19 Roll pin
20 Differential cage

7 Withdraw the housing and gaskets (if fitted), followed by the differential unit (photos).
8 Prise the oil seals from the side covers and housing (photo).
9 If a complete new differential unit is being fitted, proceed to paragraph 25, but remember that the final drive gear and pinion should be renewed together as a set if either the gear or pinion is worn excessively. If the unit is being overhauled proceed as follows.
10 Using a two-legged puller, pull the side bearings from the differential cage and identify each bearing side for side.
11 Scratch identification marks on the final drive gear and differential cage so that they can be refitted in the original position.
12 Bend back the locktabs, then unscrew the final drive gear securing bolts evenly and in diagonal sequence.
13 Withdraw the final drive gear together with the left-hand differential gear.
14 Identify the left-hand differential gear, then remove it from the final drive gear together with the thrust washer.
15 Using a suitable punch, drive the pinion pin retaining roll pin from the differential cage in a right-to-left direction, ie towards the final drive gear flange.
16 Drive out the pinion pin, and remove the thrust block, pinions and thrust washers.
17 Clean all components in paraffin and wipe dry. Examine the gears for wear, chipping, and damage. Spin the bearings by hand and check them for rough running. Hold the outer races and attempt to move the inner races laterally; any movement indicates a worn bearing. Check the fit of the differential gears in the final drive gear, differential cage and side cover bushes. If worn, drive out the old bushes with a suitable drift, then drive the new bushes into position. Make sure that the oil holes in the side cover bushes are correctly aligned. Renew all components as necessary and obtain new side cover gaskets and oil seals. Obtain new differential housing gaskets if fitted. Note that although the differential pinions and gears are not a complete matched set, they should nevertheless be renewed together and not individually. The same applies to the final drive gear and pinion; refer to Section 3 if necessary.
18 Commence reassembly by fitting the right-hand differential gear together with a new thrust washer into the differential cage.
19 Install the pinions, new thrust washers, and thrust block, at the same time gradually inserting the pinion pin into the cage. Before fully installing the pin, make sure that the roll pin hole is positioned in line with the hole in the cage.
20 Secure the pinion pin by driving the roll pin into the cage from the right-hand side.
21 Locate the final drive gear on the differential cage with the previously made marks aligned, and insert the bolts together with the locktabs.
22 Tighten the bolts evenly in diagonal sequence to the specified torque. Bend the locktabs against one flat of each bolt to lock them.
23 Using a suitable length of tube against the inner races, drive the side bearings onto the differential unit. If refitting the old bearings, make sure that they are located on the correct sides. The flanged side of the outer races must face outwards.
24 With the side covers and housing resting on a wooden block, drive the new oil seals squarely into position (photo).
25 Check that the differential housing and gearbox casing mating faces are clean.
26 Position the differential unit onto the gearbox casing and engage

the final drive gear with the pinion. Push the unit slightly towards the right (flywheel) side of the casing to facilitate the subsequent preload adjustment.
27 On manual gearbox models, position tool 18G 1236 or adhesive tape over the selector shaft.
28 If gaskets were originally fitted, fit new gaskets over the studs. If no gaskets were fitted, do not use any sealant at this stage.
29 Install the differential housing, locktabs and washers, and tighten the securing nuts evenly in diagonal sequence sufficiently to hold the differential unit firmly. However, it must be possible to move the unit when refitting the side cover in order to adjust the preload.
30 On manual gearbox models, insert the selector shaft detent ball, spring, sleeve, and O-ring into the right-hand side of the gearbox casing.
31 Fit the right-hand (flywheel side) side cover together with a new gasket, making sure that the oil holes in the cover and differential housing are aligned (photo).
32 Insert the securing bolts and washers and tighten them evenly in diagonal sequence to the specified torque after locating the exhaust bracket in position (photo).
33 Fit the previously removed shims against the left-hand bearing outer race. If new components have been fitted, fit a nominal amount of shims.
34 Fit the left-hand side cover without a gasket, insert the securing bolts and washers, and tighten them evenly in diagonal sequence just sufficiently for the side cover to fully contact the bearing outer race. Do not overtighten the bolts, otherwise the side cover will be distorted.
35 If no gap exists between the side cover and the housing/casing, remove the side cover and add more shims.
36 Using a feeler blade, check the gap between the side cover and the housing/casing (photo). If the bolts have been tightened evenly, the gap will be identical at all points around the cover. Compare the measured gap with *the preload figure plus the compressed gasket thickness*. The compressed gasket thickness can be assumed to be 0.007 in (0.18 mm), therefore the figure to compare the gap with is 0.011 in (0.28 mm). Calculate the shim thickness as follows:

   (a) If the measured gap is greater than 0.011 in (0.28 mm) subtract 0.011 in (0.28 mm) from the measured gap to determine the thickness of shims to **remove** *from the shim pack*

   (b) If the measured gap is less than 0.011 in (0.28 mm), subtract the measured gap from 0.011 in (0.28 mm) to determine the thickness of shims to **add** *to the shim pack*

37 Remove the left-hand side cover and adjust the shim pack as necessary.
38 *If no gaskets are fitted between the differential housing and gearbox casing,* remove the right-hand side cover and gasket, remove the nuts and withdraw the differential housing sufficiently to apply an unbroken bead of RTV sealant on each of the two mating faces. Do not disturb the position of the differential unit. After applying the sealant, the differential housing nuts must be fully tightened within twenty minutes. However, first refit the housing and install the locktabs, washers and nuts. Tighten the nuts as described in paragraph 29, then refit the right-hand side cover and gasket, insert the securing bolts and washers, and tighten them evenly in diagonal sequence to the specified torque.
39 *On gasket and non-gasket types* grease the adjustment shims

2.7A Removing the differential housing

2.7B Removing the differential unit

2.8 Removing a side cover oil seal

2.24 Installing a new side cover oil seal

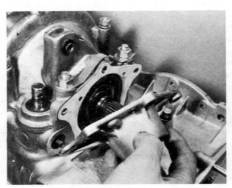

2.31 Installing the right-hand side cover

2.32 Exhaust bracket location on right-hand side cover

2.36 Differential bearing preload shim checking

2.42 Tightening differential housing nuts

and locate them against the differential bearing outer race.

40 Fit the left-hand side cover together with a new gasket, making sure that the oil holes in the cover and differential housing are aligned.

41 Insert the securing bolts and washers and tighten them evenly in diagonal sequence to the specified torque.

42 Tighten the differential housing nuts evenly and in diagonal sequence to the specified torque (photo). Lock the nuts by bending up the locktabs.

43 Remove the tape or tool 18G 1236 where applicable, and refit the engine/gearbox assembly as described in Chapter 1.

3 Final drive pinion (manual gearbox models) – removal and refitting

Note: *Although the final drive pinion and gear are not a matched set, they must nevertheless be renewed together if either is worn*

1   Remove the differential unit as described in Section 2.

2   Remove the bolt and clamp securing the speedometer pinion to the housing.

3   Withdraw the speedometer pinion together with the bushes and gasket (photo).

4   Unscrew the speedometer pinion housing nuts and bolts evenly, noting the location of the engine mounting brackets.

5   Remove the engine mounting bracket, then withdraw the housing and gear from the gearbox casing (photo). Remove the gasket.

6   Turn the gear selector shaft anti-clockwise to disengage the stub and interlock spool from the bellcrank levers.

7   Working through the differential aperture in the gearbox casing, use a screwdriver to push the centre bellcrank lever inwards in order to select 4th gear. Lever the 1st/2nd selector fork towards the final drive pinion in order to select 1st gear. The gears are now locked together.

8   Flatten the locktabs, then, using a $1\frac{1}{2}$ inch AF socket, unscrew and remove the final drive pinion nut and lockwasher (photo).

9   Mark the final drive pinion in relation to the third motion shaft, then slide it off (photo). Note the line of notches on the pinion teeth to

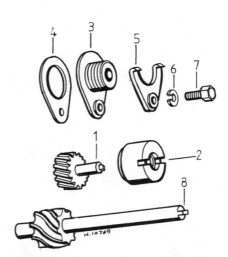

Fig. 7.3 Speedometer drivegear components (Sec 3)

1	Speedometer pinion	5	Clamp
2	Plain bush	6	Spring washer
3	Pinion bush with seal	7	Bolt
4	Gasket	8	Speedometer gear

indicate the final drive gear mesh position.

10 Fit the new final drive pinion on the third motion shaft, making sure that it is the correct way round.

11 Fit the locktab and nut and tighten the nut to the specified torque (photo). Bend the locktab onto one flat of the nut to lock it.

12 Lever the 1st/2nd selector fork into neutral. Pull the centre bellcrank lever outwards to select neutral.

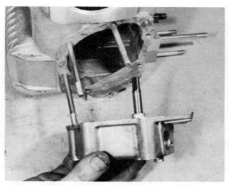

3.3 Removing the speedometer pinion

3.5 Removing the speedometer pinion housing and gear

3.8 Removing the final drive pinion nut lockwasher

3.9 Removing the final drive pinion

3.11 Tightening the final drive pinion nut

13 Clean the speedometer gear housing and gearbox casing mating faces, and install the housing with a new gasket.
14 Install the engine mounting bracket, then fit and tighten the housing retaining nuts and bolts evenly and in diagonal sequence to the specified torque.

15 Turn the gear selector shaft clockwise to engage the stub and interlock spool with the bellcrank levers.
16 Insert the speedometer pinion together with the bushes and a new gasket. Fit the clamp to the housing and tighten the bolt.
17 Fit the differential unit as described in Section 2.

4 Fault diagnosis – final drive

Symptom	Reason(s)
Noise on turns	Worn differential gear Worn driveshaft joints (see Chapter 8)
Loss of drive (manual gearbox models)	Final drive pinion nut loose and pinion out of mesh (note that speedometer will work with car stationary and forward gear engaged)

Chapter 8 Driveshafts

For modifications and information applicable to later models, see Supplement at end of manual

Contents

Fault diagnosis – driveshafts 4
General description 1
Inner constant velocity (CV) joint – removal and refitting 3

Outer constant velocity (CV) joint and driveshaft – removal and refitting 2

Specifications

Type	Solid shafts splined to constant velocity inner and outer joints

Torque wrench settings	lbf ft	kgf m
Upper and lower balljoint nuts	37	5.1
Steering balljoint nut	22	3.0
Driveshaft-to-drive flange nut (see text)	160	22.3

1 General description

Drive is transmitted from the splined final drive differential gears to the inner constant velocity joints. Splined solid driveshafts are connected to the inner and outer constant velocity joints and drive is transmitted through the splined driving flange to the front wheels.

Overhaul of the constant velocity joints is not possible. However, it is possible to renew the rubber boots which are available in repair kits. If the outer constant velocity joints are worn excessively, they will 'click' loudly on full left or right turns under load.

2 Outer constant velocity (CV) joint and driveshaft – removal and refitting

Note: *Before starting work, obtain tools 18G304, 18G304F, 18G1342, and a suitable balljoint separator (see Figs. 8.1 and 8.2).*
1 Working beneath the front of the car, remove the cross-head screws and withdraw the square rebound rubber from under the upper suspension arm. Insert a suitable large size nut or block of wood between the arm and subframe to retain the front suspension in the normal running position.
2 Apply the handbrake, then jack up the front of the car and support it on axle stands. Remove the roadwheel.
3 Grease the tapered end of tool 18G1342, then slide it along the top of the driveshaft and carefully insert it under the neck of the rubber boot and into contact with the inner joint extension tube.
4 Fit the clamp and plate of the tool to the underside of the driveshaft so that it contacts the subframe. On the left-hand side, rest the tapered part of the tool on the U-bolt.
5 Drive the tapered part of the tool towards the differential to release the inner joint from the driveshaft spring ring. Remove the tool.
6 Have an assistant firmly apply the brake pedal, then remove the

Fig. 8.1 Tools 18G304 and 18G304F for removing drive flange (Sec 2)

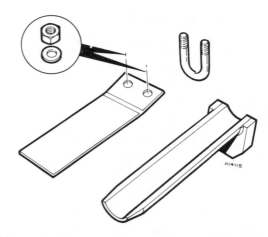

Fig. 8.2 Tool 18G1342 for releasing driveshaft from inner CV joint (Secs 2 and 3)

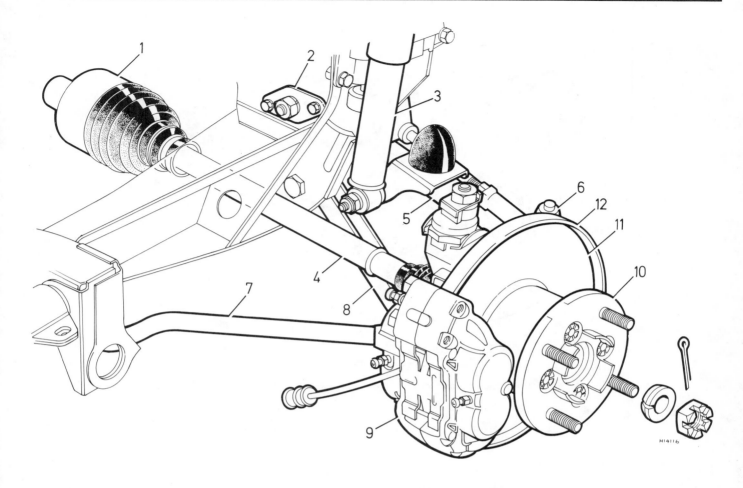

Fig. 8.3 Left-hand side driveshaft and components (Sec 1)

1	Inner joint	4	Driveshaft	7	Anti-roll bar	10	Drive flange
2	Upper suspension arm pivot plate	5	Upper suspension arm	8	Lower suspension arm	11	Disc
3	Shock absorber	6	Steering balljoint	9	Brake caliper	12	Shield

split pin and unscrew the drive flange nut (photo). Remove the split collar.

7 Refer to Chapter 9 and remove the brake disc caliper without disconnecting the hydraulic hoses. Suspend the caliper to one side without straining the hoses.

8 Refer to Chapter 9 and remove the drive flange and disc.

9 Unscrew the self-locking nut from the steering balljoint. Using a separator tool, disconnect the balljoint from the steering arm.

10 Remove the disc brake shield from the swivel hub assembly.

11 Unscrew the nuts from the swivel hub upper and lower balljoints. Using a separator tool, disconnect the upper and lower suspension arms from the swivel hub.

12 Withdraw the swivel hub and driveshaft assembly from the inner constant velocity joint.

13 Drive the outer constant velocity joint from the swivel hub assembly using a soft metal drift. If the inner bearing inner race remains on the CV joint stubshaft, the ball-bearings will be displaced and should be examined for damage and wear. Renew the bearing if necessary, with reference to Chapter 11.

14 Tap the water shield from the CV joint.

15 Examine the outer CV joint rubber boot for damage and splits and, if necessary, renew it as follows, provided the joint is in good condition. If the joint is being renewed, note that it is serviced with the driveshaft as a complete assembly.

16 To renew the rubber boot, first obtain a repair kit. Cut the old clips from the boot using snips.

2.6 Drive flange nut and split pin

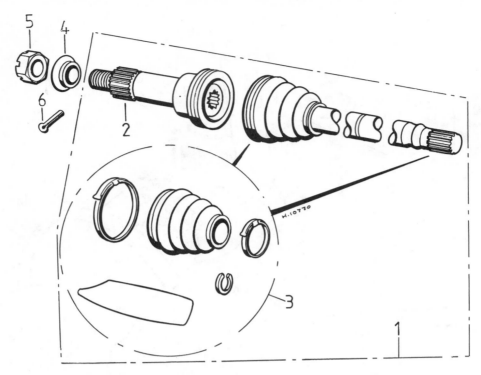

Fig. 8.4 Outer constant velocity joint and driveshaft components (Sec 2)

1	Driveshaft and joint	4	Collar
	assembly	5	Nut
2	Bell joint	6	Split pin
3	Repair kit		

17 Slide the rubber boot off the driveshaft.

18 Hold the driveshaft vertically over the workbench with the outer CV joint downwards. Using a soft-faced mallet, strike the outer edge of the joint sharply and remove the joint from the driveshaft.

19 Extract the spring ring from the outer end of the driveshaft.

20 Fit the new spring ring from the repair kit, and drive the driveshaft into the outer CV joint while compressing the ring to facilitate entry.

21 Pack the CV joint with 66 cc of the molybdenum disulphide based grease supplied with the repair kit.

22 Slide the new rubber boot into position over the CV joint and driveshaft, making sure that the mating surfaces are clean.

23 Refer to Fig. 8.5 and note that the clip must be fitted with the fold facing the forward direction of rotation. Wrap the large clip around the rubber boot and pull the free end tightly between the front tabs. Flatten the tabs with a screwdriver, and bend the clip back between the rear tabs. Flatten the rear tabs to secure the clip.

24 Check that the rubber boot is not stretched or compressed, then secure it to the driveshaft with the small clip, using the method described in paragraph 23.

25 Fit the water shield squarely onto the outer end of the CV joint and fill the sealing face with grease. Refer to Chapter 11 for the fitting dimension.

26 Insert the driveshaft through the swivel hub, and pull it fully into the hub without displacing the outer bearing. If available, tools 18G1104 and 18G1104B can be used, but failing this, rest the outer bearing inner race on a suitable length of tubing and tap the driveshaft assembly down through the bearings.

27 Lubricate the inner joint rubber boot, then insert the driveshaft and push it sharply to engage the spring ring.

28 Locate the swivel hub ball-pins into the upper and lower suspension arms and refit the tab washers and nuts. Tighten the nuts to the specified torque and bend up the tab washers to lock them.

29 Locate the disc brake shield on the swivel hub assembly.

30 Fit the steering balljoint to the steering arm, but do not fully

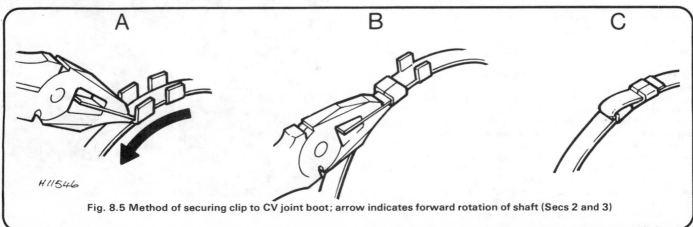

Fig. 8.5 Method of securing clip to CV joint boot; arrow indicates forward rotation of shaft (Secs 2 and 3)

3.7A Inner constant velocity joint removing tool

3.7B Using levers to remove the inner constant velocity joints

tighten the self-locking nut at this stage.
31 Fit the drive flange and disc assembly, followed by the brake caliper (Chapter 9).
32 Place a plain washer over the end of the driveshaft. The washer dimensions should be: 50 mm (1.97 in) outside diameter, 25 mm (0.98 in) inside diameter, 6.5 mm (0.26 in) thickness. Fit the driveshaft nut and tighten it firmly — say to half the final specified torque — whilst an assistant applies the brake, then unscrew the nut and remove the washer. The purpose of this operation is to make sure that the shaft is fully home.
33 Oil the driveshaft threads.
34 Tighten the steering balljoint self-locking nut to the specified torque.
35 Fit the split collar and the driveshaft nut. Have an assistant apply the brake, or bolt a bar to two of the wheel studs, and tighten the driveshaft nut to the specified torque. If the split pin holes are not aligned at this torque, tighten further until the holes are aligned. Insert a new split pin and bend back the legs.
36 Refit the roadwheel and lower the car to the ground.
37 Remove the nut or wooden block, and refit the rebound rubber to the subframe.

3 Inner constant velocity (CV) joint – removal and refitting

Note: *Before starting work, obtain tool 18G1342 and a suitable balljoint separator*
1 Follow the procedure given in Section 2, paragraphs 1 to 5.
2 Refer to Chapter 9 and remove the brake disc caliper without disconnecting the hydraulic hoses. Suspend the caliper to one side without straining the hoses.
3 Unscrew the self-locking nut from the steering balljoint. Using a separator tool, disconnect the balljoint from the steering arm.
4 Unscrew the nuts from the swivel hub upper and lower balljoints. Using a separator tool, disconnect the upper and lower suspension arms from the swivel hub.
5 Withdraw the swivel hub and driveshaft assembly from the inner constant velocity joint and place it to one side.
6 Drain the oil from the engine/gearbox unit.
7 Lever the inner constant velocity joint from the differential side gear. If available, use tool 18G1240 against the final drive cover, otherwise careful use of two levers will be required (photos).
8 Examine the inner CV joint rubber boot for damage and splits, and if necessary, renew it as follows. First obtain a repair kit, then cut the old clip from the boot using snips.
9 Remove the rubber boot from the joint.
10 Pack the CV joint with 75 cc of the molybdenum disulphide based grease supplied with the repair kit.
11 Clean the mating surfaces of the boot and joint, then slide the new rubber boot in position.

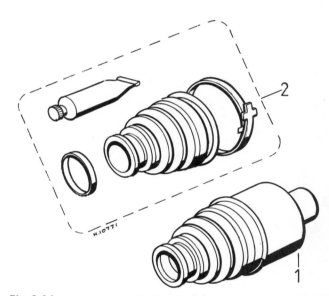
Fig. 8.6 Inner constant velocity joint (1) and repair kit (2) (Sec 3)

12 Refer to Fig. 8.5 and note that the clip must be fitted with the fold facing the forward direction of rotation. Wrap the clip around the rubber boot and pull the free end tightly between the front tabs. Flatten the tabs with a screwdriver, and bend the clip back between the rear tabs. Flatten the rear tabs to secure the clip.
13 Fit the ring over the small diameter end of the rubber boot.
14 Smear the differential side cover oil seal clip with engine oil.
15 Wipe clean the CV joint oil seal surface, then fit the CV joint to the differential side gear and sharply push it in to engage the spring ring.
16 Lubricate the inner joint rubber boot, then insert the driveshaft complete with swivel hub and push it sharply to engage the spring ring.
17 Locate the swivel hub ball-pins into the upper and lower suspension arms, and refit the tab washers and nuts. Tighten the nuts to the specified torque and bend up the tab washers to lock them.
18 Fit the steering balljoint to the steering arm, but do not fully tighten the self-locking nut at this stage.
19 Refit the brake disc caliper with reference to Chapter 9.
20 Tighten the steering balljoint self-locking nut to the specified torque.
21 Refit the roadwheel and lower the car to the ground.
22 Remove the wooden block, and refit the rebound rubber to the subframe.
23 Refill the engine/gearbox unit with oil.

4 Fault diagnosis – driveshafts

Symptom	Reason(s)
Vibration and noise on lock	Worn driveshaft joints
Noise on taking up drive	Worn drive flange and driveshaft splines Loose driveshaft-to-flange nut Worn driveshaft joints Loose roadwheel nuts

Chapter 9 Braking system

For modifications and information applicable to later models, see Supplement at end of manual

Contents

Brake disc – examination, removal and refitting 7
Brake drum – inspection and renovation 10
Disc caliper – removal, overhaul and refitting 6
Disc pads – inspection and renewal 4
Fault diagnosis – braking system 22
Footbrake pedal – removal and refitting 19
General description 1
Handbrake – adjustment 16
Handbrake cable – removal and refitting 17
Handbrake lever and switch – removal and refitting 18
Hydraulic brake lines and hoses – inspection, removal
and refitting 14

Hydraulic system – bleeding 15
Master cylinder – removal, overhaul and refitting 12
Pressure compensating valve – removal, overhaul and refitting ... 13
Rear brake – adjustment 3
Rear brake adjuster – removal and refitting 9
Rear brake backplate – removal and refitting 11
Rear brake shoes – inspection and renewal 5
Rear wheel cylinder – removal, overhaul and refitting 8
Routine maintenance 2
Vacuum servo unit – description 20
Vacuum servo unit – removal and refitting 21

Specifications

System type .... Four wheel hydraulic, with discs on front and drums on rear. Dual hydraulic feeds with rear brake pressure regulating valve. Servo assistance on 1.3 models. Cable-operated handbrake on rear wheels

Discs
Working diameter .... 8.35 in (213 mm)
Thickness .... 0.37 in (9.6 mm)
Minimum pad thickness .... 0.125 in (3 mm)

Drums
Internal diameter .... 7.0 in (177.9 in)
Minimum lining thickness .... 0.0625 in (1.6 mm)

Servo boost ratio 2.04:1

Brake fluid type/specification .... Hydraulic fluid to FMVSS 116 DOT 3 or SAE J1703C (Duckhams Universal Brake and Clutch Fluid)

Torque wrench settings

	lbf ft	kgf m
Backplate to radius arm	19	2.6
Caliper	38	5.3
Compensating valve end plug	40	5.4
Disc to flange	38	5.2
Master cylinder/brake servo mounting (1.3)	9	1.2
Master cylinder mounting (1.0)	19	2.6
Master cylinder reservoir flange	5	0.7
Master cylinder mounting plate to bulkhead	8.5	1.2

1 General description

The braking system is of four wheel hydraulic, dual circuit type with discs at the front and manually adjusted drum brakes at the rear. The dual circuit system is of the H-I type, where the primary circuit feeds both front and rear brakes, and the secondary circuit feeds the front brakes only. Each front brake caliper incorporates four pistons and two independent hydraulic feeds. A direct acting brake servo unit is fitted to 1.3 models.

A pressure compensating valve is installed in the rear hydraulic circuit to prevent the rear wheels locking in advance of the front wheels during heavy applications of the brakes (photo).

The handbrake operates on the rear wheels only, and incorporates a switch which illuminates a warning light on the instrument panel when the handbrake is applied. Driver warning lights are provided for the brake pad wear and brake fluid low level.

2 Routine maintenance

1   The brake fluid level should be checked every week and, if necessary, topped up with the specified brake fluid to the bottom of the filler neck. The reservoir is translucent and the check can be made without removing the filler cap.
2   Every 12 000 miles (20 000 km), or 12 months if this occurs sooner, the hydraulic pipes and unions should be checked for chafing, leakage, cracks and corrosion. At the same time, check the disc pads and rear brake linings for wear and renew then as necessary. Adjust the rear brakes and handbrake, and lubricate the handbrake cables and linkages. Where a servo is fitted, check the vacuum hose for condition and security.
3   The disc pad warning indicators should also be checked at the interval given in paragraph 2. To do this, first locate the twin terminal black plastic sockets located on the wiring harness over each wheel

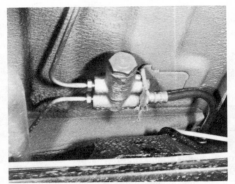

1.1 Pressure compensating valve

3.3 Adjusting the rear brakes

4.2 Removing the disc pad anti-rattle spring

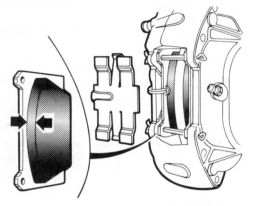
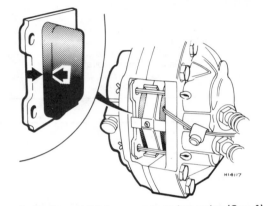

Fig. 9.1 Alternative types of front brake pads – arrows indicate pad thickness measuring point (Sec 4)

arch. Switch on the ignition and connect a bridging wire between the terminals of one socket; the pad wear warning light should be illuminated on the instrument panel. If not, either the warning bulb is blown or there is a fault in the circuit. Repeat the check on the remaining front brake. On some models the pad wear system is only fitted to the right-hand side inner pad.

4 Renew the brake fluid every 18 000 miles (30 000 km) or 18 months, and renew all fluid seals and flexible hoses every 36 000 miles (60 000 km) or 3 years.

3 Rear brakes – adjustment

1 Chock the front wheels, then jack up the rear of the car and support it on axle stands.
2 Fully release the handbrake and make sure that both rear wheels can be rotated freely.
3 Working beneath the car, turn the adjuster on the rear face of one backplate clockwise until the wheel is locked (photo).
4 Loosen the adjuster by two or three flats until the wheel can be rotated freely.
5 Repeat the procedure on the remaining rear wheel, then lower the car to the ground.

4 Disc pads – inspection and renewal

1 Apply the handbrake, then jack up the front of the car and support it on axlestands. Remove the roadwheels.
2 Using a screwdriver, move the anti-rattle spring upwards to release it from the bottom split pin, then withdraw it downwards from the upper split pin (photo).
3 Measure the thickness of the lining material on each disc pad, and if either one is at or below the specified minimum, renew the complete set of front disc pads. Note that the instrument panel warning lamps should glow if either inner pad wears to the minimum thickness.
4 To remove the pads, straighten the split pins and extract them from the caliper.
5 Where fitted, disconnect the wear indicator wiring from the

harness and detach the rubber clip (photo).
6 Press each pad slightly against its pistons, then withdraw it from the caliper using pliers (photo).
7 Brush the dust and dirt from the caliper, pistons, disc and pads, *but do not inhale it as it is injurious to health.* Scrape any scale or rust from the disc and pad backing plate.
8 Using a piece of wood, press the pistons back into the caliper. At the same time check the level of brake fluid in the reservoir: if this is near the top of the reservoir, unscrew the relevant bleed screw to release the fluid while the piston is being depressed. Tighten it immediately afterwards.
9 Smear brake grease lightly on the metal-to-metal contact surfaces of each pad backing plate.
10 Insert the pads into the caliper with the linings facing the disc. Note that only one pad has a wear indicator; fit this on the inner side of the disc.
11 Connect the wear indicator wiring and clip where fitted.
12 Insert the split pins through the caliper and pads. Bend the ends to lock them.
13 Fit the anti-rattle spring under the bottom split pin, then hook it under the top split pin.
14 Repeat the procedure on the remaining wheel, then refit the wheels and lower the car to the ground.
15 Depress the footbrake pedal several times to set the pads, then check and, if necessary, top up the level of brake fluid in the master cylinder reservoir.

5 Rear brake shoes – inspection and renewal

1 Chock the front wheel, then jack up the rear of the car and support it on axle stands. Remove the rear wheels.
2 Release the handbrake. Remove the two cross-head screws and withdraw the brake drum over the wheel studs (photo). If the drum is tight, release the adjuster one or two turns, and if necessary tap the periphery of the drum with a soft-faced mallet to release it from the studs.
3 Brush the dust from the brake drum, brake shoes, and backplate,

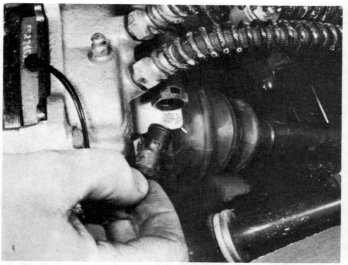

4.5 Disc pad wear indicator wiring connector

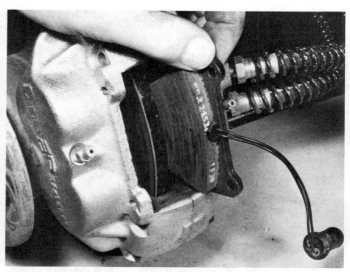

4.6 Removing a disc pad from the caliper

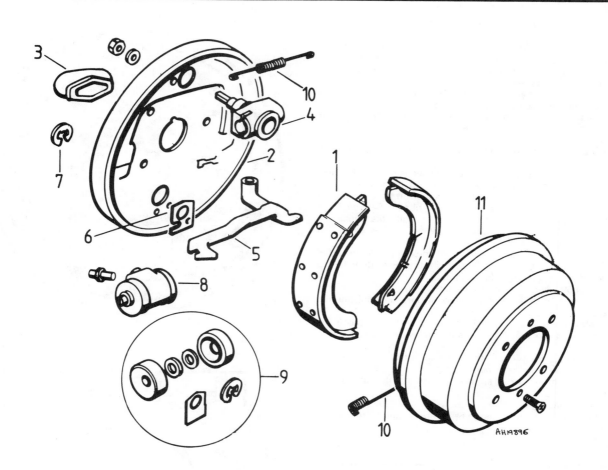

Fig. 9.2 Exploded view of the rear brakes – left-hand side shown (Secs 5 and 8)

1 Brake shoes	4 Adjuster	7 Circlip	10 Return springs
2 Backplate	5 Lever assembly	8 Wheel cylinder	11 Brake drum
3 Rubber boot	6 Gasket	9 Repair kit	

5.2 Removing the brake drum

5.5 Rear brake shoe upper return spring location and adjuster

but do not inhale it as it is injurious to health. Scrape any scale or rust from the drum.

4   Measure the brake shoe lining thickness. If it is worn down to the specified minimum amount, or if it is nearly worn down to the rivets, renew all four rear brake shoes. If the linings are in good condition, refit the drum and adjust the brakes as described in Section 3.

5   To remove the brake shoes, first note the location of the return springs, and to which holes thay are fitted (photo).

6   Release each shoe from the adjuster pegs using a screwdriver or adjustable spanner. Similarly release the shoes from the wheel cylinder pistons.

7   Disengage the handbrake levers and withdraw the shoes. Detach both return springs.

8   Clean the brake backplate. If there are any signs of loss of grease from the rear hub bearings, the oil seal should be renewed with reference to Chapter 11. If hydraulic fluid is leaking from the wheel cylinder, it must be repaired or renewed as described in Section 8. Do not touch the brake pedal or handbrake lever while the shoes are removed. Position an elastic band over the wheel cylinder pistons to retain them.

9   Lay the new shoes on a flat surface in their approximate fitted attitude. The leading edges must face in the opposite direction to forward movement of the drum (see Fig. 9.3).

10   Hook the bottom return spring to the shoes with the middle section to the bottom; this will ensure that it does not foul the hub when fitted.

11   Fit the shoes and spring to the handbrake levers. Remove the elastic band and locate the shoe webs in the wheel cylinder piston slots.

12   Hook the top return spring to the shoes from the rear, then lever the shoe webs into the adjuster peg slots.

13   Fully unscrew the adjuster. Tap the shoes so that they are located concentric to the hub.

14   Fit the drum and tighten the two screws.

15   Refit the roadwheel and adjust the rear brakes and handbrake as described in Sections 3 and 16.

16   Lower the car to the ground.

6   Disc caliper – removal, overhaul and refitting

1   Jack up the front of the car and support it on axle stands. Remove the roadwheel.

2   Remove the disc pads as described in Section 4.

3   Unscrew the two bolts securing the caliper and disc shield to the swivel hub. Remove the spring washers.

4   Withdraw the caliper and support it on a stand without straining the hydraulic hoses.

5   Clean the caliper thoroughly with methylated spirit and allow to dry.

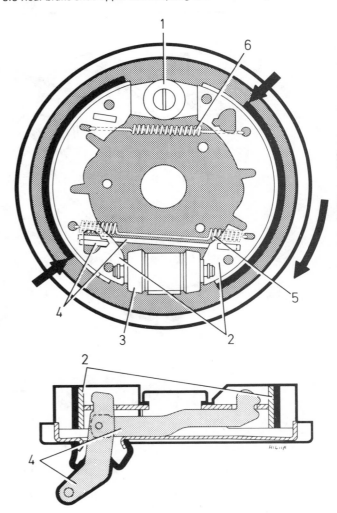

Fig. 9.3 Sectional view of the rear brakes (Sec 5)

1   Adjuster   4   Handbrake lever assembly
2   Brake shoes   5   Bottom return spring
3   Wheel cylinder   6   Top return spring

Arrows indicate brake shoe leading edges and forward rotation of drum

6   Make a piece of hardwood of the shape shown in Fig. 9.4 and insert it into the caliper. Have an assistant slowly depress the footbrake pedal until the free piston is almost out of its bore. Remove the hardwood block and pull out the piston; soak up the released brake fluid with a piece of cloth.

7   Using a non-metallic instrument such as a plastic needle, prise the retainer and wiper seal from the mouth of the bore. Similarly remove the fluid seal from the groove inside the bore.

8   Clean the piston, bore and grooves with a lint-free cloth, then inspect their surfaces for damage, wear and corrosion. If the piston surface alone is unserviceable, it may be possible to obtain a new piston. However, it is more common for both sealing surfaces to be affected, in which case the complete caliper must be renewed. If the components are in good condition, obtain a repair kit of new seals.

9   Dip the new fluid seal in clean brake fluid and manipulate it into the bore groove using the fingers only. Note that the groove is designed to hold the inner edge of the seal slightly raised.

10   Fit the wiper seal to the retainer and press them both into the mouth of the bore.

11   Loosen the bleed screw for the piston removed (one screw is provided for both upper pistons), then smear the piston with clean brake fluid and insert it into the bore leaving approximately 0.15 in (4 mm) projecting. Tighten the bleed screw and top up the reservoir as necessary.

12   Repeat the procedure given in paragraphs 6 to 11 for the remaining pistons.

13   If the caliper is to be renewed, identify each brake fluid hose for position, then unscrew the unions. Note that two types of caliper are fitted, and it is important to fit the correct type; the information (type A or type B) is to be found on the bonnet lock crossmember. Also note that bleed nipples for both types are not interchangeable; the nipple taper must contact the seat before the hexagon contacts the body. *Do not separate the caliper halves.*

14   If necessary, the disc shield can be removed at this stage.

15   Reconnect the hoses to the caliper and tighten the unions.

16   Refit the caliper and disc shield to the swivel hub, and tighten the bolts to the specified torque.

17   Refit the disc pads as described in Section 4.

18   Refit the roadwheel and lower the car to the ground.

19   Bleed the complete brake hydraulic circuits as described in Section 15.

7   Brake disc – examination, removal and refitting

1   Jack up the front of the car and support it on axle stands. Apply the handbrake and remove the roadwheel.

2   Rotate the disc and examine it for deep scoring or grooving. Light scoring is normal, but, if excessive, the disc should be removed and either renewed or ground by a suitably qualified engineering works.

3   To remove the brake disc, first refit the roadwheel and lower the car to the ground. Remove the split pin, and loosen the driveshaft nut while an assistant depresses the footbrake pedal.

4   Jack up the front of the car again and support it on axle stands. Remove the roadwheel.

5   Remove the disc caliper as described in Section 6, leaving the hydraulic hoses connected and supporting the caliper on a stand.

6   Remove the driveshaft nut and the split collar from the end of the driveshaft.

7   Pull the drive flange and disc assembly from the driveshaft, using a suitable puller if necessary.

8   Mark the drive flange and disc in relation to each other, then unscrew the special bolts and separate the two components.

9   Refitting is a reversal of removal, but make sure that the mating faces of the disc and flange are clean, and tighten the bolts in diagonal sequence to the specified torque. Grease the hub outer oil seal before inserting the drive flange. Refer to Chapter 8 for details of driveshaft nut tightening.

8   Rear wheel cylinder – removal, overhaul and and refitting

1   Remove the rear brake shoes as described in Section 5.

2   Remove the cap from the brake fluid reservoir. Place a sheet of thin polythene over the warning switch assembly, then tighten the cap.

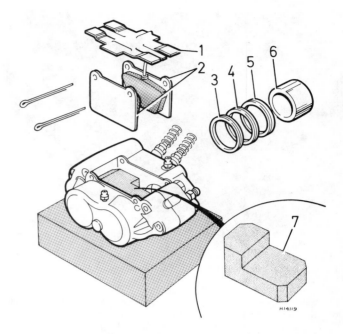

Fig. 9.4 Exploded view of front brake caliper (Sec 6)

1   Anti-rattle spring   5   Fluid seal
2   Pads   6   Piston
3   Retainer   7   Wooden block for removing
4   Wiper seal   pistons

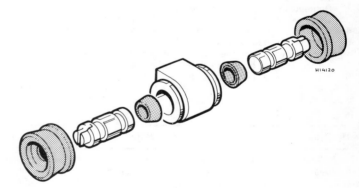

Fig. 9.5 Exploded view of the rear wheel cylinder (Sec 8)

This will help prevent the loss of brake fluid in the subsequent procedure.

3   Working under the car, unscrew the union nut and remove the brake pipe from the wheel cylinder.

4   Unscrew and remove the bleed screw.

5   Using a screwdriver, prise out the retaining circlip.

6   Withdraw the wheel cylinder and gasket from the backplate (photo).

7   Disconnect the dust covers from the body, and withdraw the pistons. Identify the pistons side for side.

8   Remove the dust covers and seals from the pistons.

9   Clean all the components in methylated spirit and allow to dry. Examine the surfaces of the pistons and cylinder bores for wear, scoring and corrosion. If evident, renew the complete wheel cylinder. If they are in good condition, discard the seals, retaining circlip and gasket, and obtain a repair kit.

10   Dip the inner seals in clean brake fluid, and fit them to the piston inner grooves, using the fingers only to manipulate them. Make sure that the larger diameter end faces the inner end of the piston.

11   Carefully insert the pistons half way into the cylinders.

8.6 Rear brake wheel cylinder

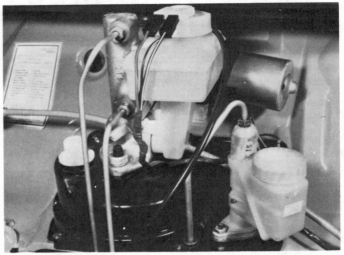

12.5 Brake master cylinder location (left) showing fluid level warning switch wires – clutch master cylinder on right

12 Coat the sealing surfaces of the dust covers with rubber lubricant, then fit them into the groove on the pistons and wheel cylinder body.
13 Refitting is a reversal of removal, but use the new gasket and circlip. adjust the brakes as described in Section 3, and bleed the hydraulic system as described in Section 15. Do not forget to remove the polythene sheet from the brake fluid reservoir.

9 Rear brake adjuster – removal and refitting

1   Remove the rear brake shoes as described in Section 5.
2   Remove the rubber boot from the backplate.
3   Unscrew the two nuts and remove the spring washers.
4   Withdraw the adjuster from the backplate.
5   Remove the pegs and identify them side for side. Check that the adjuster screw moves freely and lubricate the threads with grease. Grease the pegs and reinsert them in the adjuster.
6   Refitting is a reversal of removal, but adjust the brakes as described in Section 3. Note that the adjuster can only be fitted one way round.

10 Brake drum – inspection and renovation

1   Whenever the brake drums are removed, they should be checked for wear and damage. Light scoring of the friction surface is normal, but if excessive, it is recommended that the drums are renewed as a pair.
2   After a high mileage, the friction surface may become oval. Where this has occurred, it may be possible to grind the surface true, but this should only be carried out by a qualified engineering works. It is preferable to renew the drums as a pair.

11 Rear brake backplate – removal and refitting

1   Remove the rear brake shoes as described in Section 5.
2   Remove the rear wheel cylinder and adjuster as described in Sections 8 and 9.
3   Remove the hub assembly as described in Chapter 11.
4   Remove the clevis pin and disconnect the handbrake cable from the operating lever. Withdraw the lever assembly and rubber boot from the backplate.
5   Unscrew and remove the three nuts and washers, and withdraw the backplate from the radius arm.
6   If necessary, remove the bolts and cable bracket from the radius arm, noting the location of the spacers.
7   Refitting is a reversal of removal, but make sure that the mating surfaces of the flange and radius arm are clean. Adjust the rear brakes and handbrake as described in Sections 3 and 16.

12 Master cylinder – removal, overhaul and refitting

1   If a servo unit is fitted, depress the footbrake pedal several times to dissipate the vacuum.
2   Working in front of the car, connect bleed tubes to the primary and secondary bleed nipples on the passenger-side brake caliper. The nipples are located on one side of the caliper.
3   Loosen the bleed nipples half a turn, and place the ends of the tubes in a jar.
4   Operate the footbrake pedal until the fluid reservoir is empty, then tighten the bleed screws and remove the tubes.
5   Pull the wiring connectors from the reservoir filler cap terminals (photo).
6   Unscrew the primary and secondary union nuts, and remove the hydraulic pipes from the master cylinder. Plug the ends of the pipes, and place cloth rags around the bottom of the master cylinder to protect the surrounding paintwork.
7   *Where a servo unit is fitted,* unscrew the retaining nuts and washers, and withdraw the master cylinder and gasket from the servo unit.
8   *Where the master cylinder is mounted directly on the bulkhead plate,* remove the clevis pin securing the pushrod to the brake pedal inside the car, then unbolt the master cylinder and remove it together with the gasket.
9   Do not spill any brake fluid on the paintwork otherwise repainting may be necessary. If accidentally spilt, swill off immediately with copious amounts of cold water.
10 Drain and discard the fluid remaining in the reservoir.
11 Clean the exterior of the master cylinder with methylated spirit, then mount it horizontally in a soft-jawed vice with the reservoir uppermost.
12 Unbolt the reservoir from the body (non-servo models) or remove the clips and pull out the pins (servo models).
13 Prise the sealing washers from the body with a screwdriver.
14 Push the pushrod/piston fully into the cylinder, and use long-nosed pliers to remove the secondary piston stop pin from the secondary inlet. Release the pushrod.
15 *On the non-servo type* prise the rubber boot from the end of the master cylinder.
16 *On both types* depress the piston and extract the circlip from the mount of the master cylinder using circlip pliers.
17 Remove the pushrod (where fitted), primary piston and primary spring. Place them on the bench in order of removal.
18 Remove the cylinder from the vice and tap it on a block of wood to remove the secondary piston and spring.
19 Note the position of each item, then remove the seals, washers and spring retainers from the pistons, keeping them in their correct order of removal.
20 Clean all the components in methylated spirit and examine them

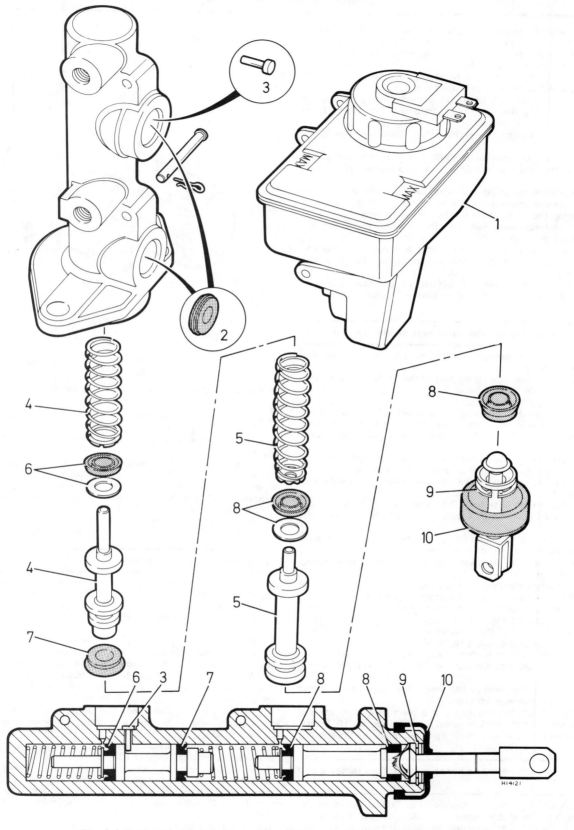

Fig. 9.6 Exploded view of the master cylinder – non-servo type shown (Sec 12)

1	Reservoir	4	Secondary piston and spring		washer		washer
2	Seals	5	Primary piston and spring	7	Secondary piston seal	9	Circlip
3	Secondary piston stop pin	6	Secondary piston seal and	8	Primary piston seals and	10	Rubber boot

for wear and damage. In particular check the surfaces of the pistons and cylinder bore for scoring and corrosion. If evident, renew the complete master cylinder, but if in good condition, discard the seals and washers and obtain a repair kit.

21 Check that the inlet and outlet ports are free and unobstructed. Dip the pistons and seals in clean brake fluid.

22 Fit the seals and washers to the pistons with the lips facing the directions shown in Fig. 9.6; use the fingers only to manipulate them into position.

23 Fit the spring retainers to the ends of the pistons, followed by the springs.

24 Insert the secondary piston and spring into the bore, taking care not to damage the seal lips. Similarly insert the primary piston and spring.

25 Push the primary piston into the bore, together with the pushrod (where fitted), and fit the retaining circlip to the groove in the mouth of the bore. Refit the rubber boot on the non-servo type.

26 Push the pushrod/piston fully into the cylinder, and insert the secondary piston stop pin.

27 Locate the seals on the cylinder inlets and refit the reservoir according to type. Only tighten the screws (where fitted) to the specified torque.

28 Refitting is a reversal of removal, but use a new mounting gasket, and bleed the hydraulic system as described in Section 15.

13 Pressure compensating valve – removal, overhaul and refitting

1   The pressure compensating valve is located to the left of the fuel tank on the underbody.

2   To remove the valve, jack up the rear of the car and support it on axle stands. Chock the front wheels, and remove the left-hand rear wheel.

3   Remove the brake fluid reservoir filler cap and place a sheet of thin polythene over the warning switch assembly, then tighten the cap. This will help prevent the loss of brake fluid in the subsequent procedure.

4   Unscrew the union nut securing the left-hand rear rigid brake pipe to the flexible hose at the bracket on top of the radius arm.

5   Unscrew the nut, remove the washer, and detach the flexible hose from the bracket.

6   Unscrew the flexible hose from the compensating valve.

7   Unscrew the two union nuts securing the rigid brake pipes to the compensating valve.

8   Remove the mounting bolt and withdraw the compensating valve.

9   Clean the exterior of the valve with methylated spirit.

10 Mount the valve in a soft-jawed vice, and unscrew the end plug. Remove the washer.

11 Remove the small diameter spring, piston, bearing, large diameter spring and seals, keeping them in the order of removal.

12 Clean all the components with methylated spirit and examine them for wear and damage. If excessive, renew the complete compensating valve, but if the components are in good condition, discard the old seals and obtain a repair kit.

13 Dip the seals and piston in clean brake fluid, then reassemble the valve in the reverse order to dismantling. Tighten the end plug to the specified torque.

14 Fit the valve to the bracket and insert the mounting bolt and flexible hose, then tighten them both.

15 The remaining refitting procedure is a reversal of removal, but when completed bleed the brakes as described in Section 15. Do not forget to remove the polythene sheet from the brake fluid reservoir.

14   Hydraulic brake lines and hoses – inspection, removal and refitting

1   It is important to note that two types of fittings are in use as shown in Fig. 9.8. The metric fittings are coloured gold or black and generally have the letter 'M' stamped on them. If there is any doubt about the compatability of fittings, check that they can be fully screwed together using the fingers only.

2   At the intervals given in Section 2, clean the rigid brake lines and flexible hoses and check them for damage, leakage, chafing and cracks (photos). If the rigid pipes are corroded excessively, they must be renewed. Check the retaining clips for security, and clean away any

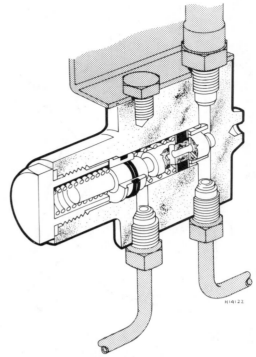

Fig. 9.7 Cutaway view of the pressure compensating valve (Sec 13)

accumulations of dirt and debris.

3   To remove a rigid brake line, unscrew the union nuts at each end, and where necessary remove the line from the clips. Refitting is a reversal of removal.

4   To remove a flexible brake hose, unscrew the union nut securing the rigid brake line to the end of the flexible hose. Remove the nut and washer, and withdraw the hose from the bracket. Unscrew the remaining end from the component or rigid pipe according to position. Refitting is a reversal of removal.

5   Bleed the complete hydraulic system as described in Section 15 after fitting a rigid brake line or flexible brake hose.

15 Hydraulic system – bleeding

1   The correct functioning of the brake hydraulic system is only possible after the removal of all air from the components and circuit; this is achieved by bleeding the system. Note that only clean unused brake fluid, which has remained unshaken for at least 24 hours, must be used.

2   If there is any possibility of incorrect fluid being used in the system, the brake lines and components must be completely flushed with uncontaminated fluid and new seals fitted to the components.

3   *Never* reuse brake fluid which has been bled from the system.

4   During the procedure, do not allow the level of brake fluid to drop more than half way down the reservoir.

5   Before starting work check that all pipes and hoses are secure, unions tight, and bleed screws closed. Take great care not to allow hydraulic fluid to come into contact with the car paintwork, otherwise the finish will be seriously damaged. Wash off any spilled fluid immediately with cold water.

6   There are a number of one-man, do-it-yourself, brake bleeding kits currently available from motor accessory shops. It is recommended that one of these kits is used wherever possible, as they greatly simplify the bleeding operation, and also reduce the risk of expelled air and fluid being drawn back into the system. If one of these kits is not available, it will be necessary to gather together a clean jar and two suitable lengths of clear plastic tubing which is a tight fit over the bleed screw, and also to engage the help of an assistant.

7   If hydraulic fluid has been lost from the master cylinder due to a leak in the system, ensure that the cause is traced and rectified before proceeding further.

8   If the hydraulic system has only been partially disconnected and

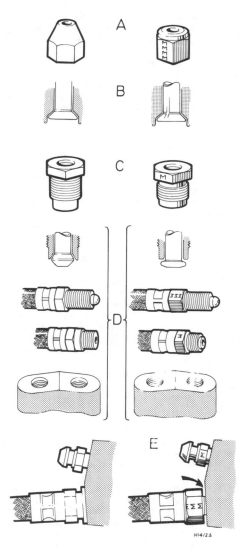

Fig. 9.8 Unified and Metric fittings used in the braking system (Sec 14)

14.2A Primary circuit four-way connector location

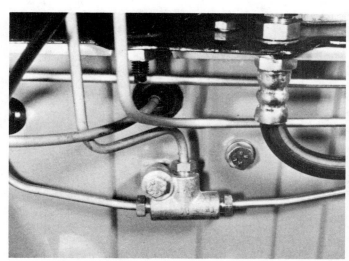

14.2B Secondary circuit connector to front brakes

A — Metric pipe nuts, unions, bleed screws and hose ends are coloured black or gold. Most are also identified by the letter M

B — The correct Unified or Metric pipe flares must be used

C — The end of a Metric hose is coloured black or gold

D — Metric fittings are not counterbored. Some Unified fittings may also not be counterbored. If the thread type is not known on a fitting, screw the item in by finger pressure only. If the fit is slack, or the item will not screw fully in, the threads may be of different types.

E — A Metric hose seals against the bottom of the port, with a gap between the cylinder or caliper and the hose hexagon

suitable precautions were taken to prevent further loss of fluid, it should only be necessary to bleed that part of the system (ie primary or secondary circuit). However, note that if the front part of the primary circuit has been disconnected, the rear part must also be bled in the correct order.

9   To bleed the system, first clean the area around the right-hand rear wheel cylinder bleed screw and fit the bleed tube. If necessary, top up the master cylinder reservoir with brake fluid.

10 If a one-man brake bleeding kit is being used, open the bleed screw half a turn and position the unit so that it can be viewed from the car. Depress the brake pedal to the floor and slowly release it; the one-way valve in the kit will prevent expelled air from returning to the system. Repeat the procedure then top up the brake fluid level.

Continue bleeding until clean hydraulic fluid, free from air bubbles, can be seen coming through the tube. Now tighten the bleed screw and remove the tube.

11 If a one-man brake bleeding kit is not available, immerse the free end of the bleed tube in the jar and pour in sufficient brake fluid to keep the end of the tube submerged. Open the bleed screw half a turn and have your assistant depress the brake pedal to the floor and then slowly release it. Tighten the bleed screw at the end of the downstroke to prevent the expelled air and fluid from being drawn back into the system. Repeat the procedure then top up the brake fluid level. Continue bleeding until clean hydraulic fluid, free from air bubbles, can be seen coming through the tube. Now tighten the bleed screw and remove the tube.

12 Repeat the procedure described in paragraphs 9 to 11 on the left-hand rear wheel cylinder, then follow the order shown in Figs. 9.9 or 9.10, dependent on brake system type – see label on bonnet lock crossmember. Note that the lower pair of pistons in the front brake calipers must be bled simultaneously, and therefore two bleed tubes are necessary. This also applies to one-man brake bleeding kits (photo); therefore two bleed tubes must be obtained.

13 When completed, recheck the fluid level in the reservoir, top up if necessary, and refit the cap. Depress the brake pedal several times; it should feel firm and free from 'sponginess' which would indicate air still present in the system.

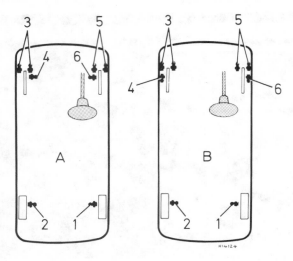

Fig. 9.9 Brake bleeding sequence for right-hand drive cars (Sec 15)

A – type A brakes   *B – type B brakes*

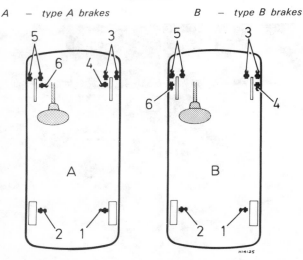

Fig. 9.10 Brake bleeding sequence for left-hand drive cars (Sec 15)

A – type A brakes   *B – type B brakes*

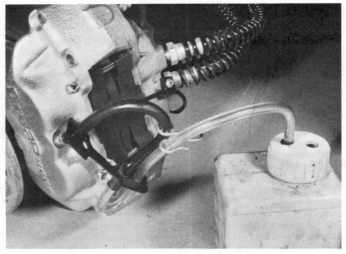

15.12 Typical brake bleeding kit connected to front brake caliper – note that two tubes are required for lower circuit

16 Handbrake – adjustment

1   Chock the front wheels, then jack up the rear of the car and support it on axle stands.
2   Adjust the rear brakes as described in Section 3.
3   Apply the handbrake to the third notch. It should just be possible to rotate the rear wheels with heavy hand pressure.
4   To adjust the handbrake, loosen the cable locknut using a spanner through the access slot in the carpet behind the handbrake. Turn the adjusting nut until the correct tension is achieved, then tighten the locknut.
5   Release the handbrake and check that the wheels rotate freely, then lower the car to the ground.

17 Handbrake cable – removal and refitting

1   Remove one front seat with reference to Chapter 12.
2   Unbolt the central seat belt arms from the underbody tunnel.
3   Lift the rear carpet, move the cable guide aside and remove the seal.
4   Remove the clevis pin and disconnect the cable from the hand-brake lever.
5   Jack up the rear of the car and support it on axle stands. Chock the front wheels.
6   Working beneath the car, remove the cable from the underbody bracket and fuel tank, and pull the cable through the floor.
7   Remove the clevis pins and disconnect the cables from the rear brake levers (photo).
8   Release the cables from the radius arm brackets, abutment brackets and subframe.
9   Lift the compensator link from its guide, and withdraw the cable assembly (photo).
10   Refitting is a reversal of removal, but adjust the handbrake as described in Section 16.

18 Handbrake lever and switch – removal and refitting

1   Remove one front seat with reference to Chapter 12.
2   Unbolt the central seat belt arms from the underbody tunnel.
3   Lift the rear carpet. Remove the clevis pin and disconnect the cable from the handbrake lever.
4   Pull off the wires from the switch terminals, remove the securing screws, and withdraw the switch (photo).
5   Unbolt the handbrake lever from the floor bracket.
6   Refitting is a reversal of removal, but adjust the handbrake as described in Section 16.

19 Footbrake pedal – removal and refitting

1   Disconnect the battery negative lead.
2   Working inside the car, remove the clevis pin and disconnect the pushrod from the pedal.
3   Pull the wires from the stoplight switch, then unscrew the switch from the bracket (photo).
4   Unbolt the end pedal bracket from the bulkhead and unhook the return spring.
5   Unscrew the pivot nut, then withdraw the bracket, spring and pedal.
6   Refitting is a reversal of removal.

20 Vacuum servo unit – description

1   A vacuum servo unit is fitted to 1.3 models, and provides assistance to the driver when the brake pedal is depressed.
2   The unit operates by vacuum from the inlet manifold, and it basically comprises a booster diaphragm and non-return valve.
3   With the brake pedal released, vacuum is channeled to both sides of the diaphragm, but when the pedal is depressed, one side is opened to the atmosphere. The resultant unequal pressures are harnessed to assist in depressing the master cylinder pistons.
4   Under normal operating conditions the vacuum servo unit is very

Fig. 9.11 Handbrake cable components (Secs 17 and 18)

17.7 Handbrake cable backplate location

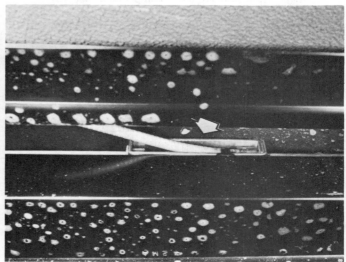

17.9 Handbrake cable compensator link location (arrowed)

18.4 Handbrake lever switch location (arrowed)

19.3 Stoplight switch location (arrowed)

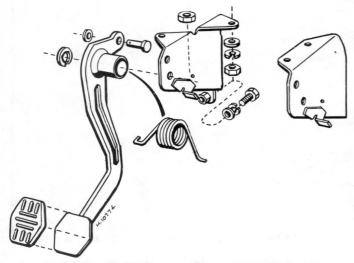

Fig. 9.12 Footbrake pedal components (Sec 19)

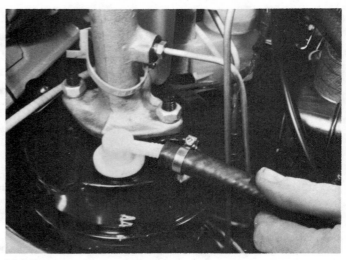

21.2 Removing the vacuum hose from the servo

reliable, and when a fault does occur the first action should be renewal of the non-return valve. If this does not help, the servo should be renewed. In the event of a failure, the hydraulic system is in no way affected, except that higher pedal pressure will be necessary.

21 Vacuum servo unit – removal and refitting

1   Remove the master cylinder as described in Section 12.

2   Disconnect the vacuum hose from the non-return valve (photo).
3   Working inside the car, remove the clevis pin and disconnect the pushrod from the brake pedal.
4   Unscrew the mounting nuts and remove the servo unit from the engine compartment.
5   Refitting is a reversal of removal, with reference to Section 12.

22 Fault diagnosis – braking system

Symptom	Reason(s)
Excessive pedal travel	Rear brake shoes out of adjustment Brake fluid leak Air in hydraulic system
Uneven braking and pulling to one side	Contaminated linings Seized wheel cylinder or caliper Incorrect adjustment Unequal tyre pressures Loose suspension anchor point Different lining material at each wheel
Brake judder	Worn drums and/or discs Loose suspension anchor point
Brake pedal feels 'spongy'	Air in hydraulic system Faulty master cylinder seals
Excessive effort to stop car	Servo unit faulty (where fitted) Seized wheel cylinder or caliper Incorrect lining material Contaminated linings New linings not yet bedded-in Compressed brake line due to damage

Chapter 10 Electrical system

For modifications and information applicable to later models, see Supplement at end of manual

Contents

Alternator – fault finding and testing 8
Alternator – maintenance and special precautions 6
Alternator – removal and refitting 7
Alternator brushes – removal, inspection and refitting 9
Auxiliary circuits relay and circuit diode – description 25
Battery – charging 5
Battery – electrolyte replenishment 4
Battery – maintenance 3
Battery – removal and refitting 2
Cigar lighter – removal and refitting 20
Combination switches – removal and refitting 17
Courtesy light switch – removal and refitting 21
Direction indicator and hazard flasher system – general 15
Fault diagnosis – electrical system 35
Fuses – general 14
General description 1
Headlamps – alignment 27
Headlamps and headlamp bulbs – removal and refitting 26
Horn – removal and refitting 33

Ignition switch/steering column lock – removal and refitting 16
Instrument panel and instruments – removal and refitting 23
Instrument panel printed circuit and voltage stabilizer – removal
and refitting 24
Lamp bulbs – renewal 28
Lighting switch – removal and refitting 18
Radio – removal and refitting 34
Speedometer cable – removal and refitting 22
Starter motor – removal and refitting 11
Starter motor – testing in the car 10
Starter motor (inertia type) – overhaul 12
Starter motor (pre-engaged type) – overhaul 13
Switch panel switches – removal and refitting 19
Tailgate wiper motor and gearbox – removal, overhaul and
refitting 32
Windscreen wiper linkage – removal, overhaul and refitting 31
Windscreen wiper motor – removal and refitting 30
Wiper blades – renewal 29

Specifications

System type ....
12 volt, negative earth

Battery
Capacity ....
30 amp hr or 40 amp hr
Type:
    Lucas ....
OA7 or OA9
    Chloride ....
170/60/89 or 190/60/90

Alternator
Type ....
Lucas 18ACR or Motorola 9AR2683G
Output at 14 volt and 3000 engine rpm ....
43 amp (Lucas), 45 amp (Motorola)
Rotor winding resistance at 20°C (68°F) ± 5% ...
3.2 ohm
Regulated output at 3000 engine rpm with current less
than 10 amp ....
13.6 to 14.6 volt, depending on type – see text
Minimum brush length protruding from moulding ....
0.3 in (8 mm)

Starter motor
Type ....
Lucas M35J (inertia) or M35JPE (pre-engaged)
Minimum brush length ....
0.375 in (9.5 mm)
Commutator thickness (minimum) ....
0.08 in (2.03 mm)

Fuses

	Current rated	Blow rated
Fuse 1	17 amp	35 amp
Fuse 2	12 amp	25 amp
Fuse 3	8 amp	15 amp
Fuse 4	8 amp	15 amp

Bulbs

	Wattage
Headlamps – Metro and Metro L	45/40
Headlamps – Metro HLE, Metro 1.3S, and Metro 1.3HLS	60/50
Sidelamps	4
Direction indicators	21
Reverse lamps	21
Side repeater lamps	5
Stop and tail lamps	5/21
Rear number plate lamp	6

	Wattage
Interior lamp	10
Switch illumination lamps	0.75
Heated rear window switch	1.2
Instrument panel lamps	1.2
Rear fog lamp	21

Torque wrench settings

	lbf ft	kgf m
Alternator adjusting link to alternator	9	1.2
Aternator adjusting link to front plate	27	3.7
Alternator bracket to crankcase	16	2.2
Alternator pulley nut	27	3.7
Alternator top fixings	16	2.2
Starter motor retaining bolts	27	3.7
Wiper crank lock nut	11.5	1.7

1 General description

The electrical system is of 12 volt negative earth type. The battery is charged by a belt-driven alternator which incorporates a voltage regulator. The starter motor is of inertia or pre-engaged type and incorporates four brushes and a face-type commutator. On the inertia type, the drive pinion is thrown into engagement with the flywheel ring gear by the movement of the starter motor. On the pre-engaged type, a solenoid moves the drive pinion into engagement before the starter motor is energised.

Although repair procedures are given in this Chapter, it may well be more economical to renew worn components as complete units.

2 Battery – removal and refitting

1 The battery is located on the right-hand side of the engine compartment.
2 Lift the plastic cover from the negative terminal, loosen the clamp bolt, and remove the lead.
3 Lift the plastic cover from the positive terminal, loosen the clamp bolt, and remove the lead (photo).
4 Loosen the battery retaining bar nuts and completely remove the nuts from one side.
5 Swivel the bar to one side, and unhook the two rods.
6 Lift the battery from the carrier platform, taking care not to spill any electrolyte on the bodywork.
7 Refitting is a reversal of removal, but make sure that the polarity is correct before connecting the leads, and do not overtighten the clamp bolts.

3 Battery – maintenance

1 Normal weekly battery maintenance consists of checking the electrolyte level of each cell to ensure that the separators are covered with electrolyte. On some batteries the check can be made without removing the battery covers, since the case is translucent and is marked as shown in Fig. 10.1.
2 If the electrolyte level has dropped, remove the covers and add distilled or de-ionized water to each cell until the separators are just covered.
3 At the same time, the top of the battery should be wiped clean with a dry cloth, to prevent the accumulation of dust and dampness which may cause the battery to become partially discharged over a period.
4 Every 12 000 miles (20 000 km) or 12 months, whichever occurs first, disconnect and clean the battery terminals and leads. After refitting them and before fitting the plastic covers, smear the exposed metal with petroleum jelly.
5 At the same time, inspect the battery bar and carrier for corrosion. If evident, remove the battery and clean the deposits away, then treat the affected metal with a proprietary anti-rust liquid and paint with the original colour.
6 When the battery is removed for whatever reason, it is worthwhile checking it for cracks and leakage. Cracks can be caused by topping up the cells with distilled water in winter *after* instead of *before* a run. This gives the water no chance to mix with the electrolyte, so the former freezes and splits the battery case. If the battery case is fractured, it

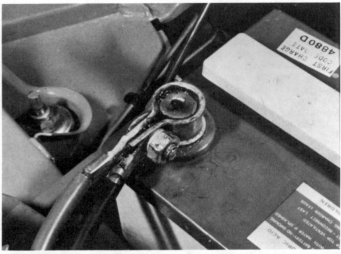

2.3 Battery positive terminal and lead

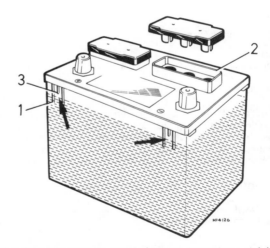

Fig. 10.1 Electrolyte level marks (certain batteries only) (Sec 3)

1	Low mark	3	High mark
2	Filler trough		Arrows show electrolyte level

may be possible to repair it with a proprietary compound, but this depends on the material used for the case. If electrolyte has been lost from a cell, refer to Section 4 for details of adding a fresh solution.
7 If topping up the battery becomes excessive and the case is not fractured, the battery is being over-charged and the voltage regulator will have to be checked.
8 If the car covers a very small annual mileage, it is worthwhile checking the specific gravity of the electrolyte every three months to determine the state of charge of the battery. Use a hydrometer to make the check, and compare the results with the following table.

	Ambient temperature above 25°c (77°F)	Ambient temperature below 25°C (77°F)
Fully charged	1.210 to 1.230	1.270 to 1.290
70% charged	1.170 to 1.190	1.230 to 1.250
Fully discharged	1.050 to 1.070	1.110 to 1.130

Note that the specific gravity readings assume an electrolyte temperature of 15°C (60°F); for every 10°C (18°F) below 15°C (60°F) subtract 0.007, or above, add 0.007.
9   If the battery condition is suspect, first check the specific gravity of electrolyte in each cell. A variation of 0.040 or more between any cells indicates loss of electrolyte or deterioration of the internal plates.
10   A further test can be made using a battery heavy discharge meter. The battery should be discharged for a maximum of 15 seconds at a load of three times the ampere-hour capacity (at the 20 hour discharge rate). Alternatively, connect a voltmeter across the battery terminals, and spin the engine on the starter with the coil low tension negative lead disconnected and the headlamps, heated rear window and heater blower switched on.
11   If the voltmeter reading remains above 9.6 volts, the battery condition is satisfactory. If the voltmeter reading drops below 9.6 volts and the battery has already been charged as described in Section 5, it is faulty and should be renewed.

4   Battery – electrolyte replenishment

1   If, after fully charging the battery, one of the cells maintains a specific gravity which is 0.040 or more lower than the others, but the battery also maintains 9.6 volts during the heavy discharge test (Section 3), it is likely that electrolyte has been lost.
2   If a significant quantity of electrolyte has been lost through spillage, it will not suffice merely to refill with distilled water. Top up the cell with a mixture of 2 parts sulphuric acid to 5 parts distilled water.
3   When mixing the electrolyte, *never* add water to sulphuric acid – *always* pour the acid slowly onto the water in a glass container. *If water is added to sulphuric acid, it will explode!*
4   After topping up the cell with fresh electrolyte, recharge the battery, and check the hydrometer readings again.

5   Battery – charging

1   In winter when a heavy demand is placed on the battery, such as when starting from cold and using more electrical equipment, it is a good idea to occasionally have the battery fully charged from an external source at a rate of 3.5 to 4 amps. Note that *both* battery terminal leads must be disconnected before charging; in order to prevent possible damage to any semi-conductor electrical components.
2   Continue to charge the battery until no further rise in specific gravity is noted over a four hour period.
3   Alternatively, a trickle charger, charging at a rate of 1.5 amps can be safely used overnight.
4   Special rapid 'boost' charges, which are claimed to restore the power of the battery in 1 to 2 hours, can be dangerous unless they are thermostatically controlled, as they can cause serious damage to the battery plates through overheating.
5   While charging the battery, ensure that the temperature of the electrolyte never exceeds 37.8°C (100°F).

6   Alternator – maintenance and special precautions

1   Periodically wipe away any dirt which has accumulated on the outside of the unit, and also check that the plug is pushed firmly on the terminals. At the same time, check the tension of the drivebelt and adjust it if necessary as described in Chapter 2.
2   Take extreme case when making electrical circuit connections on the car, otherwise damage may occur to the alternator or other electrical components employing semi-conductors. Always make sure that the battery leads are connected to the correct terminals. Before using electric-arc welding equipment to repair any part of the car,

disconnect the battery leads and alternator multi-plug. Disconnect the battery leads before using a mains charger. Never run the alternator with the multi-plug or a battery lead disconnected.

7   Alternator – removal and refitting

1   Disconnect the battery negative lead.
2   Pull the multi-plug(s) from the alternator terminals (photo).
3   Loosen the adjustment link nut and the mounting pivot bolts.
4   Swivel the alternator in towards the engine, and slip the drivebelt from the pulley.
5   Remove the adjustment link nut and washers. Remove the pivot bolts, nuts and washers. Withdraw the alternator from the engine (photo).
6   Refitting is a reversal of removal, but before tightening the mounting bolts and the adjustment nut, tension the drivebelt as described in Chapter 2.

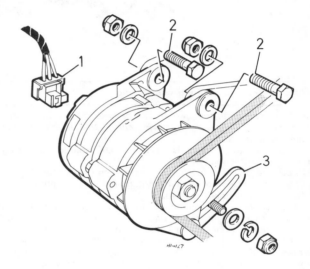

Fig. 10.2 Alternator mounting (Sec 7)

1   Multi-plug
2   Pivot bolts
3   Adjusting link

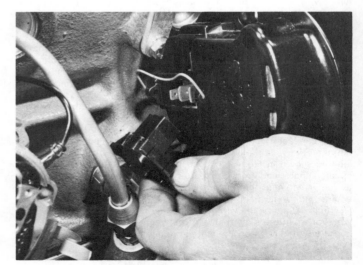

7.2 Removing the multi-plug from the alternator

7.5 Removing the alternator

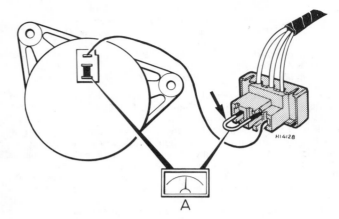

Fig. 10.3 Checking the alternator output (Sec 8)

Arrow shows bridging wire, 'A' indicates ammeter connections

8   Alternator – fault finding and testing

Note: *To carry out the complete test procedure, use only the following test equipment – 0 to 20 volt moving coil voltmeter, 0 to 100 amp moving coil ammeter*

1   Check that the battery is at least 70% charged by using a hydrometer as described in Section 3.
2   Check the drivebelt tension with reference to Chapter 2.
3   Check the security of the battery terminal leads, alternator multi-plug(s), and interconnecting wire.
4   *To check the cable continuity,* pull the multi-plug(s) from the alternator terminals and switch on the ignition, being careful not to crank the engine. Connect the voltmeter between a good earth and each of the terminals in the multi-plug in turn. If battery voltage is not indicated, there is an open circuit in the wiring, which may be due to a blown ignition warning light bulb if on the small terminal.
5   *To check the alternator output,* disconnect the mutli-plug(s), and connect the ammeter between either of the large alternator output terminals and a bridging wire connected between the large terminals in the multi-plug. Connect a further bridging wire between the small terminals of the multi-plug and alternator (see Fig. 10.3). Run the engine at approximately 3000 rpm with the headlamps, heated rear window, and heater blower switched on, for one minute only. The ammeter should indicate the specified output of the alternator; if not, the alternator is faulty.
6   *To check the charging circuit voltage drop,* remove all previously fitted bridging wires and refit the multi-plug(s) to the alternator. Remove the cover from the multi-plug and connect the voltmeter between the battery positive terminal and either of the large alternator output terminals. Switch on the headlamps, heated rear window, and heater blower, and run the engine at approximately 3000 rpm. A dirty connection in the charging circuit is indicated if the voltmeter reads more than 0.5 volts.
7   *To check the alternator voltage regulator,* refit the multi-plug cover, connect the voltmeter across the battery, and connect the ammeter between the positive battery lead and the main circuit supply lead as shown in Fig. 10.4. If no terminal is fitted, unbolt the main circuit supply lead from the battery positive lead and connect the ammeter between them. With all accessories switched off, start the engine and run it at approximately 3000 rpm until the ammeter reads less than 10 amps; the voltmeter should read between 13.8 and 14.6 volts for a Motorola alternator, or between 13.6 and 14.4 volts for a Lucas alternator. If not, the voltage regulator is faulty.

9   Alternator brushes – removal, inspection and refitting

1   Remove the alternator as described in Section 7.

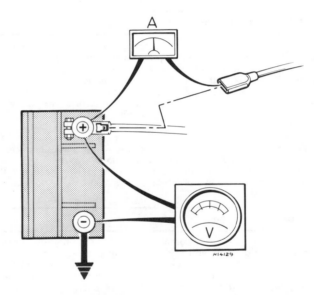

Fig. 10.4 Checking the voltage regulator (Sec 8)

'A' indicates ammeter connections
'V' indicates voltmeter connections

Lucas type

2   Remove the two securing screws and withdraw the end cover.
3   Disconnect the Lucar connector from the rectifier pack, and remove the brush moulding and regulator case retaining screws. Remove the brush moulding and regulator.
4   Check that the brushes protrude from the moulding by more than the specified minimum amount. If not, remove the screws, withdraw them from the moulding, and renew them.

Motorola type

5   Remove the two screws securing the voltage regulator to the rear of the alternator. Withdraw the regulator and release the two wires.
6   Remove the screw and withdraw the brush holder, taking care not to damage the brushes.
7   Check that the brushes protrude from the moulding by more than the specified minimum amount. If not, renew the brushes by unsoldering them and fitting new ones.

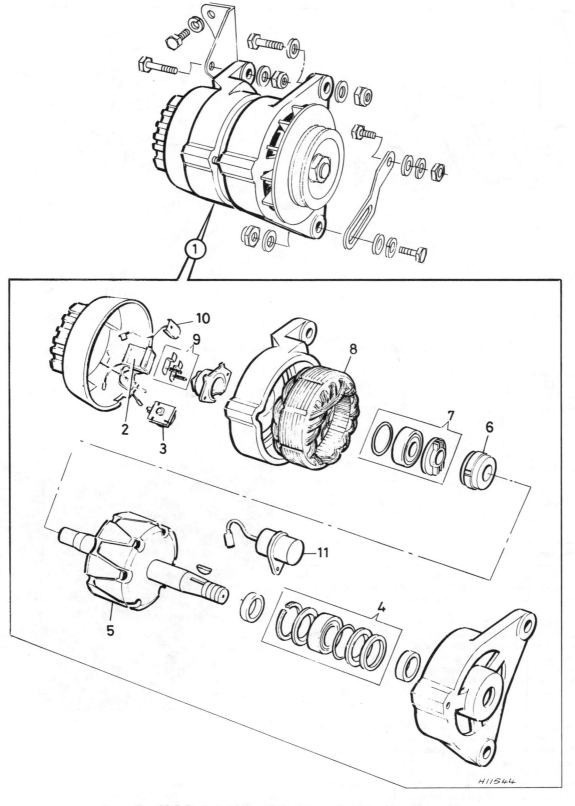

Fig. 10.5 Exploded view of the Lucas alternator (Sec 9)

1	Alternator assembly	4	Bearing assembly	7	Bearing assembly	10	Surge protection diode
2	Regulator	5	Rotor	8	Stator	11	Suppression capacitor
3	Rectifier	6	Slip ring	9	Brush set		

H11544

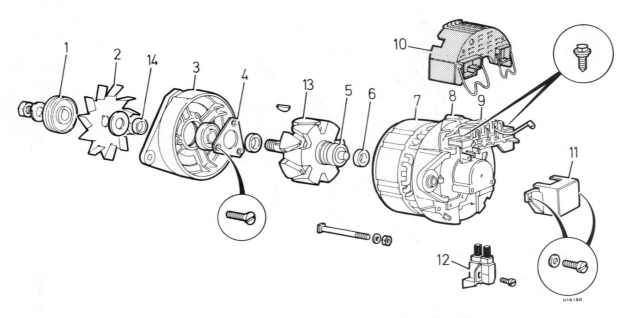

Fig. 10.6 Exploded view of the Motorola alternator (Sec 9)

1 Pulley	5 Slip ring	9 Diode bridge	12 Brush holder
2 Fan	6 Bearing	10 Cover	13 Rotor
3 Drive end housing	7 Stator	11 Regulator	14 Spacer
4 Plate	8 Slip ring end housing		

Lucas and Motorola types

8   Refitting is a reversal of removal, but make sure that the brushes move freely in their holders. If necessary, clean them with petrol and, if this is not sufficient, use a fine file. Clean the slip rings with fine glasspaper and wipe them with a petrol-soaked cloth.

10 Starter motor – testing in the car

1   If the starter motor fails to operate, first check the condition of the battery by switching on the headlamps. If they glow brightly, then gradually dim after a few seconds, the battery is in an uncharged condition.
2   If the battery is in good condition, check the starter motor main terminal and the engine earth cable for security. Check the terminal connections on the starter solenoid located on the battery carrier (inertia starter) or over the starter (pre-engaged starter).
3   If the starter still fails to turn, use a voltmeter or 12 volt test lamp and leads to check that current is reaching the solenoid terminal with the Lucar terminals. Connect one lead to earth and the other to the terminal, when a reading should be obtained or the test lamp should glow.
4   With the ignition switched on and the ignition key in position III, check that current is reaching the remaining solenoid terminal and the starter main terminal. If a voltmeter is being used, there should not be any significant voltage drop at the main terminal, otherwise a bad connection or faulty solenoid is indicated.
5   If current at the correct voltage is available at the starter motor, yet it does not operate, the starter motor is faulty.

11 Starter motor – removal and refitting

1   Disconnect the battery negative lead.
2   *On the inertia type starter,* disconnect the supply cable from the starter main terminal (photo).
3   *On the pre-engaged type starter,* disconnect the supply cables

11.2 Disconnecting the starter supply lead

from the solenoid.
4   Unscrew the bottom then top retaining bolts, and withdraw the starter motor from the engine (photo). Remove the lead bracket.
5   Refitting is a reversal of removal, but tighten the retaining bolts to the specified torque.

12 Starter motor (inertia type) – overhaul

1   Mark the commutator end bracket in relation to the yoke. Remove the retaining screws and withdraw the end bracket sufficient to slide

11.4 Removing the starter motor

the field brushes from the holder.

2   Slide the thrust washer from the armature.

3   Remove the two screws, and withdraw the drive end bracket complete with armature from the yoke and pole pieces.

4   Using a proprietary tool, compress the drive pinion cushion spring and extract the jump ring from the armature.

5   Slide the collar, cushion spring, bush, pinion assembly and drive end bracket from the armature.

6   Clean all the components in paraffin and wipe dry. Examine the bushes for wear, and if necessary renew them. Remove the endplate from the commutator end bracket and remove the felt bush. Drive out the bushes using a drift of suitable diameter, but before fitting the new bushes, soak them in clean engine oil at room temperature for 24 hours, or at 100°C (212°F) for 2 hours.

7   Check the length of the brushes, and renew them if they are less than the specified minimum. Note that the field brushes must be soldered to the terminal.

8   Check the continuity of the field windings by connecting a 12 volt test lamp (with 12 watt bulb) and leads between each field bush in turn and the yoke. The bulb will glow if the field windings are good.

9   If the field winding insulation is suspect, remove the rivet securing the field winding wire to the yoke and hold the wire away from the yoke. Repeat the test described in paragraph 8. If the bulb glows, the windings are faulty. If available, use an 110 volt ac supply and 15 watt bulb for this test as this will give more accurate results.

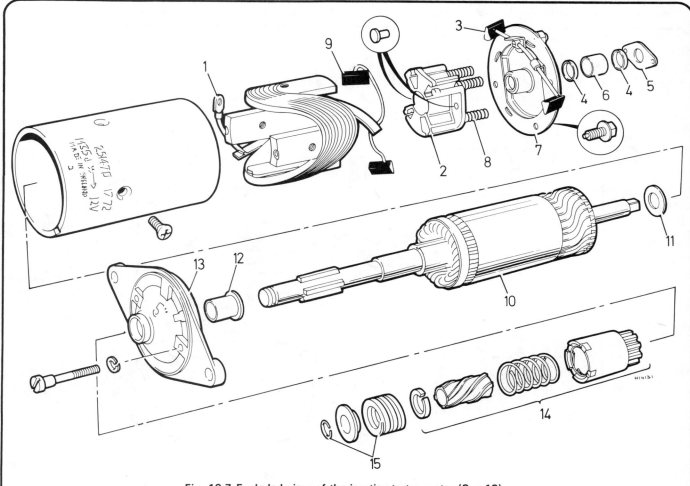

Fig. 10.7 Exploded view of the inertia starter motor (Sec 12)

1 Field winding connection	5 End cover	9 Field brush	13 Drive end bracket
2 Brush box	6 Bush	10 Armature	14 Drive pinion assembly
3 Input brush	7 Commutator end bracket	11 Thrust washer	15 Cushion spring and
4 Felt bushes	8 Brush spring	12 Bush	retaining ring

10 Check the armature shaft for distortion, and examine the commutator for excessive scoring, wear and burrs. If necessary, the commutator should be skimmed in a lathe and then polished with fine glasspaper. Make sure that it is not reduced below the specified minimum thickness, and do not undercut the mica insulation.

11 Check the armature windings for good insulation by connecting a test lamp and leads between each commutator segment in turn and the armature shaft; if the bulb glows, the insulation is faulty.

12 Temporarily insert each brush in the brush holder and check that they move freely against the springs.

13 Check the teeth of the drive pinion for wear and chipping and, if necessary, renew the pinion and barrel complete.

14 Reassembly is a reversal of dismantling, but make sure that the yoke is correctly aligned with the end brackets; a notch is provided to locate the drive end bracket. Mount the starter motor in a vice and use jump leads from a battery to test its operation.

13 Starter motor (pre-engaged type) – overhaul

1   Remove the plastic cap from the commutator end plate, and extract the split pin from the armature shaft.

2   Remove the thrust washer and any shims, noting the order of removal.

3   Disconnect the link wire from the solenoid.

4   Unscrew the two nuts and remove the washers, then withdraw the solenoid from the drive end housing. Pull back the rubber boot (if fitted), and unhook the solenoid armature from the actuating lever.

5   Remove the drive end housing retaining screws, and withdraw the housing and armature from the yoke.

6   Remove the armature from the end housing, and at the same time disengage the actuating arm from the pinion assembly.

7   Remove the rubber block and sleeve from the end housing.

8   Prise off the special retaining washer, then drive out the pivot pin and remove the actuating lever.

9   Tap the thrust collar towards the pinion, then extract the jump ring from the armature shaft.

10 Remove the thrust collar and drive pinion assembly.

11 Mark the commutator end bracket in relation to the yoke. Remove the retaining screws and withdraw the end bracket sufficiently to slide the field brushes from the holder, then remove the end bracket.

12 Remove the thrust washer from the commutator end of the armature.

13 The starter motor is now fully dismantled, and the inspection procedure is basically the same as that described in Section 12, paragraphs 6 to 12 inclusive. In addition, check the drive pinion assembly, drive end housing, actuating lever, and solenoid for wear and damage. Make sure that the drive pinion one-way clutch operates correctly, and renew the complete assembly if necessary.

14 Reassembly is a reversal of dismantling, but make sure that the notches in the yoke are correctly aligned with the protrusions on the end bracket and end housing. The starter motor may be tested in a vice, using jump leads from the motor terminal and yoke.

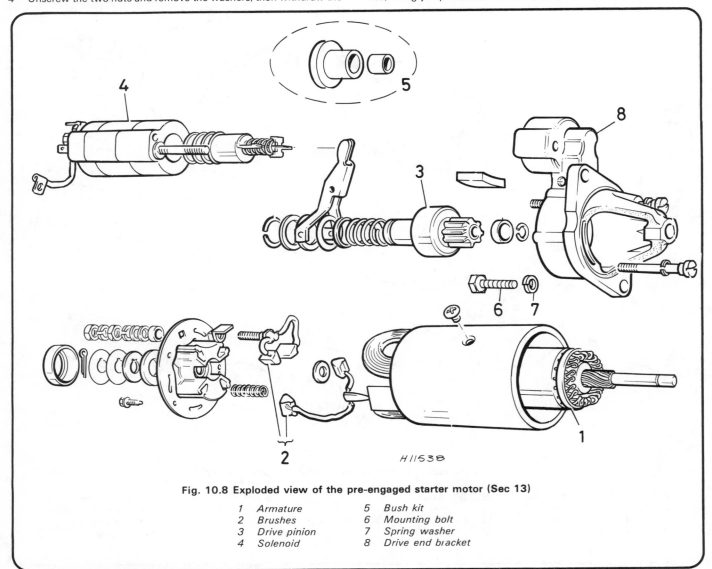

H11538

Fig. 10.8 Exploded view of the pre-engaged starter motor (Sec 13)

1	Armature	5	Bush kit
2	Brushes	6	Mounting bolt
3	Drive pinion	7	Spring washer
4	Solenoid	8	Drive end bracket

14 Fuses – general

1   The fuses are located behind the switch panel on the right-hand side of the dash panel. Access to them, is gained by removing the two screws from the front of the switch panel, and pivoting the panel downwards (photo).

2   The fuse locations are numbered together with the respective current rating, and the circuits protected are as follows:

> *Fuse 1 ....*   *Direction indicators, stop lamps, reverse lamps, heated rear window and warning light*
> *Fuse 2 ....*   *Interior lamp, hazard warning, lighter*
> *Fuse 3 ....*   *Sidelamps, tail lamps, number plate lamps, panel lamps*
> *Fuse 4 ....*   *Tailgate wiper motor, tailgate washer motor*

3   In addition to the main fuses, in-line fuses are provided to protect the following circuits:

> *Rear fog lamps, wiper motor, washer motor, heater motor*

4   Always renew a fuse with one of identical rating, and never renew it more than once without finding the source of the trouble (usually a short circuit).

15 Direction indicator and hazard flasher system – general

1   The flasher units are located on the fuseboard behind the switch panel on the right-hand side of the dash panel.

2   To remove either one of them, disconnect the battery negative lead, then remove the two screws and pivot the switch panel downwards. The direction indicator flasher unit is located on the left of the fuseboard, and the hazard flasher unit is located to the right of it. Pull the required unit directly from the fuseboard to remove it.

3   Should the flashers become faulty in operation, check the bulbs for security and make sure that the contact surfaces are not corroded. Check all the relevant wiring and terminals. If the flashers are still faulty and the relevant fuse has not blown, renew the flasher unit. If the fuse has blown, a short circuit may be the cause of the failure.

16 Ignition switch/steering column lock – removal and refitting

1   The ignition switch is an integral part of the steering column lock, and removal and refitting procedures are given in Chapter 11.

17 Combination switches – removal and refitting

1   Remove the steering wheel as described in Chapter 11.

2   Disconnect the battery negative lead.

3   Remove the screws retaining the steering column cowls together and to the outer column bracket.

4   Separate the cowls and withdraw the right-hand cowl over the wash/wipe switch (photo).

5   Disconnect the multi-plug connectors to the wash/wipe switch, direction indicator switch and lighting switch.

6   Remove the left-hand cowl over the direction indicator switch, leaving the choke cable attached.

7   Loosen the securing screw, and withdraw the combined switches from the upper column.

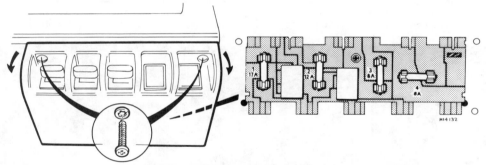

Fig. 10.9 Fuse locations (Sec 14)

14.1 Switch board and fuses

17.4 Removing the right-hand steering column cowl

8   Refitting is a reversal of removal, but after tightening the switch assembly clamp screw, position the striker bush with the arrow pointing towards the direction indicator switch.

18 Lighting switch – removal and refitting

1   Remove the steering wheel as described in Chapter 11.
2   Disconnect the battery negative lead.
3   Remove the screws retaining the steering column cowls together and to the outer column bracket.
4   Separate the cowls and withdraw the right-hand cowl over the wash/wipe switch.
5   Disconnect the multi-plug connector to the lighting switch.
6   Remove the left-hand cowl over the direction indicator switch. The lighting switch can now be removed from the cowl by depressing the plastic ears (photo).
7   Refitting is a reversal of removal, but make sure that the switch is fully entered into the cowl.

19 Switch panel switches – removal and refitting

1   Disconnect the battery negative lead.
2   Remove the two screws from the front of the switch panel, and pivot the panel downwards (photos).
3   Depress the plastic ears of the relevant switch, push it from the fuseboard, and remove it from the switch panel.
4   Refitting is a reversal of removal, but make sure that the switch is fully entered into the panel.

20 Cigar lighter – removal and refitting

1   Disconnect the battery negative lead.
2   If a radio is fitted, disconnect the supply and earth leads, and the aerial. Remove the rear mounting bolt and two side screws, and place the radio to one side.
3   Remove the cigar lighter button.
4   Pull the supply wire from the cigar lighter terminal.
5   Unscrew and remove the cigar lighter and earth lead (photo).
6   Refitting is a reversal of removal.

21 Courtesy light switch – removal and refitting

1   Disconnect the battery negative lead.
2   Open the door and locate the courtesy light switch on the front door pillar. Remove the single screw and withdraw the switch (photo).
3   Disconnect the supply wire and tie a loose knot in it to prevent it dropping into the pillar. Remove the switch.
4   Refittiing is a reversal of removal.

22 Speedometer cable – removal and refitting

1   Prise the speedometer cable grommet from the engine compartment side of the bulkhead.
2   Pull the cable straight out of the bulkhead to release it from the speedometer head (photo).
3   Unclip the cable from the swivel clip.
4   Remove the windscreen washer bottle and place it to one side.
5   Unscrew the knurled nut and pull the cable from the pinion housing on the left-hand side of the gearbox.
6   Withdraw the speedometer cable, and if necessary remove the inner cable and grommet. If either the inner or outer cable is damaged or worn, renew the complete assembly.
7   Refitting is a reversal of removal.

23 Instrument panel and instruments – removal and refitting

1   Disconnect the battery negative lead.
2   Prise out the speedometer cable grommet from the bulkhead, and

18.6 Lighting switch and multi-plug

19.2A Removing the switch panel screws

19.2B Lowering the switch panel

20.5 Removing the cigar lighter

21.2 Removing the courtesy light switch

22.2 Removing the speedometer cable from the head

23.4 Disconnecting the instrument panel multi-plugs

23.5 Removing a bulb holder from the instrument panel

23.6 Removing an instrument panel section screw

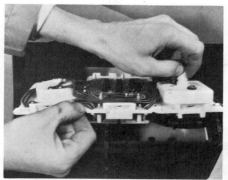
23.7 Removing the instrument panel sections

23.8 Removing the instrument panel front

24.3 Extracting the voltage stabilizer

pull out the cable to release it from the speedometer head.
3   Remove the two screws securing the switch panel to the facia and lower the panel. Pull the pivots from the supports and allow the panel to hang by its harness.
4   Unscrew the nuts securing the instrument panel housing to the facia. Withdraw the housing and at the same time disconnect the multi-plug connectors from the printed circuit board (photo).
5   From the rear of the housing, twist the three upper bulb holders, anti-clockwise and remove them (photo).
6   Remove the screws securing the three instrument panel sections, noting that the centre section screws are shorter (photo).
7   Carefully withdraw the instrument panel sections and printed circuit, taking care not to damage the latter (photo).
8   Each individual instrument can now be removed by removing the nuts or screws securing it to the panel. On 1.3 models, the digital clock can be removed from the tachometer by loosening the dial screws and withdrawing the clock reset control. If necessary, remove the front panel (photo).
9   Refitting is a reversal of removal, but make sure that the reset controls, where fitted, pass through the holes in the instrument panel window.

24 Instrument panel printed circuit and voltage stabilizer – removal and refitting

1   Remove the instrument panel as described in Section 23, paragraphs 1 to 4.
2   Remove all the bulb holders from the rear of the housing.
3   Pull the voltage stabilizer from the blade connectors (photo).
4   Remove the cross-head screws and withdraw the blade connectors from the printed circuit.
5   Unscrew the retaining nuts and prise out the plastic retainers from the printed circuit.
6   Where a digital clock is fitted in the base of the tachometer, remove the brass screw, lift the printed circuit, then refit the screw to retain the clock.

7   Remove the remaining screws and withdraw the printed circuit.
8   Refitting is a reversal of removal, with reference to Section 23 as necessary.

25 Auxiliary circuits relay and circuit diode – description

An auxiliary circuits relay is fitted in the wiring harness on all models, and is located on the right-hand side, wheel arch on right-hand drive models and on the left-hand side wheel arch on left-hand drive models. The relay is connected in the heater and wiper circuit and protects the ignition switch from overloading (photo).
All models are equipped with a circuit junction diode to protect the various instruments fitted with semi-conductors devices.

26 Headlamps and headlamp bulbs – removal and refitting

Metro and Metro L models
1   With the bonnet open, pull the socket connector from the rear of the headlamp, and withdraw the rubber cover.
2   Release the clip and remove the headlamp bulb.
3   To remove the headlamp unit, first remove the plastic radiator grille. Prise off the mounting clips and lower the unit from the adjustment screws.
4   Refitting is a reversal of removal, but make sure that the lug on the bulb flange engages with the notch on the reflector, and adjust the headlamp alignment as described in Section 27. Do not touch the bulb glass; if touched, clean it with methylated spirit.

Metro HLE, 1.3S and 1.3 HLS models
5   With the bonnet open, pull the rubber cover from the rear of the headlamp (photo).
6   Pull the socket connector from the bulb (photo).
7   Release the clip and remove the headlamp bulb (photo).
8   To remove the headlamp unit, first remove the plastic radiator grille.

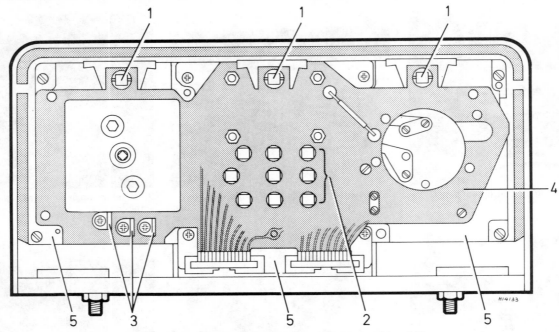

Fig. 10.10 Rear view of the instrument panel (Sec 23)

1   Panel illumination lamps   3   Voltage stabilizer   4   Printed circuit
2   Warning lamps   connections   5   Instrument panel sections

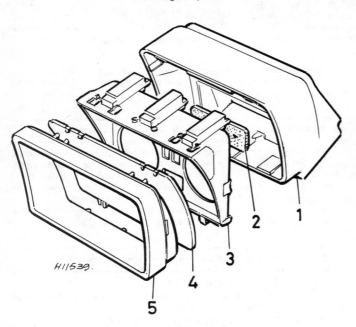

**Fig. 10.11 Exploded view of instrument panel less printed circuit
(Sec 23)**

1   Case   4   Window
2   Warning light panel   5   Surround
3   Mask

9   Remove the sidelamp and direction indicator bulbs.
10 Unscrew the four mounting nuts, one of which is located under the
front wing (photo). Remove the washers.
11 Withdraw the headlamp unit from the front of the car (photo).
12 Refitting is a reversal of removal, with reference to paragraph 4.

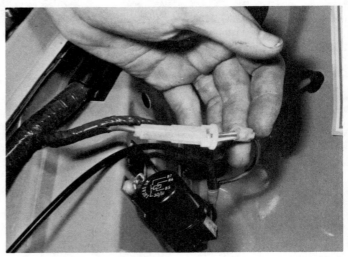

25.1 Auxiliary circuits relay and fuse

27 Headlamps – alignment

1   The headlamp alignment should be checked every 12 000 miles
(20 000 km) or 12 months, whichever occurs first.
2   It is recommended that the alignment is carried out by a BL garage
using modern beam setting equipment. However, in an emergency, the
following procedure will provide an acceptable light pattern.
3   Position the car on a level surface with tyres correctly inflated,
approximately 10 metres (33 feet) in front of, and at right-angles to, a
wall or garage door.
4   Draw a horizontal line on the wall or door at headlamp centre
height. Draw a vertical line corresponding to the centre line of the car,
then measure off a point either side of this, on the horizontal line,
corresponding with the headlamp centres.
5   Switch on the main beam and check that the areas of maximum
illumination coincide with the headlamp centre marks on the wall. If

26.5 Headlamp rear cover (1.3 HLS)

26.6 Removing the headlamp bulb socket (1.3 HLS)

26.7 Removing the headlamp bulb (1.3 HLS)

26.10 Removing the headlamp retaining nuts (1.3 HLS)

26.11 Removing the headlamp unit (1.3 HLS)

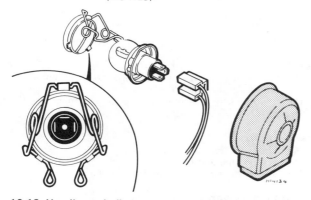

Fig. 10.12 Headlamp bulb components for Metro and Metro L models (Sec 26)

Fig. 10.13 Headlamp unit components for Metro and Metro L models (Sec 26)

not, turn the plastic knobs located on the rear of the headlamps; turn both knobs to raise or lower the beam, and one knob (either will do) to move the beam horizontally.

28 Lamp bulbs – renewal

Note: *Lamp bulbs should always be renewed with ones of similar type and rating as listed in the Specifications*

Sidelamps and front indicator lamps
Metro and Metro L models
1   Remove the lens from the front bumper (2 screws).
2   Push and twist the bulbs to remove them.

Metro HLE, 1.3 S, and 1.3 HLS models
3   To remove the sidelamp bulb, pull back the rubber cover and pull

out the bulb holder (photo). Push and twist the bulb to remove it.
4   To remove the indicator bulb, pull back the rubber cover and turn the bulb holder anti-clockwise from the headlamp reflector. Push and twist the bulb to remove it (photo).

Side repeater lamp
5   Reach up under the front wing, and pull the bulb holder from the lamp body.
6   A wedge type bulb is fitted; pull it straight from the bulb holder.
7   When refitting the bulb holder, support the lamp body and lens from the outside. If the lamp body is displaced use adhesive to stick it to the wing (photo).

28.3 Removing the front sidelamp bulb holder (1.3 HLS)

28.4 Removing the front direction indicator bulb (1.3 HLS)

28.7 The side repeater lamp being refitted with adhesive

28.8 Removing the rear lamp cluster air vent

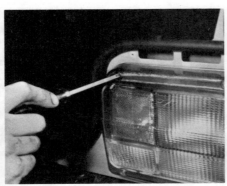

28.9A Removing the screws ...

28.9B ... and rear lamp lens

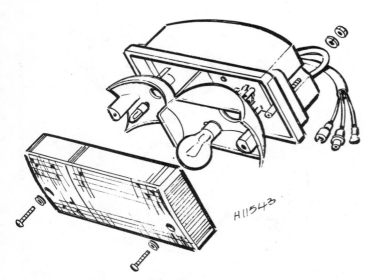

H11543

Fig. 10.14 Sidelamp and front indicator lamp components for Metro and Metro L models (Sec 28)

Rear lamp cluster

8   Open the tailgate. Remove the two screws and the air vent (photo).
9   Remove the four screws and withdraw the lamp lens (photos).
10   Push and twist the faulty bulb to remove it (photo). Note that the stop/tail bulb has offset pins and can only be fitted in one position.

Rear number plate lamp

11   Press and twist the lamp lens to remove it (photo).
12   Push and twist the bulb to remove it (photo).

Rear foglamp

13   Remove the two screws and withdraw the lens (photo).
14   Push and twist the bulb to remove it.
15   Note that the lens is tapered; the narrow end must face the side of the car.

Interior lamp

16   Prise the lamp from the roof (photo).
17   Depress the bulb and turn it through 90° to remove it.
18   Do not trap the wires when refitting the lamp.

Switch illumination

19   Disconnect the battery negative lead.
20   Remove the two screws from the front of the switch panel, and pivot the panel downwards.
21   Remove the bulb holder from the switch. A wedge type bulb is fitted; pull it straight from the bulb holder.

Instrument panel warning lamps

22   Remove the instrument panel as described in Section 23.
23   Twist the relevant bulb holder anti-clockwise and remove it.
24   A wedge type bulb is fitted; pull it straight from the bulb holder.

29 Wiper blades – renewal

1   The wiper blades should be removed when they no longer clean the windscreen or tailgate window effectively.
2   Lift the wiper arm away from the windscreen or tailgate window.
3   Lift the spring retainer, then separate the blade from the wiper arm (photo).
4   Insert the new blade into the arm and make sure that the spring retainer is engaged correctly.

28.10 Removing a stop light bulb

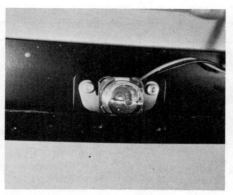
28.11 Rear number plate lamp

28.12 Removing the rear number plate lamp lens (lamp removed for clarity)

28.13 Removing the rear foglamp lens

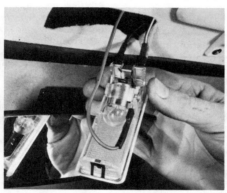
28.16 Interior lamp

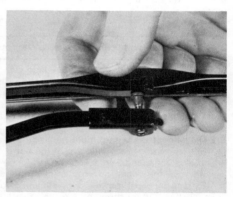
29.3 Disconnecting the windscreen wiper blade

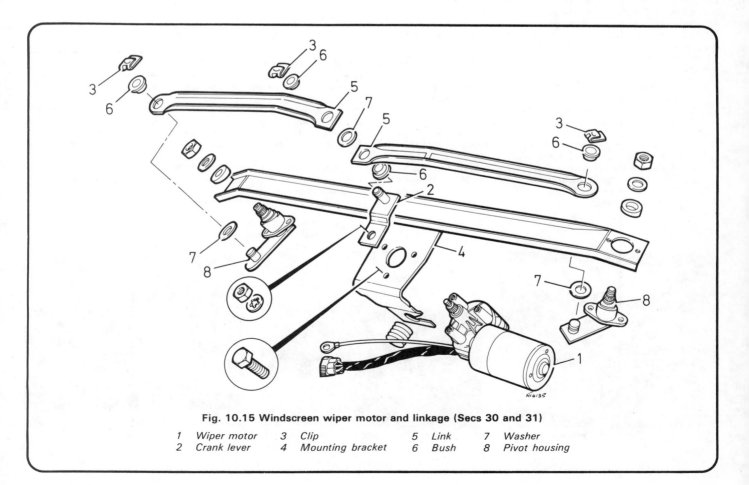

Fig. 10.15 Windscreen wiper motor and linkage (Secs 30 and 31)

1	Wiper motor	3	Clip	5	Link	7	Washer
2	Crank lever	4	Mounting bracket	6	Bush	8	Pivot housing

30 Windscreen wiper motor – removal and refitting

1   Disconnect the battery negative lead.
2   Remove the air cleaner as described in Chapter 3.
3   Extract the clip from the linkage pivot on the motor crank lever.
4   Remove the bushes, washer and links from the crankpin.
5   Unscrew the nut and remove the washer and crank lever from the motor spindle.
6   Unscrew the motor mounting screws and disconnect the wiring multi-plug.
7   Disconnect the earth lead and withdraw the wiper motor.
8   Refitting is a reversal of removal, but before fitting the crank lever, temporarily reconnect the battery and switch on the ignition (wiper switch 'off') to set the motor in the 'parked' position. Fit the crank lever horizontally and facing the driver's side of the car. Lubricate the linkage bushes, crankpin and linkages with a molybdenum disulphide based grease.

31 Windscreen wiper linkage – removal, overhaul and refitting

1   Disconnect the battery negative lead.
2   Remove the air cleaner as described in Chapter 3.
3   Lift the hinged covers on the wiper arms and unscrew the nuts (photo). Prise the wiper arms from the spindles with a screwdriver.
4   From each pivot housing, unscrew the nut and remove the washer and spacer.
5   Disconnect the wiring multi-plug and the earth lead.
6   Slide the rubber mounting from the bottom of the bracket, noting which slot engages the bracket.
7   Remove the wiper motor and linkage together from the car.
8   Extract the clips from the crankpin and pivot arms, and remove the links, bushes and washers, noting their relative positions.
9   Remove the wiper motor as described in Section 30.
10 Remove the bottom spacers from the pivot housings, drill out the rivets, and remove the housings from the bracket.
11 Press the bushes out of the links.
12 Examine the bushes and pivot housings for wear, and if worn excessively, obtain a kit of bushes and clips.
13 Refitting is a reversal of removal, but note the following additional points:

(a) *Lubricate the pivots and bushes with a molybdenum disulphide based grease*
(b) *Press the bushes into the links in the direction shown in Fig. 10.15; note that the rounded ends of the links must face outwards*
(c) *Fit the pivot housings (with the longer lever to the driver's side of the bracket), using new rivets.*
(d) *Tighten the pivot housing nuts to the specified torque*
(e) *With the motor in the 'parked' position, fit the wiper arms to the spindles so that the blades are parallel to the lower edge of the windscreen.*

32 Tailgate wiper motor and gearbox – removal, overhaul and refitting

1   Disconnect the battery negative lead.
2   Lift the hinged cover on the wiper arm and unscrew the nut. Prise the wiper arm from the spindle with a screwdriver, together with the spacer.
3   Unscrew the nut and remove the washer and spacer from the motor spindle.
4   Prise the trim panel from the tailgate inner panel using a wide-bladed screwdriver (photo).
5   Disconnect the earth lead and the wiring multi-plug.
6   Remove the mounting bracket screws, and withdraw the wiper motor and gearbox (photo).
7   Note the location of the wires in the multi-plug, then depress the tags and remove the pins.
8   Remove the insulating sleeve, and detach the pins from the wires.
9   Unscrew the through-bolts and withdraw the motor from the gearbox.
10 The motor and gearbox can be renewed separately if necessary.
11 Reassembly and refitting are a reversal of the removal procedure, but note the following additional points:

(a) *Make sure that the lug on the motor is engaged with the notch on the gearbox*
(b) *Adjust the armature endfloat by loosening the locknut on the gearbox, turning the screw to eliminate the endfloat, then loosening the screw very slightly to give a small endfloat. Tighten the locknut*
(c) *Before fitting the wiper arm, switch on the ignition and operate the motor to set the spindle in the 'parked' position. Fit the wiper arm to the spindle so that the blade is parallel to the lower edge of the tailgate window.*
(d) *Note that the tailgate washer bottle and motor are located on the left-hand rear inner panel (photo)*

33 Horn – removal and refitting

1   The single-note horn is located in the engine compartment on the left-hand side (photo).
2   To remove the horn, first disconnect the battery negative lead.
3   Disconnect the wires from the horn terminals.
4   Unbolt the mounting bracket and remove the horn.
5   If the horn emits an unsatisfactory sound, it may be possible to adjust it, assuming the internal circuit and contact points are in good condition. The adjustment is best made with the horn mounted on the car. Turn the hexagon head (Mixo type) or screw (Lucas type) until the best sound is achieved.
6   Refitting is a reversal of removal.

31.3 Unscrewing the wiper arm spindle nut

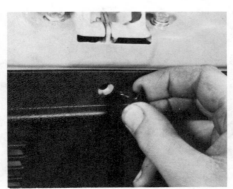
32.4 Removing a tailgate trim panel fastener

32.6 Tailgate wiper motor and gearbox

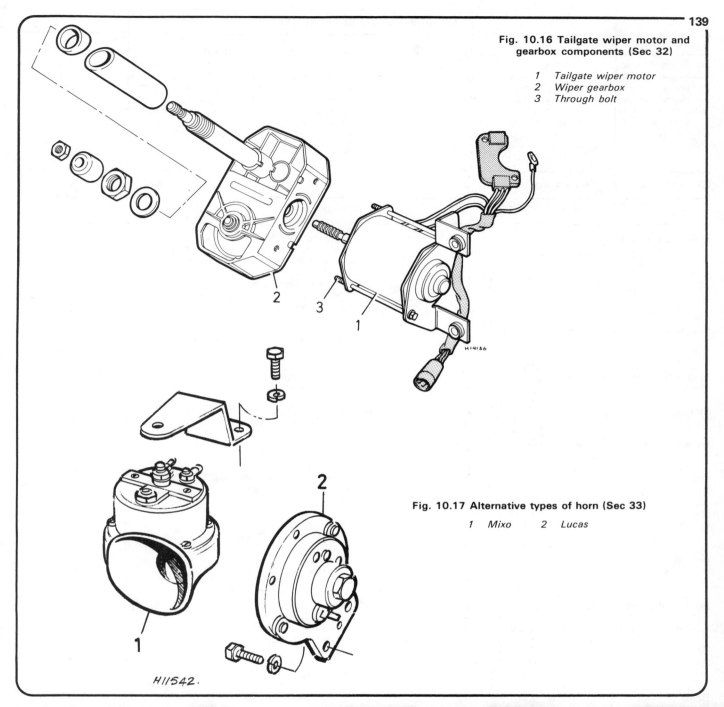

Fig. 10.16 Tailgate wiper motor and gearbox components (Sec 32)

1 Tailgate wiper motor
2 Wiper gearbox
3 Through bolt

Fig. 10.17 Alternative types of horn (Sec 33)

1 Mixo   2 Lucas

32.11 Tailgate washer bottle and motor

33.1 Horn location

34.4 Removing the radio

34 Radio – removal and refitting

1   Disconnect the battery negative lead.
2   Disconnect the supply and earth wires from the radio, leaving the in-line fuse and choke intact.
3   Remove the aerial from the radio.
4   Unscrew the rear mounting bolt and two side screws and withdraw the radio from the car (photo).
5   Using a small hooked instrument (a length of welding rod will do), pull out the bottom of the radio grille and remove it.
6   Remove the cross-head screws and withdraw the speaker and wiring from the facia.
7   If necessary, remove the radio earth wire from the speaker compartment.
8   Refitting is a reversal of removal.

35 Fault diagnosis – electrical system

Symptom	Reason(s)
Starter fails to turn engine	Battery discharged or defective Battery terminal and/or earth leads loose Starter motor connections loose Starter solenoid faulty Starter brushes worn or sticking Starter commutator dirty or worn Starter field coils earthed
Starter turns engine very slowly	Battery discharged Starter motor connections loose Starter brushes worn or sticking
Starter spins but does not turn engine	Pinion or flywheel ring gear teeth broken or badly worn Seized pinion (inertia type)
Starter noisy	Pinion or flywheel ring gear teeth badly worn Mounting bolts loose
Battery will not hold charge for more than a few days	Battery defective internally Electrolyte level too low Battery terminals loose Alternator drivebelt slipping Alternator or regulator faulty Short circuit
Ignition light stays on	Alternator faulty Alternator drivebelt broken
Ignition light fails to come on	Warning bulb blown Indicator light open circuit Alternator faulty
Instrument readings increase with engine speed	Voltage stabilizer faulty
Fuel or temperature gauge gives no reading	Wiring open circuit Sender unit faulty
Fuel or temperature gauge give maximum reading all the time	Wiring short circuit Gauge faulty
Lights inoperative	Bulb blown Fuse blown Battery discharged Switch faulty Wiring open circuit Bad connection due to corrosion
Failure of component motor	Commutator dirty or burnt Armature faulty Brushes sticking or worn Armature bearings dry or misaligned Field coils faulty Fuse blown Wiring loose or broken
Failure of an individual component	Wiring loose or broken Fuse blown Bad circuit connection Switch faulty Component faulty

Key to main wiring diagrams. Not all items are fitted to all models. For later models see Chapter 13

1 Rear fog guard lamps
2 Front fog lamps (if fitted)
3 Panel illumination lamp
4 Cigar lighter illumination
5 LH tail lamp
6 Number plate lamp
7 RH tail lamp
8 LH sidelamp
9 RH sidelamp
10 Headlamp dipped beams
11 Main beam warning lamp
12 Headlamp main beams
13 Front fog lamp relay (if fitted)
14 Horn
15 Starter motor
16 Starter motor solenoid
17 Rear fog guard lamp switch and warning light
19 Headlamp dipswitch
20 Headlamp flasher switch
21 Horn push
22 Front fog lamp switch (if fitted)
23 Fuses
24 Line fuses
25 Main lighting switch
26 Battery
27 Auxiliary circuits relay
28 Rear screen wash/wipe switch (if fitted)
29 Windscreen wash/wipe switch
30 Ignition/starter switch
31 Headlamp washer relay (if fitted)
32 Heater motor
33 Rear screen washer motor (if fitted)
34 Windscreen wiper motor
35 Cigar lighter
36 Clock
37 Headlamp washer motor
38 Rear screen washer motor
39 Windscreen washer motor
40 Radio (if fitted)
41 Interior light and switch
42 Heater motor switch
43 Door switches
44 Brake failure warning lamp relay
45 Alternator
46 Hazard warning flasher unit
47 Hazard switch and warning light

49 Ballast resistor cable
50 Direction indicator flasher unit
51 Heated rear screen switch and warning lamp
53 Brake fluid level sensor
54 Direction indicator switch
55 Brake failure warning light
56 Reversing lamp switch
57 Stop-lamp switch
58 Voltage stabilizer
59 Brake pad wear warning light
60 Ignition warning light
61 Tachometer (if fitted)
62 Ignition coil
63 Brake pad wear sensors
64 Choke warning light
65 Oil pressure warning light
66 Handbrake warning light
67 Seat belt warning light
68 Fuel gauge
69 Water temperature gauge
70 Induction heater and thermostat (if fitted)
71 Suction chamber heater (if fitted)
72 Direction indicator repeater lamps
73 RH front indicator lamp
74 RH rear indicator lamp
75 Indicator warning light
76 LH rear indicator lamp
77 LH front indicator lamp
78 Heated rear screen
79 Reversing lamps
80 Gearbox selector panel illumination (Automatics only)
81 Stop-lamps
82 Choke warning light switch
83 Oil pressure light switch
84 Handbrake warning light switch
85 Passenger seat switch
86 Passenger seat belt switch
87 Driver's seat belt switch
88 Fuel gauge tank unit
89 Water temperature transducer
90 Radiator cooling fan
91 Radiator cooling fan thermostat
92 Distributor
93 Heater control illumination
94 Panel switch illumination

Cable colour code

B	Black	P	Purple
G	Green	R	Red
K	Pink	S	Slate
LG	Light green	U	Blue
N	Brown	W	White
O	Orange	Y	Yellow

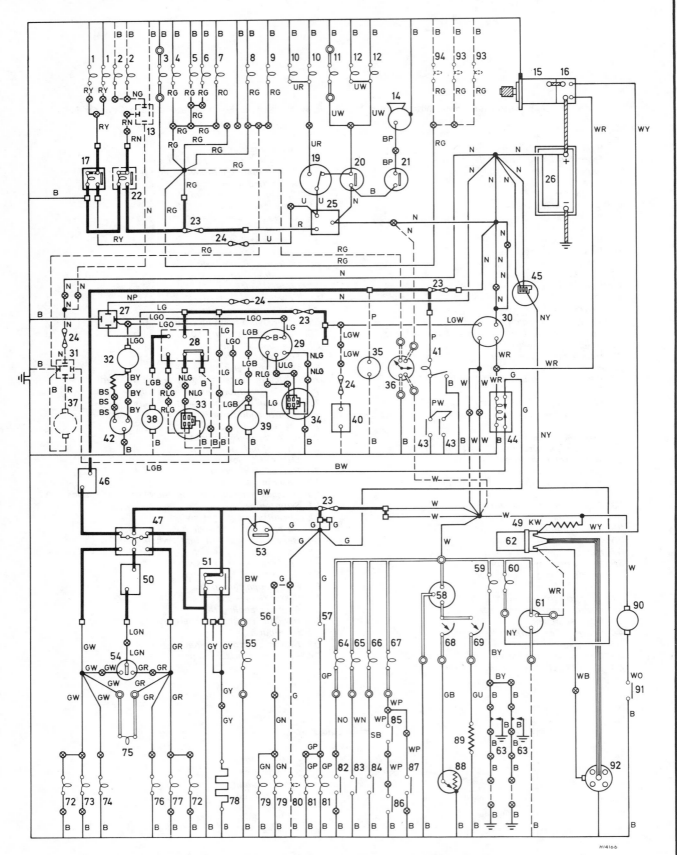

Fig. 10.18 Wiring diagram for right-hand drive models 1980 to 1982. For key see page 141

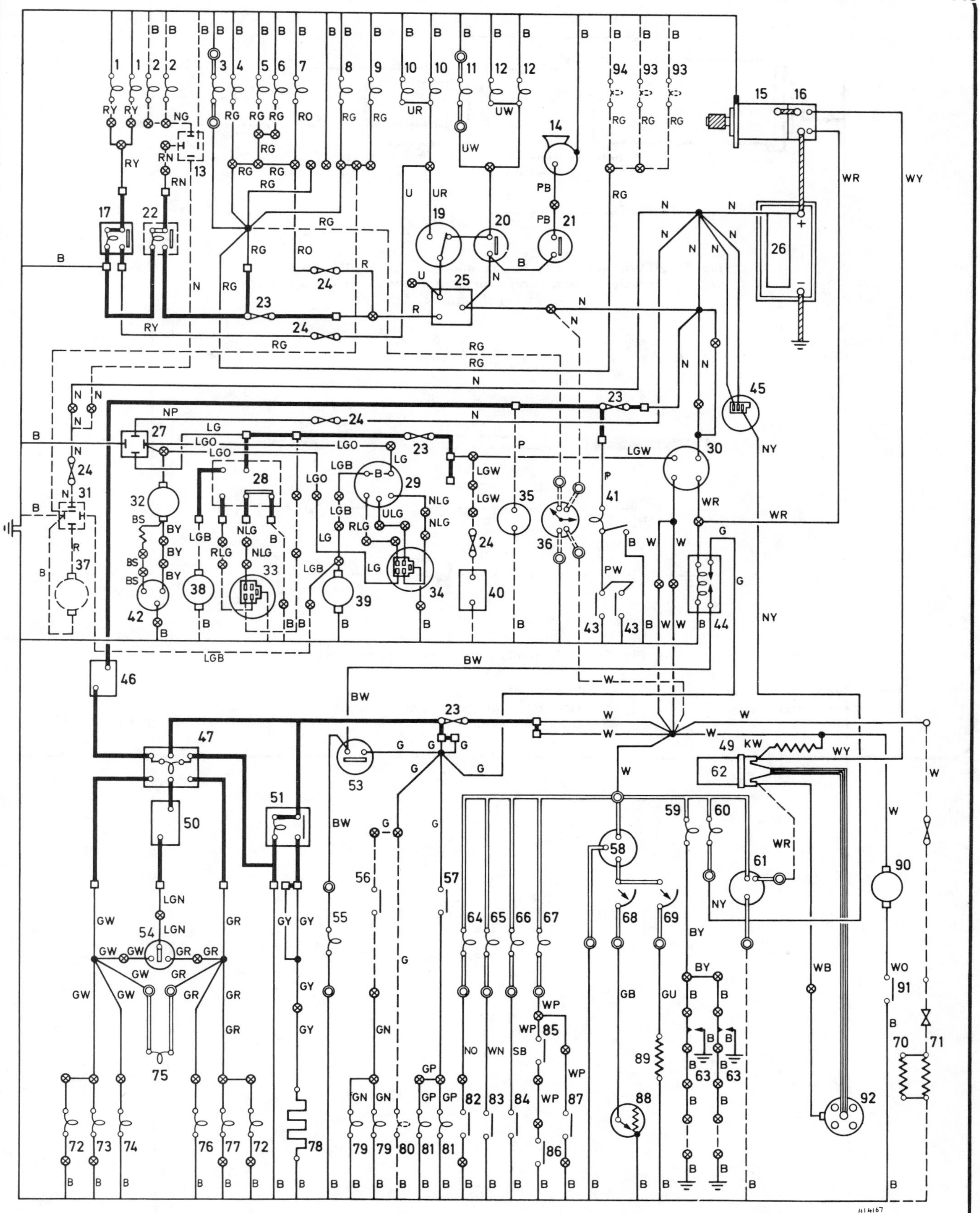

Fig. 10.19 Wiring diagram for left-hand drive models 1980 to 1983. For key see
page 141

H14167

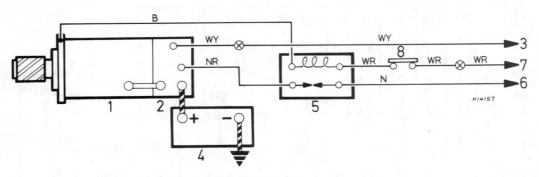

Fig. 10.20 Wiring diagram for pre-engaged starter fitted to models
with automatic transmission. For colour code see key to main
wiring diagrams

1	Starter motor	3	To ignition coil	5	Solenoid relay	7	From ignition switch
2	Solenoid	4	Battery	6	Feed from battery	8	Starter inhibitor switch

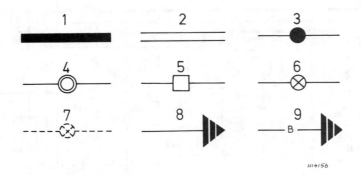

Fig. 10.21 Symbols used in wiring diagrams

1	Fuse board printed circuit	4	Instrument printed circuit connector	7	When fitted
2	Instrument printed circuit	5	Fuse board printed circuit connector	8	Component earthed via mounting
3	Sealed joint	6	Other connector	9	Component earthed via cable

Chapter 11 Suspension and steering

For modifications and information applicable to later models, see Supplement at end of manual

Contents

Anti-roll bar − removal and refitting 6
Fault diagnosis − suspension and steering 22
Front hub assembly − removal, overhaul and refitting 10
Front Hydragas unit − removal and refitting 4
Front shock absorber − removal and refitting 5
Front suspension lower arm − removal, overhaul and refitting 8
Front suspension upper arm − removal, overhaul and refitting 7
Front suspension upper or lower balljoint − renewal 9
General description 1
Hydragas units − testing 3
Rear hub assembly − removal, overhaul and refitting 13

Rear Hydragas unit − removal and refitting 11
Rear suspension radius arm − removal, overhaul and refitting 12
Roadwheels and tyres − general 21
Routine maintenance 2
Steering column − removal, overhaul and refitting 15
Steering column lock/ignition switch − removal and refitting 16
Steering rack and pinion − removal, overhaul and refitting 20
Steering rack gaiter − renewal 18
Steering wheel − removal and refitting 14
Tie-rod end balljoint − removal and refitting 17
Wheel alignment − checking and adjusting 19

Specifications

Front suspension
Type .... Independent, unequal length upper and lower arms, anti-roll bar, Hydragas spring units, telescopic shock absorbers

Rear suspension
Type .... Independent, trailing arms, operating interconnected Hydragas spring units via arms and pushrods

Suspension grease points
Grease type .... Multi-purpose lithium based grease (Duckhams LB 10)

Steering
Type .... Rack-and-pinion, flexible coupling
Number of turns lock-to-lock 3.3
Steering wheel diameter .... 14.96 in (380 mm)
Rack pinion bearing preload .... 0.001 to 0.004 in (0.025 to 0.102 mm)
Pinion bearing shim gap .... 0.011 to 0.013 in (0.28 to 0.33 mm)
Pinion bearing standard shim .... 0.092 in (2.337 mm)
Pinion bearing shims available .... 0.005 in, 0.0075 in, 0.010 in (0.127 mm, 0.1905 mm, 0.254 mm)
Yoke-to-cover plate clearance .... 0.002 to 0.005 in (0.05 to 0.12 mm)
Yoke-to-cover plate shims available .... 0.0024 in (0.061 mm)
Rack ball-pin centre dimension .... 44.2 to 44.3 in (112.2 to 112.5 mm)

Front wheel alignment
Toe-out .... 0 to 0.125 in (0 to 3 mm)
Inner wheel angle (with outer wheel at 20°) .... 23.75° ± 1.5°
Camber angle .... 0' ± 30'
Caster angle .... 2° 6' positive ± 1°

Rear wheel alignment
Toe-in/out .... 0°30' toe-in to 0°30' toe-out
Camber angle .... 1° negative ± 30'

Wheels
Type .... Pressed steel disc, with vented centre
Size:
    Standard .... 4.50B x 12 in
    Denovo .... 95 x 320 mm

Tyres
Size:
    Metro, Metro L and Metro HLE .... 135SR x 12 or 155/70R x 12 radial
    Metro 1.3 L, Metro 1.3 S and Metro 1.3 HLS ...... 155/70R x 12 radial
    Denovo 2 .... 160/65R x 320

Pressures (cold) – lbf/in² (kgf/cm²):	Front	Rear
Metro, Metro L, and Metro HLE with 135 SR tyres	32 (2.2)	28 (2.0)
Metro, Metro L, and Metro HLE with 155/70 tyres	33 (2.3)	28 (2.0)
Metro 1.3 L, Metro 1.3 S and Metro 1.3 HLS	28 (2.0)	26 (1.8)
Denovo 2	28 (2.0)	26 (1.8)

Torque wrench settings

	lbf ft	kgf m
Front suspension		
Anti-roll bar to subframe	19	2.6
Anti-roll bar end nut (see text)	30 to 80	4.1 to 11.1
Hub balljoint socket	75	10.3
Hub balljoint nut to arm	37	5.1
Lower arm pivot	75	10.3
Shock absorber upper nut	27.5	3.8
Shock absorber lower nut	35	4.8
Upper arm pivot	55	7.6
Rear suspension		
Hub nut	60	8.3
Radius arm pivot	53	7.3
Steering		
Column clamp to bracket	19	2.6
Column clamp to column	8.5	1.2
Coupling cover to body	6.5	0.9
Flexible coupling to pinion	11	1.5
Flexible coupling to column	19	2.6
Column bracket to shelf	19	2.6
Coupling to pinion	19	2.6
Column to bracket	19	2.6
Column lock shear bolt (minimum)	14	1.9
Steering arm to hub	38	4.5
Rack U-bolts	19	2.6
Steering wheel	35	48
Tie-rod end	22	3.0
Tie-rod to rack	35	4.8
Upper steering column	8.5	1.2
Wheels		
Wheel nuts	42	5.8

1 General description

The front suspension is of independent, upper and lower arm type incorporating separate Hydragas spring units on each side, telescopic shock absorbers, and an anti-roll bar.

The rear suspension is of independent, trailing arm type incorporating interconnected Hydragas spring units, which are operated via pushrods from the trailing arms. The rear Hydragas units are each preloaded with a coil spring.

The Hydragas units comprise a chamber of pressurized nitrogen gas contained by a rubber diaphragm, and a further chamber of pressurized fluid consisting of water, alcohol and additives. Movement of the suspension causes the pushrod to compress the fluid, which causes the intermediate diaphragm to deflect into the nitrogen chamber. The unit acts as a variable rate gas spring.

Although the front and rear Hydragas units function in an identical manner, the rear units incorporate an internal damper flap valve, whereas the front units are damped by separate telescopic shock absorbers. The front units are not interconnected but the rear units are via a pipe containing a flow restrictor. The front and rear ride heights are set by pressurizing the fluid in the Hydragas units.

Due to the high pressures involved and the special equipment required, the Hydragas units must only be depressurized, evacuated and pressurized by a BL garage. In the event of loss of pressure, the car may be driven to the place of repair over metalled roads at up to 20 mph (32 kph).

The steering is of rack-and-pinion type mounted on the rear of the front subframe. The steering column is attached to the rack pinion by a flexible coupling. Note that a minor steering column modification was carried out on all cars early in 1981; if in doubt as to whether this modification has been carried out on your vehicle, consult your dealer. All service procedures should remain basically unchanged.

2 Routine maintenance

1   Every 12 000 miles (20 000 km) or 12 months, whichever occurs first, the front and rear suspension should be lubricated with a grease gun. The front grease nipple is located on the upper suspension arm at the pivot end. The rear nipple is located on the outer end of the radius arm pivot. Always clean the nipple before using the grease gun.
2   At the same time examine the Hydragas units for leaks, and check all the suspension joints and mountings for security and damage.
3   Check, and if necessary adjust, the front wheel alignment.
4   Check the steering gaiters for splitting, and examine the steering balljoints for wear. Check the steering gear for security.

3 Hydragas units – testing

1   A fault in a Hydragas unit can be determined by checking the car ride height as shown in Fig. 11.3. If the measurements are less than those specified, first check the units and rear interconnecting pipe for signs of leakage, which will appear as a slight residue left after the fluid has evaporated.
2   If the cause is a union, tighten the nut and have the system repressurized at a BL garage.
3   If it is determined that a Hydragas unit is leaking fluid, renew the unit and again have it repressurized by a BL garage.
4   If no fluid leak can be found, it is possible that nitrogen has leaked from the unit. To check this, the car must be taken to a BL garage and the unit checked with the pressure pump. The fluid pressure should increase rapidly to the pressure of the nitrogen, and thereafter increase at a noticeably slower rate. If nitrogen has been leaking, the pressure will have dropped and the fluid pressure will increase rapidly above the

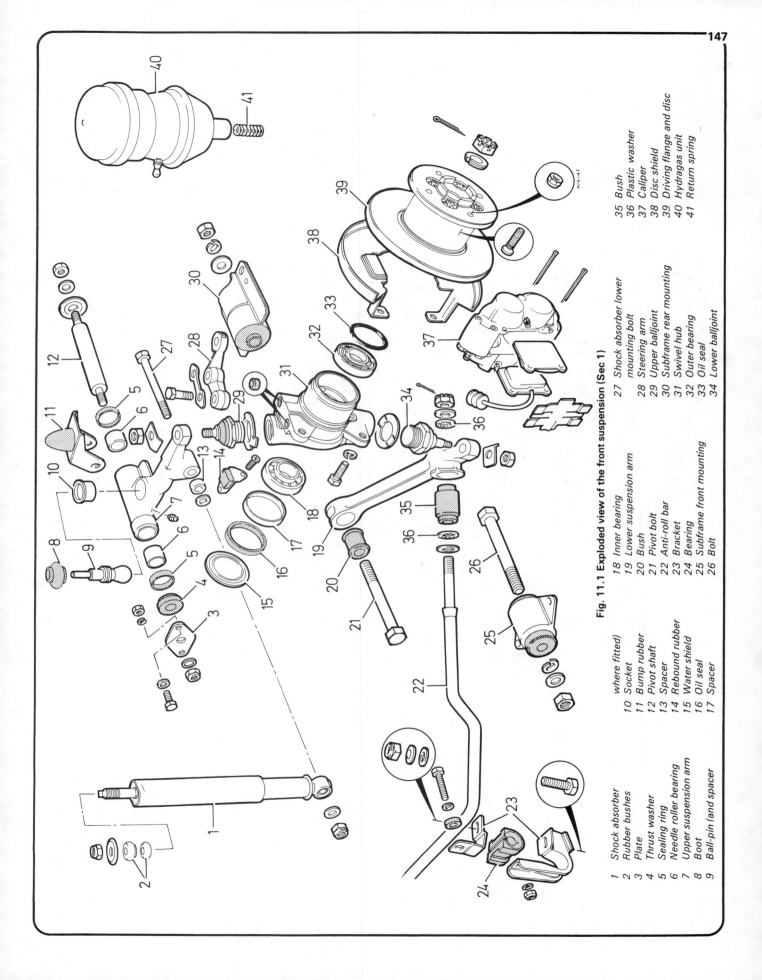

Fig. 11.1 Exploded view of the front suspension (Sec 1)

1 Shock absorber
2 Rubber bushes
3 Plate
4 Thrust washer
5 Sealing ring
6 Needle roller bearing
7 Upper suspension arm
8 Boot
9 Ball-pin (and spacer

where fitted)
10 Socket
11 Bump rubber
12 Pivot shaft
13 Spacer
14 Rebound rubber
15 Water shield
16 Oil seal
17 Spacer

18 Inner bearing
19 Lower suspension arm
20 Bush
21 Pivot bolt
22 Anti-roll bar
23 Bracket
24 Bearing
25 Subframe front mounting
26 Bolt

27 Shock absorber lower
    mounting bolt
28 Steering arm
29 Upper balljoint
30 Subframe rear mounting
31 Swivel hub
32 Outer bearing
33 Oil seal
34 Lower balljoint

35 Bush
36 Plastic washer
37 Caliper
38 Disc shield
39 Driving flange and disc
40 Hydragas unit
41 Return spring

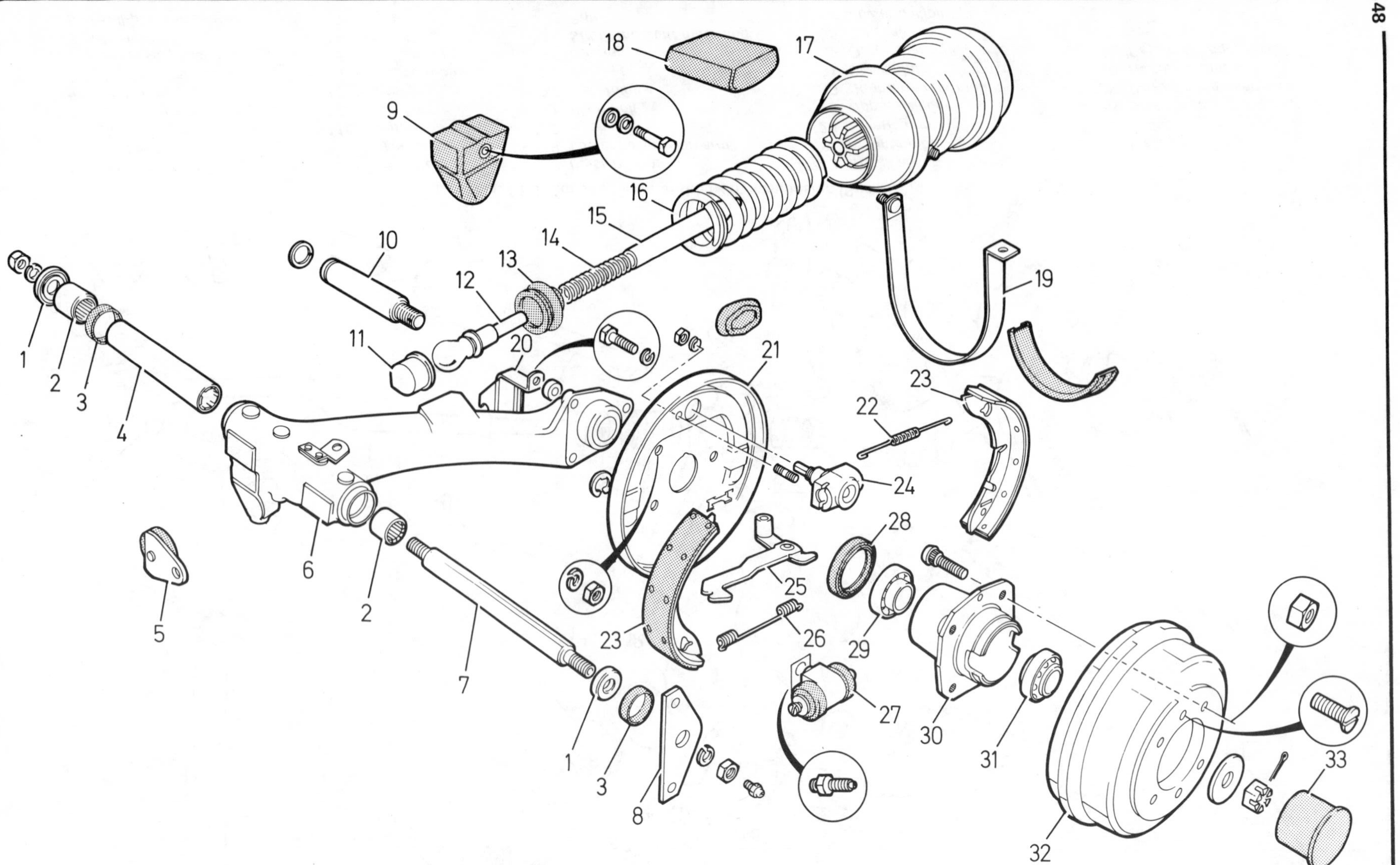

H14142

Fig. 11.2 Exploded view of the rear suspension (Sec 1)

1 Thrust washer
2 Needle roller bearing
3 Sealing ring
4 Lubricating tube
5 Rebound rubber
6 Radius arm
7 Pivot shaft

8 Retaining plate
9 Bump rubber
10 Stub shaft
11 Socket
12 Ball-pin
13 Boot
14 Return spring

15 Strut
16 Helper spring
17 Hydragas unit
18 Mounting pad
19 Reaction strap
20 Handbrake cable mounting
     bracket

21 Backplate
22 Upper return spring
23 Brake shoe
24 Brake adjuster
25 Handbrake levers
26 Lower return spring
27 Wheel cylinder

28 Oil seal
29 Inner bearing
30 Hub
31 Outer bearing
32 Brake drum
33 Grease retaining cap

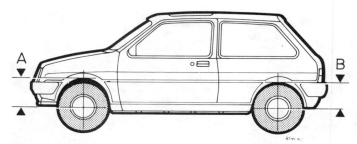

Fig. 11.3 Suspension ride height dimensions (Sec 3)
A = 12.87 + 0.4 in (327 + 10 mm)
B = 12.64 ± 0.4 in (321 ± 10 mm)

normal nitrogen pressure. The nitrogen pressures are as follows:

Front Hydragas unit ....325 lbf/in^2 ± 6.5 lbf/in^2
(2241 kN/m^2 ± 44.8 kN/m^2)
Rear Hydragas unit ....230 lbf/in^2 ± 4.6 lbf/in^2
(1586 kN/m^2 ± 31.7 kN/m^2)

Note that the rear Hydragas units must be checked for a nitrogen leak separately, by removing the interconnecting pipe and using an adaptor.
5   If it is determined that a Hydragas unit has leaked nitrogen, renew it and have the suspension repressurized by a BL garage.

4   Front Hydragas unit – removal and refitting

1   Have the Hydragas unit depressurized by a BL garage.
2   Apply the handbrake, then jack up the front of the car and support it on axle stands. Remove the roadwheel.
3   Unbolt the outer bracket from the subframe tower, and withdraw the Hydragas unit together with its return spring (photo).
4   Remove the piston spacer(s) from the the knuckle joint on the driver's side.
5   Refitting is a reversal of removal, but have the Hydragas unit pressurized by a BL garage.

5   Front shock absorber – removal and refitting

1   If the left-hand shock absorber is being removed, remove the retaining screws and place the cooling system expansion tank to one side.
2   For both left and right-hand sides unscrew the self-locking nut

from the upper mounting, and remove the cup washer and large diameter rubber bush.
3   Turn the steering to allow access from the front, then unscrew the bottom mounting nut and remove the washer (photo).
4   Slide the shock absorber, washer and distance sleeve from the bottom mounting bolt, leaving the bolt and bump stop in position.
5   Withdraw the shock absorber from the upper mounting together with the small diameter rubber bush.
6   Note that if the shock absorber is to be refitted, it must be stored in an upright position.
7   Before fitting, grip the shock absorber lower mounting in a vice with the unit upright, then compress and extend it at least six times until there is no free travel when changing the direction of stroke. This will remove any trapped air from the internal fluid.
8   Refitting is a reversal of removal, but tighten the self-locking mounting nuts to the specified torque.

6   Anti-roll bar – removal and refitting

1   Turn the steering as necessary to allow access from the front, and remove the rebound buffers from the subframe on both sides. The buffers are located beneath the suspension upper arms and are secured by two cross-head screws (photo).
2   Insert distance pieces such as suitably-sized nuts in place of the buffers to retain the suspension in the normal running position.
3   Apply the handbrake, jack up the front of the car, and support it on axle stands. Remove both front wheels.
4   Extract the split pin from one end of the anti-roll bar and unscrew the nut (photo). Remove the plain washer and plastic washer. Similarly remove the nut and washers from the remaining end of the anti-roll bar.
5   Unbolt the bearing brackets from the front of the subframe, noting the position of the components (photo).
6   Unbolt and detach one of the subframe rear mountings.
7   Remove the nut, spring and plain washer from the mounting pivot bolt, then drive the bolt through the mounting and lower suspension arm.
8   Pull the lower suspension arm from the subframe and detach the anti-roll bar from both lower suspension arms. Withdraw the anti-roll bar from the car. Remove the washers.
9   To refit the anti-roll bar, first fit one steel washer against the shoulder on each end of the bar, followed by one plastic washer.
10   Insert the bar in the fixed lower suspension arm, then in the free lower suspension arm.
11   Locate the lower suspension arm in the subframe and insert the pivot bolt through the arm and mounting from the front. Fit the plain washer and spring washer and tighten the nut finger tight.
12   Fit the mounting to the underbody and tighten the bolts.
13   Fit the bearing brackets to the front of the subframe and tighten

4.3 Front Hydragas unit

5.3 Front shock absorber and lower mounting

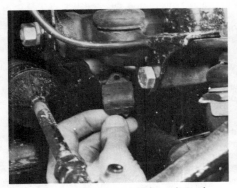

6.1 Removing a front suspension rebound buffer

6.4 Anti-roll bar-to-lower suspension arm joint

6.5 Anti-roll bar and front bearing bracket

7.5 Hydragas unit-to-upper arm knuckle joint

7.9 Front suspension upper arm pivot front retaining plate

the nuts finger tight.

14 Fit one plain washer on the ends of the bar against the lower arms, followed by the steel washers and nuts. Tighten the nuts finger tight.

15 Fit the roadwheels and lower the car to the ground.

16 Remove the distance pieces and fit the rebound buffers to the subframe.

17 With the weight of the car on the suspension, tighten the lower arm pivot bolts and the anti-roll bar bracket bolts to the specified torque.

18 Tighten the anti-roll bar end nuts to the lower of the torque wrench settings specified. Tighten further if necessary to align the split pin holes, but do not exceed the higher specified torque. Insert new split pins and bend over the ends to secure.

7 Front suspension upper arm – removal, overhaul and refitting

1   Have the relevant Hydragas unit depressurized by a BL garage.

2   Jack up the front of the car and support it on axle stands. Apply the handbrake and remove the roadwheel.

3   Unscrew the shock absorber lower mounting nut, and remove the shock absorber, washers and distance sleeve.

4   Remove the bolt and bump stop.

5   Remove the knuckle joint from the upper arm and extract it from the Hydragas unit together with the return spring (photo).

6   Support the driving flange and disc assembly with a trolley jack or block of wood.

7   Flatten the tab washer and unscrew the swivel hub upper balljoint nut. Remove the tab washer.

8   Using a separator tool, release the upper arm from the balljoint.

9   Unscrew the upper arm shaft rear nut, and unbolt the front retaining plate from the subframe (photo).

10 If removing the left-hand side upper arm, move the windscreen washer reservoir to one side.

11 Withdraw the pivot shaft assembly from the front of the subframe and recover the rear washers.

12 Lift the suspension upper arm from the subframe and recover the sealing rings and rear thrust washer.

13 To overhaul the upper arm, unscrew the grease nipple and grip the arm in a soft-jawed vice.

14 Remove the needle roller bearings with a soft metal drift.

15 Clean all the components in paraffin and wipe dry. Examine the needle roller bearings and the pivot shaft for damage, wear and pitting. If evident, renew the bearings and shaft. Make sure that the grease nipple lubrication drilling is unobstructed.

16 Drive the needle roller bearings into the upper arm with the marked ends facing outwards. Lubricate the bearings with multi-purpose lithium based grease, then refit the grease nipple.

17 Refitting is a reversal of removal, but note the following additional points:

(a) The thrust washers must be fitted with their grooved sides against the upper arm. Initially, fit the sealing rings and locate the rear thrust washer in the ring

(b) Lubricate the knuckle joint with a multi-purpose lithium based grease

(c) Tighten all nuts to the specified torque, and lock the swivel hub upper balljoint nut by bending the tab washer over the upper arm and nut

(d) After having the Hydragas unit pressurized by a BL garage, fully loosen the shock absorber lower mounting nut and retighten it to the specified torque with the weight of the car on the suspension

8 Front suspension lower arm – removal, overhaul and refitting

1   Turn the steering as necessary to allow access from the front, and remove the rebound buffer from the subframe on the relevant side. The buffer is located beneath the suspension upper arm is secured by two cross-head screws.

2   Insert a distance piece such as a suitably-sized nut in place of the buffer to retain the suspension in the normal running position.

3   Apply the handbrake, jack up the front of the car, and support it on axle stands. Remove the roadwheel.

4   Extract the split pin from the end of the anti-roll bar and unscrew the nut. Remove the plain washer and plastic washer abutting the

lower arm.

5   Unbolt the anti-roll bar bearing brackets from the front of the subframe, noting the position of the components.

6   Flatten the tab washer and unscrew the swivel hub lower balljoint nut. Remove the tab washer.

7   Using a separator tool, release the lower arm from the balljoint.

8   Unbolt and detach the relevant subframe rear mounting.

9   Remove the nut, spring and plain washer from the pivot bolt, then drive the bolt through the mounting and lower suspension arm.

10 Pull the lower suspension arm from the subframe, and remove it from the anti-roll bar. Recover the plastic and steel washers from the anti-roll bar.

11 To overhaul the lower arm, the pivot bush and anti-roll bar bush should be renewed. To remove the bushes, use a length of metal tubing, a long bolt, nut and packing pieces. Tighten the nut to draw out the bush. To fit the new bushes, dip them in a soapy water solution or use a rubber lubricant. Pull them into the lower arm using a nut and bolt and packing pices.

12 Refitting is a reversal of removal, but note the following additional points:

(a) *The anti-roll bar plastic washers must be fitted against the lower arm*

(b) *Tighten all nuts and bolts to the specified torque; the lower arm pivot bolt and the anti-roll bar mounting nuts and bolts should be fully tightened with the weight of the car on the suspension*

(c) *Lock the swivel hub lower balljoint nut by bending the tab washer over the lower arm and nut*

(d) *Lock the anti-roll bar-to-lever arm retaining nut with a new split pin.*

9   Front suspension upper or lower balljoint – renewal

1   To prevent problems by not being able to unscrew the balljoint socket, it is recommended that tool 18G1341 is obtained from a tool hire agent.

2   Turn the steering as necessary to allow access from the front, and remove the rebound buffer from the subframe on the relevant side. The buffer is located beneath the suspension upper arm and is secured by two cross-head screws.

3   Insert a distance piece such as a suitably-sized nut in place of the buffer to retain the suspension in the normal running position.

4   Apply the handbrake, jack up the front of the car, and support it on axle stands. Remove the roadwheel.

5   Flatten the tab washer and unscrew the swivel hub upper or lower balljoint nut (as applicable). Remove the tab washer.

6   Using a separator tool release the balljoint from the suspension arm. If removing the upper balljoint, support the swivel hub assembly with a trolley jack.

7   Flatten the lockwasher tabs, and if available fit tool 18G1341 to the balljoint socket, retaining it in position with the balljoint nut.

8   Hold the driving flange and swivel hub stationary, then unscrew the balljoint socket and remove the lockwasher. Remove the tool if used.

9   Fitting a new balljoint is a reversal of the removal procedure. Apply two beads of Loctite 245, diametrically opposite each other, to the thread. Tighten the balljoint and nut to the specified torques within 15

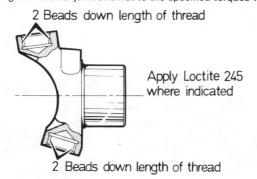

2 Beads down length of thread

Apply Loctite 245 where indicated

2 Beads down length of thread

Fig. 11.4 Sectional view of swivel hub upper balljoint, showing application of thread locking compound (Sec 9)

minutes of Loctite application. Lock the balljoint by bending two opposite tabs of the lockwasher over the sides of the swivel hub. Lock the balljoint nut by bending the tab washer over the suspension arm and nut.

10 Front hub assembly – removal, overhaul and refitting

1   Turn the steering as necessary to allow access from the front, and remove the rebound buffer from the subframe on the relevant side. The buffer is located beneath the suspension upper arm and is secured by two cross-head screws.

2   Insert a distance piece such as a suitably-sized nut in place of the buffer to retain the suspension in the normal running position.

3   Extract the split pin from the end of the driveshaft and loosen the nut while an assistant depresses the footbrake pedal.

4   Apply the handbrake, jack up the front of the car, and support it on axle stands. Remove the roadwheel.

5   Remove the brake caliper as described in Chapter 9, but leave the hydraulic hoses connected, and support the caliper on a stand without straining the hoses. Remove the disc shield.

6   Unscrew the driveshaft nut and remove the split collar.

7   Slide the drive flange and disc assembly from the driveshaft, using a puller if necessary.

8   Flatten the tab washers and unscrew the swivel hub upper and lower balljoint nuts (photo). Remove the tab washers.

9   Unscrew and remove the tie-rod end nut.

10 Using a separator tool, release the tie-rod end from the steering arm, and the suspension arms from the balljoints.

11 While tapping the end of the driveshaft with a mallet, withdraw the swivel hub assembly. If the inner bearing inner race remains on the driveshaft, use a suitable puller to remove it.

12 If necessary, remove the water shield from the driveshaft.

13 Prise out the inner oil seal and remove the spacer.

14 Prise out the outer oil seal. Note that the oil seals are not the same.

15 Using a soft metal drift, drive out one of the bearing inner races, then invert the hub and drive out the complete opposite bearing. Invert the hub again and drive out the remaining outer race.

16 Clean the hub, bearings and driveshaft stub with paraffin and wipe dry. Examine the components for wear and damage. Inspect the bearing balls and races for wear and pitting. Renew the components as necessary and obtain new oil seals.

17 Lubricate the bearings with multi-purpose lithium based grease, then drive them into the swivel hub with the marked ends facing outwards. Use a length of tubing on the outer races only.

18 Fit the spacer against the inner bearing.

19 Dip the oil seals in engine oil, then press them into the swivel hub with their lips facing inwards. Use a block of wood to locate the outer seal flush with the hub, and use a length of metal tubing to locate the

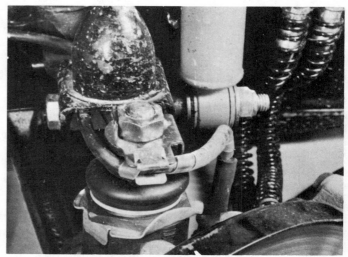

10.8 Swivel hub upper balljoint

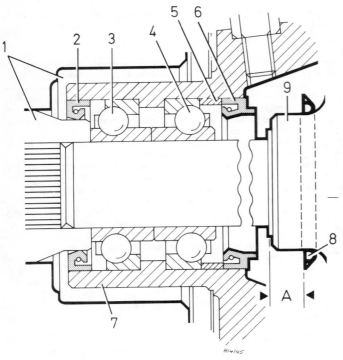

Fig. 11.5 Cross-sectional view of the front hub (Sec 10)

1 Driving flange and disc	5 Spacer
2 Outer oil seal	6 Inner oil seal
3 Outer bearing	7 Swivel hub
4 Inner bearing	8 Water shield
	9 Driveshaft

Dimension 'A' = 0.25 in (6.4 mm)

inner seal against the spacer.

20 Press grease into the spaces between the bearings and oil seals.

21 Press the water shield onto the driveshaft with reference to dimension 'A' Fig. 11.5. Fill the water shield groove with grease.

22 Locate the swivel hub over the end of the driveshaft and, using a length of metal tubing against the outer bearing inner race, tap the inner races fully onto the driveshaft.

23 The remaining refitting procedure is a reversal of removal, but tighten the nuts to the specified torque. Lock the balljoint nuts by bending the tab washers over the suspension arms and nuts. Refer to Chapter 8 for the driveshaft nut tightening procedure.

11 Rear Hydragas unit – removal and refitting

1 Have the rear Hydragas units depressurized by a BL garage.

2 Chock the front wheels, jack up the rear of the car and support it on stands. Remove the roadwheel.

3 Disconnect and plug the interconnecting pipe from the Hydragas unit.

4 Unbolt the bump rubber and reaction strap from the body (photos).

5 Unbolt the shield and clamp plate from the subframe.

6 Withdraw the Hydragas unit, helper spring and strut, together with the return spring from the subframe and knuckle joint.

7 Prise the knuckle joint assembly from the radius arm.

8 Note that if the three-way connector in front of the left-hand rear wheel is removed, it must always be refitted with the restricted drilling in the line between the two rear Hydragas units (photo).

9 Check the knuckle joint for wear, and renew it if necessary.

10 Refitting is a reversal of removal, but lubricate the knuckle joint with a multi-purpose lithium based grease. Have the rear Hydragas units pressurized by a BL garage.

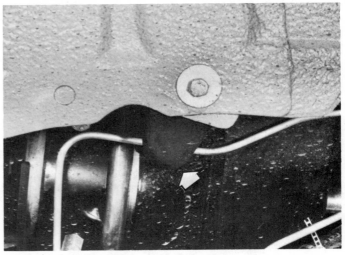

11.4A Rear suspension bump rubber (arrowed) ...

11.4B ... Hydragas unit ...

11.4C ... and reaction strap inner mounting nut (arrowed)

11.8 Rear Hydragas interconnecting pipe and three-way connector

12 Rear suspension radius arm – removal, overhaul and refitting

1   Remove the rear Hydragas unit as described in Section 11.
2   Release the handbrake, then remove the clevis pin and disconnect the handbrake cable from the backplate and bracket.
3   Remove the brake fluid reservoir filler cap, wrap thin polythene over the level warning switch and tighten the cap onto the polythene. This will help prevent brake fluid from being lost in the subsequent procedure.
4   Unscrew the rigid brake pipe union, then unscrew the nut and remove the flexible hose from the bracket in the radius arm (photo).
5   Unscrew the nuts from each end of the pivot shaft, and unbolt the retaining plate from the subframe (photos). Remove the outer thrust washer.
6   Support the radius arm with a jack, then tap out the pivot shaft from the inside.
7   Withdraw the radius arm and collect the inner thrust washer and both sealing rings.
8   If necessary, remove the brake shoes and backplate as described in Chapter 9.
9   If the bearings are to be renewed, drive them out of the radius arm and remove the lubricating tube.
10   Clean all the components with paraffin and examine them for wear and damage. Renew them as necessary and obtain new sealing rings. Make sure that the lubricating drillings in the shaft are unobstructed.
11   Drive one needle roller bearing into the outer end of the radius arm with its stamped end outwards and to a depth of 0.2 in (5 mm).
12   Insert the lubricating tube with the splined end towards the outer bearing, and drive the second needle roller bearing into the radius arm

with the stamped end facing outwards.
13   Locate the large thrust washer with its grooved side against the inner end of the radius arm, and fit the wide sealing ring over it.
14   Fit the narrow sealing ring to the outer end of the radius arm.
15   Support the radius arm in the subframe, and insert the pivot shaft with the grease nipple outwards.
16   Fit the small thrust washer with the chamfer against the shaft, install the retaining plate, and tighten the bolts.
17   Fit the spring washers and nuts to the pivot shaft and tighten them to the specified torque.
18   Using a grease gun, lubricate the radius arm bearings with the recommended grease.
19   Reconnect the brake flexible hose and rigid pipe to the bracket. Reconnect the handbrake cable.
20   Remove the polythene from the brake fluid reservoir, then adjust and bleed the brakes as described in Chapter 9.
21   Refit the rear Hydragas unit as described in Section 11.

13 Rear hub assembly – removal, overhaul and refitting

1   Chock the front wheels, jack up the rear of the car, and support it on axle stands. Remove the roadwheel and release the handbrake.
2   Remove the securing screws and withdraw the brake drum; loosen the adjuster if necessary.
3   Brush clean the backplate, but do not inhale the brake dust as it is injurious to health.
4   Using a soft metal punch, tap the grease cap on alternate sides, and remove it (photo).
5   Extract the split pin and unscrew the hub nut. Remove the plain washer.
6   Using a suitable puller, remove the hub from the stub shaft. If the inner bearing inner race remains in the stub shaft, use a puller to remove it.
7   Prise out the oil seal with a screwdriver.
8   Using a soft metal drift, drive out one of the bearing inner races, then insert the hub and drive out the complete opposite bearing. Insert the hub again and drive out the remaining outer race.
9   Clean all the components in paraffin and examine them for damage and wear. Check the bearing balls and races for wear and pitting. Renew the components as necessary and obtain a new oil seal. If the wheel studs are worn or damaged, drive them out and install new ones.
10   Lubricate the bearings with multi-purpose lithium based grease, then drive them into the hub with their marked ends outwards, using a length of metal tube on the outer races.
11   Dip the oil seal in engine oil, then press it into the hub with the lip facing inwards.
12   Wipe clean the stub shaft and oil seal bearing surface. Locate the hub on the stub shaft and use a length of metal tube to drive the inner races onto the shaft.
13   Fit the plain washer and tighten the nut to the specified torque.
14   Lock the nut with a new split pin and tap the grease cap into the hub.
15   Refit the brake drum and wheel, adjust the brakes, and lower the car to the ground.

12.4 Brake pipe and hose connection on rear suspension radius arm

12.5A Rear suspension arm pivot shaft inner nut

12.5B Rear suspension arm outer mounting

13.4 Removing the rear hub grease cap

14.2 Removing the steering wheel central cover

15.3 Steering column and wiring multi-plug

17.3A Steering tie-rod end balljoint

17.3B Using a separator tool to release the tie-rod end balljoint

14 Steering wheel – removal and refitting

1   Set the front wheels in the straight-ahead position.
2   Prise the cover from the centre of the steering wheel (photo).
3   Unscrew and remove the retaining nut and mark the steering wheel and inner column in relation to each other.
4   Withdraw the steering wheel from the inner column splines.
5   Refitting is the reversal of removal, but align the previously made marks, and tighten the retaining nut to the specified torque.

15 Steering column – removal, overhaul and refitting

1   Remove the steering wheel as described in Section 14.
2   Lift the carpet, remove the coupling cover, and unbolt the inner column from the flexible coupling. Carefully note how the bolts are positioned to ensure they are refitted correctly.
3   Remove the steering column cowls with reference to Chapter 10. Disconnect the multi-plugs (photo).
4   Unscrew the top and bottom mountings and withdraw the steering column assembly from the car.
5   Remove the switch assembly. Unbolt the upper column, withdraw the inner column, and remove the top bush halves.
6   Clean the components in paraffin and wipe dry. Examine the bush for wear and renew it if necessary.
7   Reassembly and refitting is a reversal of removal and dismantling, but it is important to tighten the column mounting bolts in the following manner after loosening the lower clip. With the mounting bolts finger tight and the inner column attached to the flexible coupling, move the outer column until it is concentric with the inner column. Tighten the mounting bolts and lower clip while holding the outer column in the same position.

16 Steering column lock/ignition switch – removal and refitting

1   Remove the steering column as described in Section 15.
2   Drill out the shear bolt heads from the lock clamp, and remove the lock/ignition switch from the outer column.
3   Locate the lock body centrally over the slot in the outer column, and lightly bolt the clamp into position without shearing the heads.
4   Refit the steering column as described in Section 15, but before fitting the cowls, check that the lock and ignition switch operate correctly.
5   Tighten the clamp bolts until the bolt heads shear off, then refit the cowls.

17 Tie-rod end balljoint – removal and refitting

1   Apply the handbrake, jack up the front of the car, and support it on axle stands. Remove the roadwheel.
2   Loosen the tie-rod end adjustment locknut a quarter of a turn.
3   Unscrew the balljoint nut and detach the balljoint from the steering arm using a separator tool (photos).
4   Unscrew the tie-rod end from the tie-rod.
5   Refitting is a reversal of removal, but tighten the nuts to the specified torque. and check the front wheel alignment, making any adjustment as necessary (see Section 19).

18 Steering rack gaiter – renewal

1   Remove the tie-rod end balljoint as described in Section 17.
2   Loosen the clips on the tie-rod and steering gear housing, and remove the gaiter.
3   Lubricate the contact surfaces of the gaiter with steering gear

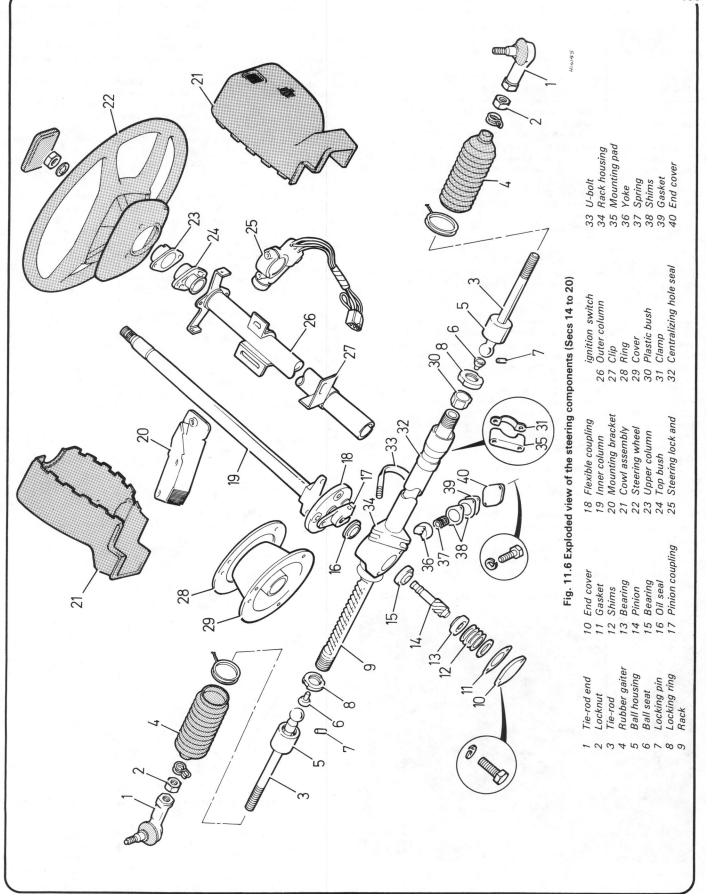

H14145

Fig. 11.6 Exploded view of the steering components (Secs 14 to 20)

1 Tie-rod end
2 Locknut
3 Tie-rod
4 Rubber gaiter
5 Ball housing
6 Ball seat
7 Locking pin
8 Locking ring
9 Rack

10 End cover
11 Gasket
12 Shims
13 Bearing
14 Pinion
15 Bearing
16 Oil seal
17 Pinion coupling

18 Flexible coupling
19 Inner column
20 Mounting bracket
21 Cowl assembly
22 Steering wheel
23 Upper column
24 Top bush
25 Steering lock and

ignition switch
26 Outer column
27 Clip
28 Ring
29 Cover
30 Plastic bush
31 Clamp
32 Centralizing hole seal

33 U-bolt
34 Rack housing
35 Mounting pad
36 Yoke
37 Spring
38 Shims
39 Gasket
40 End cover

grease, then locate it over the tie-rod and housing.
4   Secure the gaiter with the two clips.
5   Refit the tie-rod end balljoint as described in Section 17.

19 Wheel alignment – checking and adjusting

1   Accurate wheel adjustment is essential for good steering and slow tyre wear. Before checking it, make sure that the car is only loaded to kerbside weight (ie with a full fuel tank), the tyres are correctly inflated, and the suspension trim heights are correct.
2   Place the car on level ground with the wheels in the straight-ahead position, then roll the car backwards 12 ft (4 metres) and forwards again.
3   Using a wheel alignment gauge, check that the front wheel toe-out dimension is as given in the Specifications.
4   If adjustment is necessary, loosen the tie-rod end locknuts on both tie-rods and release the small gaiter clips.
5   Rotate each tie-rod by equal amounts until the alignment is correct. There must be equal amounts of visible thread on each tie-rod.
6   Tighten the locknuts and refit the gaiter clips.
7   Camber and castor angles are preset and cannot be adjusted. However, if their accuracy is suspect, they can be checked by a suitably equipped garage.

20 Steering rack and pinion – removal, overhaul and refitting

1   Disconnect the battery negative lead.
2   Jack up the front of the car and support it on stands. Apply the handbrake and remove both front wheels. Centralize the steering.
3   Lift the carpet, remove the coupling cover, and disconnect the pinion coupling from the flexible coupling. Carefully note how the bolts are positioned to ensure they are refitted correctly.
4   Unscrew the tie-rod end balljoint nuts and use a separator tool to detach the balljoints from the steering arms.
5   Unscrew the nuts and bolts and remove the U-bolt and mounting pad and clamp (photo).
6   Rotate the rack assembly and withdraw it from the driver's side of the subframe.
7   Remove the tie-rod ends, locknuts, gaiters and clips with reference to Sections 17 and 18.
8   The inner tie-rod ball housings are locked to the rack by pins. Drill out the pins with a $\frac{5}{32}$ in (4 mm) drill to a depth of 0.248 in (6.3 mm).
9   Loosen the locking rings, then unscrew the ball housings using a pipe wrench. Identify the housings and tie-rods side for side.
10 Remove the ball seats and unscrew the locking rings.
11 Unbolt the damper cover plate and remove the gasket, shims, spring and yoke.
12 Remove the clamp bolt and pull the coupling from the pinion.

13 Unbolt the pinion end cover, remove the gasket and shims, and drive out the pinion and lower bearing.
14 Withdraw the rack from the pinion end of the housing, drive out the pinion upper bearing and oil seal, and remove the plastic bush from the housing.
15 Clean all components in paraffin and wipe dry. Examine them for wear and damage, and renew them as necessary.
16 During reassembly pack the pinion end of the rack with 80cc of semi-fluid grease (such as Duckhams Adgear 00), and the opposite end with 20cc.
17 Commence reassembly by engaging the plastic bush with the slots in the support end of the housing.
18 Insert the pinion upper bearing, then insert the rack from the pinion end. Centralize the rack with a 6 mm bolt through the centre of the housing.
19 Insert the pinion and the lower bearing. Fit the end cover without a gasket and with an excess of shims. Note that the *damper* bolts are longer and must not be used on the pinion end cover. Determine the gap ('A' in Fig. 11.7) using feeler blades, and adjust the shim pack to obtain the specified gap which takes into consideration the gasket thickness. The specified standard shim must be next to the cover. Fit the gasket and tighten the bolts.
20 Press a new pinion oil seal into the housing.
21 Fit the coupling to the pinion with the studs parallel to the rack.
22 Install the damper yoke without the spring, and the cover plate without a gasket. Lightly tighten the bolts to clamp the rack, remove the centralizing bolt, and rotate the pinion half a turn in each direction. If necessary loosen the bolts fractionally to allow free rack movement. Determine the gap ('B' in Fig. 11.7) using feeler blades. The shims to fit are the measured gap plus the specified yoke-to-cover plate clearance, less 0.005 in (0.13 mm) for the gasket thickness.
23 Remove the cover plate, and fit the spring, shim pack and gasket. Refit the plate and tighten the bolts. Check that the pinion turns freely. If possible check that the pinion starting torque is between 5 and 18 lbf in (0.06 and 0.21 kgf m).
24 Centralize the rack again with the bolt.
25 Smear grease on the tie-rod ball, the install the locking ring, ball seat, tie-rod, and ball housing.
26 Tighten the ball housing until the tie-rod is just pinched, then

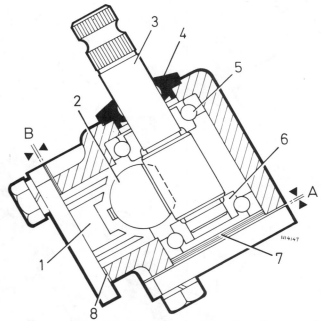

Fig. 11.7 Cross-sectional view of the steering pinion bearing
(Sec 20)

1	Yoke	5	Upper bearing
2	Rack	6	Lower bearing
3	Pinion	7	Preload shims
4	Oil seal	8	Yoke shims

A and B – see text

20.5 Steering rack and pinion U-bolt mounting nuts (arrowed)

tighten the locking ring.

27 Using a spring balance, check that the torque required to move the tie-rod 25 degrees from the rack centre line is between 50 and 65 lbf in (0.57 and 0.73 kgf m). If necessary, loosen the locking ring and adjust the ball housing.

28 Lock the ball housing and locking ring by drilling to a depth of 0.41 in (10.3 mm) with a $\frac{5}{32}$ in (4 mm) drill, and driving in a new pin. Note that the new hole must be at least 90 degrees from any previous holes, and that only three holes may be drilled (refer to Fig. 11.8).

29 Retain the pin by peening the hole in four places.

30 Repeat the procedure given in paragraphs 25 to 29 on the remaining side.

31 Fit the gaiters, locknuts and tie-rod ends with reference to Sections 17 and 18, noting that the gaiters and inner clips are different for each side. Adjust the tie-rod ends equally on each side to obtain the specified rack ball-pin centre dimension.

32 Remove the rack centralizing bolt and move the rubber band over the hole.

33 Refitting is a reversal of removal, but tighten all nuts and bolts to the specified torque, and adjust the front wheel alignment as described in Section 19.

21 Roadwheels and tyres – general

1 Clean the insides of the roadwheels whenever they are removed. If necessary, remove any rust and repaint them.

2 At the same time remove any flints or stones which may have become embedded in the tyres. Examine the tyres for damage and splits. Where the depth of tread is almost down to the legal minimum, renew them.

3 The wheels should be rebalanced half way through the life of the tyres to compensate for loss of rubber.

4 Check and adjust the tyre pressures regularly and make sure that the dust caps are correctly fitted. Remember to also check the spare tyre.

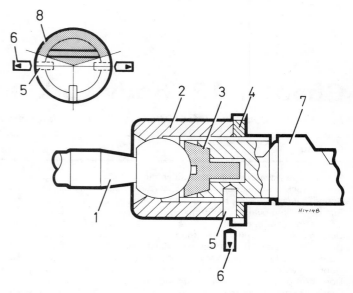

Fig. 11.8 Cross-sectional view of the steering rack end joint (Sec 20)

1 Tie-rod	7 Rack
2 Ball housing	8 Rack end view showing
3 Ball seat	permissible locking pin
4 Locking ring	drillings – do not drill
5 Drilled hole	in shaded area
6 Locking pin	

22 Fault diagnosis – suspension and steering

Symptom	Reason(s)
Excessive play in steering	Worn rack and pinion or tie-rods Worn tie-rod end balljoints Worn swivel hub balljoints
Wanders or pulls to one side	Incorrect wheel alignment Worn tie-rod end balljoints Worn swivel hub balljoints Uneven tyre pressures
Heavy or stiff steering	Seized balljoint Incorrect wheel alignment Low tyre pressures Lack of lubricant in rack and pinion
Wheel wobble and vibration	Roadwheels out of balance Roadwheels damaged Worn shock absorbers Worn wheel bearings
Excessive tyre wear	Incorrect wheel alignment Worn shock absorbers Incorrect tyre pressures Roadwheels out of balance
Low suspension ride height	Leaking Hydragas unit or rear interconnecting pipe

Chapter 12 Bodywork and fittings

For modifications and information applicable to later models, see Supplement at end of manual

Contents

Bonnet – removal, refitting and adjustment	8
Bonnet lock – adjustment	16
Bonnet release cable – removal and refitting	15
Bumpers – removal and refitting	24
Door – removal and refitting	18
Door glass – removal and refitting	21
Door lock – removal, refitting and adjustment	19
Door private lock – removal and refitting	20
Door rattles – tracing and rectification	7
Door trim pad – removal and refitting	17
Facia – removal and refitting	25
Front wing – removal and refitting	9
General description	1
Heater – adjustment	27
Heater and heater radiator – removal and refitting	26
Heater motor – removal and refitting	28
Maintenance – bodywork and underframe	2
Maintenance – hinges and locks	6
Maintenance – upholstery and carpets	3
Major body damage – repair	5
Minor body damage – repair	4
Rear quarterlight glass – removal and refitting	14
Seats – removal and refitting	23
Subframes – removal and refitting	29
Tailgate – removal and refitting	10
Tailgate glass – removal and refitting	13
Tailgate support strut – removal and refitting	11
Window regulator – removal and refitting	22
Windscreen glass – removal and refitting	12

1 General description

The bodyshell and underframe is of all-steel welded construction and is of computer based design. The assembly and welding of the main body unit is completed entirely by computer controlled robots, and the finished unit is checked for dimensional accuracy using modern computer and laser technology.

The front wings are bolted in position and are detachable should renewal be necessary after a front end collision.

2 Maintenance – bodywork and underframe

1 The general condition of a car's bodywork is the thing that significantly affects it value. Maintenance is easy but needs to be regular. Neglect, particularly after minor damage, can lead quickly to further deterioration and costly repair bills. It is important also to keep watch on those parts of the car not immediately visible, for instance the underside, inside all the wheel arches and the lower part of the engine compartment.

2 The basic maintenance routine for the bodywork is washing – preferably with a lot of water, from a hose. This will remove all the loose solids which may have stuck to the car. It is important to flush these off in such a way as to prevent grit from scratching the finish. The wheel arches and underframe need washing in the same way to remove any accumulated mud which will retain moisture and tend to encourage rust. Paradoxically enough, the best time to clean the underframe and wheel arches is in wet weather when the mud is thoroughly wet and soft. In very wet weather the underframe is usually cleaned of large accumulations automatically and this is a good time for inspection.

3 Periodically, it is a good idea to have the whole of the underframe of the car steam cleaned, engine compartment included, so that a thorough inspection can be carried out to see what minor repairs and renovations are necessary. Steam cleaning is available at many garages and is necessary for removal of the accumulation of oily grime which sometimes is allowed to become thick in certain areas. If steam cleaning facilities are not available, there are one or two excellent grease solvents available which can be brush applied. The dirt can then be simply hosed off.

4 After washing paintwork, wipe off with a chamois leather to give an unspotted clear finish. A coat of clear protective wax polish will give added protection against chemical pollutants in the air. If the paintwork sheen has dulled or oxidised, use a cleaner/polisher combination to restore the brilliance of the shine. This requires a little effort, but such dulling is usually caused because regular washing has been neglected. Always check that the door and ventilator opening drain holes and pipes are completely clear so that water can be drained out (photos). Bright work should be treated in the same way as paintwork. Windscreens and windows can be kept clear of the smeary film which often appears, by adding a little ammonia to the water. If they are scratched, a good rub with a proprietary metal polish will often clear them. Never use any form of wax or other body or chromium polish on glass.

3 Maintenance – upholstery and carpets

1 Mats and carpets should be brushed or vacuum cleaned regularly to keep them free of grit. If they are badly stained remove them from the car for scrubbing or sponging and make quite sure they are dry before refitting. Seats and interior trim panels can be kept clean by a wipe over with a damp cloth. If they do become stained (which can be more apparent on light coloured upholstery) use a little liquid detergent and a soft nail brush to scour the grime out of the grain of the material. Do not forget to keep the head lining clean in the same way as the upholstery. When using liquid cleaners inside the car do not over-wet the surfaces being cleaned. Excessive damp could get into the seams and padded interior causing stains, offensive odours or even rot. If the inside of the car gets wet accidentally it is worthwhile taking some trouble to dry it out properly, particularly where carpets are involved. *Do not leave oil or electric heaters inside the car for this purpose.*

4 Minor body damage – repair

The photographic sequences on pages 166 and 167 illustrate the operations detailed in the following sub-sections.

Repair of minor scratches in the car's bodywork

If the scratch is very superficial, and does not penetrate to the metal of the bodywork, repair is very simple. Lightly rub the area of the scratch with a paintwork renovator, or a very fine cutting paste, to remove loose paint from the scratch and to clear the surrounding bodywork of wax polish. Rinse the area with clean water.

Apply touch-up paint to the scratch using a fine paint brush; continue to apply thin layers of paint until the surface of the paint in

2.4A Clearing a front valance drain hole with a piece of wire

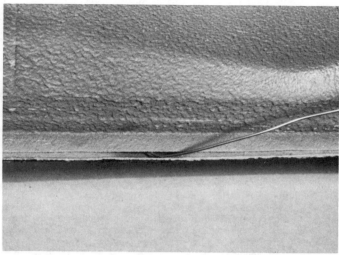

2.4B Clearing a sill panel drain hole with a piece of wire

the scratch is level with the surrounding paintwork. Allow the new paint at least two weeks to harden: then blend it into the surrounding paintwork by rubbing the scratch area with a paintwork renovator or a very fine cutting paste. Finally, apply wax polish.

Where the scratch has penetrated right through to the metal of the bodywork, causing the metal to rust, a different repair technique is required. Remove any loose rust from the bottom of the scratch with a penknife, then apply rust inhibiting paint to prevent the formation of rust in the future. Using a rubber or nylon applicator fill the scratch with bodystopper paste. If required, this paste can be mixed with cellulose thinners to provide a very thin paste which is ideal for filling narrow scratches. Before the stopper-paste in the scratch hardens, wrap a piece of smooth cotton rag around the top of a finger. Dip the finger in cellulose thinners and then quickly sweep it across the surface of the stopper-paste in the scratch; this will ensure that the surface of the stopper-paste is slightly hollowed. The scratch can now be painted over as described earlier in this Section.

Repair of dents in the car's bodywork

When deep denting of the car's bodywork has taken place, the first task is to pull the dent out, until the affected bodywork almost attains its original shape. There is little point in trying to restore the original shape completely, as the metal in the damaged area will have stretched on impact and cannot be reshaped fully to its original contour. It is better to bring the level of the dent up to a point which is about $\frac{1}{8}$ in (3 mm) below the level of the surrounding bodywork. In cases where the dent is very shallow anyway, it is not worth trying to pull it out at all. If the underside of the dent is accessible, it can be hammered out gently from behind, using a mallet with a wooden or plastic head. Whilst doing this, hold a suitable block of wood firmly against the outside of the panel to absorb the impact from the hammer blows and thus prevent a large area of the bodywork from being 'belled-out'.

Should the dent be in a section of the bodywork which has double skin or some other factor making it inaccessible from behind, a different technique is called for. Drill several small holes through the metal inside the area – particularly in the deeper section. Then screw long self-tapping screws into the holes just sufficiently for them to gain a good purchase in the metal. Now the dent can be pulled out by pulling on the protruding heads of the screws with a pair of pliers.

The next stage of the repair is the removal of the paint from the damaged area, and from an inch or so of the surrounding 'sound' bodywork. This is accomplished most easily by using a wire brush or abrasive pad on a power drill, although it can be done just as effectively by hand using sheets of abrasive paper. To complete the preparation for filling, score the surface of the bare metal with a screwdriver or the tang of a file, or alternatively, drill small holes in the affected area. This will provide a really good 'key' for the filler paste.

To complete the repair see the Section on filling and re-spraying.

Repair of rust holes or gashes in the car's bodywork

Remove all paint from the affected area and from an inch or so of the surrounding 'sound' bodywork, using an abrasive pad or a wire brush on a power drill. If these are not available a few sheets of abrasive paper will do the job just as effectively. With the paint removed you will be able to gauge the severity of the corrosion and therefore decide whether to renew the whole panel (if this is possible) or to repair the affected area. New body panels are not as expensive as most people think and it is often quicker and more satisfactory to fit a new panel than to attempt to repair large areas of corrosion.

Remove all fittings from the affected area except those which will act as a guide to the original shape of the damaged bodywork (eg headlamp shells etc). Then, using tin snips or a hacksaw blade, remove all loose metal and any other metal badly affected by corrosion. Hammer the edges of the hole inwards in order to create a slight depression for the filler paste.

Wire brush the affected area to remove the powdery rust from the surface of the remaining metal. Paint the affected area with rust inhibiting paint; if the back of the rusted area is accessible treat this also.

Before filling can take place it will be necessary to block the hole in some way. This can be achieved by the use of aluminium or plastic mesh, or aluminium tape.

Aluminium or plastic mesh is probably the best material to use for a large hole. Cut a piece to the approximate size and shape of the hole to be filled, then position it in the hole so that its edges are below the level of the surrounding bodywork. It can be retained in position by several blobs of filler paste around its periphery.

Aluminium tape should be used for small or very narrow holes. Pull a piece off the roll and trim it to the approximate size and shape required, then pull off the backing paper (if used) and stick the tape over the hole; it can be overlapped if the thickness of one piece is insufficient. Burnish down the edges of the tape with the handle of a screwdriver or similar, to ensure that the tape is securely attached to the metal underneath.

Bodywork repairs – filling and re-spraying

Before using this Section, see the Sections on dent, deep scratch, rust holes and gash repairs.

Many types of bodyfiller are available, but generally speaking those proprietary kits which contain a tin of filler paste and a tube of resin hardener are best for this type of repair. A wide, flexible plastic or nylon applicator will be found invaluable for imparting a smooth and well contoured finish to the surface of the filler.

Mix up a little filler on a clean piecce of card or board – measure the hardener carefully (follow the maker's instructions on the pack) otherwise the filler will set too rapidly or too slowly.

Using the applicator apply the filler paste to the prepared area; draw the applicator across the surface of the filler to achieve the correct contour and to level the filler surface. As soon as a contour that approximates the correct one is achieved, stop working the paste – if you carry on too long the paste will become sticky and begin to 'pick up' on the applicator. Continue to add thin layers of filler paste at twenty-minute intervals until the level of the filler is just proud of the surrounding bodywork.

Once the filler has hardened, excess can be removed using a metal plane or file. From then on, progressively finer grades of sandpaper should be used, starting with a 40 grade production paper and finishing with 400 grade wet-and-dry paper. Always wrap the abrasive paper around a flat rubber, cork, or wooden block – otherwise the surface of the filler will not be completely flat. During the smoothing of the filler surface the wet-and-dry paper should be periodically rinsed in water. This will ensure that a very smooth finish is imparted to the filler at the final stage.

At this stage the 'repair area' should be surrounded by a ring of bare metal, which in turn should be encircled by the finely 'feathered' edge of the good paintwork. Rinse the repair area with clean water, until all of the dust produced by the rubbing-down operation has gone.

Spray the whole repair area with a light coat of primer – this will show up any imperfections in the surface of the filler. Repair these imperfections with fresh filler paste or bodystopper, and once more smooth the surface with abrasive paper. If bodystopper is used, it can be mixed with cellulose thinners to form a really thin paste which is ideal for filling small holes. Repeat this spray and repair procedure until you are satisfied that the surface of the filler, and the feathered edge of the paintwork are perfect. Clean the repair area with clean water and allow to dry fully.

The repair area is now ready for final spraying. Paint spraying must be carried out in warm, dry, windless and dust free atmosphere. This condition can be created artificially if you have access to a large indoor working area, but if you are forced to work in the open, you will have to pick your day very carefully. If you are working indoors, dousing the floor in the work area with water will help to settle the dust which would otherwise be in the atmosphere. If the repair area is confined to one body panel, mask off the surrounding panels; this will help to minimise the effects of a slight mis-match in paint colours. Bodywork fittings (eg chrome strips, door handles etc) will also need to be masked off. Use genuine masking tape and several thicknesses of newspaper for the masking operations.

Before commencing to spray, agitate the aerosol can thoroughly, then spray a test area (an old tin, or similar) until the technique is mastered. Cover the repair area with a thick coat of primer; the thickness should be built up using several thin layers of paint rather than one thick one. Using 400 grade wet-and-dry paper, rub down the surface of the primer until it is really smooth. While doing this, the work area should be thoroughly doused with water, and the wet-and-dry paper periodically rinsed in water. Allow to dry before spraying on more paint.

Spray on the top coat, again building up the thickness by using several thin layers of paint. Start spraying in the centre of the repair area and then, using a circular motion, work outwards until the whole

repair area and about 2 inches of the surrounding original paintwork is covered. Remove all masking material 10 to 15 minutes after spraying on the final coat of paint.

Allow the new paint at least two weeks to harden, then, using a paintwork renovator or a very fine cutting paste, blend the edges of the paint into the existing paintwork. Finally, apply wax polish.

5 Major body damage – repair

Where serious damage has occurred or large areas need renewal due to neglect, it means certainly that completely new sections or panels will need welding in and this is best left to professionals. If the damage is due to impact, it will also be necessary to completely check the alignment of the bodyshell structure. Due to the principle of construction, the strength and shape of the whole car can be affected by damage to one part. In such instances the services of a BL agent with specialist checking jigs are essential. If a body is left misaligned, it is first of all dangerous as the car will not handle properly, and secondly uneven stresses will be imposed on the steering, engine and transmission, causing abnormal wear or complete failure. Tyre wear may also be excessive.

6 Maintenance – hinges and locks

1   Oil the hinges of the bonnet, tailgate and door with a drop or two of light oil every 12 000 miles (20 000 km) or 12 months, whichever occurs first.
2   At the same time, lightly oil the bonnet release mechanism and all door locks.
3   Do not attempt to lubricate the steering lock.

7 Door rattles – tracing and rectification

1   Check first that the door is not loose at the hinges, and that the latch is holding the door firmly in position. Check also that the door lines up with the aperture in the body. If the door is out of alignment, adjust it as described in Sections 18 and 19.
2   If the latch is holding the door in the correct position but the latch still rattles, the lock mechanism is worn and should be renewed.
3   Other rattles from the door could be caused by wear in the window operating mechanism, interior lock mechanism, or loose glass channels.

8 Bonnet – removal, refitting and adjustment

1   Support the bonnet in its open position, and place some cardboard or rags beneath the corners by the hinges.
2   Mark the location of the hinges with a pencil, then loosen the four retaining nuts and bolts (photo).
3   With the help of an assistant, release the stay, unscrew and remove the retaining bolts, and withdraw the bonnet from the car.
4   Refitting is a reversal of removal, but adjust the hinges to their original positions. The bonnet rear edge should be flush with the scuttle and the gaps at either side equal.

9 Front wing – removal and refitting

1   Support the bonnet in its open position.
2   Pull the bulb holder from the side repeater lamp.
3   Unscrew the bolt from behind the wing and remove the bumper end capping. Remove the aerial where applicable.
4   Loosen the wing retaining bolt in the top of the door shut, and remove the remaining bolts.
5   Withdraw the front wing from the car.
6   Refitting is a reversal of removal, but use a sealer compound to seal the wing to the body.

10 Tailgate – removal and refitting

1   Disconnect the battery negative lead.

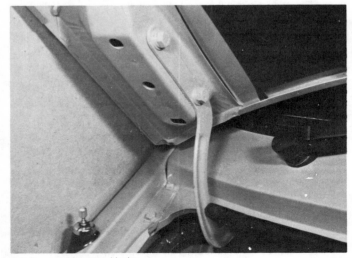
8.2 Bonnet hinge and bolts

2   Unhook the parcel shelf support cords.

3   Prise out the tailgate trim pad.

4   Disconnect the washer tube from the jet and the wiper wires from the multi-plug, tape them together, and tie a draw cord to them.

5   Prise out the rubber grommet and pull the wires and tube through the tailgate until the cord emerges, then untie the cord but leave it in the tailgate.

6   Disconnect the wire from the heated rear window and attach a cord to it. Prise out the grommet and pull the wire through, then untie the cord but leave it in position.

7   Using a pencil, mark the position of the hinges.

8   With the help of an assistant, support the tailgate, then prise out the locking pegs and detach the support struts from the tailgate.

9   Using an impact screwdriver, remove the hinge screws from the tailgate, then withdraw the tailgate from the car (photo).

10 Refitting is a reversal of removal, but adjust the hinges to their original positions and if necessary adjust the striker (photo).

11 Tailgate support strut – removal and refitting

1   With the tailgate open, unhook the parcel shelf support cords and have an assistant support the tailgate.

2   Using a small screwdriver, prise out the locking pegs and detach the support strut from the tailgate and body (photos).

3   Refitting is a reversal of removal.

12 Windscreen glass – removal and refitting

1   If the windscreen has shattered, cover the facia panel and air vents with a large sheet of polythene to catch the pieces of glass. If available, adhesive sheeting will facilitate the removal of the shattered windscreen. Remove all of the glass.

2   Remove the windscreen wiper arms and the interior mirror.

3   If the windscreen is to be removed intact, release the rubber surround from the bodywork with a blunt screwdriver, taking care not to damage the paintwork. Have an assistant support the windscreen, then sit inside and push the screen and rubber from the aperture using the feet (suitably padded) if necessary.

4   Remove the rubber surround.

5   Examine the rubber surround for damage or deterioration and renew it if necessary. Clean the sealer from the body aperture and repair any damage or distortion of the flange.

6   Fit the rubber surround to the windscreen with the drain holes at the bottom.

7   Obtain a length of strong cord and insert it into the flange groove of the rubber surround with the free ends overlapping at the bottom.

8   Locate the windscreen on the aperture and have an assistant press gently from the outside.

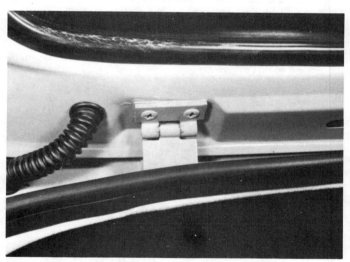

10.9 Tailgate hinge and bellows

10.10 Tailgate striker

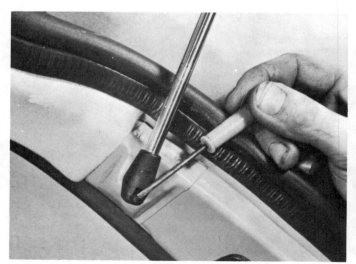

11.2A Releasing the tailgate strut locking peg

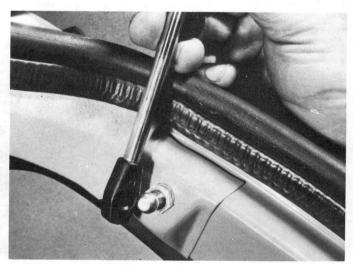

11.2B Removing the tailgate strut

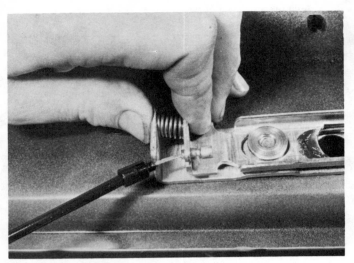

15.2 Removing the bonnet release cable

16.1 The bonnet lockpin

9   From inside the car, pull each end of the cord in turn to locate the rubber surround onto the flange. Tap the glass with the palm of the hand to make sure that it is fully seated.
10 Fit the interior mirror and wiper arms.

13 Tailgate glass – removal and refitting

1   The procedure is similar to that for the windscreen described in Section 12, except that it is necessary to unhook the parcel shelf support cords, disconnect the heated rear window feed wire and earth strap, and remove the wiper arm and rubber grommet.
2   Refitting is a reversal of removal.

14 Rear quarterlight glass – removal and refitting

1   The procedure is similar to that for the windscreen described in Section 12, except that it is necessary to fold the relevant rear seat forwards.
2   When fitting the glass, apply sealer between the outer part of the rubber surround and the glass and flange.

15 Bonnet release cable – removal and refitting

1   Working inside the car, remove the bonnet release lever and disconnect the cable.
2   Working in the engine compartment, disconnect the cable from the lock and release the cable straps (photo).
3   Withdraw the cable and grommet from the scuttle.
4   Refitting is a reversal of removal.

16 Bonnet lock – adjustment

1   Adjustment is only possible at the lock pin mounted on the bonnet (photo).
2   Loosen the locknut and use a screwdriver to adjust the length of the lock pin so that the bonnet closes easily and is held firmly in place.
3   Tighten the locknut.

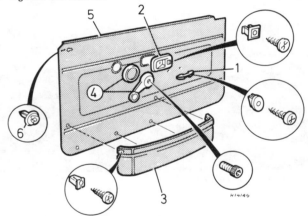

Fig. 12.1 Door trim pad and fittings (Sec 17)

1   Armrest   4   Window regulator handle
2   Door handle surround   5   Trim pad
3   Pocket   6   Clip

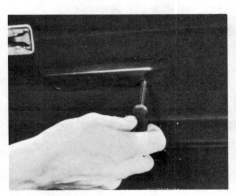

17.1A Removing the armrest

17.1B Removing the interior door handle surround screw ...

17.1C ... and surround

17.1D Removing the door pocket (1.3 HLS)

17.2A Removing the window regulator handle

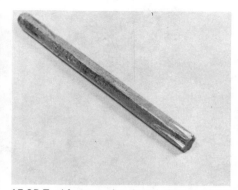

17.2B Tool for removing the window regulator handle screw

17.3 Removing the trim pad

18.3A Front door upper hinge

18.3B Front door lower hinge

17 Door trim pad – removal and refitting

1   Remove the screws and withdraw the armrest, interior door handle surround, and door pocket where fitted (photos).
2   Fully close the window and note the fitted position of the window regulator handle. Remove the screw and withdraw the handle and bezel. Ideally the screw should be removed with a special splined tool, but an Allen key may be used instead (photos).
3   With a wide-bladed screwdriver, release the trim pad retaining clips from the door inner panel starting at the bottom rear corner. Withdraw the trim pad (photo).
4   Refitting is a reversal of removal.

18 Door – removal and refitting

1   Remove the trim pad as described in Section 17.
2   Carefully pull off the polythene sheet.
3   Using a pencil, mark the position of the hinges on the door (photos).
4   With the help of an assistant, support the door and unscrew the hinge nuts.
5   Withdraw the hinge plates and door.
6   Refitting is a reversal of removal, but locate the hinges in their original positions. Check that the front edge of the door is flush or slightly recessed to the front wing, and if necessary adjust the hinges.

19 Door lock – removal, refitting and adjustment

1   Remove the trim pad as described in Section 17.
2   Carefully pull off the polythene sheet.
3   Unscrew the locking button, then refit the handle and fully raise the window.

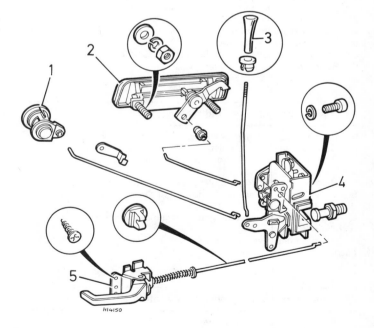

Fig. 12.2 Door lock components (Sec 19)

1   Private lock
2   Outer door handle
3   Locking button
4   Lock assembly
5   Interior door handle

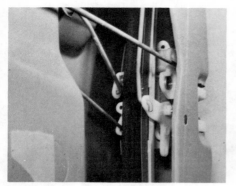

19.4 Door lock and control rods

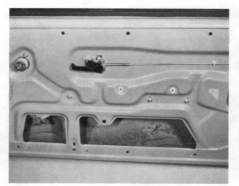

19.5 Inner door handle and rod

19.7 Door lock retaining screws

4   Unclip the control rods from the outer door handle and private lock (photo).
5   Remove the cross-head screw from the inner door handle, pull the control rod from the clip and disconnect it from the lock (photo).
6   Remove the screw from the rear window channel.
7   Remove the lock assembly screws and withdraw the lock from the door aperture (photo).
8   Refitting is a reversal of removal, but adjust the lock striker pin as follows.
9   Check that the latch disc is in the open position, then loosen the striker pin nut and position the pin so that the door can be closed easily and is held firmly. Close the door gently but firmly when making the adjustment.
10   Tighten the striker pin nut.

20 Door private lock – removal and refitting

1   Remove the trim pad as described in Section 17.
2   Carefully pull off the polythene sheet.
3   Refit the handle and fully raise the window.
4   Working through the aperture, unclip the control rod from the private lock and slide out the retaining clip.
5   Withdraw the private lock from the outside of the door.
6   Refitting is a reversal of removal.

21 Door glass – removal and refitting

1   Remove the trim pad as described in Section 17.
2   Carefully pull off the polythene sheet.
3   Remove the cross-head screw retaining the window channel guides.
4   Remove the window regulator with reference to Section 22.
5   Fully lower the glass to the bottom of the door and release it from the channel.
6   Remove the outer weatherseal, lift the rear edge of the glass, and withdraw it from the door.
7   Refitting is a reversal of removal, with reference to Section 22 as necessary.

22 Window regulator – removal and refitting

1   Remove the trim pad as described in Section 17.
2   Carefully pull off the polythene sheet.
3   Refit the handle and raise the window to 2 inches (50 mm) from the top. Wedge the window in this position.
4   Remove the regulator securing screws and the regulator channel securing screws.
5   Slide the regulator arms from the glass lower channel, then withdraw the regulator from the door aperture.
6   Refitting is a reversal of removal.

23 Seats – removal and refitting

1   Ideally a special splined tool should be obtained to remove the seat mounting screws, but it may be possible to remove them using an Allen key.

Front seat
2   Adjust the seat as necessary for access, remove the rotating screws, and withdraw the seat through the door aperture.

Rear seat
3   Unhook the parcel shelf support cords and fold down the rear seat. Remove the shelf.

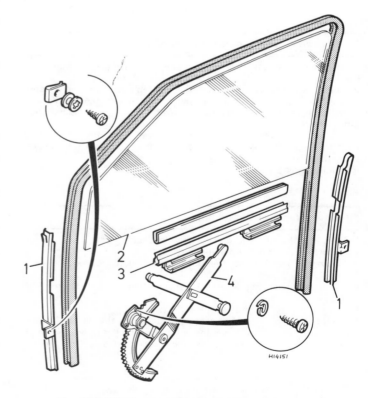

H14151

Fig. 12.3 Window regulator and glass components
(Secs 21 and 22)

1	Window channel	3	Lower channel
2	Glass	4	Regulator

4 Detach the carpet from the seat, then remove the mounting screws.
5 Withdraw the seat assembly through the tailgate aperture.

Front and rear seats

6 Refitting is a reversal of removal, but before tightening the rear seat mounting screws, secure the squabs to ensure correct alignment.

24 Bumpers – removal and refitting

1 The bumper sections are shown in Fig. 12.4.
2 To remove a front bumper, it will probably be necessary to remove the radiator (Chapter 2) to gain access to the mounting bolts.
3 To remove either a front or rear bumper, first remove the end cappings, which are each retained in place by a single bolt.
4 Where applicable, disconnect the wiring from the fog lamps, front sidelamps, and rear number plate lamps.
5 Unscrew the mounting bolts and withdraw the bumper from the car.
6 Refitting is the reversal of removal.

25 Facia – removal and refitting

1 Remove the instrument panel as described in Chapter 10.
2 Open the glovebox, remove the two pivot screws and bushes, and withdraw the glovebox (photo).
3 Remove the two screws and pull back the carpet from the top of the glove compartment area.
4 Unclip and remove the three facia retaining rods (photo).
5 Disconnect the tubes from the vent ducts (photo).
6 Prise out the ash tray and remove the centre facia retaining screw (photos). Remove the remaining retaining screws from under the shelf.
7 Pull the facia from the bulkhead, starting at the top, and withdraw it through the passenger door aperture (photo).
8 If necessary, prise out the speaker grille and detach the demister ducts (1 screw each).
9 Refitting is a reversal of removal.

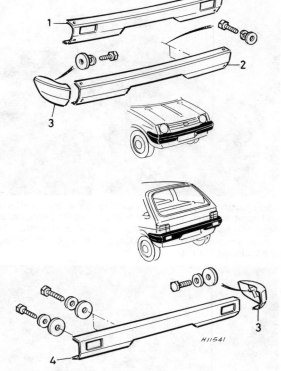

Fig. 12.4 Bumper components (Sec 24)

1 *Front bumper (standard and L models)*
2 *Front bumper (HLE and*
   1.3 models)
3 *End capping*
4 *Rear bumper*

25.2 Removing the glovebox

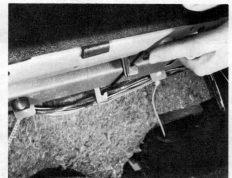

25.4 Facia retaining rod location

25.5 Disconnecting the vent duct tubes

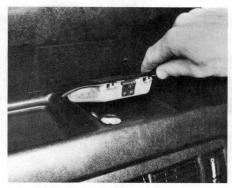

25.6A Removing the ashtray

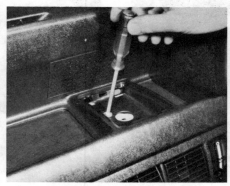

25.6B Removing the centre facia retaining screw

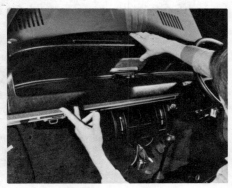

25.7 Removing the facia

This sequence of photographs deals with the repair of the dent and paintwork damage shown in this photo. The procedure will be similar for the repair of a hole. It should be noted that the procedures given here are simplified — more explicit instructions will be found in the text

In the case of a dent the first job — after removing surrounding trim — is to hammer out the dent where access is possible. This will minimise filling. Here, the large dent having been hammered out, the damaged area is being made slightly concave

Now all paint must be removed from the damaged area, by rubbing with coarse abrasive paper. Alternatively, a wire brush or abrasive pad can be used in a power drill. Where the repair area meets good paintwork, the edge of the paintwork should be 'feathered', using a finer grade of abrasive paper

In the case of a hole caused by rusting, all damaged sheet-metal should be cut away before proceeding to this stage. Here, the damaged area is being treated with rust remover and inhibitor before being filled

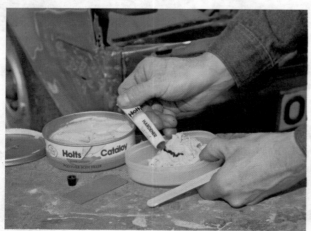

Mix the body filler according to its manufacturer's instructions. In the case of corrosion damage, it will be necessary to block off any large holes before filling — this can be done with aluminium or plastic mesh, or aluminium tape. Make sure the area is absolutely clean before ...

... applying the filler. Filler should be applied with a flexible applicator, as shown, for best results; the wooden spatula being used for confined areas. Apply thin layers of filler at 20-minute intervals, until the surface of the filler is slightly proud of the surrounding bodywork

Initial shaping can be done with a Surform plane or Dreadnought file. Then, using progressively finer grades of wet-and-dry paper, wrapped around a sanding block, and copious amounts of clean water, rub down the filler until really smooth and flat. Again, feather the edges of adjoining paintwork

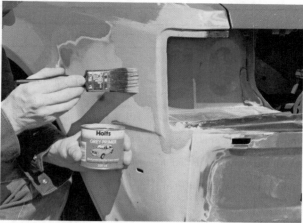

The whole repair area can now be sprayed or brush-painted with primer. If spraying, ensure adjoining areas are protected from over-spray. Note that at least one inch of the surrounding sound paintwork should be coated with primer. Primer has a 'thick' consistency, so will find small imperfections

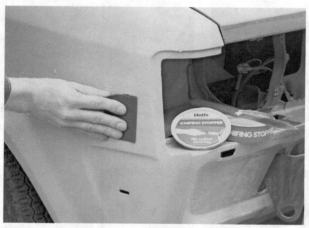

Again, using plenty of water, rub down the primer with a fine grade wet-and-dry paper (400 grade is probably best) until it is really smooth and well blended into the surrounding paintwork. Any remaining imperfections can now be filled by carefully applied knifing stopper paste

When the stopper has hardened, rub down the repair area again before applying the final coat of primer. Before rubbing down this last coat of primer, ensure the repair area is blemish-free — use more stopper if necessary. To ensure that the surface of the primer is really smooth use some finishing compound

The top coat can now be applied. When working out of doors, pick a dry, warm and wind-free day. Ensure surrounding areas are protected from over-spray. Agitate the aerosol thoroughly, then spray the centre of the repair area, working outwards with a circular motion. Apply the paint as several thin coats

After a period of about two weeks, which the paint needs to harden fully, the surface of the repaired area can be 'cut' with a mild cutting compound prior to wax polishing. When carrying out bodywork repairs, remember that the quality of the finished job is proportional to the time and effort expended

26 Heater and heater radiator – removal and refitting

1   Drain the cooling system (Chapter 2), and remove the air cleaner (Chapter 3).
2   Identify the heater hoses on the engine side of the bulkhead, then disconnect them from the heater (photo).
3   Remove the facia with reference to Section 25.
4   If fitted, remove the radio (Chapter 10), and cigar lighter (Chapter 10).
5   Remove the demister elbows and tubes and disconnect the heater multi-plug (photo).
6   Remove the heater mounting bolts and the left-hand air inlet duct nut (photos).
7   Withdraw the heater unit from the car.
8   Pull off the heater control knobs, then unscrew the securing screws and withdraw the cover (photos).
9   Remove the screws and withdraw the inlet duct and blanking plate after releasing the sealant.
10 Withdraw the radiator pipe seal and drill out the rivets securing the flange.
11 Note the position of the air temperature control rod, then loosen the locking screws (photo).
12 Remove the clips and screws retaining the two halves, loosen the control bracket screws, and withdraw the upper casing half.
13 Remove the screws, withdraw the retaining plate, and lift out the radiator and seals.
14 Refitting is a reversal of removal, but it will be necessary to use a riveting tool to secure the pipe flange. Use sealing compound to seal the inlet duct and blanking plate to the housing. If necessary adjust the air temperature control as described in Section 27. Fill the cooling system with reference to Chapter 2.

26.2 Disconnecting the heater hoses

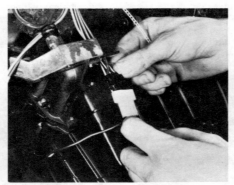
26.5 Disconnecting the heater wiring multi-plug

26.6A Removing the front heater mounting bolts

26.6B Removing the rear heater mounting bolt

26.8A Removing the heater control knobs

26.8B Removing the heater cover panel

26.8C Removing the heater case

26.11 Air temperature controls on the heater

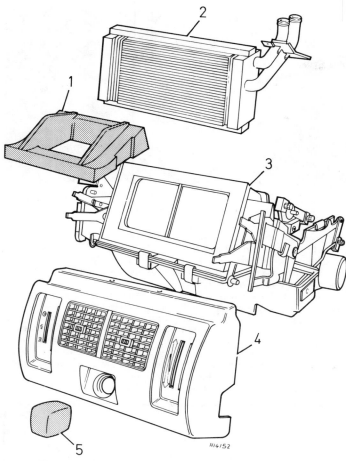

Fig. 12.5 Heater radiator and components (Sec 26)

1   Seal   4   Cover
2   Radiator   5   Control knob
3   Heater assembly

27 Heater – adjustment

Air distribution
1   Position the air distribution control knob fully upwards.
2   Loosen the rod-to-lever locking screw, and turn the lever fully clockwise.
3   Tighten the locking screw.

Temperature control and face level ventilation
4   Remove the facia as described in Section 25.
5   If fitted, remove the radio. Remove the cigar lighter as described in Chapter 10.
6   Pull off the heater control knobs, and remove the heater cover bottom screws.
7   Remove the heater mounting bolts and the left-hand air inlet duct nut.
8   Lower the heater sufficiently to remove the heater cover top screws and withdraw the cover.
9   Position the temperature control lever fully upwards and loosen the control locking screws.
10 Turn the upper flap lever fully clockwise, then tighten the upper screw.
11 Turn the lower flap lever fully anti-clockwise then tighten the lower screw with the upper flap held fully clockwise.
12 Position the face level ventilation lever fully upwards and loosen the control linkage screw (photo).
13 Turn the flap lever fully clockwise then tighten the locking screw.
14 Reverse the procedure given in paragraphs 4 to 8.

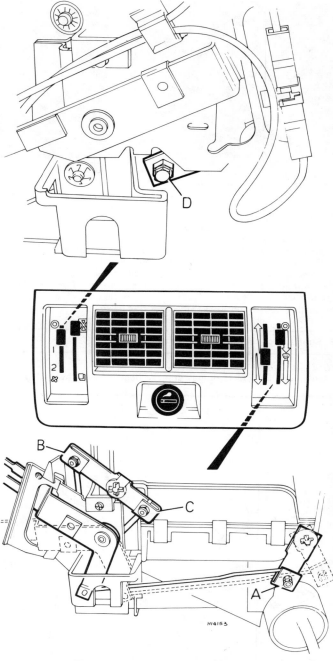

Fig. 12.6 Heater adjustments (Sec 27)

A   Air distribution   C   Air temperature lower flap
B   Air temperature upper flap   D   Face level ventilation

28 Heater motor – removal and refitting

1   Disconnect the battery negative lead.
2   On right-hand drive models, remove the air cleaner (Chapter 2) and unbolt the cooling system expansion tank for access.
3   On left-hand drive models, unscrew the clutch hose bracket nut.
4   Disconnect the heater motor wiring multi-plug.
5   Remove the mounting plate retaining bolts and withdraw the inlet box assembly from the car.
6   Disconnect the wires from the heater motor, noting their locations.
7   Remove the screws and withdraw the mounting plate.
8   Unclip the drain tube and inlet seal, then remove the clips and

27.12 Heater ventilation controls

29.6 A front subframe rear mounting

29.7 A front subframe front mounting

screws retaining the inlet box halves.
9   Break the joint and separate the inlet box halves.
10 Withdraw the inlet baffle, heater motor and mounting strip.
11 Remove the fan from the heater motor spindle.
12 Clean the sealant from the inlet box halves.
13 Refitting is a reversal of removal, but position the fan outer face 4.02 to 4.04 in (102.25 to 102.75 mm) from the motor tag rear face. Use sealing compound to seal the inlet box halves.

29 Subframes – removal and refitting

Front subframe
1   Remove the front Hydragas units as described in Chapter 11.

2   Remove the engine and gearbox assembly, and the engine mountings as described in Chapter 1.
3   Remove the steering rack and pinion as described in Chapter 11.
4   Remove the swivel hub assemblies as described in Chapter 11 together with the driveshafts.
5   Remove the exhaust system, gearchange rod and support stay, and disconnect the shock absorber lower mountings.
6   Support the rear of the subframe and remove the lower suspension arms, anti-roll bar, and rear subframe mountings (photo).
7   Support the front of the subframe and remove the front subframe mountings (photo).
8   Withdraw the subframe from under the car, and remove the upper suspension arms with reference to Chapter 11.
9   Refitting is a reversal of removal.

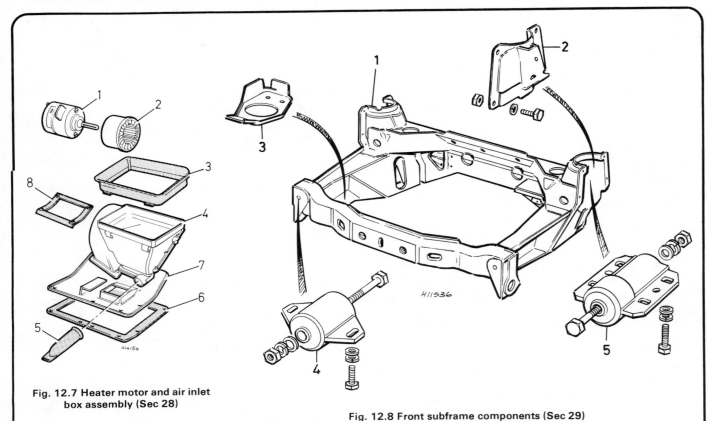

Fig. 12.7 Heater motor and air inlet box assembly (Sec 28)

1 Motor   5 Drain tube
2 Fan   6 Seal
3 Seal   7 Mounting plate
4 Air inlet box 8 Seal

Fig. 12.8 Front subframe components (Sec 29)

1 Front subframe   4 Front mounting
2 Tower bracket   5 Rear mounting
3 Engine mounting bracket

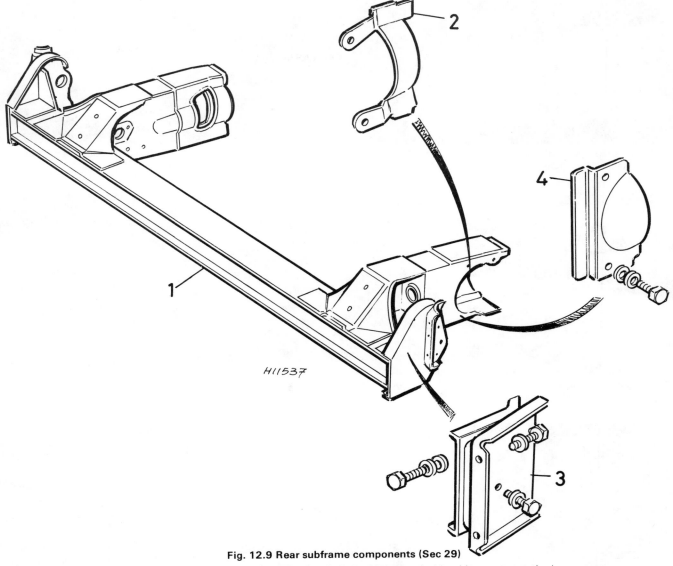

H11537

Fig. 12.9 Rear subframe components (Sec 29)

1 Rear subframe
2 Clamp plate

3 Mounting (with rubber centre section)
4 Hydragas unit shield

Rear subframe

10 Chock the front wheels. Jack up the rear of the car and support on axle stands, leaving a clear space beneath the rear subframe.
11 Remove both rear wheels.
12 Release the handbrake, then disconnect the cable end fittings from the rear brake levers by extracting the split pins and removing the clevis pins (photo).
13 Cut the plastic straps holding the handbrake cable to each rear radius arm (photo).
14 Fit brake hose clamps to the flexible brake hoses attached to the radius arms (photo). If clamps are not available, tighten the brake fluid reservoir cap onto a piece of polythene to help reduce the loss of fluid when the hoses are disconnected.
15 Working on each side in turn, unscrew the rigid pipe union nuts, then unscrew the locknuts and disconnect the flexible hoses from the brackets on the radius arms.
16 Support the rear subframe on axle stands or trolley jacks.
17 Unbolt the Hydragas straps from the underbody. If preferred, the outer bolts only can be unscrewed and the straps uncurled to release the Hydragas units, otherwise unscrew the inner strap mountings accessible within the spare wheel well (photos).
18 Unbolt the front of the subframe from the mountings (photo).
19 Disconnect the handbrake cables from the radius arm brackets by

29.12 Handbrake cable end fitting and clevis pin

29.13 Plastic strap (arrowed) holding handbrake cable to rear radius arm

29.14 Clamp fitted to rear flexible brake hose

29.17A Hydragas unit outer strap bolt (arrowed)

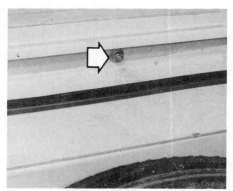
29.17B Hydragas unit inner strap bolt viewed from the spare wheel well

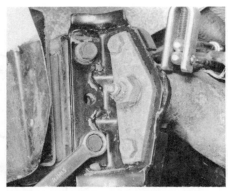
29.18 Unbolting the subframe from the front mountings

29.19A Pull out the clip (arrowed) ...

29.19B ... and disconnect the handbrake cable from the radius arm bracket

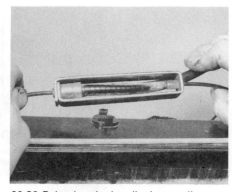
29.20 Releasing the handbrake equaliser from the plastic clip on the front of the subframe

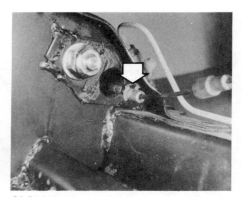
29.21A Pull out the clip (arrowed) ...

29.21B ... and withdraw the handbrake cable ends through the access holes

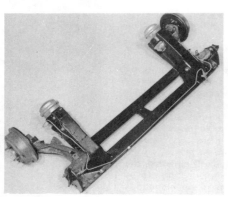
29.22 Rear subframe removed from the car

29.23 Hydragas Schrader valve and union (arrowed)

29.24A Unscrew the bolts (arrowed) ...

29.24B ... and remove the rear subframe mounting

29.25 Bleeding the rear brakes

pulling out the clips and sliding the inner cables through the bracket slots (photos).
20 Lower the rear subframe three or four inches, then unclip the equaliser from the plastic clip on the front of the subframe (photo).
21 Disconnect the handbrake cables from the front of the subframe by pulling out the clips, removing the rubber covers and withdrawing the cable ends through the access holes (photos).
22 Lower the rear subframe to the ground and withdraw it from under the car (photo).

23 To dismantle the radius arms and Hydragas units, depressurize the units and follow the procedure given in Chapter 11. Unbolt the Schrader valve and union, and unclip the fluid pipes (photo).
24 Unbolt the subframe mountings from the body and examine them for deterioration and damage (photos). Renew them if necessary.
25 Refitting is a reversal of removal, but have the Hydragas units pressurized by a BL garage, bleed the brake hydraulic system (Chapter 9) (photo), and adjust the handbrake cable (Chapter 9). Attach the handbrake cables to the radius arms with new plastic straps.

Chapter 13 Supplement:
Revisions and information on later models

Contents

Introduction 1
Specifications 2
Engine 3
  Engine/gearbox removal and refitting – later models
  Engine mounting modifications
  Cylinder head (MG Turbo) – removal and refitting
  Inlet valve oil seals (998 cc)
  Timing cover removal and refitting (engine in vehicle)
  Crankshaft pulley bolt – removal and refitting
  Plain main bearing shells
  Crankcase ventilation system – MG Turbo
  Pistons and connecting rods
  Oil coolers – description
  Oil cooler (water-cooled) – removal and refitting
  Oil cooler (air-cooled) – removal and refitting
  Camshaft/distributor driveshaft (1985-on 1.3 models) – refitting
Cooling system 4
  Expansion tank leakage
  Radiator bottom hose fitting
  Cooling system (1985-on models) – general description
  Radiator (1985-on models) – removal and refitting
  Cooling fan assembly (1985-on models) – removal and refitting
  Thermostat – fitting
Fuel and exhaust systems 5
  Air cleaner (MG 1300 and Vanden Plas models) – description
  and testing
  Air cleaner (MG Turbo models) – removal and refitting
  Fuel filter (MG Turbo models) – renewal
  Fuel pump knock (all models except MG Turbo) – rectification
  Fuel pump (MG Turbo models) – description and testing
  Fuel pump (MG Turbo models) – removal and refitting
  Fuel pump (automatic transmission models) – renewal
  Fuel tank (MG Turbo models) – removal and refitting
  Fuel tank (5-door models) – removal and refitting
  Choke control cable (1985-on models) – removal and refitting
  Idle speed and idler gear noise
  Throttle damper deleted (later models)
  Anti run-on valve (MG 1300 models) – removal and refitting
  Carburettor – dismantling and reassembly
  Turbocharger and associated components – description
  Turbocharger – cautions
  Turbocharger – removal, inspection and refitting
  Turbocharger control components – testing, removal and
  refitting
  Carburettor (MG Turbo models) – description and maintenance
  Carburettor (MG Turbo models) – removal and refitting
  Idle speed adjustment – all later models
  Inlet and exhaust manifolds (MG and Vanden Plas models) –
  description, removal and refitting
  Exhaust elbow gasket (MG Turbo models) – removal and
  refitting
  Exhaust system (all later models) – description, removal and
  refitting
  Exhaust downpipes – modification
  Fault diagnosis – turbocharger

Ignition system 6
  Electronic ignition system – description
  Electronic ignition system – maintenance
  Electronic ignition system – static timing
  Electronic ignition distributor (pre-1985 models) – dismantling
  and reassembly
  Electronic ignition amplifier (pre-1985 models) – general
  Electronic ignition distributor (1985-on models) – dismantling
  and reassembly
  Electronic ignition amplifier (1985-on models) – general
  Distributor – removal and refitting
  Timing marks – all models
  Fault diagnosis – electronic ignition
Clutch 7
  Clutch (non-Verto) – removal precaution
  Clutch hydraulic damper – description, removal and refitting
  Clutch judder – causes and remedies
  Clutch linkage lubrication – all models
  Verto clutch – description
  Verto clutch – removal, overhaul and refitting
  Verto clutch – throw-out stop adjustment
  Verto clutch – release bearing removal and refitting
  Clutch cable (1985-on models) – removal and refitting
Manual gearbox 8
  Third motion shaft bearing – general
  Selector shaft oil seal – general
  Reverse gear – disengagement
Automatic transmission 9
  Gear selection problems – general
  Selector cable – adjustment checking procedure
  Loss of drive when cold
  Speedometer drivegear – removal and refitting
Final drive 10
  Differential thrust block – general
Driveshafts 11
  Lubrication of CV joints
  Driveshaft knock
Braking system 12
  Use of anti-squeal paste on front brake pads
  Rear brake squeal
  Rear brake shoe linings (1985-on models) – inspection
  Brake disc wear measurement (all models except MG Turbo and
  1985-on models)
  Brake disc renewal (all models)
  Ventilated disc orientation (MG Turbo and all 1985-on models)
  Stones trapped between disc and shield
  Water entering rear brake drums
  Brake judder
  Master cylinder (1985-on models) – description
  Inertia/pressure regulating valve (Van models) – description,
  removal and refitting
  Pressure reducing valve (1985-on Saloon models) – description,
  removal and refitting
  Hydraulic system (1985-on models) – bleeding
  Handbrake – adjustment

Electrical system 13
Part A General equipment
 Lucas A115 alternator – brush renewal
 Ignition warning light bulb wattage
 Starter solenoid (inertia starters) – earthing
 Starter relay – general
 Fuses (1985-on models) – general
 Veglia instrument panels
 Instrument panel dismantling – pre-1985 MG Turbo models
 Instrument panel and instruments (1985-on models) – removal
 and refitting
 Speedometer cable (1985-on models) – removal and refitting
 Dim-dip headlamps
 Clock (pre-1985 MG Turbo models) – removal and refitting
 Clock (1985-on models) – removal and refitting
 Combination switch (1985-on models) – removal and refitting
 Instrument panel surround switch (1985-on models) – removal
 and refitting
 Electric window switch and relay – removal and refitting
 Windscreen and tailgate window washers – general
 Screen washer pumps (MG Turbo models) – removal and
 refitting
 Windscreen washer tube (MG Turbo models) – removal and
 refitting
 Headlamp washer system – general
 Trip computer – general
 Heater control illumination bulb – removal and refitting
 Automatic transmission selector illumination bulb – removal and
 refitting
 Radio cassette player (electronic) – removal and refitting
Part B Mobile radio equipment
 Aerials – selection and fitting
 Loudspeakers
 Interference
 Suppression methods – ignition
 VHF/FM broadcasts
Suspension and steering 14
 General description
 Leaks from Hydragas units

 Front suspension spacers
 Front shock absorber rubber bush
 Front anti-roll bar knock – rectification
 Rear suspension spacers
 Rear Hydragas struts
 Rear anti-roll bar (MG Turbo) – removal and refitting
 Steering column (1985 models) – removal, overhaul and
 refitting
 Steering rack and pinion, (1985 models) – removal, overhaul
 and refitting
 Steering column (1986-on models)
 Steering rack and pinion – removal and refitting
 Wheels and tyres – general
Bodywork and fittings 15
 Maintenance – bodywork and underframe
 Plastic components
 Front spoiler (MG Turbo models) – removal and refitting
 Wheel arch finishers (MG Turbo models) – removal and refitting
 Rear spoiler (MG and 1985-on models) – removal and refitting
 Opening rear quarterlight – removal and refitting
 Increasing front seat rearward adjustment
 Seat belt lowering kit
 Rear bumper fixings (1983 models)
 Sunroof – general
 Tailgate lock – removal and refitting
 Remote control door mirror – removal and refitting
 Door trim pad (5-door models) – removal and refitting
 Front door lock (central locking models) – removal and refitting
 Rear door lock – removal and refitting
 Door glass (central locking models) – removal and refitting
 Door (1985-on models) – removal and refitting
 Central locking door lock motor – removal and refitting
 Electric window motor – removal and refitting
 Facia (1985-on models) – removal and refitting
 Heater and heater radiator (1985-on models) – removal and
 refitting
 Heater (1985-on models) – adjustment
 Front seat release lever cable (3-door models) – removal and
 refitting

1 Introduction

This Chapter contains information which has become available since the book was first written. Most of the information, therefore, deals with changes made to later models, or with models such as the MG Metro introduced at a later date.

The Sections in this Chapter follow the same order as the first twelve Chapters of the book. The Specifications are all grouped together for convenience, but they too are arranged in Chapter order.

It is suggested that before undertaking a particular job, reference be made first to this Supplement for the latest information, then to the appropriate Chapter earlier in the book. In this way any revisions can be noted before starting.

2 Specifications

The Specifications listed below are revisions of, or supplementary to, the Specifications at the beginning of each of the preceding Chapters.

998 cc engine – 1982-on
Compression ratio
1982:
  1.0, L and Van .... 8.3 : 1
  City .... 9.6 : 1
  HLE .... 10.3 : 1
1983 (otherwise as 1982):
  Low compression models .... 8.3 : 1
  1.0 L and Gala .... 9.6 : 1
1984 (otherwise as 1983):
  1.0, L, City and Van (engine 99H907P) .... 9.6 : 1
  1.0, L, HLE, City X and Van (engine 99HA06P) .... 10.3 : 1
  L, HLE and City X (engine 99HA08P) .... 10.3 : 1
1985-on (all models):
Note: *Space restrictions have necessitated the abbreviation of the engine codes shown below. To obtain the full code, substitute the numbers listed into the code in place of the dashes.*

  99HA – – P:
    64, 68, 69 .... 8.3 : 1 (Low compression)
    67, 71 .... 9.6 : 1 (Standard compression)
    65, 66, 70, 75 .... 10.3 : 1 (High compression)

99HB – – P:

39, 96, 97, 98, 99	8.3 : 1 (Low compression)
38, 87, 88, 89	9.6 : 1 (Standard compression)
90, 91, 92, 93	10.3 : 1 (High compression)

Valve clearances (cold) – inlet and exhaust

All models except 1983 1.0, L, HLE and City	0.012 to 0.014 in (0.30 to 0.36 mm)
1983 1.0, L, HLE and City	0.012 in (0.30 mm)

Valve guides

Fitted height (head modified for inlet valve oil seals)	0.540 in (13.72 mm)

1275 cc engine – 1982-on (except MG Turbo)
Compression ratio

1982:

Low compression models	8.0 : 1
1.3, L, Vanden Plas manual and Van	9.4 : 1
MG	10.5 : 1

1983 (otherwise as 1982):

Gala, Moritz and Automatic	9.4 : 1
HLE	9.75 : 1
1984	as 1983

1985-on (all models):

Note: *Space restrictions have necessitated the abbreviation of some of the engine codes shown below. To obtain the full code, substitute the numbers listed into the code in place of the dashes.*

12HA73AA, 12HA84AA, 12HB37AA, 12HC18AA, 12HC19AA	8.0 : 1 (Low compression)
12HA – – AA:	
60, 61, 62, 71, 72, 80, 86, 87	9.75 : 1 (Standard compression)
12HB – – AA:	
09, 22, 36	9.75 : 1 (Standard compression)
12HC – – AA:	
01, 02, 03, 04, 05, 06, 07, 08, 09, 10, 11	9.75 : 1 (Standard compression)
12HA83AA, 12HA42AA, 12HC14AA, 12HC15AA	10.5 : 1 (High compression)

Valve clearances (cold)

1982 and 1983 MG:

Inlet	0.012 to 0.014 in (0.30 to 0.36 mm)
Exhaust	0.015 to 0.017 in (0.38 to 0.43 mm)
1982 Vanden Plas (inlet and exhaust)	0.012 in (0.30 mm)
1983 L, HLE and 1.3 Automatic (inlet and exhaust)	0.012 in (0.30 mm)
1985-on MG and Vanden Plas manual (inlet and exhaust)	0.013 to 0.015 in (0.33 to 0.38 mm)
All other models (inlet and exhaust)	0.012 to 0.014 in (0.30 to 0.36 mm)

Valves

Head diameter (MG 1300 models only)	1.401 to 1.406 in (35.58 to 35.71 mm)

Valve timing (at valve clearance of 0.021 in/0.53 mm):

HLE models:

Inlet opens	9° BTDC
Inlet closes	41° ABDC
Exhaust opens	49° BBDC
Exhaust closes	11° ATDC

MG 1300 models:

Inlet opens	16° BTDC
Inlet closes	56° ABDC
Exhaust opens	59° BBDC
Exhaust closes	29° ATDC

1275 cc engine (MG Turbo)
Compression ratio

	9.4 : 1

Valve clearances (cold)

1982 and 1983:

Inlet	0.014 in (0.35 mm)
Exhaust	0.016 in (0.40 mm)

1984-on:

Inlet	0.012 to 0.014 in (0.30 to 0.35 mm)
Exhaust	0.014 to 0.016 in (0.35 to 0.40 mm)

Valves

Stem diameter:

Exhaust	0.3131 to 0.3137 in (7.955 to 7.970 mm)

Clearance in guide:

Exhaust	0.0031 to 0.0032 in (0.079 to 0.081 mm)

Valve guides:

Inside diameter (reamed) – exhaust	0.3164 to 0.3169 in (8.036 to 8.049 mm)

Valve springs free length:
    Inner .... 1.703 in (43.256 mm)
    Outer .... 1.740 in (44.196 mm)

Torque wrench settings

	lbf ft	kgf m
Crankshaft pulley bolt	105	14.5
Cylinder head bypass plug	12	1.7
Cylinder head nuts (oiled)	55	7.6
Sump drain plug	28	3.9
Sump screws	8	1.1
Water outlet elbow nuts	16	2.2
Engine mountings:		
$^3/_8$ in UNC	30	4.1
M8	22	3.0
M10	33	4.6
M12	53	7.3
Right-hand, from late 1986	21 to 26	2.9 to 3.6

Cooling system
Torque wrench settings (MG Turbo)

	lbf ft	kgf m
Coolant drain plug	27	3.7
Coolant temperature transmitter	40	5.5

Fuel and exhaust systems (998 cc engine – 1982-on)
Carburettor – general

Type	HIF 38
Piston spring colour	Red
Jet size	0.090 in
Exhaust gas CO content	1.5 to 3.5%

Carburettor data
1982 1.0, L and Van:
    Specification number:
        Low compression .... FZX 1413
        Standard compression .... FZX 1279
    Needle:
        Low compression .... ADU
        Standard compression .... ADP
    Idling speed .... 750 rpm
    Fast idle speed .... 1300 rpm

1982 HLE and City:
    Specification number:
        HLE .... FZX 1414
        City .... FZX 1278
    Needle:
        HLE .... ADS
        City .... ADP
    Idling speed:
        HLE .... 600 to 700 rpm
        City .... 750 rpm
    Fast idle speed:
        HLE .... 1100 rpm
        City .... 1300 rpm

1983 Gala:
    Specification number .... FZX 1279
    Needle .... ADP
    Idling speed .... 750 rpm
    Fast idle speed .... 1300 rpm

1983 1.0, L, HLE and City:
    Specification number:
        Low compression .... FZX 1413
        1.0 and L .... FZX 1279
        HLE .... FZX 1414
    Needle:
        Low compression .... ADU
        1.0 and L .... ADP
        HLE .... ADS
    Idling speed:
        All models except HLE .... 750 rpm
        HLE .... 650 rpm
    Fast idle speed .... 1300 rpm

1984 Low compression 1.0, L and Van:
Specification number .... FZX 1413
Needle .... ADU
Idling speed .... 750 rpm
Fast idle speed .... 1300 rpm

1984 Standard compression 1.0, L and Van:
Specification number:
   Engine 99HA06P .... FZX 1414
   Engine 99HA07P .... FZX 1279
Needle:
   Engine 99HA06P .... ADS
   Engine 99HA07P .... ADP
Idling speed:
   Engine 99HA06P .... 650 rpm
   Engine 99HA07P .... 750 rpm
Fast idle speed:
   Engine 99HA06P .... 1100 rpm
   Engine 99HA07P .... 1300 rpm

1984 City X (Low compression) and City:
Specification number .... FZX 1413 or FZX 1279
Needle .... ADU or ADP
Idling speed .... 750 rpm
Fast idle speed .... 1300 rpm

1984 L, HLE and City X:
Specification number .... FZX 1414
Needle .... ADS
Idling speed .... 650 rpm
Fast idle speed .... 1100 rpm

1985-on Low compression models:
Specification number:
   All except engine 99HA69P and 99HB97P .... FZX 1413
   Engine 99HA69P and 99HB97P .... FZX 1458
Needle .... ADU
Idling speed .... 700 to 800 rpm
Fast idle speed .... 1250 to 1350 rpm

1985-on Standard compression models (including Mayfair):
Specification number .... FZX 1279
Needle .... ADP
Idling speed .... 700 to 800 rpm
Fast idle speed .... 1250 to 1350 rpm

1985-on High compression models:
Specification number .... FZX 1414
Needle .... ADS
Idling speed .... 600 to 700 rpm
Fast idle speed .... 1050 to 1150 rpm

Fuel and exhaust systems (1275 cc engine – 1982-on)
Carburettor – general
Type .... HIF 44
Piston spring colour .... Red
Jet size .... 0.100 in
Exhaust gas CO content .... 1.5 to 3.5%

Carburettor data
1982 1.3, L and Van:
Specification number .... FZX 1412
Needle .... BEJ
Idling speed:
   Low compression .... 650 rpm
   Standard compression .... 750 rpm
Fast idle speed .... 1100 rpm

1982 MG and Vanden Plas:
Specification number:
   MG .... FZX 1409
   Vanden Plas .... FZX 1280
Needle:
   MG .... BDL
   Vanden Plas .... BEJ

Idling speed:
    MG .... 850 rpm
    Vanden Plas .... 750 rpm
  Fast idle speed .... 1100 rpm

1983 L, HLE and Automatic:
  Specification number:
    Low compression .... FZX 1412
    HLE .... FZX 1429
    All other models .... FZX 1281
  Needle:
    HLE .... BER
    All other models .... BEJ
  Idling speed:
    Low compression and HLE .... 650 rpm
    All other models .... 750 rpm
    Fast idle speed .... 1100 rpm

1983 Gala and Moritz:
  Specification number .... FZX 1281
  Needle .... BEJ
  Idling speed .... 750 rpm
  Fast idle speed .... 1100 rpm

1984 1.3, L and Van:
  Specification number .... FZX 1412
  Needle .... BEJ
  Idling speed:
    Low compression .... 650 rpm
    Standard compression .... 750 rpm
  Fast idle speed .... 1100 rpm

1984 L and Automatic:
  Specification number .... FZX 1281
  Needle .... BEJ
  Idling speed .... 750 rpm
  Fast idle speed .... 1100 rpm

1984 HLE:
  Specification number .... FZX 1429
  Needle .... BER
  Idling speed .... 650 rpm
  Fast idle speed .... 1100 rpm

1984 MG:
  Specification number .... FZX 1409
  Needle .... BDL
  Idling speed .... 850 rpm
  Fast idle speed .... 1100 rpm

1984 Vanden Plas:
  Specification number .... FZX 1412
  Needle .... BEJ
  Idling speed .... 750 rpm
  Fast idle speed .... 1100 rpm

1985-on Low compression models:
  Specification number .... FZX 1412
  Needle .... BEJ
  Idling speed .... 600 to 700 rpm
  Fast idle speed .... 1050 to 1150 rpm

1985-on Standard compression models (including Mayfair):
  Specification number .... FZX 1429
  Needle .... BER
  Idling speed .... 600 to 700 rpm
  Fast idle speed .... 1050 to 1150 rpm

1985-on Automatic and Vanden Plas Automatic:
  Specification number .... FZX 1462
  Needle .... BFZ
  Idling speed .... 750 to 850 rpm
  Fast idle speed .... 950 to 1050 rpm

1985-on MG and Vanden Plas manual:
   Specification number:
      Engine 12HA83AA and 12HC14AA .... FZX 1409
      Engine 12HB42AA and 12HC15AA .... FZX 1469
   Needle:
      Engine 12HA83AA and 12HC14AA .... BDL
      Engine 12HB42AA and 12HC15AA .... BFY
   Idling speed .... 800 to 900 rpm
   Fast idle speed:
      Engine 12HA83AA and 12HC14AA .... 1000 to 1100 rpm
      Engine 12HB42AA and 12HC15AA .... 1100 to 1200 rpm

Fuel and exhaust systems (MG Turbo)
Carburettor data
Type .... HIF 44
Piston spring colour .... Yellow
Jet size .... 0.100 in
Exhaust gas CO content .... 0.5 to 2.5%
Specification number:
   1982 to 1984 .... FZX 1411
   1985-on .... FZX 1435
Needle .... BDD
Idling speed .... 800 to 900 rpm
Fast idle speed .... 1050 to 1150 rpm

Turbocharger
Boost pressure .... 4 to 7 lbf/in² (0.28 to 0.49 kgf/cm²)
Wastegate operating pressure .... 4 lbf/in² (0.28 kgf/cm²)
Permissible bearing clearance:
   Radial .... 0.003 to 0.006 in (0.08 to 0.15 mm)
   Axial .... 0.001 to 0.003 in (0.03 to 0.08 mm)

Torque wrench settings

	lbf ft	kgf m
Turbocharger to exhaust manifold	28	3.8
Turbocharger to exhaust elbow	15	2.1
Oil drain adaptor screws	16	2.2
Oil feed banjo bolts	11	1.5
Wastegate bracket screws	16	2.2
Plenum chamber to carburettor	16	2.2
Non-return valve to manifold	18	2.5

Ignition system (998 cc engine – 1982-on)
Coil
Type:
   1982 to 1984 .... Lucas 16C6 or AC Delco 9977230
   1985-on .... Bosch 0-221-119-353 or Ducellier 520068A

Distributor
Type .... Lucas 59D4 or Ducellier
Ignition timing at 1500 rpm (with vacuum disconnected)
1982:
   HLE .... 7° BTDC
   All other models .... 15° BTDC
1983:
   HLE .... 5 to 7° BTDC
   All other models .... 15° BTDC
1984:
   Engines 99HA06P and 99HA08P .... 5 to 7° BTDC
   All other models .... 15° BTDC
1985-on:
   High compression .... 5 to 7° BTDC
   All other models .... 14 to 16° BTDC

Spark plugs

	Type	Electrode gap
1982	Unipart GSP 263	0.025 in (0.64 mm)
1983:		
1.0, L and City	Unipart GSP 263	0.025 in (0.64 mm)
HLE	Unipart GSP 263	0.035 in (0.90 mm)
Gala	Unipart GSP 163	0.035 in (0.90 mm)
1984 to 1986	Unipart GSP 163, GSP 4362	0.025 in (0.64 mm)
1987	Unipart GSP 4382	0.025 in (0.64 mm)

Ignition system (1275 cc engine – 1982-on)
Coil
Type:

1982	Lucas 16C6, Ducellier 520025A or AC Delco 9977250
1983 and 1984	Lucas 16C6 or AC Delco 9977250
1985-on:	
Van	Bosch 0-221-119-353 or Ducellier 520068A
All other models	Bosch 0-221-122-360 or Ducellier 520067A

Distributor
Type:

1982 to 1984	Lucas 59D4 or Ducellier
1985-on:	
Van	Lucas 59D4
All models	Lucas 65DM4 (electronic)
Air gap:	
Lucas 65DM4	0.006 to 0.010 in (0.15 to 0.25 mm)
Ignition timing at 1500 rpm (with vacuum disconnected)	
1982:	
Low compression	13° BTDC
Standard compression	11° BTDC
MG	10° BTDC
Vanden Plas	11° BTDC
1983:	
Low compression	13° BTDC
HLE	9° BTDC
All other models	11° BTDC
1984:	
Low compression	13° BTDC
Standard compression	11° BTDC
HLE	7 to 9° BTDC
MG	10° BTDC
Vanden Plas	11° BTDC
1985-on:	
Low compression	13° BTDC
Standard compression	7 to 9° BTDC
MG and Vanden Plas manual:	
Engine 12HA83AA	10° BTDC
Engine 12HB42AA	5° BTDC

Spark plugs

	Type	Electrode gap
1982	Unipart GSP 263	0.025 in (0.64 mm)
1983:		
1.3L and Automatic	Unipart GSP 263	0.025 in (0.64 mm)
Low compression and HLE	Unipart GSP 263	0.035 in (0.90 mm)
Gala and Moritz	Unipart GSP 163	0.035 in (0.90 mm)
1984	Unipart GSP 163	0.035 in (0.90 mm)
1985-on:		
Van	Unipart GSP 163, GSP 4362	0.035 in (0.90 mm)
All other models	Unipart GSP 163, GSP 4362	0.040 in (1.0 mm)

Ignition system (MG Turbo)
Coil

1982 to 1984	Ducellier 520029
1985-on	Ducellier 520067A or Bosch 0-221-122-360

Distributor
Type:

1982 to 1984	Lucas 59DM4 (electronic)
1985-on	Lucas 65DM4 (electronic)
Air gap	0.006 to 0.010 in (0.15 to 0.25 mm)
Ignition timing at 1500 rpm (with vacuum disconnected)	
1982 to 1984	7° BTDC
1985-on	6 to 8° BTDC

Spark plugs

	Type	Electrode gap
1982 to 1984	Unipart GSP 281	0.035 in (0.90 mm)
1985-on	Unipart GSP 281, GSP 4452	0.040 in (1.0 mm)

Clutch
Type (1982-on – from VIN 532165) ....
Verto; single dry plate and pressure plate located on outer face of flywheel

Actuation

To 1984	Hydraulic
1985-on	Cable with automatic adjustment

Torque wrench settings

	lbf ft	kgf m
Pressure plate to flywheel	18	2.5
Flywheel centre bolt	112	15.5

Manual transmission

Ratios

1.0 HLE (1983 models):

1st	4.004 : 1
2nd	2.307 : 1
3rd	1.435 : 1
4th	1 : 1
Reverse	4.026 : 1

1.3 HLE (1983 models):

1st	3.647 : 1
2nd	2.184 : 1
3rd	1.425 : 1
4th	1 : 1
Reverse	3.666 : 1

All 1984-on models except 1.0 HLE:

1st	3.647 : 1
2nd	2.185 : 1
3rd	1.425 : 1
4th	1 : 1
Reverse	3.666 : 1

1.0 HLE (1984-on models):

1st	4.004 : 1
2nd	2.307 : 1
3rd	1.435 : 1
4th	1 : 1
Reverse	4.026: 1

Automatic transmission

Torque wrench setting

	lbf ft	kgf m
Drain plug	30	4.0

Final drive

Ratio (later models)

1.0 Van	3.467 : 1
1.0, 1.0L and City – to 1983	3.647 : 1 or 3.105 : 1
1.0 Gala, City, 1.0L and City X – 1984-on	3.647 : 1
1.0 HLE	3.105 : 1
Automatic	2.760 : 1
MG Turbo	3.211 : 1
1.3 HLE to 1983	3.444 : 1 or 3.105 : 1
1.3 HLE – 1984	3.105 : 1
1.3 HLE – 1985	2.950 : 1
All other 1.3 models	3.444 : 1

Driveshafts

Torque wrench settings

	lbf ft	kgf m
Driveshaft-to-drive flange nut:		
Two split pin hole type	200	27.4
Single split pin hole type	193	26.4

Braking system

Discs

Disc type (MG Turbo and all 1985-on models)	Ventilated, LH and RH not interchangeable
Disc minimum thickness:	
Plain disc	0.236 in (6.0 mm)
Ventilated disc	Information not available at time of writing
Maximum allowable run-out	0.006 in (0.15 mm)
Maximum allowable thickness variation	0.0005 in (0.013 mm)

Electrical system

Alternator (alternative type)

Make and type	Lucas A115
Output at 14V and 6000 alternator rpm	45 amps
Rotor winding resistance at 68°F (20°C)	3.2 ohms
Brush length:	
New	0.8 in (20 mm)

Wear limit	0.4 in (10 mm)
Brush spring pressure	4.7 to 9.8 oz (133 to 278 g)

Bulbs

	Wattage
Ignition (no-charge) warning light (from VIN 388652)	2

Suspension and steering

Rear suspension (MG Turbo)

Type	As other models, plus anti-roll bar
Rear wheel alignment	Parallel ± 0° 15′

Steering (MG Turbo)

Steering wheel diameter	14.0 in (355 mm)

Front wheel alignment (MG Turbo)

Inner wheel angle (with outer wheel at 29° 48′)	31° 50′

Wheels

Size and type:

MG Turbo	5.50J x 13 alloy
MG 1300 (pre 1984)	5J x 12 pressed steel
MG 1300 (1984)	12 in x 5J alloy
MG 1300 (1985-on)	315 x 120 mm alloy
1.0 and 1.3 Van	12 in x 4.5B pressed steel
All other models:	
Pre-1984	4.50B x 12 pressed steel
1984-on	315 x 105 mm pressed steel

Tyres

Size:

1982 to 1983 models:	
1.0 models	135 SR x 12 radial
1.3 models, except MG Turbo	155/70R x 12 radial
MG Turbo	165/60 HR x 13 radial
1984 models:	
1.0 Saloon models	150/65 R315 radial
1.0 and 1.3 Vans	155/70 SR12 radial
1.3 Moritz	150/65 R315 radial
MG 1300	155/70 SR12 radial
MG Turbo	165/65 HR13 radial
All other 1.3 models	160/65 R315 radial
1985-on models:	
MG Turbo	165/60 HR 13 radial
All other models	160/65 R315 radial

Pressures (cold) – lbf/in² (kgf/cm²):

	Front	Rear
1982 models:		
1.0 models	32 (2.2)	28 (2.0)
1.3 models except Automatic	32 (2.2)	26 (1.8)
1.3 Automatic	30 (2.1)	26 (1.8)
1983 models:		
1.0 models	32 (2.2)	26 (1.8)
1.3 Automatic	30 (2.1)	26 (1.8)
MG Turbo	28 (2.0)	28 (2.0)
All other 1.3 models	28 (2.0)	26 (1.8)
1984 models:		
1.0 and 1.3 Vans	28 (2.0)	32 (2.2)
All other 1.0 models	30 (2.1)	28 (2.0)
1.3 Moritz	30 (2.1)	28 (2.0)
MG Turbo	28 (2.0)	28 (2.0)
All other 1.3 models	28 (2.0)	26 (1.8)
1985-on models:		
165/65 R315 tyres (except Van)		
Up to 4 persons	28 (2.0)	26 (1.8)
Fully laden	32 (2.2)	30 (2.1)
165/65 R315 tyres (Van)	28 (2.0)	32 (2.2)
165/60 HR13 tyres	28 (2.0)	28 (2.0)

Torque wrench settings

	lbf ft	kgf m
Hydragas unit charging valve	12	1.7
Anti-roll bar U-bolt clamp nuts	16	2.2
Alloy wheel nuts:		
1985-on models	42	5.8
All other models	36	5.0

184

Under-bonnet view of MG Metro 1300

1 Battery
2 Starter motor solenoid

3 Anti run-on valve
4 Brake hydraulic reservoir

5 Carburettor damper cap
6 Air cleaner vacuum motor

7 Expansion tank filler cap
8 Windscreen washer reservoir

9 Oil filler cap
10 Engine oil dipstick

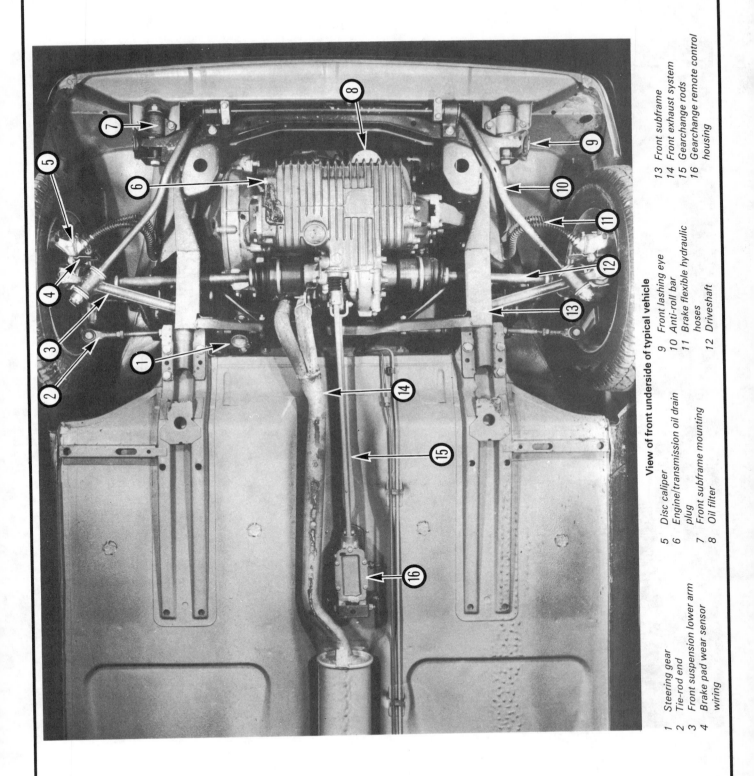

View of front underside of typical vehicle

1 Steering gear
2 Tie-rod end
3 Front suspension lower arm
4 Brake pad wear sensor wiring
5 Disc caliper
6 Engine/transmission oil drain plug
7 Front subframe mounting
8 Oil filter
9 Front lashing eye
10 Anti-roll bar
11 Brake flexible hydraulic hoses
12 Driveshaft
13 Front subframe
14 Front exhaust system
15 Gearchange rods
16 Gearchange remote control housing

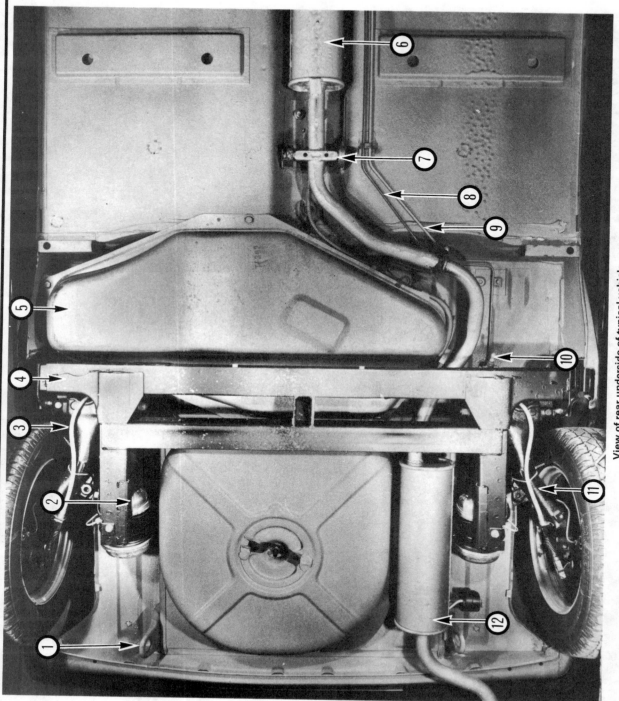

View of rear underside of typical vehicle

1 Rear lashing eye
2 Rear Hydragas unit
3 Handbrake cable
4 Rear subframe

5 Fuel tank
6 Intermediate silencer
7 Exhaust mounting

8 Brake rigid hydraulic line
9 Fuel supply pipe
10 Charging valve for Hydragas units

11 Rear suspension radius arm
12 Rear exhaust system and silencer

3 Engine

Engine/gearbox removal and refitting – later models
All models
1   During 1982 the four-point engine mounting system was superseded by a three-point system. References in Chapter 1 to front and rear left-hand mountings should therefore be disregarded. The revised mountings are shown in Fig. 13.1 (photos).

2   On 1985-on models the engine/gearbox removal and refitting procedure differs slightly to that for previous models in respect of the self-adjusting clutch cable. However, the information for disconnecting and reconnecting the cable is given in Section 7 of this Supplement.

MG Turbo models
3   Proceed as described in Chapter 1, Section 5, paragraphs 1 to 16.

4   Disconnect and remove the oil cooler.

5   Raise and securely support the front of the vehicle.

6   Disconnect the speedometer cable from the gearbox, and remove the exhaust downpipe bracket from the gearbox.

7   Drive out the roll pin and disconnect the gear selector rod from the selector shaft. Unbolt the steady rod from the gearbox.

8   Disconnect the choke and throttle cables from the carburettor.

9   Remove the left-hand roadwheel and support the suspension lower arm on a trolley jack.

10 Disconnect both top and bottom swivel hub balljoints. It is advisable, though not essential, to remove the left-hand brake caliper beforehand, to avoid straining the hydraulic hose.

11 Release the left-hand driveshaft from the differential side gear as described in Chapter 8, Section 3.

12 The weight of the engine/transmission unit should now be taken on the lifting gear. Disconnect the engine mountings and raise the unit slightly.

13 Disengage the right-hand driveshaft from the differential side gear.

14 Make a last check for any wires, cables or hoses which have been overlooked, then move the unit forwards and lift it out of the vehicle.

15 Refitting is a reversal of the removal procedure.

Engine mounting modifications
16 Apart from the changes to three-point mounting described above, improvements have been made to the damping properties of the four-point mountings. These improvements reduce 'shake' at 30 to 50 mph. The improved mountings are identified by a spot of yellow paint.

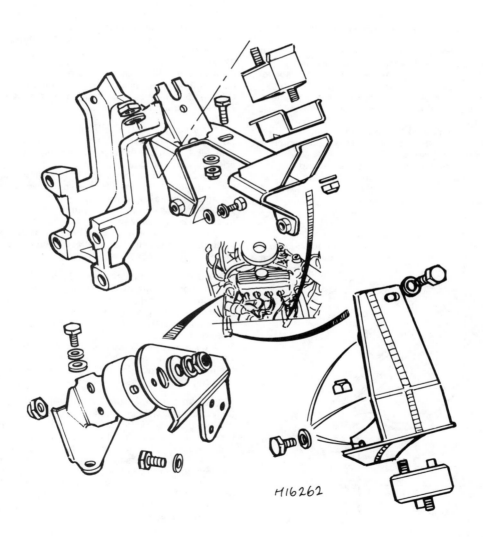

H16262

Fig. 13.1 Three-point engine mountings. Manual transmission version shown – automatic is similar (Sec 3)

3.1A Right-hand rear engine mounting

3.1B Right-hand front engine mounting

They are fitted to all positions except the left-hand rear, which is unchanged.

17 When renewing the old type mountings with the new type, discard the washers above and below the old mointings. In their place fit a cupped washer (domed side up) below, and a plain washer above. These washers should be purchased with the mountings.

18 If after fitting the improved mountings, 'shake' is still a problem, consult a reputable tyre specialist with a view to obtaining the best possible wheel and tyre balance.

19 The above remarks do not apply to the MG Turbo, which is fitted with harder mountings than standard. Additionally, the right-hand rear mounting is fitted with a retaining snubber.

20 From late 1986, the bracket attaching the right-hand rear engine mounting to the flywheel housing is increased in thickness to 0.315 in (8.0 mm). The securing bolts for the new bracket are longer than the previous bolts, and the torque setting is revised, as given in the Specifications.

Cylinder head (MG Turbo) – removal and refitting

21 To save time, it is not necessary to remove the turbocharger and exhaust manifold in order to remove the cylinder head. The inlet manifold however should be removed, then after removing the nuts

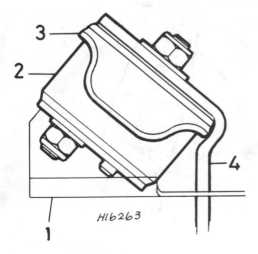

Fig. 13.2 Right-hand rear engine mounting fitted to MG Turbo models (Sec 3)

| 1 | Subframe bracket | 3 | Snubber |
| 2 | Mounting rubber | 4 | Engine bracket |

from the end studs, a stud removal tool can be used to extract both studs. Two narrow nuts locked together may alternatively be used to remove the studs.

22 When the cylinder head is lifted from the cylinder block, the exhaust manifold remains in the engine compartment. Remember to renew the exhaust manifold gasket when refitting the cylinder head. Oil the bolt threads, and tighten in the correct sequence to the specified torque.

Inlet valve oil seals (998 cc)

23 The valve stem oil seals fitted to the larger engine, as described in Chapter 1, are now fitted to the smaller engine as well. This has the effect of reducing oil consumption.

24 The fitting of the seals has also required the fitting of modified valves (with cotter grooves nearer the end of the stem). The valve spring seat has also been raised by 0.05 in (1.2 mm).

25 New type valves and seals can be fitted to old type cylinder heads, in complete sets only, with the addition of a shim 0.05 in (1.2 mm) thick underneath each spring. These shims may also be found already fitted to engines which left the factory with new type valves and seals in unmodified heads.

Timing cover removal and refitting (engine in vehicle)

26 On models with the three-point engine mounting system, the following additional operations are required when removing the timing cover with the engine *in situ*. Refer also to Chapter 1, Section 11.

27 Disconnect the windsceeen washer pump plug and move the reservoir to one side.

28 After removing the crankshaft pulley, lift the alternator so that its adjusting link is clear of the timing cover. Wedge or clamp the alternator in this position while the cover is removed.

29 Refitting is a reversal of the removal procedure.

Crankshaft pulley bolt – removal and refitting

30 When removing the crankshaft pulley bolt with the engine still in the car, there is insufficient room to use a normal socket due to the location of the right-hand engine mounting. A ring spanner may be used instead, but if the bolt is particularly tight, tool 18G 98A (Fig. 13.3) should be obtained from a tool hire agent. The tool has a strengthened tip for hitting with a heavy hammer.

31 Early crankshaft pulley bolts may be found to have a shoulder which can foul the end of the crankshaft and cause the pulley to become loose. Where this has occurred, renew the pulley and fit the later modified bolt together with a lockwasher. The later bolt does not have a shoulder.

Plain main bearing shells

32 During 1982, modifications were made to the cylinder block and main bearing caps. The lower main bearing shells fitted to these modified units are plain, ie they have no central oil groove. Both engine sizes are affected.

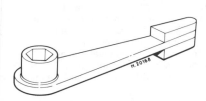

Fig. 13.3 Tool 18G 98A for unscrewing the crankshaft pulley bolt (Sec 3)

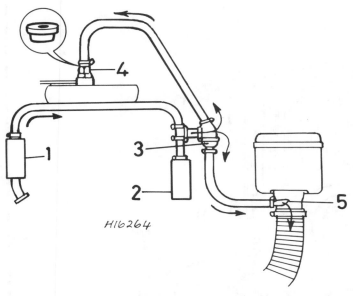

H16264

Fig. 13.4 Crankcase ventilation system fitted to MG Turbo models (Sec 3)

1   Oil separator (flywheel   3   Regulator valve
    housing)   4   One-way restrictor valve
2   Oil separator (timing cover) 5   Air cleaner nozzle

33 Make sure that the correct type shells are obtained when engine overhaul is undertaken. The new and old type bearings are **not** interchangeable.

Crankcase ventilation system – MG Turbo
34 The crankcase ventilation system on MG Turbo models is modified slightly from the standard design in order to prevent the turbocharger pressurising the crankcase.
35 At low engine speeds and on the overrun, fumes are drawn into the inlet manifold via the one-way restrictor valve.
36 As the engine speed rises and the inlet manifold becomes pressurised, the one-way restrictor valve closes. Fumes are then inducted via the regulator valve into the air cleaner.
37 Maintenance is as described in Chapter 1, Section 18. Additionally, the valves should be cleaned periodically and renewed if their operation is suspect.

Pistons and connecting rods
38 From early 1987, on the 998 cc engine, the piston gudgeon pins are a press fit in the connecting rods instead of being retained by circlips in the pistons. This arrangement is as used on the 1275 cc engine, making piston and connecting rod renewal a job best left to a BL garage.

Oil coolers – description
39 Two types of oil cooler may be encountered. The first type, fitted to MG 1300 and Vanden Plas models, uses engine coolant as the heat exchange medium. This type of cooler fits in between the oil filter head and the oil filter itself. The second type of cooler, fitted to Automatic and MG Turbo models, uses air as the heat exchange medium and is similar in appearance to a coolant radiator.
40 Depending on operating territory and production date, oil coolers may be encountered on models other than those mentioned above.

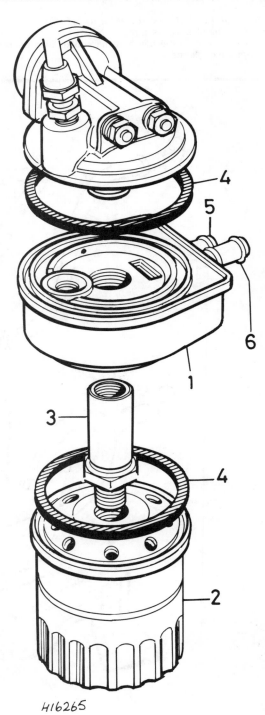

H16265

Fig. 13.5 Oil cooler – water-cooled type (Sec 3)

1   Oil cooler   4   Sealing rings
2   Oil filter   5   Coolant inlet
3   Fixing bolt   6   Coolant outlet

Oil cooler (water-cooled) – removal and refititng

41 Drain the cooling system as described in Chapter 2.
42 Disconnect the coolant hoses from the oil cooler.
43 Remove the oil filter cartridge as described in Chapter 1.
44 Unscrew the centre fixing bolt and remove the oil cooler. Recover the sealing ring if this did not come away with the cooler.
45 Refitting is a reversal of the removal procedure. Use a new sealing ring and a new oil filter cartridge. Refill the cooling system and check the engine oil level after running the engine.

Oil cooler (air-cooled) – removal and refitting

46 Remove the air cleaner assembly to improve access.
47 Disconnect and plug the hoses at the cooler. Be prepared for oil spillage from the cooler itself.

48 Release the cooler from its mounting brackets and bushes. (In the case of the MG Turbo, release the top bracket from the body and remove the bracket and bush with the cooler.)
49 With the cooler removed, flush it through with petrol or cellulose thinner if internal blockage or contamination was the reason for removal. Blow through with compressed air to dry out the cleaning solvent. Clean the fins with paraffin or a suitable detergent. Do not forget to flush the hoses too if necessary.
50 Refitting is a reversal of the removal procedure. Use new mounting bushes if the old ones were in poor condition. On MG Turbo models, fit the outlet hose in line with the oil cooler, and the inlet hose offset at an angle of 10°.
51 Top up the engine oil level (by approximately the amount lost), start the engine and check for leaks. On MG Turbo models, **do not** rev

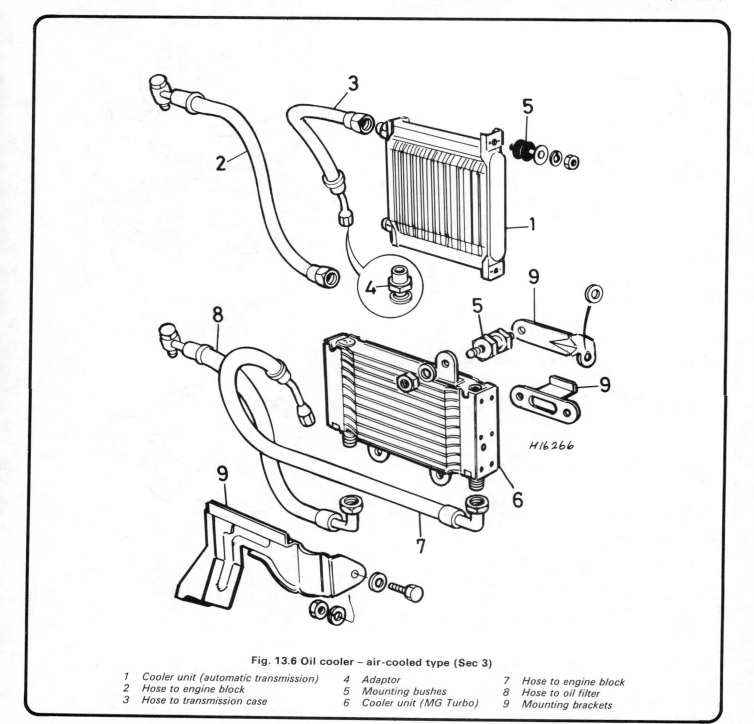

Fig. 13.6 Oil cooler – air-cooled type (Sec 3)

1 Cooler unit (automatic transmission)	4 Adaptor	7 Hose to engine block
2 Hose to engine block	5 Mounting bushes	8 Hose to oil filter
3 Hose to transmission case	6 Cooler unit (MG Turbo)	9 Mounting brackets

the engine for at least 10 seconds after this start-up, otherwise there is a danger of damaging the turbocharger bearings. Recheck the oil level after stopping the engine.

Camshaft/distributor driveshaft (1985-on 1.3 models) – refitting

52 As a result of 1985-on 1.3 models being fitted with the electronic ignition 65 DM4 distributor, incorporating an external amplifier module, the angle at which the distributor driveshaft is fitted is different to that given in Chapter 1, Section 33.

53 The revised slot angle is shown in Fig. 13.7, but, with this exception, the procedure is identical.

4 Cooling system

Expansion tank leakage

1 Under certain operating conditions, small quantities of coolant may be discharged from the pressure relief valve hole in the expansion tank filler neck. This coolant may collect along the expansion tank seam, giving the impression that the tank itself is leaking at the seam.

2 If expansion tank leakage is suspected, therefore, be sure that the apparent leakage is not due to the normal behaviour of the pressure relief cap and hole. Talcum powder dusted over the outside of the tank will show the source of small leaks.

Radiator bottom hose fitting

3 On models where the radiator bottom hose incorporates a take-off point for the oil cooler and/or heater matrix, take care not to push the connecting pipe so far into the hose that the take-off point is blocked (photo).

4 Correct fitting of this hose should be checked if problems are experienced with poor heater output.

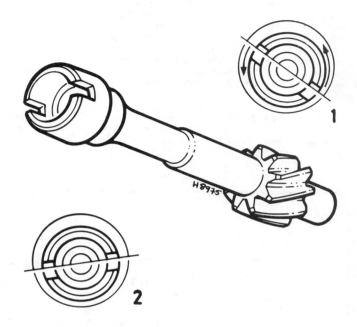

Fig. 13.7 Distributor driveshaft fitting procedure for 1985-on 1.3 models (Sec 3)

1 Initial fitting position   *2 Fitted position (TDC)*

4.3 Bottom hose with take-off for oil cooler

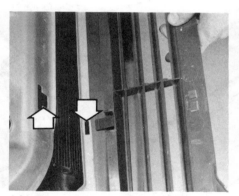

4.6A Front grille location slots (arrowed)

4.6B Removing the front cross panel strut bolt

4.6C Removing the front cross panel mounting screws

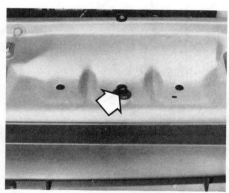

4.6D Radiator upper left-hand mounting (arrowed)

4.6E Radiator fitted to 1985 models

Cooling system (1985-on models) – general description

5   The cooling system components for 1985-on models are shown in Fig. 13.8. The radiator thickness has been reduced considerably, but its length has been increased. The cooling fan assembly is now attached to the radiator by nuts instead of bolts. The radiator top hose inlet is now at the top right-hand side of the radiator. The cylinder block drain plug is still located on the rear right-hand side of the cylinder block, but the reference in Chapter 2, Section 2 to the clutch slave cylinder does not apply.

Radiator (1985-on models) – removal and refitting

6   The procedure is identical to that given in Chapter 2, however the upper right-hand mounting is concealed beneath the bonnet lock cross panel, and extra care is necessary to ensure that the locating pin enters the mounting bush. The front grille is no longer retained with

screws, but must be lifted and withdrawn from the location slots (photos).

Cooling fan assembly (1985-on models) – removal and refitting

7   The removal procedure is as described in Chapter 2, except that the assembly is retained by nuts instead of bolts.
8   To remove the fan motor from the cowl, drill out the three rivets. It is not possible to overhaul the motor.
9   Use new pop-rivets to secure the fan motor to the cowl.

Thermostat – fitting

10 When fitting the thermostat, make sure that the spring support pillars do not obstruct the heater outlet in the sandwich plate.

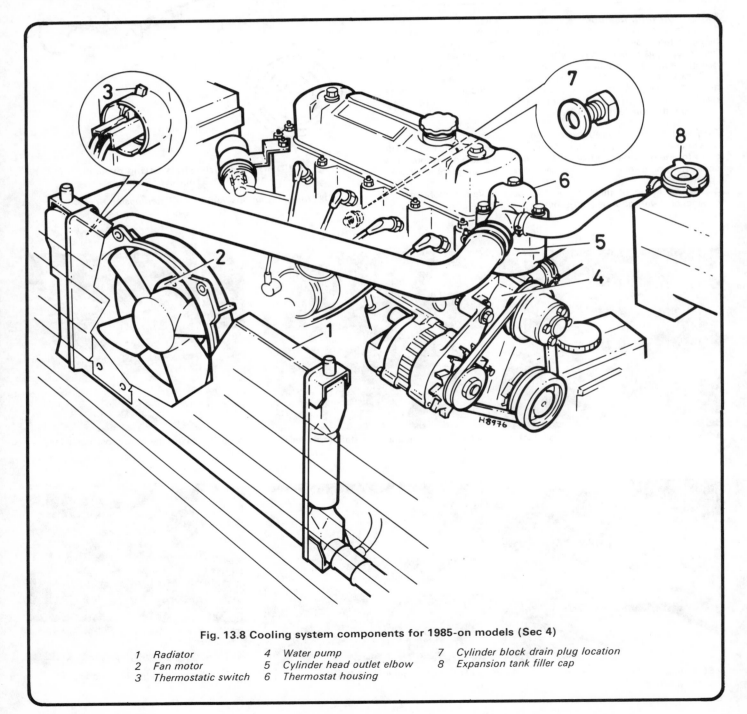

Fig. 13.8 Cooling system components for 1985-on models (Sec 4)

1	Radiator	4	Water pump	7	Cylinder block drain plug location
2	Fan motor	5	Cylinder head outlet elbow	8	Expansion tank filler cap
3	Thermostatic switch	6	Thermostat housing		

5 Fuel and exhaust systems

Air cleaner (MG 1300 and Vanden Plas models) – description and testing

1 MG 1300 non-Turbo models, pre-1985 LHD Vanden Plas and 1985-on manual transmission Vanden Plas models are fitted with an air cleaner similar to that described in Chapter 3, with the addition of a vacuum-operated flap valve to control the intake air temperature.

2 Removal and refitting are as described in Chapter 3, but additionally the vacuum hose must be disconnected and reconnected (photo).

3 A visual check may be made to determine correct operation of the temperature control system. On starting the engine from cold, the flap in the air cleaner snout should be positioned so that air is drawn only from the hot air pick-up shroud. As the engine warms up, or if the vacuum hose is disconnected, the flap should move to close the hot air intake in favour of the cold air.

4 Malfunction of the temperature control system may be due to a faulty temperature sensor (photo), a faulty vacuum motor, or a failure in the vacuum supply (hose blocked or leaking). The temperature sensor is available separately from the air cleaner body, but the vacuum motor is not.

Air cleaner (MG Turbo models) – removal and refitting

5 The air cleaner on MG Turbo models is remote from the carburettor, being mounted on the left-hand side of the engine compartment.

6 To renew the air cleaner element, release the spring clips and take off the cover. Extract the element, wipe clean the inside of the housing and fit a new element. Refit the cover and secure with the spring clips.

7 To remove the air cleaner unit complete, first disconnect the large supply hose and the small crankcase ventilation system hose.

8 Unbolt the air cleaner bracket from the car body and remove the air cleaner complete with bracket. The air cleaner bracket and body can be separated after removing the four screws from the base.

9 Refitting is a reversal of the removal procedure.

Fuel filter (MG Turbo models) – renewal

10 The fuel filter is located in the fuel line between the pressure regulator and the carburettor. It should be renewed at the intervals specified in *Routine Maintenance,* or more frequently if filter blockage is suspected.

11 Take precautions against fire when removing the filter, and do not smoke. Residual pressure in the fuel lines may lead to significant fuel spillage when the filter is removed.

12 Release the hose clamps on each side of the filter and carefully pull off the hoses. Inspect the hoses and clips; renew these too, if necessary. Mop up any fuel spilt.

13 Fit the new filter. A directional arrow or an 'OUT' marking should point towards the carburettor; an 'IN' marking should face the pressure regulator. In the absence of any markings the filter may be fitted either way round.

14 Secure the new filter with the hose clamps. When all spilt fuel has been removed from the engine bay, start the engine and check for leaks.

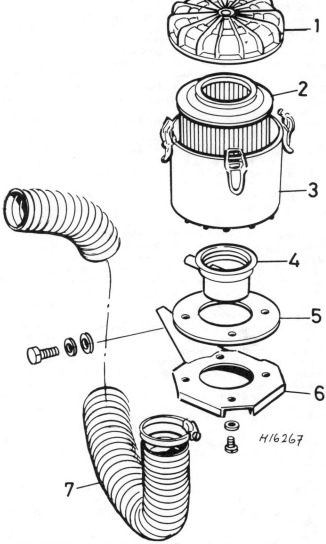

Fig. 13.9 Air cleaner components – MG Turbo models (Sec 5)

1 Cover	5 Seal
2 Element	6 Bracket
3 Housing	7 Supply hose
4 Adaptor	

5.2 Air cleaner vacuum hose connection

5.4 Air cleaner temperature sensor (inside air cleaner body)

5.40 Anti-run-on valve is mounted on bulkhead

Fuel pump knock (all models except MG Turbo) – rectification

15 Under certain conditions it is possible for the normal operation of the fuel pump to give rise to a knocking noise. From inside the car this noise may be mistaken for a sign of serious engine problems.

16 Diagnosis of fuel pump knock requires the help of an assistant. One person should sit in the car and hold the engine speed at the level where the knock is most pronounced, whilst another person squeezes and releases the fuel pump inlet flexible hose. If the noise changes or disappears when the hose is squeezed, this confirms that the fuel pump is the source of the noise.

17 Fuel pump knock can be eliminated by attention to the following points:

  (a) Make sure that the metal fuel pipe from the tank fits into its clip on the bulkhead without strain
  (b) Make sure that the flexible pipes are not touching the bulkhead, nor their clips
  (c) If the flexible pipes are under tension, fit longer pipes to relieve this

Fuel pump (MG Turbo models) – description and testing

18 The fuel pump fitted to MG Turbo models is electrically operated. The pump is located next to the fuel tank, at the rear of the vehicle.

19 Electrical supply to the pump is via a relay energised by the starter motor solenoid when the engine is being started; thereafter the relay is controlled by the oil pressure warning switch. This means that the pump will stop if the engine stalls, or if there is a catastrophic fall in oil pressure when the engine is running.

20 The fuel pump output is at high pressure. The fuel pressure regulator valve in the engine bay reduces the fuel pressure according to the requirements of the carburettor.

21 If the pump output is reckoned to be insufficient, this can be checked by disconnecting the oil pressure warning light switch, turning on the ignition and removing the fuel filler cap. Fuel should be coming out of the return line with a sufficient force to hit the far side of the filler neck. If not, check the pipes.

22 Before condemning the pump on the test above, make sure that it is not the relay which is faulty. Disconnect the fuel pump relay multiplug (under the bonnet) and join the white/green and white/purple leads (relay terminals 85 and 30/51). If the pump output is now satisfactory, the relay is faulty.

Fuel pump (MG Turbo models) – removal and refitting

23 Disconnect the battery earth lead, then raise and securely support the rear of the car. Temporarily remove the fuel filler cap to release any residual pressure in the tank, then refit it.

24 Disconnect the fuel hoses from the pump and plug them. Be prepared for some fuel spillage. Release the inlet hose from its clip.

25 Disconnect the electrical leads from the pump, identifying them if necessary.

26 Remove the nuts which secure the fuel pump mountings to the support bracket. Work the pump over to the right-hand side of the car so that it can be extracted through the rear of the subframe.

27 Separate the pump from its mounting bracket. The pump cannot be repaired, but must be renewed if defective. If it is wished to renew the pump inlet and outlet hoses, the fuel tank must first be removed.

28 Refitting the fuel pump is a reversal of the removal procedure. Position the pump in its mounting bracket so that the positive (+) connector will be vertically above the negative (−) connector when the pump is installed.

29 Run the engine and check for leaks on completion.

Fuel pump (automatic transmission models) – renewal

30 If the new fuel pump has a larger diameter body flange than the original, the kickdown rod may also need to be renewed.

Fuel tank (MG Turbo models) – removal and refitting

31 The operations are as described in Chapter 3, Section 4, but the fuel pump must be removed as described above before the tank can be removed.

Fuel tank (5-door models) – removal and refitting

32 The operations are as described in Chapter 3, Section 4, except for the information given in paragraph 4. Do not detach the right-hand side Hydragas suspension unit or lower the subframe, but instead carry out the procedure in the following paragraphs.

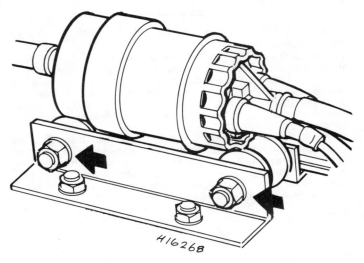

H1626B

Fig. 13.10 MG Turbo fuel pump. Remove nuts (arrowed) to release pump and mountings from support bracket (Sec 5)

33 Unscrew the nut from the exhaust system rear mounting and support the system on an axle stand.

34 Loosen the filler hose clips and slide the hose off the fuel tank stub.

35 When refitting the fuel tank make sure that the filler hose is positioned equally on the tank stub and filler tube before tightening the clips.

Choke control cable (1985-on models) – removal and refitting

36 On 1985-on models the choke control cable has been repositioned to the facia panel. However, the removal and refitting procedure is basically as given in Chapter 3.

Idle speed and idler gear noise

37 Particularly on high mileage engines, noise from the idler gear at idle is a fairly common occurence. Should the owner wish to reduce this noise it is permissible to increase the idle speed, up to the following maximum values. Note that this procedure is not permitted on MG, Vanden Plas or Turbo models.

998 cc engine	880 rpm maximum
1275 cc engine	930 rpm maximum

38 Having increased the idle speed, check that engagement of gears and overrun characteristics are not adversely affected.

Throttle damper deleted (later models)

39 The throttle damper described in Chapter 3, Section 11, is not fitted to vehicles manufactured from early 1982. The instructions for its adjustment may therefore be ignored.

Anti run-on valve (MG 1300 models) – removal and refitting

40 The anti run-on valve is mounted on a bracket on the bulkhead (photo). Its function is to prevent the engine running-on ('dieseling') after the ignition is switched off. If it is disconnected or broken it may prevent the engine from idling or running at low speeds.

41 To remove the valve, disconnect the electrical connectors and the hose from it.

42 Undo the bracket securing nut and remove the valve complete with bracket.

43 Refit in the reverse order, and check for correct operation on completion.

Carburettor – dismantling and reassembly

44 On later models the carburettor piston may have a circlip fitted to the tip of the guide rod. Where this is so, push the piston fully into the suction chamber and remove the circlip before separating the components.

45 A modified float is fitted from early 1987, and the float level setting has been changed both for the early and modified floats (see Fig. 13.11). The method of checking the setting is as described in Chapter 3, Section 13, but adjustment of the later type is by bending the float arm instead of the brass tab.

Turbocharger and associated components – description

46 The turbocharger fitted to the MG Turbo model is of the 'blow through' type, ie the compressor blows air into the carburettor. The turbocharger is made up of three housings; exhaust, centre and compressor.

47 The exhaust housing is connected to the exhaust manifold. It contains the turbine wheel and the wastegate.

48 The centre housing contains the shaft which connects the turbine and compressor wheels, together with the associated seals and bearings. Oil for bearing lubrication and heat transfer is fed to the centre housing from the engine's lubrication system.

49 The compressor housing contains the compressor wheel. It is connected to the plenum chamber and thence to the carburettor. Boost pressure sensing connections and a dump valve (to release excess pressure) are located in the plenum chamber.

50 Exhaust gas flowing past the turbine wheel causes the wheel to rotate at speeds of up to 130 000 rpm. The compressor wheel, on the same shaft, compresses air into the engine's induction system at a pressure of up to 7 lbf/in² (0.5 kgf/cm²), thus improving efficiency and performance. Boost pressure is limited in several ways. A device known as a wastegate diverts part of the exhaust gas flow away from the turbine wheel when boost pressure has reached a certain value. The pressure at which the wastegate operates is increased as engine speed rises; this is achieved by the electronic control unit (ECU), which opens a pressure reducing valve, thus reducing the pressure available for operating the wastegate. The dump valve, already mentioned, releases excess pressure from the plenum chamber.

51 The increased fuel demand at high speed and large throttle openings is catered for by the fuel pressure regulating valve. This valve increases fuel delivery in proportion to boost pressure. A boost gauge on the dashboard, linked to the ECU, displays to the driver the boost pressure being developed.

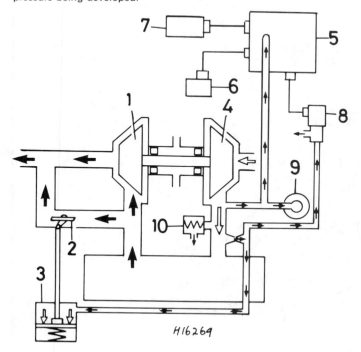

Fig. 13.12 Schematic diagram of turbocharger control systems (Sec 5)

1 Turbine wheel	6 Ignition amplifier
2 Wastegate	7 Boost gauge
3 Wastegate actuator	8 Pressure reducing valve
4 Compressor wheel	9 Fuel pressure regulator
5 Electronic control unit	10 Dump valve

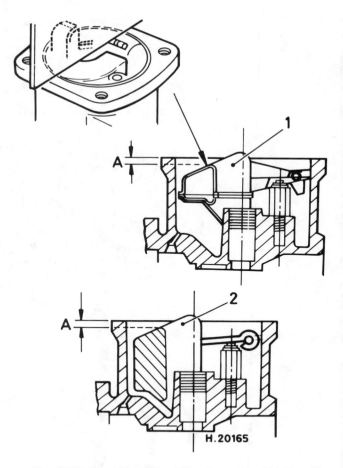

H.20165

Fig. 13.11 Float level checking dimension (A) (Sec 5)

Arrows indicate checking point

Early float (1) = 0.040 ± 0.020 in (1.0 ± 0.5 mm)
Later float (2) = 0.080 ± 0.020 in (2.0 ± 0.5 mm)

Turbocharger – cautions

52 Although the turbocharger is a simple unit, it operates at very high speeds and high temperatures. Certain precautions should be observed, both for personal safety and to avoid damage to the unit. These are as follows.

53 **Do not** *run the engine with the air intake hose disconnected*. The compressor rotates fast enough to cause grave personal injury, and there is a chance of foreign bodies being sucked in and damaging the compressor.

54 **Do not** *rev the engine immediately after start-up*. Wait a few seconds for oil pressure to become established at the turbine shaft bearings. This is especially important after an oil filter change, when the pressure may take a significant time to build up.

55 **Do not** *switch the engine off without allowing it to idle for at least 10 seconds*. Switching off immediately after a run can leave the turbine rotating at high speed with no oil pressure available at the bearings.

56 The above points also serve to stress the importance of regular oil and filter changes, and conscientious checking of the oil level between changes. Neglect of these items could prove very costly.

Turbocharger – removal, inspection and refitting

57 Disconnect the battery earth lead. Chock the rear wheels, then raise and securely support the front of the car.

58 Remove the U-bolt and clamp plate which secure the exhaust downpipe.

59 Release the hose clip which secures the oil drain hose to the turbochargers. Free the hose from the adaptor.

60 Disconnect and plug the coolant hoses which supply the inlet manifold. Be prepared for some coolant spillage.

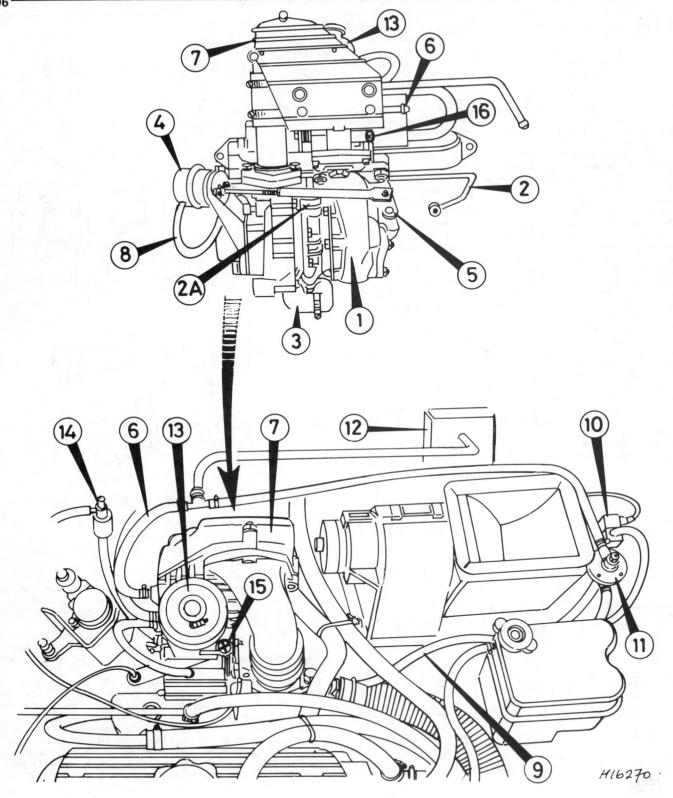

Fig. 13.13 MG Turbo engine compartment and rear of turbocharger (Sec 5)

1	Turbocharger	6	Pressure sensing hose (to	9	Pressure hose (to pressure	13	Carburettor
2	Oil inlet pipe		ECU and fuel regulator)		reducing valve)	14	Float chamber venting valve
2A	Oil inlet pipe union	7	Plenum chamber	10	Pressure reducing valve and		(if fitted)
3	Oil drain hose	8	Pressure hose (to wastegate		solenoid	15	Idle speed adjustment screw
4	Wastegate actuator		actuator)	11	Fuel pressure regulator	16	Idle mixture adjustment
5	Wastegate operating arm			12	Electronic control unit		screw

61 Disconnect and plug the fuel hose from the carburettor. Be prepared for some fuel spillage.
62 Disconnect the air pressure hose from the plenum chamber. Remove the heat shield from the plenum chamber, slacken the inlet hose clip, undo the two through-bolts and remove the plenum chamber.
63 Free the crankcase ventilation system oil trap from the flywheel housing. Disconnect the banjo union from the inlet manifold and the vacuum advance pipe from the carburettor. Move the hoses to one side.
64 Remove the heat shields from the clutch master cylinder and from the flywheel housing.
65 Release the manifold securing nuts. Unscrew the nuts which secure the inlet manifold as far as the ends of their studs.
66 Work the inlet manifold and carburettor free of the manifold gasket and off the studs. Move the assembly to one side.
67 Disconnect the air intake hose and the boost control hose from the turbocharger housing.
68 Remove the clamp which secures the exhaust pipe to the turbocharger elbow.
69 Disconnect the oil supply pipe at the warning light switch adaptor.
70 Support the engine/gearbox assembly with a jack (preferably a trolley jack), using a piece of wood to spread the load.
71 Remove the nut and washers from the rear right-hand engine mounting. Depending on the flexibility of the remaining mountings, the front right-hand mounting may also need to be disconnected.
72 Remove the nuts from the manifold studs. Raise the engine on the jack sufficiently to extract the exhaust manifold and turbocharger together, at the same time freeing the drain hose.
73 Separate the turbocharger from the exhaust manifold. If necessary,

remove the oil feed pipe and drain elbow, and the exhaust pipe adaptor.
74 **Do not** immerse the turbocharger in solvent for cleaning purposes. Use solvent if necessary to clean the outside of the wastegate housing, and use a scraper or wire brush to remove carbon. Make sure that the wastegate moves freely.
75 If a dial gauge indicator is available, the radial and axial clearances of the turbine bearings may be measured (Fig. 13.14). The clearances must not exceed the values given in the Specifications.
76 If a regulated compressed air supply is available, apply air pressure to the wastegate actuator and check that the wastegate operates at 4 lbf/in² (0.28 kgf/cm²).
77 No DIY repair to the turbocharger is possible. If the bearings are worn, or some other malfunction is evident, it should be traded in for a new one.
78 If a new turbocharger is being fitted, lubricate the bearings by pouring clean engine oil into the oil inlet port, rotating the compressor wheel at the same time. Drain the oil afterwards.
79 Refitting the turbocharger is a reversal of the removal procedure, but note the following points.

(a) Use a copper-based anti-seize compound on all nuts, bolts and studs
(b) Use new gaskets for the inlet manifold-to-engine and manifold-to-carburettor joints (the latter only if it has been disturbed). Make sure that the mating faces are clean
(c) Make sure that the oil feed pipe is not strained or kinked, and that both its unions are tightened to the specified torque
(d) Remember to give the unit time to fill with oil before revving the engine

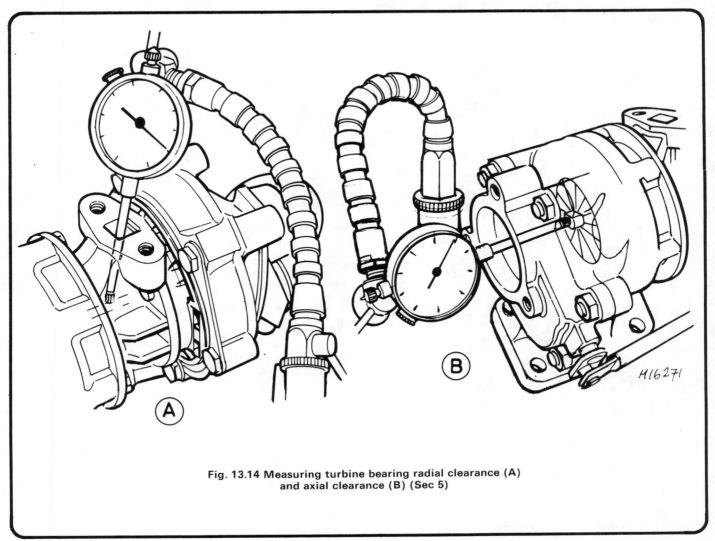

Fig. 13.14 Measuring turbine bearing radial clearance (A)
and axial clearance (B) (Sec 5)

Turbocharger control components – testing, removal and refitting

Pressure reducing valve

80 The pressure reducing valve and solenoid (sometimes together referred to as the boost solenoid valve) are located next to the fuel pressure regulator. Access is improved by moving aside the expansion tank and the cooling fan relay.

81 The solenoid may be tested *in situ* by applying the battery voltage directly to its terminals, when it should be heard to operate. It may be removed independently of the valve.

82 To remove the solenoid and valve together, unscrew the fuel regulator valve bracket. Turn the bracket on its side and unscrew the fuel regulator valve from the bracket.

83 Disconnect the pressure hose and unbolt the valve and solenoid.

84 Separate the solenoid and valve if wished. No repair is possible.

85 Refitting is a reversal of removal. Make sure that the vent hole in the valve is clear – in the case of a new valve, a blanking plug may be fitted for protection in transit, and this plug should be removed before fitting the valve.

Dump valve

86 Disconnect the pressure hose from the plenum chamber and remove the heat shield.

87 Slacken the compressor hose clip, undo the bolts and remove the plenum chamber from the carburettor.

88 Remove the diffuser pipe from the plenum chamber (two bolts at the front and one nut at the back). Be prepared for the dump valve piston and spring to be released.

89 Renew the piston and spring if the operation of the dump valve is suspect. There is no easy way of testing the components except by substitution.

90 Refit in the reverse order to removal, using new gaskets throughout.

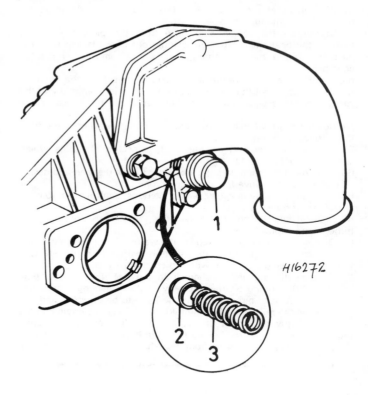

Fig. 13.15 Dump valve components (Sec 5)

1   Valve housing   3   Spring
2   Piston

Wastegate actuator

91 The wastegate actuator may be tested *in situ* by applying compressed air at 4 lbf/in² (0.28 kgf/cm²) to its pressure hose connection.

92 If the actuator fails to operate, temporarily remove its connecting rod and repeat the test. Continued failure means that the fault is in the actuator itself; if the actuator now operates, the fault is seizure of the wastegate, which may be rectified by removal and thorough cleaning (paragraph 67).

93 At the time of writing, the actuator unit was not available separately from the complete turbocharger. Removal and refitting are self-explanatory, but take care not to alter the actuating rod adjustment.

Electronic control unit

94 The electronic control unit (ECU) is reached from inside the vehicle. Begin by removing the glovebox (Chapter 12, Section 25) and pulling back the carpet.

95 Remove the closing panel and unscrew the mounting bracket from the front panel.

96 Unplug the electrical connector and disconnect the pressure hose, then remove the ECU complete with bracket.

97 No DIY testing procedures exist for the ECU, other than testing by substitution of a known good unit.

98 Refitting is the reverse of removal.

Fuel pressure regulator

99 Disconnect the battery earth lead.

100 Free the fuel pump relay and the expansion tank, and move them to one side.

101 Disconnect the pressure hose from the pressure reducing valve.

102 Unscrew the fuel pressure regulator bracket and turn the bracket to gain access to the regulator screws. Unscrew the regulator from the bracket.

103 Slide back the hose clips and disconnect the air pressure hose and the fuel hoses. Be prepared for some fuel spillage. Plug the fuel hoses.

104 No repairs to the fuel pressure regulator are possible. **Do not** attempt to alter the adjustment screw, which is preset and must not be moved.

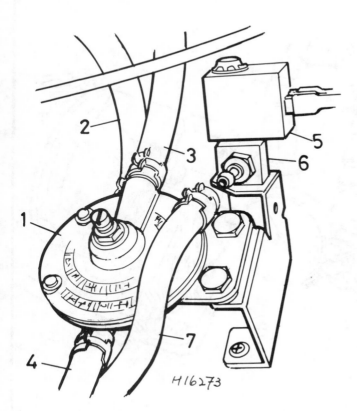

Fig. 13.16 Fuel pressure regulator and pressure reducing valve (Sec 5)

1   Fuel pressure regulator   5   Pressure reducing valve
2   Fuel outlet hose   solenoid
3   Pressure sensing hose   6   Pressure reducing valve
4   Fuel inlet hose   7   Pressure hose

105 Refitting is the reverse of removal. Use new hoses and/or clips if the condition of the old items is in doubt.

Carburettor (MG Turbo models) – description and maintenance

106 The SU HIF44 carburettor fitted to MG Turbo models works on the same principle as the normally aspirated versions. However, the Turbo carburettor is sealed against atmospheric pressure in order to maintain proper functioning throughout the range of boost pressures used, and to prevent fuel or fuel/air mixture being discharged into the engine compartment under conditions of high boost pressures.

107 The only maintenance required is a periodic check of the damper oil level. This is carried out in the same way as for the 'normal' carburettor, except that there is a securing clamp which must be released first and secured afterwards. *Failure to secure the damper cap may result in dangerous fuel leakage.*

108 The carburettor **must not** be dismantled as, at the time of writing, no repair kits are available. It is planned to make repair kits available only when pressure testing equipment has been developed and is in the hands of dealers. It cannot be emphasised too strongly that haphazard or ill-informed attempts at repair may result in dangerous fuel leakage.

109 If float chamber flooding is experienced, it may be possible to rectify the problem as follows.

110 Disconnect and plug the fuel inlet pipe at the carburettor. Also plug the carburettor fuel inlet. Mop up any spilt fuel.

111 Start the engine and run it until the fuel in the float chamber has been used up (indicated by the engine stopping).

112 Remove the plugs and reconnect the fuel inlet pipe to the carburettor, then restart the engine. The surge of fuel into the float chamber should clear the needle valve of dirt or grit which may have caused the flooding. If not, renew the carburettor.

Carburettor (MG Turbo models) – removal and refitting

113 Disconnect the battery earth lead.

114 Disconnect the pressure sensing hose from the plenum chamber and remove the heat shield. Release the inlet hose clip and unbolt and remove the plenum chamber.

115 Remove the compressor exit pipe and hose.

116 Disconnect the choke and throttle cables from the carburettor.

117 Disconnect the vacuum advance and the fuel supply pipes. Plug the fuel supply pipe. Disconnect the float chamber venting valve hose (if fitted).

118 Remove the nuts which secure the carburettor to the inlet manifold. Release the throttle cable bracket and remove the carburettor.

119 Refitting is a reversal of the removal procedure, but note the following points.

   (a) Use new gaskets and make sure that the mating surfaces are clean
   (b) Adjust the choke and throttle cables as described in Chapter 3
   (c) Top up the damper, then screw the damper cap firmly home and refit its clamp

Idle speed adjustment (all later models)

120 The procedure given in Chapter 3, Section 10, holds good for all later models. Refer to Fig. 13.13 for the location of the adjustment screws on MG Turbo models.

121 Depending on operating territory and production date, the idle mixture adjustment screw may be 'tamperproofed' by means of a plastic cap or seal, which must be destroyed in order to make an adjustment. The object of fitting the seal is to discourage (and to detect) adjustment by unqualified or unskilled operators.

122 If you wish to remove a tamperproof seal, satisfy yourself that you are not breaking any local or national anti-pollution laws by so doing. If the vehicle is still under warranty, be aware that you may be in breach of warranty conditions. Fit a new seal on completion where this is required by law.

Inlet and exhaust manifolds (MG and Vanden Plas models) – description, removal and refitting

123 MG 1300 and Turbo models are fitted with separate inlet and exhaust manifolds. The inlet manifold is heated by water from the cooling system.

124 Pre-1985 LHD Vanden Plas and 1985-on manual transmission Vanden Plas models are also fitted with separate manifolds, the inlet

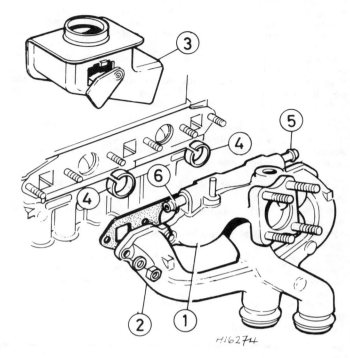

Fig. 13.17 Inlet and exhaust manifolds with coolant heating for inlet – non-Turbo models (Sec 5)

1 Inlet manifold   4 Ferrules
2 Exhaust manifold 5 Coolant inlet
3 Hot air shroud   6 Coolant outlet

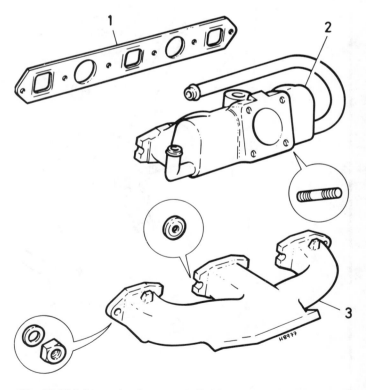

Fig. 13.18 Inlet and exhaust manifolds with coolant heating for inlet – Turbo models (Sec 5)

1 Manifold gasket   3 Exhaust manifold
2 Inlet manifold

manifold being coolant heated. However, all other Vanden Plas models are fitted with the combined manifold described in Chapter 3.

125 Removal and refitting of the manifolds on Turbo models is described earlier in this Section when dealing with turbocharger removal.

126 The procedure for non-Turbo models is basically the same as given in Chapter 3, but additionally the coolant hoses must be disconnected and plugged. If required, to prevent loss of coolant, the cooling system can be drained. Although each manifold may be removed separately, both must be removed in order to renew the gasket.

127 Before refitting the inlet manifold on non-Turbo models make sure that the ferrules are positioned correctly in the cylinder head ports. Always fit a new manifold gasket and on completion top up the cooling system as necessary.

Exhaust elbow gasket (MG Turbo models) – removal and refitting

128 Chock the rear wheels, then raise and securely support the front of the vehicle.

129 Remove the U-bolt and clamp which secure the exhaust pipe to the transmission.

130 Unscrew the clutch damper bracket and move it to one side. Remove the heat shield and disconnect the brake servo hose.

131 Remove the clamp which secures the exhaust downpipe to the elbow.

132 Relieve the locking tabs, then remove the retaining bolts from the exhaust elbow.

133 Remove the exhaust elbow and gasket.

134 Refitting is a reversal of removal. Use a new gasket and (ideally) new locktabs, and use high temperature anti-seize compound on the elbow bolts.

Exhaust system (all later models) – description, removal and refitting

135 Apart from the MG Turbo, later models have an exhaust system very much the same as that described in Chapter 3.

136 Various modifications have been made concerning the position, number and properties of exhaust mounting brackets and hangers. Consult your BL dealer, or a reputable exhaust specialist, if you wish to renew the mountings or are experiencing problems with vibration.

137 The MG Turbo shares with the 998 cc low compression model a single-downpipe exhaust system. It can safely be assumed that the two systems are not identical!

138 For removal and refitting procedures, refer to Chapter 3, Section 15.

Exhaust downpipes – modification

139 On cars subject to continual heavy use the exhaust downpipe may fracture just behind the first bend. To overcome this problem, a spring-tensioned balljoint is now fitted to allow slight flexing.

140 On MG Turbo models with a single downpipe, the balljoint is fitted with a single tensioning spring, but on twin downpipe models two springs are fitted.

141 The modified twin downpipe exhaust may be fitted instead of the earlier type, but it will be necessary to fit new exhaust mountings and new mounting brackets to the transmission and rear subframe. MG Turbo-type engine mountings should also be fitted.

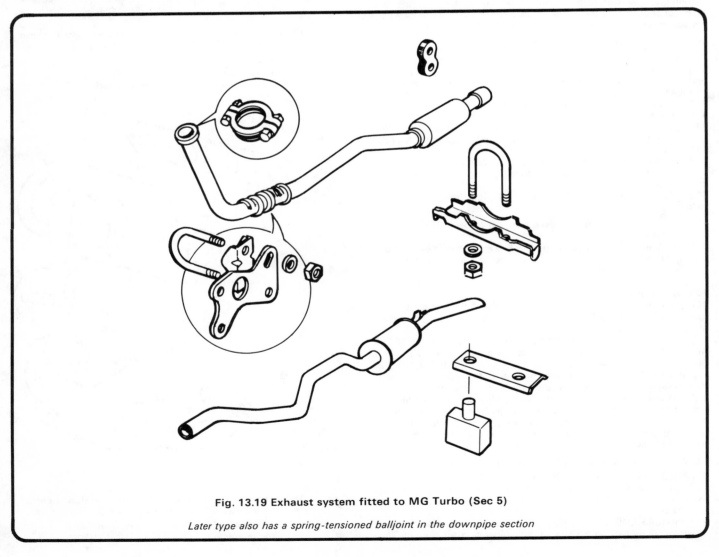

Fig. 13.19 Exhaust system fitted to MG Turbo (Sec 5)

Later type also has a spring-tensioned balljoint in the downpipe section

Fault diagnosis – turbocharger

Before attempting to diagnose faults from the table below, make sure that the air cleaner element is clean, the air intake is unrestricted, that all pressure sensing connections are tight and that the engine itself is in good condition.

Symptom	Reason(s)
Lack of engine power	Fuel starvation (check filter, regulator, pump) Exhaust manifold leak Exhaust system restricted Intake system restricted Crankcase ventilation system fault Turbocharger coked up Turbocharger internal fault Pressure reducing valve or ECU fault Float chamber venting valve (if fitted) faulty or disconnected
Blue smoke in exhaust gas	Engine oil level too high Crankcase ventilation system defective Turbo oil drain tube blocked Compressor oil seals failed
Oil consumption excessive	Oil leakage from behind compressor (unit must be removed to check)
Turbocharger excessively noisy	Intake or exhaust leak Turbine coked up Lubrication inadequate Turbocharger bearings failed

Electronic ignition system test procedure

Test	Remedy
Models fitted with 59 DM4 distributor	
1 Is the reluctor air gap set to the specified dimension?	Yes: Proceed to Test 2 No: Adjust the gap, as described in paragraph 31
2 Is the battery voltage greater than 11.5 volts?	Yes: Proceed to Test 3 No: Recharge the battery
3 Is the voltage at the coil '+' terminal more than 1 volt below battery voltage?	Yes: Faulty wiring or connector between ignition switch and coil Faulty ignition switch No: Proceed to Test 4
4 Is the voltage at the coil '–' terminal more than 2 volts?	Yes: Disconnect the wiring connector between distributor and ignition amplifier and proceed to Test 7 No: Disconnect the ignition amplifier lead at the coil '–' terminal and proceed to Test 5
5 Is the voltage at the coil '–' terminal now more than 2 volts?	Yes: Proceed to Test 6 No: Renew the ignition coil
6 Is the voltage at the ignition amplifier earth more than 0.1 volts?	Yes: Clean and/or repair the earth connection No: Renew the ignition amplifier
7 Is the pick-up coil resistance measured at the wiring connector terminals between 2.2k ohms and 4.8k ohms?	Yes: Reconnect the wiring connector between distributor and ignition amplifier and proceed to Test 8 No: Renew the pick-up coil assembly in the distributor
8 Does the voltage at the coil '–' terminal drop when the starter motor is operated?	Yes: Check and adjust the ignition timing. If the fault still exists the problem may lie with the engine internal components No: Renew the ignition amplifier
Models fitted with 65 DM4 distributor	
1 Is the battery voltage greater then 11.7 volts?	Yes: Proceed to Test 2 No: Recharge the battery
2 Is the voltage at the coil '+' terminal within 1 volt of battery voltage?	Yes: Proceed to Test 3 No: Faulty wiring or connector between ignition switch and coil, or faulty ignition switch
3 Is the resistance between the ignition coil '+' and '–' terminals between 0.4 and 0.9 ohms?	Yes: Proceed to Test 4 No: Renew the ignition coil

Test	Remedy
4 Is the resistance between the ignition coil '+' and HT terminals between 5.0 and 15.0 k ohms?	Yes: Proceed to Test 5 No: Renew the ignition coil
5 Connect a low-wattage bulb across the ignition coil '+' and '−' terminals and spin the engine on the starter. Does the bulb flash?	Yes: Proceed to Test 6 No: Proceed to Test 10
6 Is the resistance of any HT lead greater than 20 k ohms?	Yes: Renew the HT lead No: Proceed to Test 7
7 Are there signs of tracking on the ignition coil, distributor cap or rotor arm?	Yes: Renew the component as necessary No: Proceed to Test 8
8 Is the ignition timing correct?	Yes: Proceed to Test 9 No: Adjust ignition timing
9 Are the spark plugs in good condition?	Yes: Check carburettor settings and engine mechanical condition No: Renew the spark plugs
10 Are the module connections good?	Yes: Proceed to Test 11 No: Refer to paragraphs 56 to 59 of this Section
11 With the module removed, is the resistance of the distributor pick-up coil between 950 and 1150 ohms?	Yes: Refer to paragraphs 56 to 59 of this Section No: Renew the distributor pick-up coil

6 Ignition system

Electronic ignition system – description

1   The Lucas electronic ignition system consists of a distributor, an amplifier module and a coil. Externally, the distributor resembles a conventional type, but internally a reluctor and a pick-up unit take the place of the cam and contact breaker points.

2   Each time one of the reluctor teeth or arms passes through the magnetic field of the pick-up coil, an electrical signal is sent to the amplifier module which then triggers the coil in the same way as the opening of the points in a conventional system. Both centrifugal and vacuum advance are used in the accustomed manner.

3   Because there are no contact breaker points to wear out, the electronic ignition system is extremely reliable. As long as the distributor is lubricated and the spark plugs inspected or renewed at the specified intervals, and leads and connections are kept clean and dry, it is very unlikely that trouble will be experienced.

4   Because of the high voltages generated, *care should be taken to avoid receiving personal electric shocks from the HT system.* This is particularly important for anyone fitted with an artificial cardiac pacemaker.

Electronic ignition system – maintenance

5   At regular intervals (see *Routine Maintenance*) remove the distributor cap and thoroughly clean it inside and out with a dry lint-free rag. Examine the four HT lead segments inside the cap. If the segments appear badly burned or pitted, renew the cap. Make sure that the carbon brush in the centre of the cap is free to move and that it protrudes by approximately 0.1 in (3 mm) from its holder.

6   With the distributor cap removed, lift off the rotor arm. On pre-1985 models, remove the plastic anti-flash shield and carefully apply two drops of engine oil to the felt pad in the centre of the cam spindle. Also lubricate the centrifugal advance mechanism by applying two drops of oil through the square hole in the baseplate. On 1985 and later models, lubricate the bearing in the upper housing with a little engine oil, and lubricate the centrifugal advance mechanism by prising the plastic plug from the lower housing (photos). Wipe away any excess oil and refit the anti-flash shield (where fitted), rotor arm and distributor cap.

7   At the same service intervals, remove, clean and reset the spark plugs, using the procedure described in Chapter 4, Section 9. Using a stroboscopic timing light, check, and if necessary, reset the ignition timing, as described in Chapter 4, Section 6, paragraph 11 onwards.

Electronic ignition system – static timing

8   The only suitable method of ignition timing for road use is using a stroboscopic lamp. However, for initial setting-up purposes (eg after engine overhaul, or if the timing has been completely lost) the

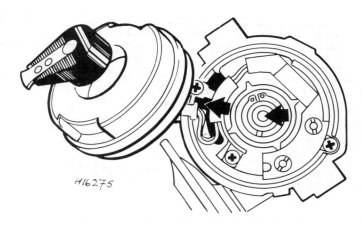

Fig. 13.20 Breakerless distributor lubrication points (arrowed) (Sec 6)

following procedure will enable the engine to be run in order to undertake dynamic timing.

9   Pull off the HT lead and remove No 1 spark plug (nearest the crankshaft pulley).

10 Place a finger over the plug hole and turn the engine in the normal direction of rotation (clockwise from the crankshaft pulley end) until pressure is felt in No 1 cylinder. This indicates that the piston is commencing its compression stroke. The engine can be turned with a socket and bar on the crankshaft pulley bolt.

11 Continue turning the engine until the notch in the crankshaft pulley is aligned with the TDC pointer on the timing scale.

12 Remove the distributor cap and check that the rotor arm is pointing towards the No 1 spark plug HT lead segment in the cap.

13 On pre-1985 models, lift off the rotor arm and anti-flash shield and observe the position of the reluctor in relation to the pick-up coil. One of the teeth on the reluctor should be aligned with, or very near to, the small pip, or limb, of the pick-up coil. Slacken the distributor clamp retaining bolt and turn the distributor body until the reluctor tooth and pick-up limb are directly in line. Tighten the distributor clamp and refit the anti-flash shield and the rotor arm.

14 On 1985-on models, if the rotor arm is not pointing towards the No 1 spark plug HT lead segment in the cap, slacken the distributor clamp bolt and turn the distributor body as necessary, then tighten the bolt. It

6.6A Lubricating the upper housing bearing on the 1985-on model electronic ignition distributor

6.6B Lubricating the centrifugal advance mechanism on the 1985-on model electronic ignition distributor

6.19A Extract the circlip

6.19B Lift off the washer and O-ring

6.20A Withdraw the reluctor ...

6.20B ... followed by the coupling ring

6.21 Disengage and withdraw the vacuum unit

6.22 Lift out the baseplate

6.24 Check the centrifugal advance mechanism for wear

6.31 Using a feeler gauge to measure the reluctor air gap

6.38 Removing the rotor arm

6.39A Amplifier module retaining screws (arrowed)

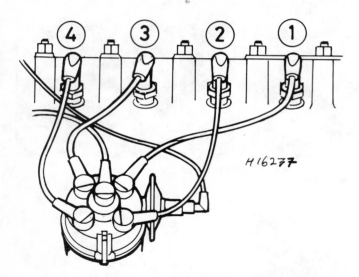

Fig. 13.21 HT lead connections and distributor orientation (Sec 6)

is not possible to align the reluctor arms as they are totally enclosed within the distributor.

15 Refit the distributor cap, No 1 spark plug and the HT lead.

16 it should now be possible to start and run the engine, enabling the ignition timing to be checked accurately using a stroboscopic timing light.

Electronic ignition distributor (pre-1985 models) – dismantling and reassembly

17 Remove the distributor as described in Chapter 4, Section 5.

18 Lift off the rotor arm, followed by the anti-flash shield.

19 Using circlip pliers, extract the retaining circlip (photo) and lift off the washer and O-ring (photo).

20 Withdraw the reluctor and coupling ring (photos) by carefully easing them off the shaft using a screwdriver if they are initially tight.

21 Undo and remove the screws securing the vacuum unit to the distributor body. Disengage the vacuum unit operating link from the peg on the underside of the baseplate using a twisting movement and withdraw the unit (photo).

22 Release the wiring harness rubber grommet and remove the two baseplate securing screws. Lift the baseplate out of its location in the distributor body (photo).

23 This is the limit of dismantling, as the parts located below the baseplate, the distributor shaft and distributor body can only be renewed as an assembly.

24 With the distributor dismantled, renew any parts that show signs of wear, or damage, and any that are known to be faulty. Pay close attention to the centrifugal advance mechanism (photo), checking for loose or broken springs, wear in the bob weight pivots and play in the distributor shaft.

25 Begin reassembly by lubricating the distributor shaft, bob weight pivots, vacuum link and baseplate sliding surfaces with engine oil.

26 Place the baseplate assembly in position, with the peg on the underside adjacent to the vacuum unit aperture. Refit and tighten the two securing screws.

27 Refit the coupling ring to the underside of the reluctor and slide this assembly over the distributor shaft. Align the broad lug of the coupling ring with the broad slot in the shaft, and push the ring and reluctor fully into place.

28 Position the O-ring and washer over the shaft and secure them with the circlip.

29 Insert the vacuum unit operating link into its aperture and manipulate the unit and baseplate until the link can be engaged with the peg. Refit and tighten the retaining screws.

30 Refit the harness leads and grommet to the slot in the distributor body.

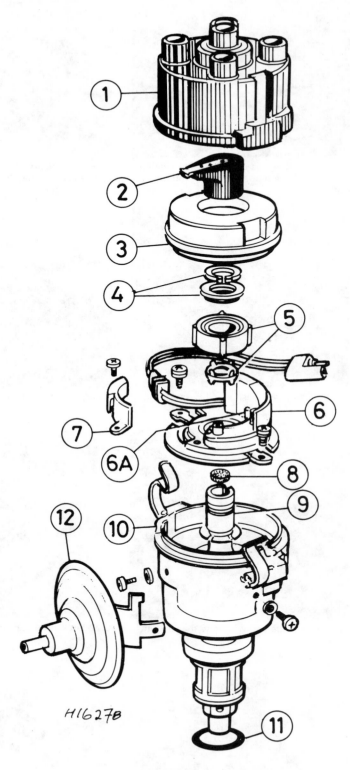

Fig. 13.22 Exploded view of 59 DM4 distributor (Sec 6)

1	Distributor cap	6A	Pick-up limb
2	Rotor arm	7	Wiring guide
3	Anti-flash shield	8	Felt pad
4	O-ring, washer and circlip	9	Distributor shaft
5	Reluctor and coupling ring	10	Distributor body
6	Pick-up coil and baseplate assembly	11	O-ring
		12	Vacuum unit

31 Position the reluctor so that one of the teeth is adjacent to the limb on the pick-up assembly. Using feeler gauges, preferably of plastic or brass, measure the air gap between the reluctor tooth and pick-up assembly (photo). If the measured dimension is outside the tolerance given in the Specifications, slacken the adjusting nuts on the pick-up assembly and reposition the unit as necessary.

32 Refit the anti-flash shield and rotor arm; then refit the distributor.

Electronic ignition amplifier (pre-1985 models) – general

33 The ignition amplifier is mounted on the bonnet lock platform, near the ignition coil. The amplifier controls the function of the ignition coil in response to signals received from the pick-up coil in the distributor.

34 The amplifier may be tested using the procedure described later in this Section. If it is found to be faulty it should be renewed.

35 To remove the unit, disconnect the battery earth lead and then disconnect the wiring plug from the end of the amplifier. Undo the bracket retaining screws and remove the bracket complete with amplifier. The amplifier can then be removed if wished.

36 Refitting is a reversal of removal. Make sure that there is good mechanical; and electrical contact between the amplifier and its bracket (which also serves as a heat sink) and between the bracket and its mounting area.

Electronic ignition distributor (1985-on models) – dismantling and reassembly

37 Remove the distributor, as described in Chapter 4, Section 5.

38 Pull off the rotor arm (photo).

39 Remove the two screws and pull the amplifier module from the connector, then remove the gasket and pull off the connector (photos).

40 Remove the screws and separate the upper housing from the lower housing (photos).

41 Remove the clamp ring and pick-up winding from the upper housing (photos).

42 Remove the vacuum unit retaining screw, then extract the circlip and thrust washer, withdraw the stator pack from the link arm, and remove the vacuum unit. Recover the remaining thrust washer from the upper housing (photos).

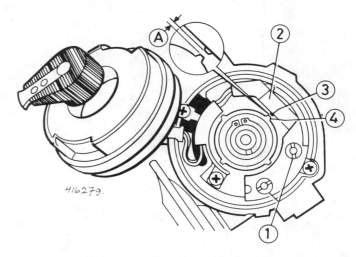

Fig. 13.23 Reluctor air gap adjustment (Sec 6)

1	Adjusting nuts	4	Reluctor tooth
2	Pick-up coil	A	Specified gap
3	Pick-up limb		

43 Further dismantling is not normally necessary. However, the shaft assembly may be removed from the lower housing by driving the roll pin from the drive dog after marking the drive dog in relation to the shaft (photos).

44 Clean and examine all the components, and renew them as required.

45 Refit the shaft assembly if removed, locate the drive dog and drive in the roll pin. Check that the drive dog offset is positioned correctly in relation to the rotor arm by referring to Fig. 13.24.

6.39B Removing the amplifier module

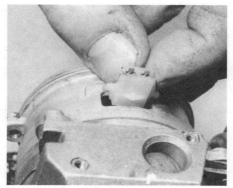

6.39C Removing the connector

6.40A Remove the screws ...

6.40B ... and withdraw the upper housing

6.41A Remove the clamp ring ...

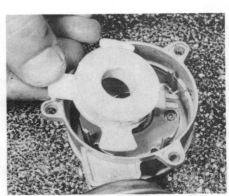

6.41B ... and pick-up winding

6.42A Vacuum unit retaining screw (arrowed)

6.42B Remove the circlip ...

6.42C ... followed by the thrust washer ...

6.42D ... stator pack ...

6.42E ... and thrust washer

6.43A Centrifugal mechanism in the distributor lower housing

6.43B Roll pin (arrowed) in the distributor drive dog

6.48 Stator pack fitted in the upper housing

6.60A Radiator moved to one side for access to the distributor (1985 1.3 model shown)

6.60B Removing the distributor cap ...

6.60C ... and wiring from the distributor (1985 1.3 model shown)

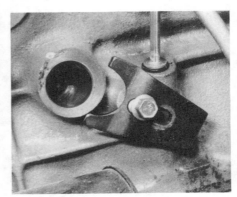

6.60D Distributor clamp and bolt

46 Lubricate the shaft bearing with a little engine oil. Also lubricate the centrifugal advance mechanism.

47 Locate the thrust washer in the upper housing.

48 Grease the end of the link arm then insert the vacuum unit in the upper housing and engage the stator pack with the link arm. Retain the stator pack with the thrust washer and circlip, and fit the vacuum unit retaining screw (photo).

49 Insert the pick-up winding in the upper housing and centralise the terminals in the aperture, then fit the clamp ring with the cut-out over the aperture.

50 Fit the lower housing to the upper housing and insert the screws finger tight. Rotate the shaft several times then fully tighten the screws.

51 Check that the reluctor arms do not touch the stator pack arms as they can easily be bent inadvertently.

52 Fit the connector and gasket.

53 Apply heat conducting silicone grease to the mounting face of the amplifier module then fit the module and tighten the screws.

54 Refit the rotor arm.

55 If necessary, renew the O-ring on the shank of the distributor, then refit the distributor, as described in Chapter 4.

Electronic ignition amplifier (1985-on models) – general

56 If, after carrying out the test procedure described at the end of this Section, the amplifier module is diagnosed as being faulty, make sure that the wiring is intact and secure.

57 As a double-check remove the module, gasket and connector, and lightly squeeze together the terminals inside the connector. Clean the terminals in the module and distributor before refitting the module, and remember to apply heat-conducting silicone grease to the mounting face on the distributor.

58 Disconnect the wiring from the module, clean the terminals, and lightly squeeze together the terminals inside the connector before refitting it. Make sure that the connector is fully located over the base.

59 Check that the LT leads are correctly fitted to the ignition coil.

Distributor – removal and refitting

60 For better access to the distributor, the radiator may be temporarily moved to one side without disconnecting the top and bottom hoses. This is particularly advantageous on 1985-on 1.3 engines where the electronic ignition amplifier module restricts access to the distributor clamp bolt. Also note that the distributor cap is retained with screws on 1985-on 1.3 models (photos).

61 Refer to Chapter 2 or Section 4 of this Supplement for the relevant procedure for removing the bonnet lock cross panel and disconnecting the wiring from the radiator.

Timing marks – all models

62 To clarify the description of the timing marks given in Chapter 4, an illustration is given here (Fig. 13.26).

Fault diagnosis – electronic ignition

63 Electronic ignition is normally very reliable; if it does fail, such failure tends to be complete. In cases of misfiring, or other intermittent faults, it is probably best to check the HT system first (as described in Chapter 4) before proceeding to the table below.

64 An electrical multi-meter which can measure voltage and resistance (ohms) will be required for testing purposes. Such a meter need not be very expensive and is a useful addition to the electrically-minded mechanic's tool kit.

---

7 Clutch

Clutch (non-Verto) – removal and precaution

1 When separating the flywheel from the crankshaft taper, care must be taken not to screw the removal tool studs through the flywheel into the clutch driven plate. This is apparently possible with certain tools, resulting in damage to the driven plate.

Clutch hydraulic damper – description, removal and refitting

2 Certain models are fitted with a damper in the hydraulic line between the clutch master and slave cylinders. The function of the damper is to provide a steady re-engagement of the clutch, regardless of the rate at which the driver releases the pedal. This is supposed to

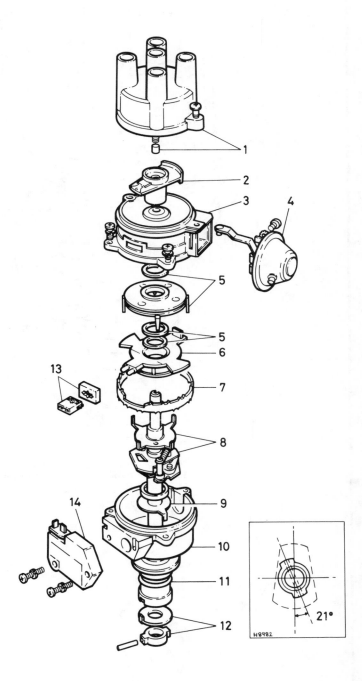

Fig. 13.24 Exploded view of 65 DM4 distributor (Sec 6)

1 Distributor cap, carbon brush and spring	8 Reluctor, centrifugal advance mechanism, and shaft assembly
2 Rotor arm	9 Thrust washer
3 Upper housing	10 Lower housing
4 Vacuum unit	11 O-ring
5 Stator pack, thrust washers and circlip	12 Drive dog and thrust washer
6 Pick-up winding	13 Connector and gasket
7 Clamp ring	14 Amplifier module

Inset indicates correct rotor arm-to-drive dog offset

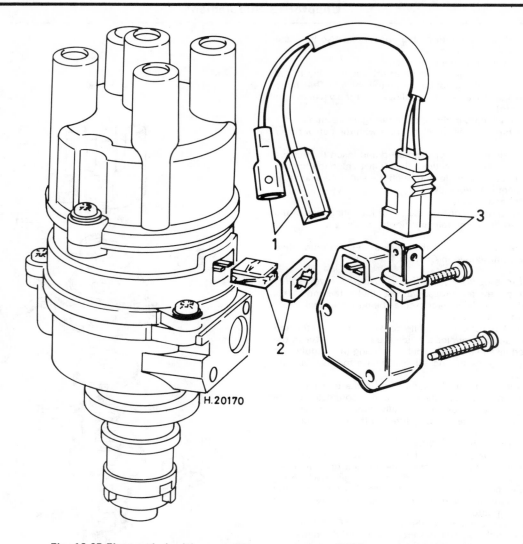

H.20170

Fig. 13.25 Electronic ignition amplifier connections (1985-on models) (Sec 6)

1 *Leads to ignition coil*   3 *Module terminals and wiring connector*
2 *Connector terminals*

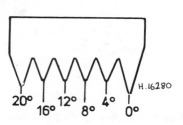

H.16280

20° 16° 12° 8° 4° 0°

Fig. 13.26 Typical timing scale. Moving mark is on crankshaft pulley (Sec 6)

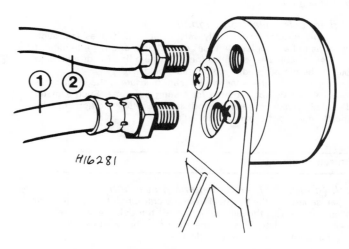

H16281

Fig. 13.27 Clutch hydraulic damper unit (Sec 7)

1 *Inlet hose*   2 *Outlet hose*

reduce clutch judder. The clutch damper is mounted on a bracket next to the clutch slave cylinder. Removal is carried out as follows.

3 Connect a length of tubing to the clutch slave cylinder bleed screw. Slacken the bleed screw and place the other end of the tubing in a jar, then empty the clutch hydraulic system by pumping the pedal. Take care not to spill hydraulic fluid on the paintwork.

4 Disconnect the inlet hose at its union with the rigid pipe. Unscrew the outlet pipe from the damper, then release the inlet hose and unscrew it.

5 Unscrew the damper unit from its bracket and remove it. Be prepared for some spillage of hydraulic fluid.

6 Refitting is a reversal of removal. Bleed the hydraulic system on completion (Chapter 5, Section 5).

Clutch judder – causes and remedies

7 Like the Mini before it, all Metros suffer to some extent from clutch judder when moving away from rest. Various modifications have been made to the clutch release components, including the hydraulic damper described above. The Verto clutch fitted in conjunction with the three-point engine mountings was a further modification, and on 1985-on models a self-adjusting cable is fitted instead of the previous hydraulic system.

8 If clutch judder is experienced on pre-1985 models fitted with the pushrod type release mechanism, it may be worthwhile fitting the old type components incorporating a release stop.

9 Apart from release mechanism components, other possible causes of clutch judder are:

(a) Damaged or distorted release bearing housing (also known as 'clutch end cover'), diaphragm spring or pressure plate
(b) Flywheel friction face damaged, taper damaged, or run-out excessive
(c) Driven (friction) plate contaminated, warped or sticking on spliners
(d) Primary gear endfloat incorrect

10 In view of the number of modifications already made, and the possibility of more to come, you are advised to consult your BL dealer or reputable parts supplier before purchasing any clutch components with a view to eliminating judder.

11 Misalignment or distortion of the release bearing housing (clutch end cover) may be checked by removing the clutch components from the housing and crankshaft, then fitting BL tool 18G 1247 onto the crankshaft and attempting to slide the housing over the alignment tool. Any reluctance to pass over the tool, or failure of the housing spigot to mate with the flywheel housing, means that the housing must be relieved until it fits, or renewed. Drilling the housing flanges and inserting $1/8$ in (3 mm) roll pins or dowels, to maintain correct alignment, is recommended at the end of this procedure.

Clutch linkage lubrication – all models

12 Whenever the clutch is overhauled, the areas of the release mechanism shown in Fig. 13.28 should be lightly greased. If stiffness of operation or restricted clutch pedal travel is experienced, it may be worth dismantling the mechanism to lubricate it.

Verto clutch – description

13 The Verto clutch differs from all previous Metro clutches in that the pressure plate and friction plate are both on the 'outside' of the flywheel, ie on the side furthest from the pistons. All references in this Supplement to the Verto clutch apply also to the factory supplied alternative manufactured by 'Automotive' (AP).

14 A heavy duty version of the clutch, similar in external appearance, is fitted to MG Turbo models. The driven (friction) plate on these models does not have any damper springs fitted.

15 The principles of operation of the Verto clutch is the same as that of previous types. The friction plate is sandwiched firmly between the flywheel and pressure plate friction surfaces when the clutch pedal is released; when the pedal is depressed, the release components cause the diaphragm spring to flex and the grip of the pressure plate is relaxed.

16 The clutch is self-adjusting in use. Adjustment of the throw-out stop should only be necessary after dismantling has taken place.

17 This type of clutch was introduced as part of a complete package of changes, the external evidence of which is the three-point engine mounting system. Consult your BL dealer or a clutch specialist if it is wished to fit the later clutch to an earlier model.

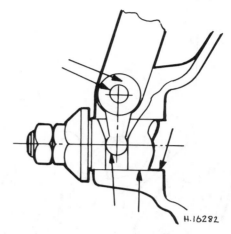

Fig. 13.28 Clutch release mechanism greasing points (arrowed) (Sec 7)

Verto clutch – removal, overhaul and refitting

18 Special tools will be required to undertake this operation. They should be available from your BL dealer or tool hire agent; details are as follows:

(a) Spanner 18G 1303, or a deep socket spanner (30 mm AF) to undo the flywheel centre bolt
(b) Puller 18G 1381 (Fig. 13.30), or equivalent, to remove the flywheel/clutch assembly from the crankshaft taper
(c) Clutch centering tool 18G 684. This tool is not essential and a way of avoiding its use is described in the text

19 Disconnect and remove the battery, then remove the battery tray.
20 Place a jack and a piece of wood under the gearbox casing and take the weight of the engine/gearbox assembly.
21 On pre-1985 models, remove the anti-roll bar clamp bolt, which is located immediately below the right-hand front engine mountings.
22 Remove the nuts and washers from the right-hand front engine mounting rubber. Raise the engine slightly, then unbolt and remove the mounting bracket and spacer from the clutch cover.
23 Remove the starter motor (refer to Chapter 10 if necessary).
24 On pre-1985 models, undo the clutch slave cylinder mounting plate bolts, retrieving the spacer. Carefully withdraw the slave cylinder from its pushrod and place the assembly of slave cylinder, bracket and (if fitted) hydraulic damper to one side. On 1985-on models extract the C-clip from the cable self-adjusting spring, then remove the split pin, washer and pin from the clevis on the release lever and release the inner cable and buffer components from the clutch cover bracket (photo).

7.24 Clutch cable and release lever fitted to 1985-on models

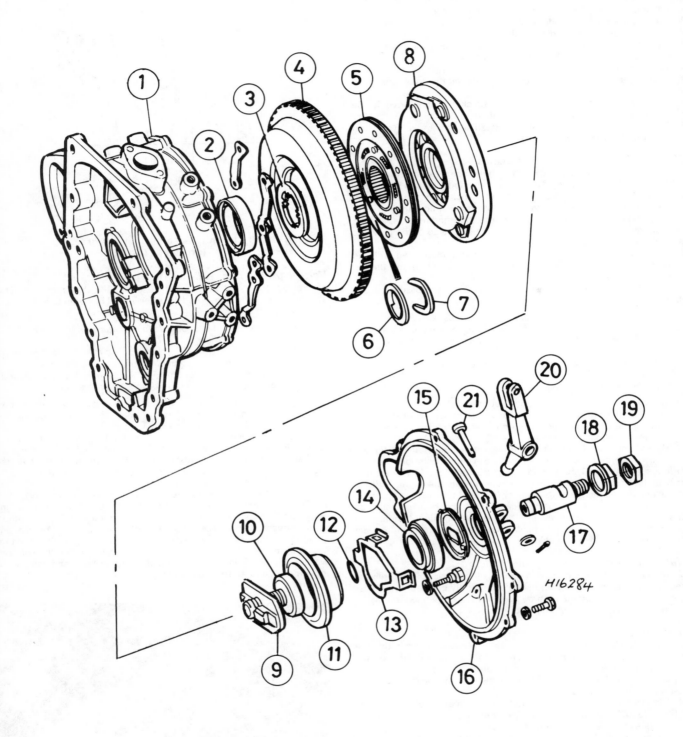

Fig. 13.29 Exploded view of Verto clutch (Sec 7)

1 Flywheel housing
2 Oil seal (primary gear)
3 Dust shield
4 Flywheel
5 Driven plate
6 Primary gear locking ring

7 C-shaped thrust washer
8 Pressure plate
9 Keyplate
10 Flywheel retaining bolt and lockwasher
11 Thrust sleeve

12 O-ring
13 Spring clip
14 Release bearing
15 Retainer plate
16 Clutch cover (release bearing housing)

17 Plunger
18 Throw-out stop
19 Locknut
20 Release lever
21 Pivot pin

25 Undo the clutch cover bolts and remove the cover. Remove the thrust bearing sleeve.

26 Make sure that the slots in the end of the crankshaft hub are horizontal (3 o'clock and 9 o'clock). Lock the flywheel by jamming a wide-bladed screwdriver between the starter ring gear and the flywheel housing.

27 Relieve the lockwasher from the slots, then undo the flywheel centre bolt using spanner 18G 1303 or equivalent. Make sure the spanner fits well, as the bolt is very tight.

28 Remove the bolt and the keyplate from the crankshaft, then fit puller 18G 1381 or equivalent to the flywheel.

29 Screw in the puller centre bolt until the flywheel/clutch assembly is released from the crankshaft taper. If the unit seems reluctant to come off, strike the centre bolt sharply with a hammer to help release the taper.

30 Remove the flywheel/clutch unit. Unscrew the pressure plate bolts, half a turn at a time in criss-cross sequence, and remove the pressure plate and driven plate from the flywheel.

31 Inspect the components for wear and damage. The driven plate should be renewed as a matter of course unless it is nearly new. It must certainly be renewed if the linings are burnt, contaminated or badly worn, or if the centre splines are worn. The source of any contamination must be dealt with.

32 The flywheel and pressure plate are not sold separately, but must be renewed as a matched assembly if wear or damage is evident. Deep grooving, cracks or crazing of the friction surfaces are grounds for renewal.

33 Consideration should also be given to renewing the release bearing whilst it is easily accessible.

34 Before commencing reassembly, check the primary gear endfloat as described in Chapter 6, Section 7.

35 Fit the driven plate to the flywheel with the hub facing the flywheel. (The plate may be marked 'FLYWHEEL SIDE' to confirm this orientation.)

36 Fit the pressure plate to the flywheel and insert the retaining bolts. Only tighten the bolts finger-tight at this stage.

37 If tool 18G 684 is available, use it to centralise the driven plate relative to the flywheel and pressure plate. If the tool is not available, offer the flywheel/clutch assembly to the crankshaft. Providing the pressure plate bolts are not too tight, the driven plate will be moved to the correct central position as it passes over the primary gear splines. Do not force the assembly onto the crankshaft if resistance is encountered, but remove it and check that the driven plate is just free to move, and approximately central.

38 When centralisation has been achieved, tighten the pressure plate retaining bolts in criss-cross sequence to the specified torque.

39 If a centralisation tool was used, remove it and fit the flywheel/clutch assembly to the crankshaft.

40 If the flywheel centre bolt is of an encapsulated type, or was secured with thread locking compound, the bolt hole threads should be thoroughly cleaned. Fit the keyplate and the flywheel centre bolt. Renew the bolt if the original one was secured by any sort of thread lock, and apply a suitable locking compound. Prevent the flywheel from rotating and tighten the centre bolt to the specified torque.

41 Stake the lockwasher into the slots in the hub, then fit the thrust bearing sleeve.

42 The remainder of the refitting process is a reversal of the removal procedure. Adjust the throw-out stop on completion as described below. On 1985-on models, compress the self-adjusting spring in order to fit the C-clip, and finally depress the clutch pedal several times to operate the automatic cable adjuster.

Verto clutch – throw-out stop adjustment

43 Unscrew the throw-out stop and locknut to the end of the thread.

44 Pull the release lever out (away from the clutch cover) by hand until you can feel the release bearing make contact with the thrust sleeve.

45 Screw the throw-out stop in until the clearance between the end of the stop and the face of the cover is as shown in Fig. 13.31.

46 Tighten the locknut, taking care not to move the throw-out stop when doing so.

Verto clutch – release bearing removal and refitting

47 Proceed as described in paragraphs 19 to 24 of this Section, but do not remove the starter motor.

48 Undo the clutch cover bolts and remove the cover.

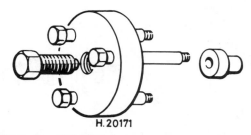

Fig. 13.30 Pulley 18G 1381 for removing the flywheel/clutch assembly from the crankshaft taper (Sec 7)

49 Pull the release bearing components off the plunger and retrieve the O-ring.

50 Separate the spring clip legs from the bearing retainer plate, then remove the bearing.

51 Examine the bearing for external damage, spin it to check for rough running and inspect it for grease leakage. If there is the slightest doubt as to its condition it should be renewed.

52 Refitting is a reversal of removal, but note the following points:

   (a) *The bearing seal faces away from the retaining plate*

   (b) *Do not forget to fit the O-ring on the plunger*

   (c) *Tighten fasteners to their specified torques, where applicable (see relevant Chapters)*

   (d) *Adjust the throw-out stop on completion*

   (e) *On 1985-on models depress the clutch pedal several times to operate the automatic cable adjuster*

Clutch cable (1985-on models) – removal and refitting

53 For better access remove the battery and battery tray.

54 Extract the C-clip from the cable self-adjusting spring.

55 Remove the split pin, washer and pin from the clevis fork on the release lever.

56 Disengage the inner cable from the retaining plate, and remove the plate and rubber buffer.

57 Working inside the car unhook the cable from the clutch pedal, then withdraw the cable from the engine compartment.

58 Refitting is a reversal of removal, but first push the outer cable fully into the self-adjuster to reduce its overall length. To facilitate inserting the outer cable through the bulkhead, smear a little brake grease inside the inter-connecting tube. After refitting, compress the self-adjusting spring and insert the C-clip, then depress the clutch pedal several times to operate the automatic cable adjuster.

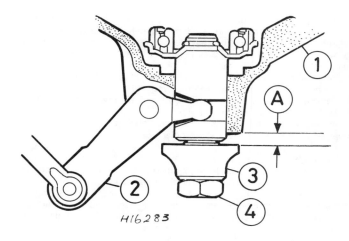

Fig. 13.31 Verto clutch throw-out stop adjustment (Sec 7)

   1   Clutch cover   *4   Locknut*
   2   Release lever   *A = 0.26 in (6.5 mm)*
   3   Throw-out stop

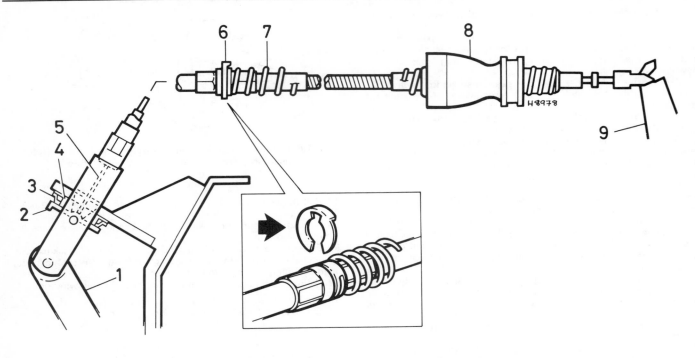

Fig. 13.32 Self-adjusting clutch cable fitted to 1985-on models (Sec 7)

1	Release lever	4	Rubber buffer	7	Self-adjusting spring
2	Retaining plate	5	Inner cable	8	Automatic adjuster
3	Support	6	C-clip	9	Clutch pedal

8 Manual gearbox

Third motion shaft bearing – general

1   From late 1981, the third motion shaft bearing retainer is secured by three screws instead of four as previously. A new lockwasher for the retainer securing bolts is another consequence of this change.

2   From VIN 083362 failure of the third motion shaft bearing has, in some cases, been due to an incorrect thrust face dimension on the rear of the first gear resulting in the fracture of the plastic bearing cage. Where this has occurred, the first gear should be renewed, together with the bearing.

Selector shaft oil seal – general

3   In order to prevent premature failure of the selector shaft oil seal, a nylon support bush has been fitted immediately behind the oil seal in the differential housing. The first bush fitted incorporated an outer groove in which an O-ring was located, but subsequenctly a larger bush without an O-ring was fitted.

4   The nylon support bush must be lubricated with lithium-based grease before fitting to the differential housing.

5   The bush with the O-ring may be fitted to models prior to VIN 650080 not originally having a bush.

6   After fitting a new bush, slight gearchange stiffness may be experienced until the correct sliding clearance is established.

Reverse gear – disengagement

7   In cases of reverse gear disengagement, first check that the centre console or gaiter is not exerting any undue pressure on the gear lever.

8   Between VIN 687000 and 732139, the problem may be due to one of the two bushes in the reverse idler gear becoming displaced, so preventing complete engagement of reverse gear. The single bush fitted originally was replaced by two bushes at VIN 687000, but the loose bush problem has been cured on models after VIN 732139.

9   If a bush is found to be displaced, renew the reverse idler gear.

10   Excessive wear of the single bush on models prior to VIN 687000 may also cause disengagement of reverse gear. To rectify this, fit a new reverse idler gear and a new shaft which has additional oil drillings for improved lubrication.

9 Automatic transmission

Gear selection problems – general

1   Owners of early Automatic Metros may experience slip or loss of drive when 'R' is selected, and perhaps a condition known as 'tie-up' (more than one gear selected) when engaging 'D'. These problems are not due to faults in the transmission, but to inaccuracies in the selector mechanisn.

2   An improved selector cable with reduced backlash is now available. This cable can be distinguished from the initial production type by a dab of red or white paint on the cable outer at the transmission end. The improved cable should be fitted if gear selection problems exist, and attention paid to the adjustment procedures.

3   On later vehicles the selector gate slot is extended somewhat at the 'D' end. Earlier vehicles can be modified by filing that end of the gate slot until the end of the slot is within 0.276 in (7 mm) of the end of the gate.

4   A revised selector valve is also fitted to later models. Consult your BL dealer if you wish to fit a later type of valve to an early transmission. The operation is beyond the scope of this book.

Selector cable – adjustment checking procedure

5   When carrying out the adjustment check detailed in Chapter 6, Section 17, paragraph 13, it may be found that either first or reverse gear does not disengage when the selector lever reaches the· 'N' position.

6   If 'R' remains engaged in position 'N', reduce the gap at the end of the selector lever travel by 0.01 in (0.25 mm).

7   If '1' remains engaged in position 'N' increase the gap at the end of the selector lever travel by 0.01 in (0.25 mm).

8   Recheck the adjustment and repeat paragraph 6 or 7 as necessary.

9   Check that the starter motor can be operated only in positions 'P' and 'N'. Adjust the inhibitor switch if necessary as described in Chapter 6, Section 19.

Loss of drive when cold

10   Some early models suffered from slip or loss of drive when cold. The condition is caused by air getting into the oil in the torque converter.

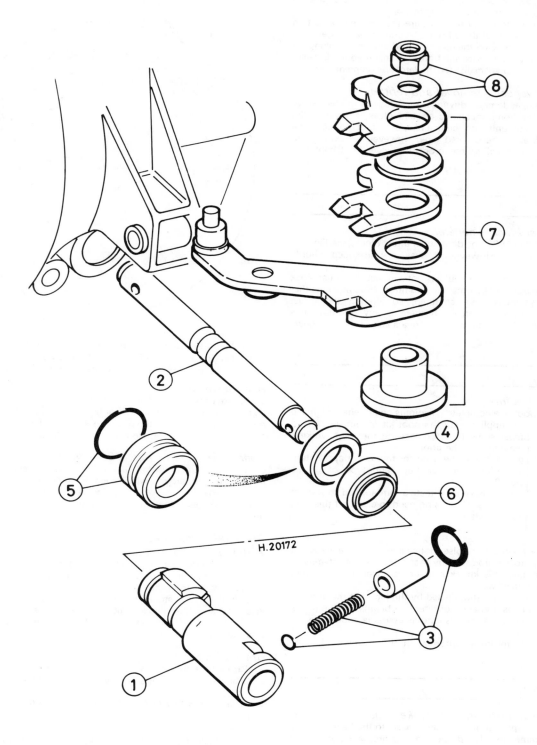

Fig. 13.33 Selector bellcrank lever and shaft components showing later nylon support bushes (Sec 8)

1   Interlock spool
2   Selector shaft
3   Detent ball, spring, sleeve and O-ring

4   Plain nylon support bush
5   Nylon support bush with O-ring
6   Oil seal

7   Bellcrank levers and pivot sleeve assembly
8   Pivot post nut and washer

H.20172

11 The simplest approach to this problem is to change the engine oil to one of 10W/40 viscosity, if not already in use.
12 If a reduction in oil viscosity fails to cure the problem, attention must be paid to the sealing of the oil pump suction pipe flange. After this, it is a question of renewing the oil pump and perhaps blanking off the lowest of the torque converter relief holes. Consult your BL dealer or automatic transmission specialist for the latest recommendations.

Speedometer drivegear – removal and refitting
13 Removal of the speedometer drivegear on 1985-on models is not recommended for the home mechanic as it involves removal of the engine and transmission unit, and the use of special tools to retain the forward clutch and align the oil feed pipe. However, removal of the pinion assembly is identical to the procedure given in Chapter 6, Section 21.

10 Final drive

Differential thrust block – general
1 For a short period in 1982, the differential thrust block (see Fig. 7.2, item 15) was omitted. However, it was re-introduced shortly afterwards.
2 If during the course of an overhaul it is noticed that the thrust block is missing, a new one should be obtained and fitted. Note however that the machining clearances have changed, so altering the thrust block-to-differential gear clearances. If there is any doubt in this respect, compare the fitted gears with new gears and fit the new gears if required.

11 Driveshafts

Lubrication of CV joints
1 When a rubber boot or a complete CV joint is being renewed, make sure that all the grease supplied with the boot kit or joint is used to lubricate the joint. Smear some of the grease on the joint working surfaces and put the remainder in the boot.
2 If for any reason grease has to be used for the above application from a bulk container, follow the quantities and type of grease recommended in Chapter 8.
3 Note that new CV joints have a protective film applied to protect them from corrosion in storage. There is no need to clean off this film, but do not mistake it for adequate lubricant.

Driveshaft knock
4 It is possible for a knocking noise, noticeable when manoeuvring the car on full lock, to be produced by loose anti-roll bar clamps or deteriorated mountings. This knock may be mistaken for driveshaft knock, indicating CV joint wear.
5 The two knocks may be distinguished by the fact that the anti-roll bar knock occurs only as a change of direction begins to take place, whilst driveshaft knock will persist as long as power is applied on full lock.
6 Refer to Section 14 for further information on anti-roll bar knock.

12 Braking system

Use of anti-squeal paste on front brake pads
1 In Chapter 9, the application of 'brake grease' to the backs of new brake pads is recommended. The purpose of this grease is two-fold: it prevents squeal and assists in the transfer of heat.
2 BL now recommend a substance known as 'Plastilube' for this purpose. Plastilube **must not** be allowed to contact the caliper piston seals, as may happen when the pistons are pushed back to receive new pads.
3 Before pushing the caliper pistons in, therefore, wipe around the side of the pistons with a clean dry cloth. This is a sensible precaution even if Plastilube is not present.
4 Other proprietary anti-squeal compounds are available. Unless it is certain that they will not attack braking system seals, the same precautions should be taken as when using Plastilube.

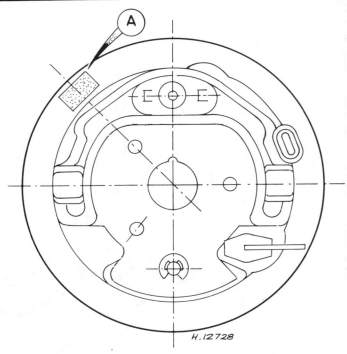

Fig. 13.34 Position (A) on right-hand rear brake backplate for fitting self-adhesive wheel balance weight to counteract rear brake squeal (Sec 12)

Rear brake squeal
5 Where persistent rear brake squeal is experienced, the problem may be cured by fitting 25 gram self-adhesive wheel balance weights to the rear brake backplates in the positions shown in Fig. 13.34. The weights can be obtained from a tyre supplier or garage.

Rear brake shoe linings (1985-on models) – inspection
6 The rear brake backplate on 1985-on models incorporates an inspection hole through which the trailing shoe lining can be checked for thickness. The use of a torch will be helpful, and, after checking, always make sure that the rubber grommet is correctly fitted in the hole.

Brake disc wear measurement (all models except MG Turbo and 1985-on models)
7 When the front brake pads have to be renewed, it is a good idea to check the thickness of the brake disc. The minimum allowable thickness is given in the Specifications.
8 A further check should be made by measuring the gap between the disc face and the caliper abutment on each side of the disc (Fig. 13.35). If this dimension exceeds 0.110 in (2.8 mm) on either side, the disc must be renewed.

Brake disc renewal (all models)
9 Brake discs should always be renewed in pairs in order to maintain even braking between the two sides of the vehicle.

Ventilated disc orientation (MG Turbo and all 1985-on models)
10 When fitting discs to MG Turbo and 1985-on models, note that the discs are 'handed', ie left-hand and right-hand discs are difference. The difference is in the angle of the cooling vanes, which are designed to function efficiently in one direction of rotation only.
11 Since the vanes are concealed inside the disc, the manufacturers have provided an external means of distinguishing the discs. The edge facing the drive flange has a concave finish on the left-hand disc, where the right-hand disc is finished with a smooth taper (Fig. 13.36).

Stones trapped between disc and shield
12 If a problem is experienced with small stones becoming trapped between a brake disc and shield, giving rise to an unpleasant squealing noise, the shield may be modified as follows.

215

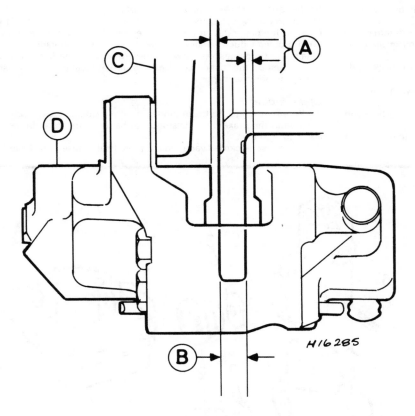

Fig. 13.35 Brake disc wear
measurement points (Sec 12)

A   Disc-to-abutment distance (see text)
B   Disc thickness
C   Swivel hub mounting lug
D   Caliper

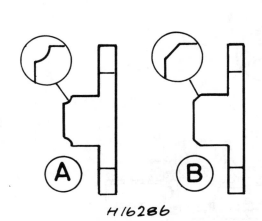

Fig. 13.36 Ventilated disc identification (Sec 12)

A   Left-hand (concave edge)

B   Right-hand (smooth edge)

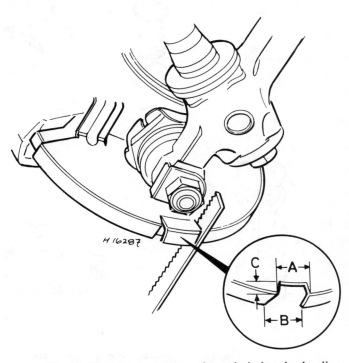

Fig. 13.37 Cutting a stone release hole in a brake disc
shield (Sec 12)

A = 0.8 in (20 mm)
B = 1.2 in (30 mm)
C = 0.25 in (6.4 mm)

13 Jack up and securely support the front of the car. Remove the front roadwheels for ease of access.
14 Carefully make two hacksaw cuts in the flange at the bottom of the disc shield. Refer to Fig. 13.37 to determine where to make the cuts. *Take care not to cut into the disc.*
15 Grip the section between the cuts with pliers. Bend it backwards and forwards, until it breaks off.
16 Smooth the cut edges with a file and paint them with anti-rust paint.
17 Check that there is a clearance of at least 0.2 in (5 mm) between the shield and the disc.
18 Repeat the operations on the other side of the car, then refit the roadwheels and lower the car to the ground.

Water entering the rear brake drums
19 To prevent water entering the rear brake drums, later models are fitted with a paper gasket between the brake drum and the flange.
20 If problems due to water entry are encountered on earlier models, obtain and fit the gaskets between the drums and their flanges. Clean off any rust on the friction surfaces and gasket mating surfaces, using fine grade abrasive paper.

Brake judder
21 When investigating brake judder, do not assume that the problem must lie in the brake discs. Distorted or badly worn brake drums will also cause judder.
22 Brake disc thickness variation is a more likely cause of brake judder

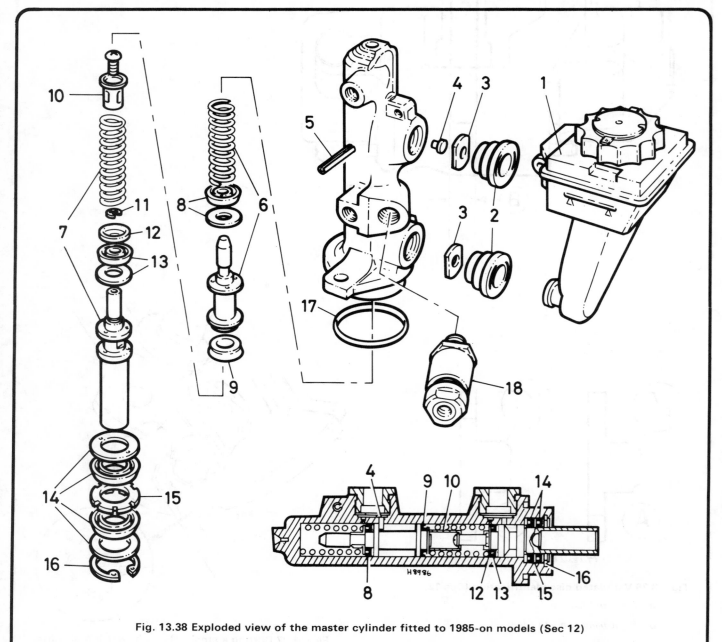

Fig. 13.38 Exploded view of the master cylinder fitted to 1985-on models (Sec 12)

1 Reservoir	6 Secondary piston and spring	10 Retainer	14 Primary piston vacuum seals
2 Sealing washers	7 Primary piston and spring	11 Circlip	and washers
3 Baffle plates	8 Secondary piston seal and	12 Spring seat	15 Spacer
4 Secondary piston stop pin	washer	13 Primary piston seal and	16 Circlip
5 Roll pin	9 Secondary piston seal	washer	17 O-ring seal
			18 Pressure reducing valve

than disc run-out. A micrometer will be needed to measure thickness variation accurately. Run-out can be measured with a dial gauge, or with feeler gauges and a fixed pointer,

23 Where disc run-out is thought to be the problem, make sure that the wheel bearings are not at fault as follows.

24 Mark the brake disc with chalk at the point of maximum run-out. Make a corresponding mark on the end of the driveshaft.

25 Remove the disc/flange assembly as described in Chapter 9. Do not separate them, but refit them 180° (half a turn) away from their original position.

26 Measure the run-out again. If the maximum run-out occurs at the same point on the disc, the disc is the source of run-out. If the run-out is reduced, or the maximum run-out occurs 180° from the previously marked point on the disc, the bearings are at least partly responsible for run-out.

27 Renew the disc and/or the bearings to bring run-out into acceptable limits (see Specifications).

Master cylinder (1985-on models) – description

28 The master cylinder fitted to 1985-on models is different to that described in Chapter 9, as can be seen in Fig. 13.38. However, the basic removal, overhaul and refitting procedure is the same.

Inertia/pressure regulating valve (Van models) – description, removal and refitting

29 1984-on Vans are fitted with an inertia/pressure regulating valve in the rear brake hydraulic circuit instead of the compensating valve described in Chapter 9.

30 To remove the valve, chock the front wheels, then jack up the rear of the car and support on axle stands.

31 Remove the brake fluid reservoir filler cap and place a sheet of thin polythene over the warning switch assembly, then tighten the cap. This will prevent unnecessary loss of brake fluid in the subsequent procedure.

32 Unscrew the union nuts from the valve then remove and plug the hydraulic pipes.

33 Unscrew the clamp bolt, prise open the clamp, and withdraw the valve.

34 Refit the valve with the vent plug uppermost and, where fitted, make sure that the valve is located on the special peg. Tighten the clamp bolt and union nuts.

35 During the bleeding of the hydraulic circuit, loosen the vent plug two or three times in order to release any trapped air. Finally lower the car to the ground.

Pressure reducing valve (1985-on Saloon models) – description, removal and refitting

36 1985-on Saloon models are fitted with a pressure reducing valve in

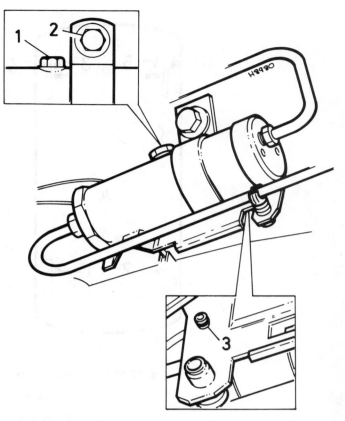

Fig. 13.39 Inertia/pressure regulating valve fitted to 1984-on Vans (Sec 12)

1 *Vent plug*   3 *Locating peg (where fitted)*
2 *Clamp bolt*

the rear brake hydraulic circuit which is located on the master cylinder, instead of the compensating valve described in Chapter 9 (photo).

37 To remove the valve, place a suitable container and rag beneath the master cylinder.

38 Unscrew the two secondary pipe unions then pull out and plug the pipes.

39 Unscrew the pressure reducing valve from the master cylinder and remove the washer.

40 Refitting is a reversal of removal, but bleed the hydraulic system on completion.

Hydraulic system (1985-on models) – bleeding

41 The basic procedure is identical to that given in Chapter 9, but the bleed screw sequence is different, as shown in Fig. 13.40.

Handbrake – adjustment

42 Apply the handbrake four times in order to settle the compensator and cable positions.

43 Adjust the rear brakes as described in Chapter 9, Section 3.

44 Apply the handbrake six notches on an old cable, or four notches on a new cable, then check that both rear wheels are locked.

45 If necessary, adjust the cable with reference to Chapter 9, Section 16, paragraphs 4 and 5.

13 Electrical system

Part A General equipment

Lucas A115 alternator – brush renewal

1 Remove the alternator as described in Chapter 10, Section 7.

2 Disconnect and remove the interference suppression capacitor from the end cover.

12.36 Rear brake pressure reducing valve (arrowed) fitted to 1985-on Saloon models

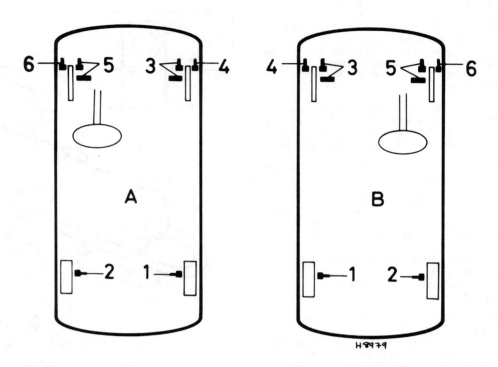

Fig. 13.40 Brake bleeding sequence for 1985-on models (Sec 12)

A   Left-hand drive models

B   Right-hand drive models

3   Undo the screws or nuts which secure the end cover. Remove the cover.
4   Unscrew the surge protection diode securing screw. Either move the diode carefully out of the way, or disconnect it from the rectifier board and remove it.
5   Make a careful note of the regulator lead colours and fitting arrangements, then disconnect the regulator leads from the rectifier board and the brushbox.
6   Remove the regulator screw and withdraw the regulator. Note that the regulator securing screw also holds one of the brush mounting plates in position.
7   Remove the two securing screws and withdraw the brushbox. Extract the free brush, then undo the securing screw to release the other brush. Remove the sealing pad.
8   Renew the brushes if they are at, or approaching, the minimum specified length. Check the brush spring pressure with the brush ends flush with the end of the brushbox; renew the springs if they have become weak.
9   Reassemble the alternator in the reverse sequence to dismantling. Refit the alternator as described in Chapter 10 and tension the drivebelt as described in Chapter 2.

Ignition warning light bulb wattage
10   The wattage of the ignition warning light bulb has been increased from 1.2W to 2W on later models. This has the effect of lowering the engine speed at which the warning light goes out (alternator cut-in speed).
11   If it is wished to lower the alternator cut-in speed on earlier models, a 2W bulb may be substituted for the existing one.

Starter solenoid (inertia starters) – earthing
12   Where an inertia starter motor is fitted, the solenoid is located on the battery carrier, and the circuit is earthed through the solenoid mounting bolts. Should the solenoid be defective the mounting bolts should be removed and cleaned, and the threads coated with a copper-based conductive grease before refitting. If the fault is not cured by this action, further investigation of the wiring will be necessary.

Starter relay – general
13   On all automatic transmission models, and other models from 1986 onwards, a relay is incorporated in the starter motor solenoid circuit.
14   The relay is located on the battery carrier, and is earthed via terminal 86 to the relay mounting screw. In the event of a malfunction, the mounting screw and battery carrier should be cleaned and coated with conductive grease to ensure good earthing. To establish that there is an earthing problem, temporarily connect a wire between the battery negative terminal and terminal 86 on the relay, and check if the fault persists.

Fuses (1985-on models) – general
15   On 1985-on models the fusebox is located below the right-hand side of the facia. To remove the cover, twist the retainers using a coin. Each fuse is colour coded as follows:

3 amp	Violet	10 amp	Red
5 amp	Tan	15 amp	Blue

16   1985-on models are also fitted with three fusible links in the first part of the battery '+' cable. If a number of circuits fail to work, check for battery voltage at the fusebox power input side.
17   If a fusible link has failed, disconnect both battery terminals ('–' first). Carefully cut back the binding and remove the sleeve from the '+' cable. Unsolder the failed fusible link and renew it with one of the same size. Cover the joints with insulating tape and reconnect the battery ('+' first).

Veglia instrument panels
18   Later models may be fitted with instrument panels made by Veglia instead of by Smiths. The two makes can be distinguished without dismantling by the fact that the mileage recorder window edges are

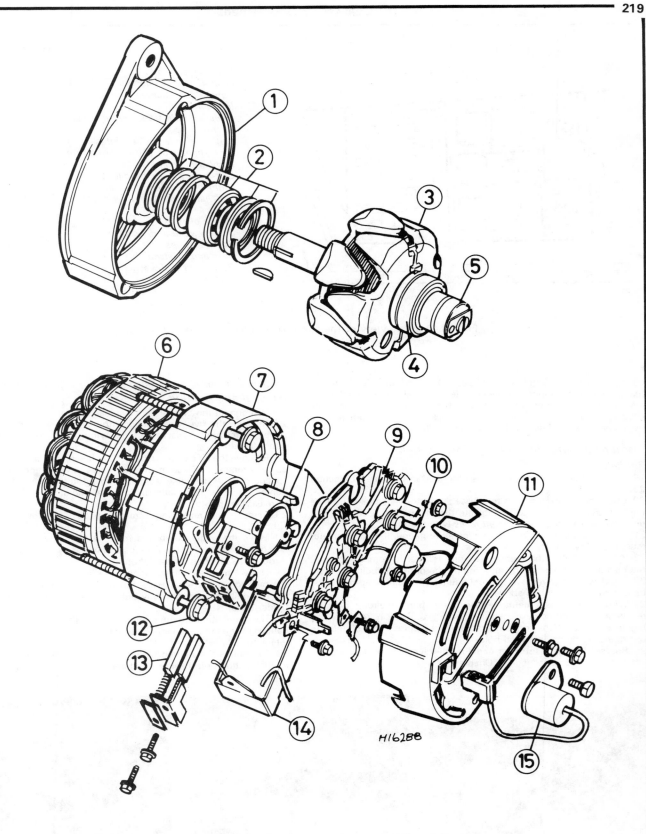

Fig. 13.41 Exploded view of Lucas A115 alternator (Sec 13A)

1 Drive end bracket
2 Drive end bearing assembly
3 Rotor
4 Slip ring end bearing
5 Slip rings
6 Stator
7 Slip ring end bracket
8 Brushbox
9 Rectifier board
10 Surge protection diode
11 End cover
12 Through-bolt
13 Brushes
14 Regulator
15 Interference suppression capacitor

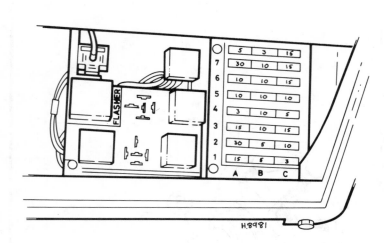

Circuit	Location	Rating (amp)
Heated rear window	A1	15
Electric front windows	A2	30
Central door locking	A3	15
Instruments	A4	3
Direction indicators, hazard lights	A5	10
Interior lamps	A6	10
Left-hand side and tail lights	B1	5
Right-hand side and tail lights, and number plate lights	B2	5
Left-hand dipped headlight	B3	10
Right-hand dipped headlight	B4	10
Left-hand main beam headlight	B6	10
Radio	C1	3
Heater blower	C2	10
Screen wiper and washers	C3	15
Rear foglamps	C4	5
Stop and reverse lights	C5	10
Rear wiper and washer	C6	15
Electric cooling fan	C7	15

Fig. 13.42 Inside view of the fusebox on 1985-on models (Sec 13A)

chamfered on the Smiths panel, but square on the Veglia panel. Instruments and components are not interchangeable between the two makes, so it is important to specify which is required if spare parts are needed. Because of the different internal design of its instruments, the Veglia panel is not fitted with a voltage stabiliser.

Instrument panel dismantling – pre-1985 MG Turbo models

19 Remove the instrument panel as described in Chapter 10, Section 23.
20 Undo the securing screws to release the instrument cluster from its housing. Release the clips to separate the instruments from the lens unit. *Do not touch the instrument faces with the fingers.*
21 If it is wished to remove the temperature gauge, the speedometer must be removed first.
22 When removing the tachometer, first release it from the casing, then extract the boost gauge and unplug the printed circuit.
23 If it is wished to remove the fuel gauge, the tachometer must first be removed as described above.
24 With all the instruments removed, the printed circuit may be renewed if wished as described in Chapter 10, Section 24. Note the higher wattage of the ignition warning light bulb – this should be distinguished by having a red holder.
25 Reassemble the instrument panel in the reverse order to dismantling, and refit it as described in Chapter 10.

Instrument panel and instruments (1985-on models) – removal and refitting

26 Disconnect the battery negative lead.
27 Remove the five screws and withdraw the surround and switch panel sufficiently to disconnect the wiring multi-plugs. Remove the panel (photos).
28 Remove the air cleaner (Chapter 3), then prise out the speedometer cable grommet. Disconnect the cable by pulling it from the speedometer. If the cable is tight, remove the fusebox cover, reach up behind the instrument panel and squeeze the outside of the connector to release it (photo).
29 Remove the remaining screws, taking care not to drop them (photo).
30 Move the panel down and rotate it to release it from the facia. Disconnect the wiring multi-plugs and withdraw the instrument panel through the steering wheel (photos).
31 The warning and illumination bulbs may be removed by twisting the bulbholder anti-clockwise, but note that the 'no-charge' bulb in the red bulbholder is the only bulb which can be separated from its holder (photos).
32 The multi-function unit incorporating the fuel and temperature gauges may be removed after withdrawing the cover (3 nuts) and unit retaining nuts.
33 To remove the printed circuit, first remove all the bulbs and the multi-function unit. Peel off the tape and remove the connector pegs.

13.27A Remove the instrument panel surround upper screws ...

13.27B ... and lower screws ...

13.27C ... and disconnect the multi-plugs

13.28 Squeeze the speedometer cable connector to release it

13.29 Instrument panel side screws (arrowed)

13.30A Disconnecting the multi-plugs

13.30B Removing the instrument panel

13.30C Front view of the 1985-on instrument panel

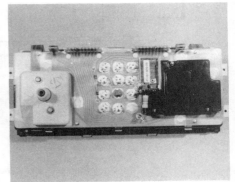

13.30D Rear view of the 1985-on instrument panel

13.31A Removing a panel light bulb

13.31B Removing a warning light bulb

13.31C Removing the 'no-charge' warning light bulb

34 To remove the speedometer head, remove the illumination bulb holders and the tape from the printed circuit. Free the wires and remove the shroud and window assembly. Release the face plate from the case and remove the trip reset control. Remove the screws and withdraw the speedometer head.

35 Removal of the tachometer is similar to the procedure for the speedometer head, but the fuel and temperature gauges must first be removed.

36 Refitting is a reversal of removal, but when fitting the multi-function unit tighten the nuts evenly to ensure good contact with the printed circuit.

Speedometer cable (1985-on models) – removal and refitting

37 The procedure is basically as described in Chapter 10, but in addition, remove the fusebox cover and if necessary the air cleaner. To release the connector from the speedometer, squeeze the knurled section.

Dim-dip headlamps

38 As from late 1986, all models are fitted with a headlamp dim-dip system, which provides headlamp illumination between the sidelight and dipped beam levels. A relay-controlled resistor circuit within a control unit in the right-hand front of the engine compartment reduces the dipped beam to one-sixth of its normal level when the sidelights are switched on with the ignition also switched on. The system effectively prevents driving with sidelights only illuminated.

Clock (pre-1985 MG Turbo models) – removal and refitting

39 Disconnect the battery earth lead.
40 Remove the ashtray away from the facia.

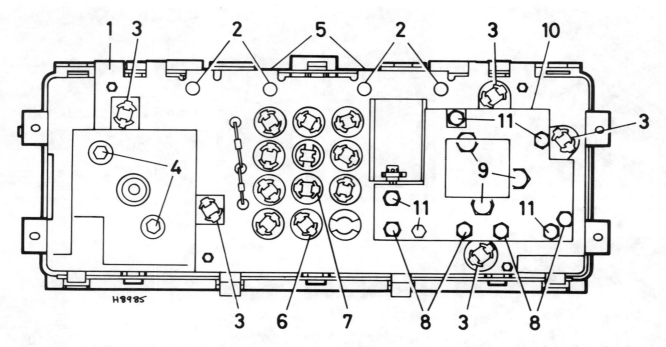

Fig. 13.43 Component location on the instrument panel fitted to 1985-on models (Sec 13A)

1 Printed circuit
2 Retaining pegs
3 Illumination bulbs
4 Speedometer head screws
5 Multi-plug connectors
6 Warning light bulbs
7 No-charge warning light bulb
8 Fuel and temperature gauge nuts
9 Tachometer nuts
10 Multi-function unit
11 Multi-function unit nuts

41 Carefully prise the clock mounting out of the facia and disconnect the multi-plug.
42 Press the retaining lugs to release the clock from its mountings.
43 Refitting is the reverse of the removal procedure.

Clock (1985-on models) – removal and refitting
44 Where the clock is mounted on the facia, prise it out and disconnect the multi-plug. Reverse the procedure when refitting.
45 Where the clock is mounted in the overhead console, prise out the interior lamp then remove the screws and lower the console. Disconnect the multi-plug and remove the clock. Refitting is a reversal of removal.

Combination switch (1985-on models) – removal and refitting
46 Remove the steering wheel as described in Chapter 11.
47 Disconnect the battery negative lead.
48 Remove the screws and withdraw the steering column cowl lower half, followed by the top half.
49 Lift the clips and pull the fibre optic guides from each side of the switch.
50 Depress the retainers and withdraw the switch. Disconnect the wiring multi-plug.
51 Refitting is a reversal of removal.

Instrument panel surround switch (1985-on models) – removal and refitting
52 Disconnect the battery negative lead.
53 Prise the switch from the surround and disconnect the multi-plug (photo).
54 Refitting is a reversal of removal.

Electric window switch and relay – removal and refitting
55 Disconnect the battery negative lead.
56 Prise the switch from the door pocket and disconnect the wiring; after noting the terminal locations.

57 The electric window relay is located on the fusebox, No 2 (centre) on the bottom row. Access is gained by removing the fusebox cover.
58 Refitting is a reversal of removal.

Windscreen and tailgate window washers – general
59 On all MG Turbo models, a combined reservoir is mounted in the left-hand rear of the luggage compartment, with two remote pumps located on the inner panel. The two identical pumps are connected to a single tube leading from the reservoir, and incorporate non-return valves in the outlet tubes to the windscreen and tailgate window.

13.53 Removing a switch from the instrument panel surround

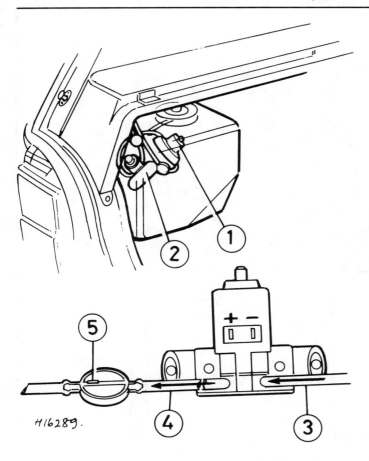

Fig. 13.44 Washer reservoir and pumps – MG Turbo models (Sec 13A)

1	Windscreen washer pump	4	Outlet pipe
2	Tailgate washer pump	5	Non-return valve
3	Inlet pipe		

60 For non-Turbo models, separate reservoirs for the windscreen and tailgate window are fitted to early models, being located on the left-hand front of the engine compartment and the left-hand rear of the luggage compartment. From VIN 556719, models with front and rear washers have a combined reservoir in the left-hand front of the engine compartment. Models with windscreen washers only have a single reservoir with an integral pump, located on the left-hand front of the engine compartment. The integral pump is retained in the reservoir by a rubber grommet.

Screen washer pumps (MG Turbo models) – removal and refitting

61 Both the windscreen and the tailgate washer pumps are located at the rear of MG Turbo models, and they share a common reservoir.
62 Open the tailgate, remove the washer reservoir and release the left-hand quarter trim.
63 Identify the pump to be removed. (The windscreen washer feed tube is blue.) Unscrew the pump mounting screws and disconnect the tubes and wires from the pump. Be prepared for some fluid spillage.
64 Release the pump bracket from the mounting rubber, but do not remove the bracket from the pump. The pump cannot be overhauled, and should be renewed if defective.
65 Refitting is a reversal of the removal procedure. Note the following points:

    (a) A new pump will need to be pop-riveted to the mounting rubber
    (b) The pump inlet is marked '−' and the outlet '+'
    (c) The non-return valve outlet is marked '−'

66 Check for correct operation on completion.

Windscreen washer tube (MG Turbo models) – removal and refitting

67 Open the tailgate and release the left-hand quarter trim.
68 Disconnect the windscreen washer tube (the blue one) from the non-return valve.
69 Secure a length of stout string to the tube, using sticky tape or some similar means. The string must be longer than the tube.
70 Open the bonnet and extract the windscreen washer jet. Disconnect the tube from the jet and from any clips. Disconnect the battery earth lead.
71 Partially withdraw the facia, as described in Chapter 12, to gain access to the aperture in the left-hand front pillar. Pull the tube through from the engine compartment, then pull the other end of the tube (with string attached) through from the rear of the car.
72 Remove the string from the old tube and secure it to the new tube. Carefully draw the new tube through from the front to the back of the car.
73 Remove the string and connect the tube to the non-return valve.
74 Feed the tube into the engine compartment, refitting the grommet if this has become displaced. Connect the tube to the jet and engage any clips.
75 Refit the disturbed trim, reconnect the battery and check the windscreen washer for correct operation. Remember that it will take a second or two for the pump to fill the new tube.

Headlamp washer system – general

76 A headlamp washer system is fitted to certain models, according to territory and trim level specified.
77 The system is similar in principle to the familiar screen washer systems, but a relay is included in the headlamp washer pump circuit so that the pump does not operate when the lights are not in use.
78 The components of the headlamp washer system are shown in Fig. 13.46. The reservoir is mounted under the left-hand wing, and the jets are positioned in the bumper overriders.
79 No specific dismantling or overhaul information is available at the time of writing. The pump cannot be repaired, and must be renewed complete if defective. It is a push fit into a grommet at the base of the reservoir.

Trip computer – general

80 A factory-fitted trip computer is available as an optional extra on certain models. The computer receives information from a speed transducer in the speedometer cable and from a fuel flow transducer in the fuel supply line. From these data and from its internal clock, the computer is able to display information relating to journey time, average speed, average and instantaneous fuel consumption and distance covered.
81 Very little is possible for the home mechanic by way of testing or repair of the computer and its transducers. In the event of malfunction, check first that all electrical connections are secure and that the battery is fully charged.
82 A faulty speed transducer (or speedometer cable) can be deduced if the trip computer fails to display distance (DIST) information. Obviously this will also affect the fuel consumption (INST and AVE) functions, but so will a faulty fuel transducer.
83 A faulty fuel transducer can be deduced if the fuel used (FUEL) information is grossly incorrect.
84 Testing of suspect transducers, or of the computer itself, is by substitution of a known good unit. No repair is possible.

Heater control illumination bulb – removal and refitting

85 Carefully work the heater control lamp free of its retainer.
86 Separate the bulbholder from the lens and extract the bulb from the holder.
87 Fit a new bulb and reassemble the lamp, then press it back into position.

Automatic transmission selector illumination bulb – removal and refitting

88 Unscrew the gear selector knob and lift the cover off the selector.
89 Remove the selector slide to expose the bulbholder.
90 Pull the bulb out of the holder and press in a new one.
91 Reassemble the selector unit.

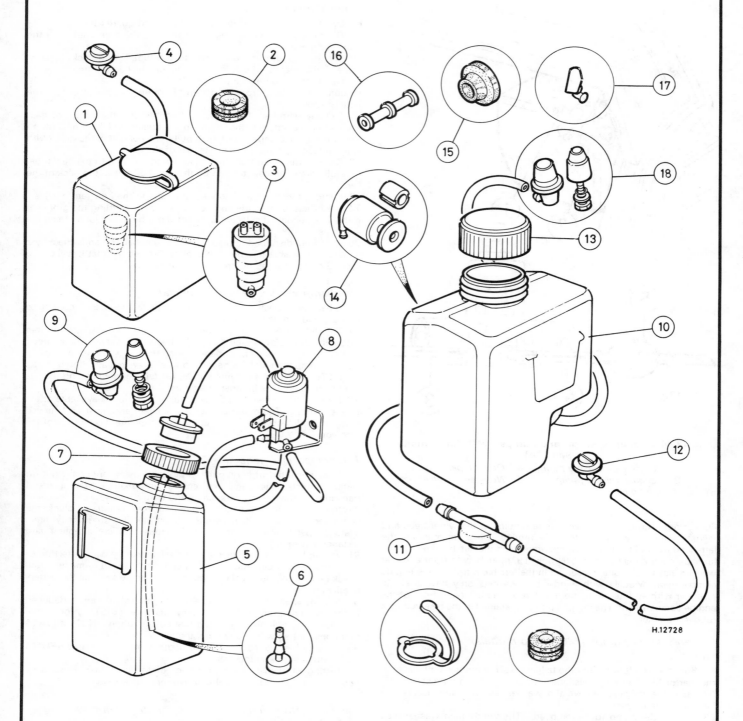

Fig. 13.45 Washer reservoirs and pumps – non-Turbo models (Sec 13A)

1	Reservoir (single)	7	Cap	13	Cap
2	Grommet	8	Pump (tailgate)	14	Pump (two integral fitted)
3	Pump (windscreen)	9	Jet	15	Grommet
4	Jet	10	Reservoir (combined)	16	Connector
5	Reservoir (single)	11	Non-return valve	17	Jet (top fitting)
6	Filter	12	Jet	18	Jet (bottom fitting)

H.12728

225

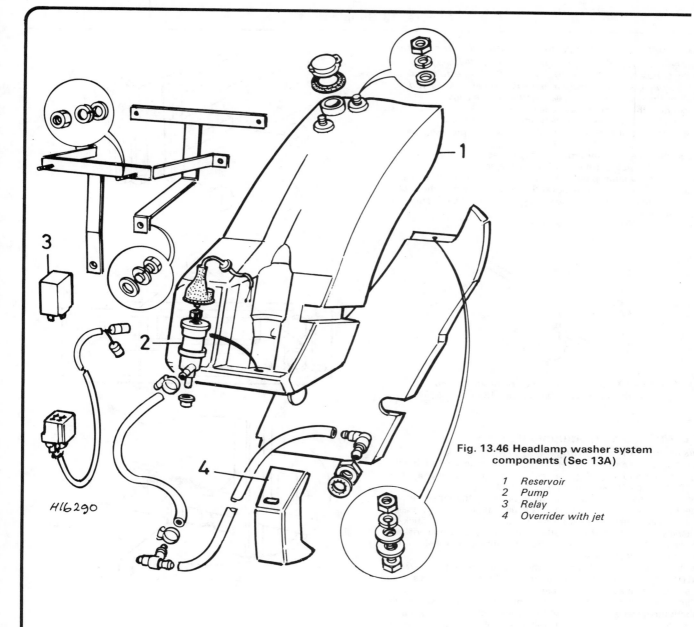

H16290

Fig. 13.46 Headlamp washer system
components (Sec 13A)

1 Reservoir
2 Pump
3 Relay
4 Overrider with jet

H.16291

Fig. 13.47 Heater control illumination bulb (Sec 13A)

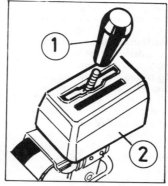
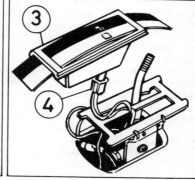

H16292

Fig. 13.48 Automatic transmission selector bulb renewal
(Sec 13A)

1 Selector knob   3 Slide
2 Cover   4 Bulbholder

Radio/cassette player (electronic) – removal and refitting

Note: *The radio/cassette player is retained with DIN clips and it is necessary to obtain tool SMD 4091 (Fig. 13.49) in order to release the clips. It may be possible to make a tool using suitable dowel rod, but the ends of the rods must be shaped to contact the clips.*

92 Disconnect the battery negative lead.
93 Prise the plastic covers from each side of the unit.
94 Insert the special tool rods into the holes until they engage the clips.
95 Press the ends of the rods outwards so that the clips are compressed, then pull out the unit from the facia.
96 Disconnect the multi-plug and aerial and remove the tool rods.
97 Refitting is a reversal of removal, but make sure that the rubber support pads are in place before pushing the unit into the facia until the clips are engaged.

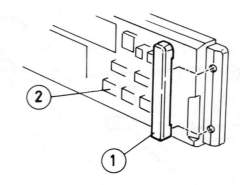

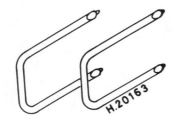

Fig. 13.49 Tool SMD 4091 for removal of the radio/cassette player (Sec 13A)

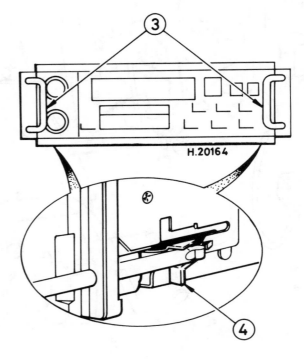

Part B Mobile radio equipment

Aerials – selection and fitting

The choice of aerials is now very wide. It should be realised that the quality has a profound effect on radio performance, and a poor, inefficient aerial can make suppression difficult.

A wing-mounted aerial is regarded as probably the most efficient for signal collection, but a roof aerial is usually better for suppression purposes because it is away from most interference fields. Stick-on wire aerials are available for attachment to the inside of the windscreen, but are not always free from the interference field of the engine and some accessories.

Motorised automatic aerials rise when the equipment is switched on and retract at switch-off. They require more fitting space and supply leads, and can be a source of trouble.

There is no merit in choosing a very long aerial as, for example, the type about three metres in length which hooks or clips on to the rear of the car, since part of this aerial will inevitably be located in an interference field. For VHF/FM radios the best length of aerial is about one metre. Active aerials have a transistor amplifier mounted at the base and this serves to boost the received signal. The aerial rod is sometimes rather shorter than normal passive types.

A large loss of signal can occur in the aerial feeder cable, especially over the Very High Frequency (VHF) bands. The design of feeder cable is invariably in the co-axial form, ie a centre conductor surrounded by a flexible copper braid forming the outer (earth) conductor. Between the inner and outer conductors is an insulator material which can be in solid or stranded form. Apart from insulation, its purpose is to maintain the correct spacing and concentricity. Loss of signal occurs in this insulator, the loss usually being greater in a poor quality cable. The quality of cable used is reflected in the price of the aerial with the attached feeder cable.

The capacitance of the feeder should be within the range 65 to 75 picofarads (pF) approximately (95 to 100 pF for Japanese and American equipment), otherwise the adjustment of the car radio aerial trimmer may not be possible. An extension cable is necessary for a long run between aerial and receiver. If this adds capacitance in excess of the above limits, a connector containing a series capacitor will be required, or an extension which is labelled as 'capacity-compensated'.

Fitting the aerial will normally involve making a $^7/_8$ in (22 mm) diameter hole in the bodywork, but read the instructions that come with the aerial kit. Once the hole position has been selected, use a centre punch to guide the drill. Use sticky masking tape around the

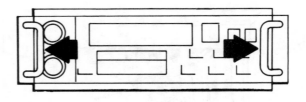

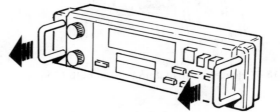

Fig. 13.50 Radio/cassette player removal sequence (Sec 13A)

1   *Plastic cover*   3   *Tool SMD 4091*
2   *Radio/cassette player*   4   *Clip*

area for this helps with marking out and drill location, and gives protection to the paintwork should the drill slip. Three methods of making the hole are in use:

(a) Use a hole saw in the electric drill. This is, in effect, a circular hacksaw blade wrapped round a former with a centre pilot drill.

(b) Use a tank cutter which also has cutting teeth, but is made to shear the metal by tightening with an Allen key.

(c) The hard way of drilling out the circle is using a small drill, say $1/8$ in (3 mm), so that the holes overlap. The centre metal drops out and the hole is finished with round and half-round files.

Whichever method is used, the burr is removed from the body metal and paint removed from the underside. The aerial is fitted tightly ensuring that the earth fixing, usually a serrated washer, ring or clamp, is making a solid connection. *This earth connection is important in reducing interference.* Cover any bare metal with primer paint and topcoat, and follow by underseal if desired.

Aerial feeder cable routing should avoid the engine compartment and areas where stress might occur, eg under the carpet where feet will be located. Roof aerials require that the headlining be pulled back and that a path is available down the door pillar. It is wise to check with the vehicle dealer whether roof aerial fitting is recommended.

Loudspeakers

Speakers should be matched to the output stage of the equipment, particularly as regards the recommended impedance. Power transistors used for driving speakers are sensitive to the loading placed on them.

Before choosing a mounting position for speakers, check whether the vehicle manufacturer has provided a location for them. Generally door-mounted speakers give good stereophonic reproduction, but not all doors are able to accept them. The next best position is the rear parcel shelf, and in this case speaker apertures can be cut into the shelf, or pod units may be mounted.

For door mounting, first remove the trim, which is often held on by 'poppers' or press studs, and then select a suitable gap in the inside door assembly. Check that the speaker would not obstruct glass or winder mechanism by winding the window up and down. A template is often provided for marking out the trim panel hole, and then the four fixing holes must be drilled through. Mark out with chalk and cut cleanly with a sharp knife or keyhole saw. Speaker leads are then threaded through the door and door pillar, if necessary drilling 10 mm diameter holes. Fit grommets in the holes and connect to the radio or tape unit correctly. Do not omit a waterproofing cover, usually supplied with door speakers. If the speaker has to be fixed into the metal of the door itself, use self-tapping screws, and if the fixing is to the door trim use self-tapping screws and flat spire nuts.

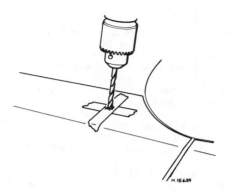

Fig. 13.51 Drilling the bodywork for aerial mounting (Sec 13B)

Rear shelf mounting is somewhat simpler but it is necessary to find gaps in the metalwork underneath the parcel shelf. However, remember that the speakers should be as far apart as possible to give a good stereo effect. Pod-mounted speakers can be screwed into position through the parcel shelf material, but it is worth testing for the best position. Sometimes good results are found by reflecting sound off the rear window.

Interference

In general, when electric current changes abruptly, unwanted electrical noise is produced. The motor vehicle is filled with electrical devices which change electric current rapidly, the most obvious being the contact breaker.

When the spark plugs operate, the sudden pulse of spark current causes the associated wiring to radiate. Since early radio transmitters used sparks as a basis of operation, it is not surprising that the car radio will pick up ignition spark noise unless steps are taken to reduce it to acceptable levels.

Interference reaches the car radio in two ways:

(a) by conduction through the wiring.
(b) by radiation to the receiving aerial.

Initial checks presuppose that the bonnet is down and fastened, the radio unit has a good earth connection *(not through the aerial downlead outer)*, no fluorescent tubes are working near the car, the aerial trimmer has been adjusted, and the vehicle is in a position to receive radio signals, ie not in a metal-clad building.

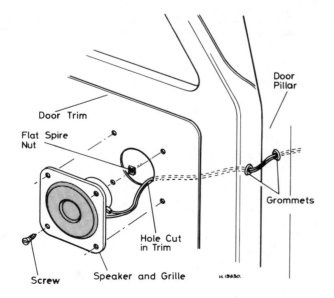

Fig. 13.52 Door-mounted speaker installation (Sec 13B)

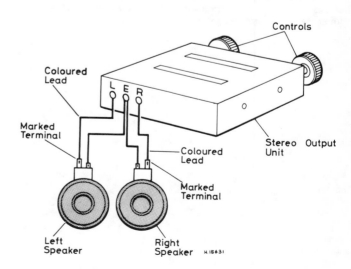

Fig. 13.53 Speaker connections must be correctly made as shown (Sec 13B)

Switch on the radio and tune it to the middle of the medium wave (MW) band off-station with the volume (gain) control set fairly high. Switch on the ignition (but do not start the engine) and wait to see if irregular clicks or hash noise occurs. Tapping the facia panel may also produce the effects. If so, this will be due to the voltage stabiliser, which is an on-off thermal switch to control instrument voltage. It is located usually on the back of the instrument panel, often attached to the speedometer. Correction is by attachment of a capacitor and, if still troublesome, chokes in the supply wires.

Switch on the engine and listen for interference on the MW band. Depending on the type of interference, the indications are as follows.

A harsh crackle that drops out abruptly at low engine speed or when the headlights are switched on is probably due to a voltage regulator.

A whine varying with engine speed is due to the alternator. Try temporarily taking off the fan belt – if the noise goes this is confirmation.

Regular ticking or crackle that varies in rate with the engine speed is due to the ignition system. With this trouble in particular and others in general, check to see if the noise is entering the receiver from the wiring or by radiation. To do this, pull out the aerial plug, (preferably shorting out the input socket or connecting a 62 pF capacitor across it). If the noise disappears it is coming in through the aerial and is *radiation noise*. If the noise persists it is reaching the receiver through the wiring and is said to be *line-borne*.

Interference from wipers, washers, heater blowers, turn-indicators, stop lamps, etc is usually taken to the receiver by wiring, and simple treatment using capacitors and possibly chokes will solve the problem. Switch on each one in turn (wet the screen first for running wipers!) and listen for possible interference with the aerial plug in place and again when removed.

Note that if most of the vehicle accessories are found to be creating interference all together, the probability is that poor aerial earthing is to blame.

Suppression methods – ignition

Suppressed HT cables are supplied as original equipment by manufacturers and will meet regulations as far as interference to neighbouring equipment is concerned. It is illegal to remove such suppression unless an alternative is provided, and this may take the form of resistive spark plug caps in conjunction with plain copper HT cable. For VHF purposes, these and 'in-line' resistors may not be effective, and resistive HT cable is preferred. Check that suppressed cables are actually fitted by observing cable identity lettering, or measuring with an ohmmeter – the value of each plug lead should be 5000 to 10 000 ohms.

A 1 microfarad capacitor connected from the LT supply side of the ignition coil to a good nearby earth point will complete basic ignition interference treatment. *NEVER fit a capacitor to the coil terminal to the contact breaker – the result would be burnt out points in a short time.*

Electronic ignition systems have built-in suppression components, but this does not relieve the need for using suppressed HT leads. In some cases it is permitted to connect a capacitor on the low tension

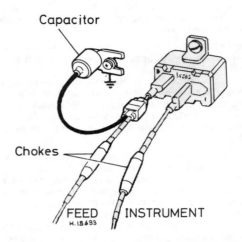

Fig. 13.54 Voltage stabiliser interference suppression (Sec 13B)

supply side of the ignition coil, but not in every case. Makers' instructions should be followed carefully, otherwise damage to the ignition semiconductors may result.

VHF/FM broadcasts

Reception of VHF/FM in an automobile is more prone to problems than the medium and long wavebands. Medium/long wave transmitters are capable of covering considerable distances, but VHF transmitters are restricted to line of sight, meaning ranges of 10 to 50 miles, depending upon the terrain, the effects of buildings and the transmitter power.

Because of the limited range it is necessary to retune on a long journey, and it may be better for those habitually travelling long distances or living in areas of poor provision of transmitters to use an AM radio working on medium/long wavebands.

For VHF/FM receiver installation the following points should be particularly noted:

(a) Earthing of the receiver chassis and the aerial mounting is important. Use a separate earthing wire at the radio, and scrape paint away at the aerial mounting.

(b) If possible, use a good quality roof aerial to obtain maximum height and distance from interference generating devices on the vehicle.

(c) Use of a high quality aerial download is important, since losses in cheap cable can be significant.

(d) The polarisation of FM transmissions may be horizontal, vertical, circular or slanted. Because of this the optimum mounting angle is at 45° to the vehicle roof.

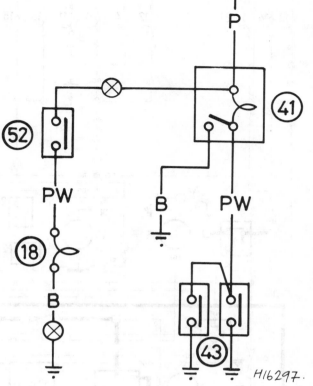

Fig. 13.56 Supplementary wiring diagram for load area light. Use in conjunction with Fig. 10.18 or 10.19

18 Load area light
41 Passenger interior light and switch
43 Door switches
52 Load area light switch

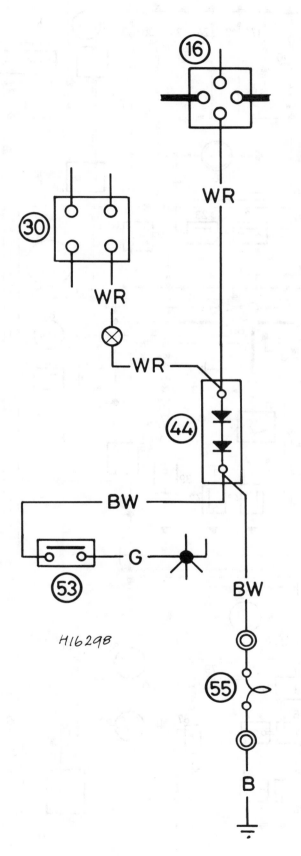

Fig. 13.55 Supplementary wiring diagram for alternative brake failure warning system. Use in conjunction with Fig. 10.18 or 10.19

16 Starter motor solenoid
30 Ignition/starter switch
44 Double blocking diode
53 Brake fluid level switch
55 Brake failure warning light

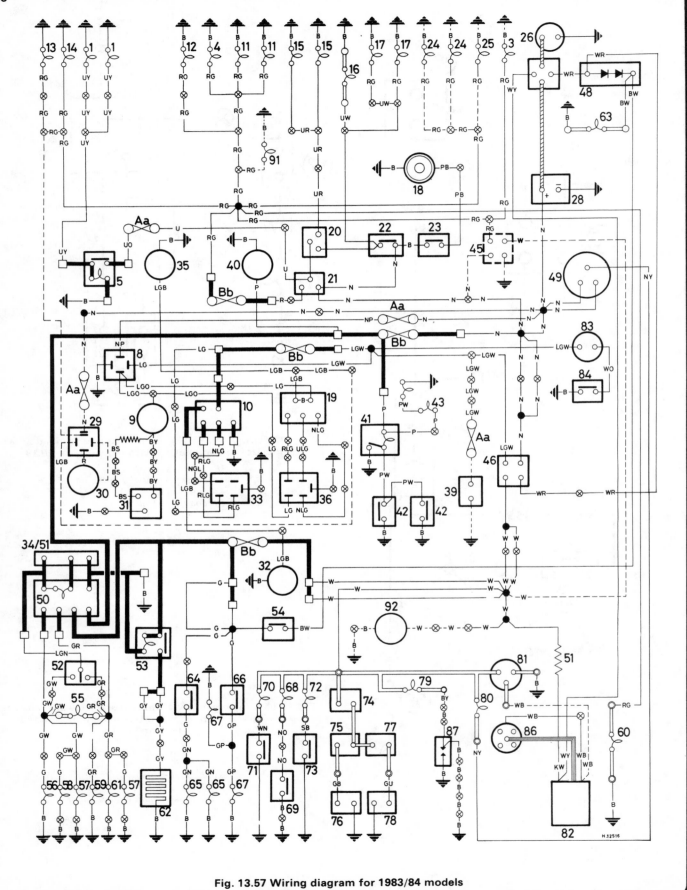

Fig. 13.57 Wiring diagram for 1983/84 models

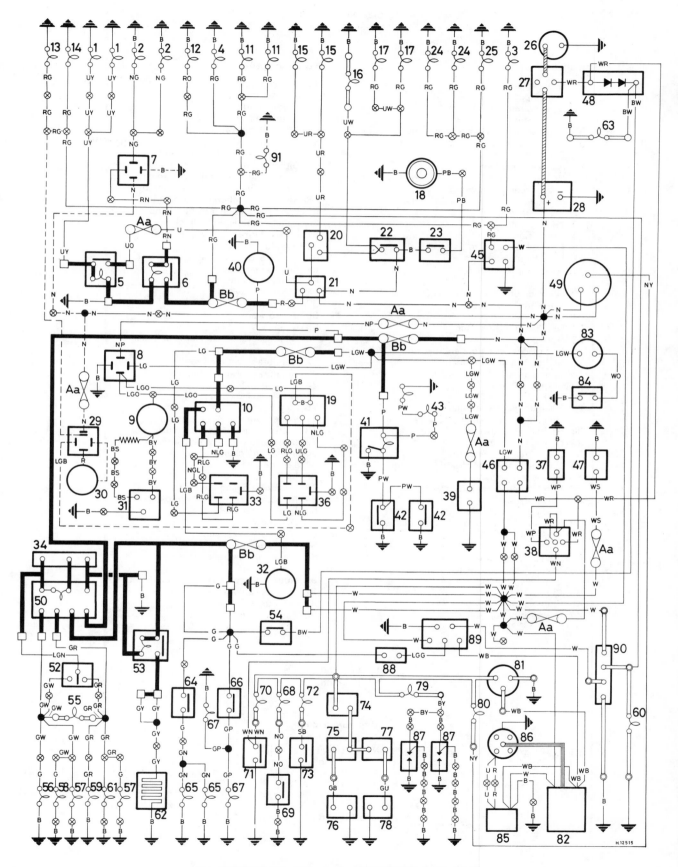

Fig. 13.58 Wiring diagram for 1983/84 Turbo models

Key to wiring diagrams – Figs. 13.57 and 13.58

No	Description
1	Rear foglamp(s)
2	Foglamps*
3	Cigar lighter illumination lamp
4	LH tail lamp
5	Rear foglamp switch and warning lamp
6	Foglamps switch and warning lamp*
7	Front foglamps relay*
8	Auxiliary circuits relay
9	Heater motor
10	Rear screen wash/wipe switch
11	Number plate illumination lamp(s)
12	RH tail lamp
13	LH sidelamp
14	RH sidelamp
15	Headlamp dip beam
16	Main beam warning lamp
17	Headlamp main beam
18	Horn(s)
19	Windscreen wash/wipe switch
20	Headlamp dip switch
21	Lighting switch
22	Headlamp flash switch
23	Horn push
24	Heater control illumination
25	Switch illumination lamp(s)
26	Starter motor
27	Starter solenoid
28	Battery
29	Headlamps washer relay
30	Headlamps wash high-pressure motor
31	Heater motor switch
32	Rear screen washer motor
33	Rear screen wiper motor
34	Direction indicator/hazard flasher unit
35	Windscreen washer motor
36	Windscreen wiper motor
37	Fuel pump
38	Fuel pump protection relay*
39	Radio or radio/cassette unit
40	Cigar lighter
41	Interior lamp(s)
42	Interior lamp door switch
43	Load space lamp switch
44	Load space lamp
45	Clock
46	Ignition/starter switch
47	Carburettor vent valve*
48	Double diode
49	Alternator
50	Hazard warning switch
51	Ballast resistor cable†
52	Direction indicator switch
53	Heated rear screen switch and warning lamp
54	Brake fluid level sensor switch
55	Direction indicator warning lamp
56	RH rear direction indicator lamp
57	Direction indicator repeater lamps
58	RH front direction indicator lamp
59	LH rear direction indicator lamp
60	Panel illumination lamp(s)
61	LH front direction indicator lamp
62	Heated rear screen
63	Brake failure warning lamp
64	Reverse lamp switch
65	Reverse lamp(s)
66	Stoplamp switch
67	Stoplamps
68	Choke warning lamp
69	Choke warning lamp switch
70	Oil pressure warning lamp or indicator
71	Oil pressure switch
72	Handbrake warning lamp
73	Handbrake warning lamp switch
74	Voltage stabiliser
75	Fuel level indicator
76	Fuel level indicator tank unit
77	Water temperature indicator
78	Water temperature transducer
79	Brake pad wear warning lamp
80	Ignition no charge warning lamp
81	Tachometer
82	Ignition coil
83	Radiator cooling fan motor
84	Radiator cooling fan thermostat
85	Ignition module*
86	Distributor
87	Brake pad wear sensor
88	Valve solenoid*
89	Electronic control unit*
90	Boost gauge*
91	Automatic gearbox selector indicator lamp
92	Anti-run-on valve
Aa	Line fuses
Bb	Fusebox printed circuit

† Non-Turbo models

* Turbo models

Wiring colour code

B	Black	N	Brown	S	Slate
G	Green	O	Orange	U	Blue
K	Pink	P	Purple	W	White
LG	Light green	R	Red	Y	Yellow

For symbols see Fig. 10.21 on page 144

Key to wiring diagrams – Figs. 13.59 and 13.60

For colour code see key to Fig. 13.57

No	Description	No	Description
1	Alternator	115	Heated rear screen switch
3	Battery	116	Heated rear screen
4	Starter solenoid	118	Windscreen washer/wiper switch
5	Starter motor	150	Heated rear screen warning lamp
6	Lighting switch	152	Hazard warning lamp
7	Headlamp dip switch	153	Hazard warning switch
8	Headlamp dip beam	165	Handbrake warning lamp switch
9	Headlamp main beam	178	Radiator cooling fan thermostat
11	RH side lamp	179	Radiator cooling fan motor
12	LH side lamp	182	Brake fluid level switch
15	Number plate illumination lamp(s)	208	Cigar lighter illumination lamp
16	Stop lamp(s)	211	Heater control illumination
17	RH tail lamp	212	Choke warning lamp switch
18	Stop lamp switch	216	Window lift switch
19	Fusebox	220	Window lift motor
20	Interior lamp	231	Headlamp relay
21	Interior lamp door switch	240	Heated rear screen relay
22	LH tail lamp	246	Glovebox illumination lamp
23	Horn	247	Glovebox illumination switch
24	Horn push	270	Rear screen wiper motor
25	Direction indicator flasher unit	271	Rear screen washer motor
26	Direction indicator switch	286	Fog rearguard lamp switch
28	RH front direction indicator lamp	287	Fog rearguard warning lamp
29	LH front direction indicator lamp	288	Fog rearguard lamp(s)
30	RH rear direction indicator lamp	296	Fuel pump relay*
31	LH rear direction indicator lamp	298	Windscreen wiper delay
32	Heater motor switch	300	Ignition switch relay
33	Heater motor	314	Header console
35	Fuel level indicator tank unit	326	Brake pad wear sensor
37	Windscreen wiper motor	336	Speaker
38	Ignition/starter switch	342	Rear screen wiper switch
39	Ignition coil	343	Rear screen wash switch
40	Distributor	344	Door lock motor
41	Fuel pump*	345	Door lock control unit
42	Oil pressure switch	347	Electronic control unit
45	Headlamp flash switch	349	Turbo boost gauge*
47	Water temperature transducer	350	Control valve solenoid*
49	Reverse lamp switch	351	Load space lamp/switch
50	Reverse lamp(s)	363	Carburettor vent valve
56	Clock†	364	Window lift relay
57	Cigar lighter	389	Column switch illumination
60	Radio or radio cassette unit	396	Footwell illumination
76	Automatic gearbox selector indicator lamp†	397	Fusebox illumination
77	Windscreen washer motor	403	Auxiliary ignition relay
82	Switch illumination lamp(s)	413	Fusible links
110	Direction indicator repeater lamps	428	Mechanical instruments

† Non-Turbo models
* Turbo models

For symbols see Fig. 10.21 on page 144

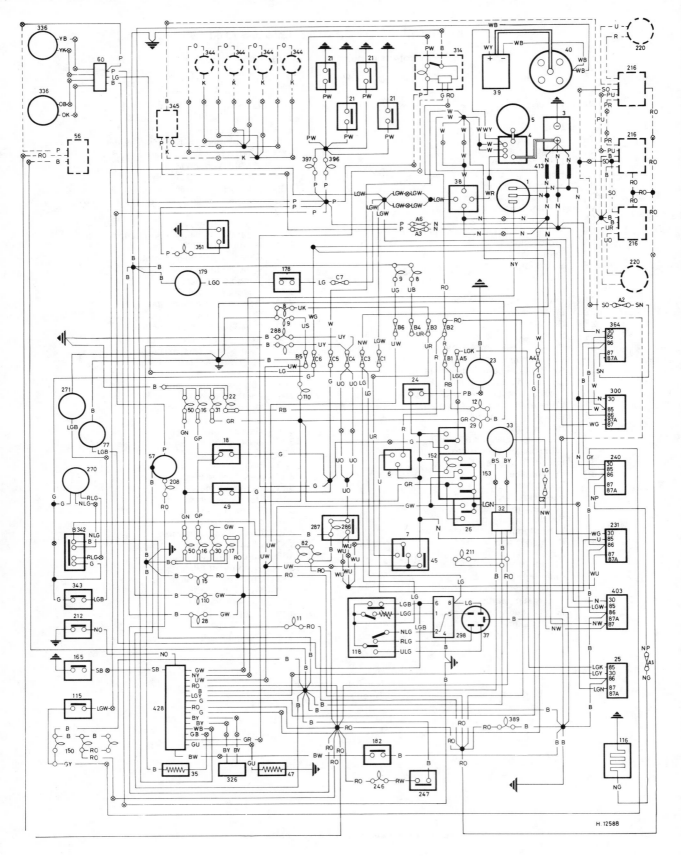

Fig. 13.59 Wiring diagram for 1985 models

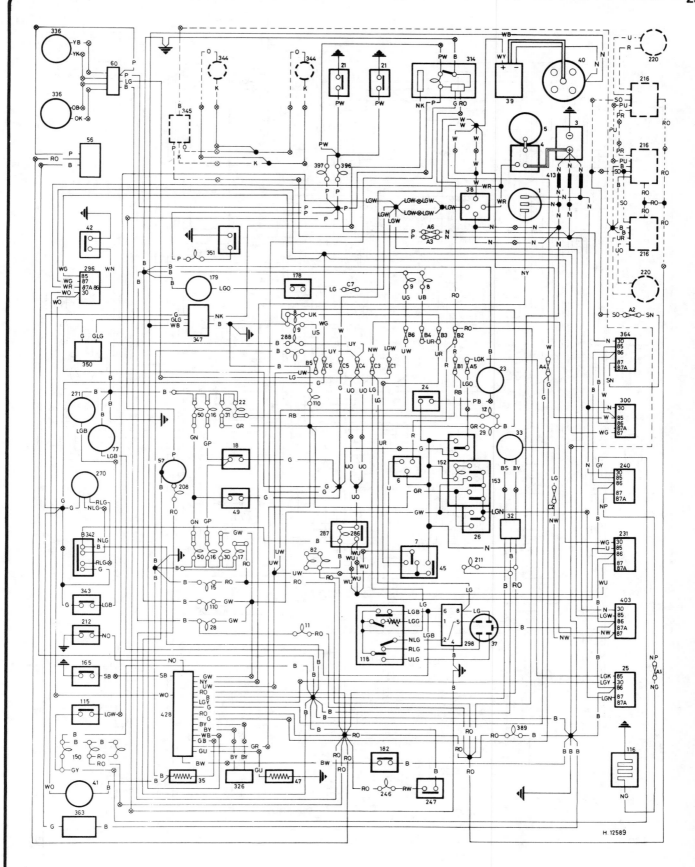

Fig. 13.60 Wiring diagram for 1985 Turbo models

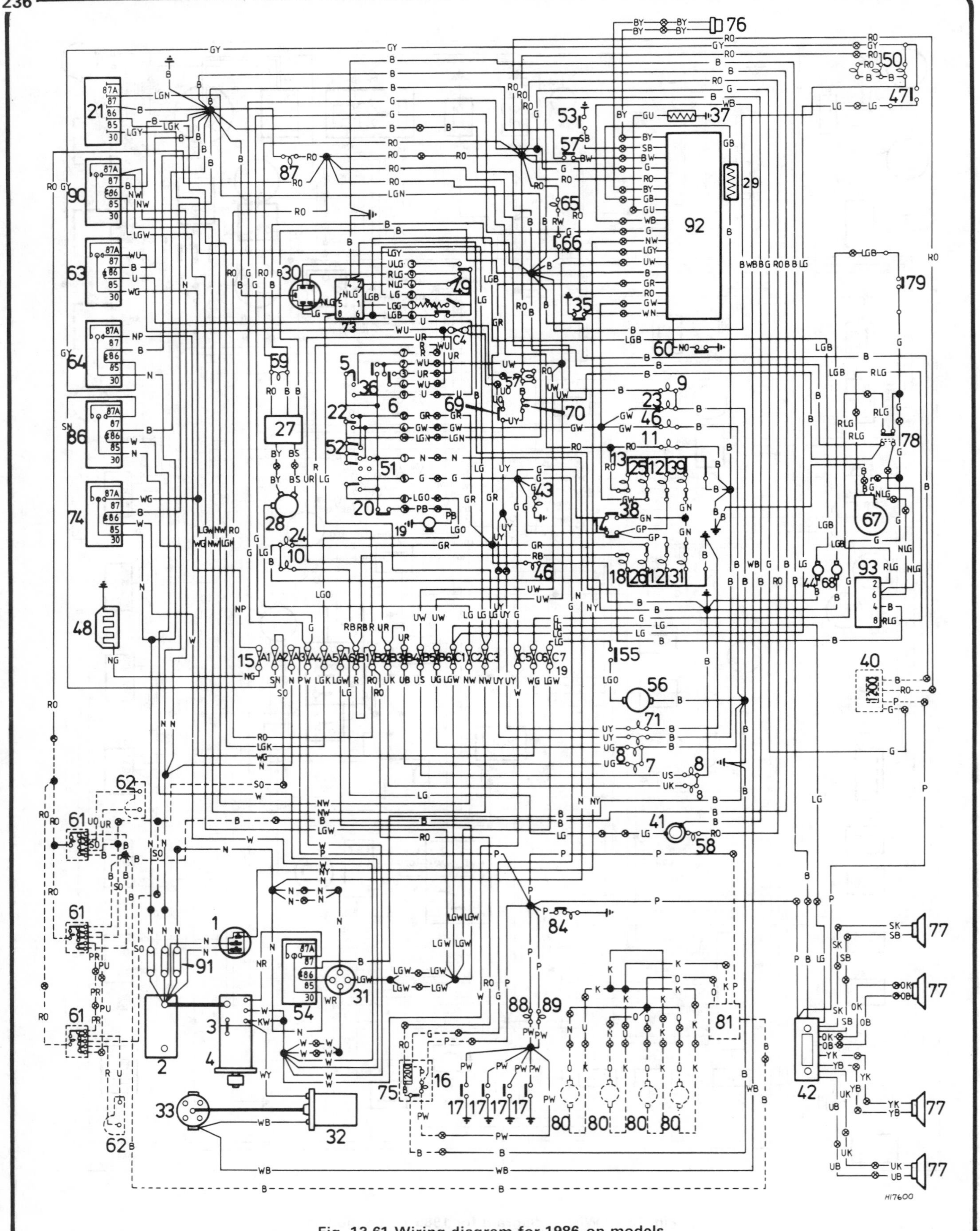

Fig. 13.61 Wiring diagram for 1986-on models

HI7600

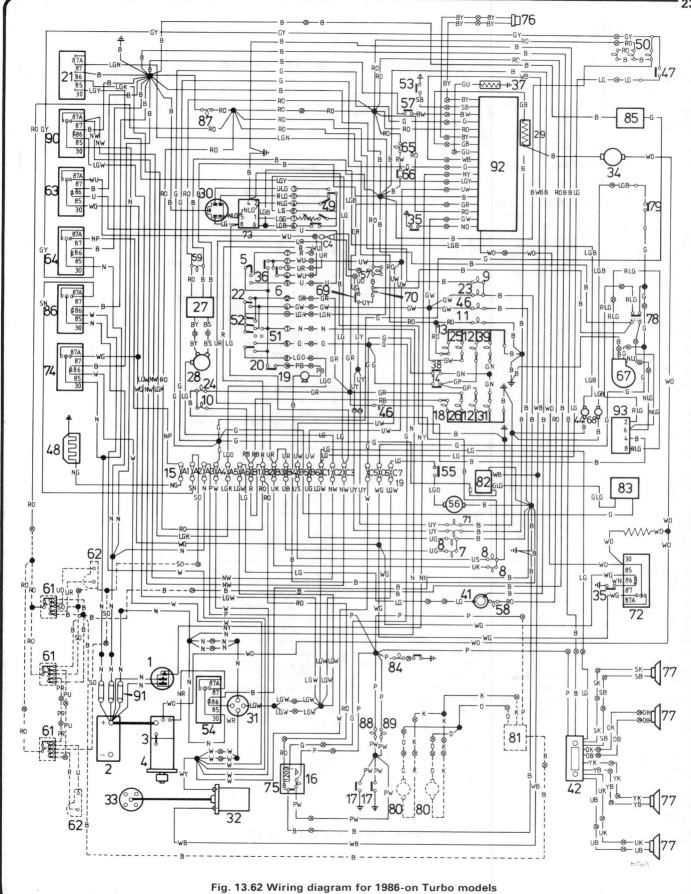

Fig. 13.62 Wiring diagram for 1986-on Turbo models

Key to wiring diagrams – Figs. 13.61 and 13.62

No	Description	No	Description
1	Alternator	48	Heated rear screen
2	Battery	49	Windscreen washer/wiper switch
3	Starter solenoid	50	Heated rear screen warning lamp
4	Starter motor	51	Hazard warning lamp
5	Lighting switch	52	Hazard warning switch
6	Headlamp dip switch	53	Handbrake warning lamp switch
7	Headlamp dip beam	54	Starter relay
8	Headlamp main beam	55	Radiator cooling fan thermostat
9	RH side lamp	56	Radiator cooling fan motor
10	LH side lamp	57	Brake fluid level switch
11	Number plate illumination lamp(s)	58	Cigar lighter illumination lamp
12	Stop-lamp(s)	59	Heater control illumination
13	RH tail lamp	60	Choke warning lamp switch
14	Stop-lamp switch	61	Window lift switch
15	Fusebox	62	Window lift motor
16	Interior lamp	63	Headlamp relay
17	Interior lamp door switch	64	Heated rear screen relay
18	LH tail lamp	65	Glovebox illumination lamp
19	Horn	66	Glovebox illumination switch
20	Horn push	67	Rear screen wiper motor
21	Direction indicator flasher unit	68	Rear screen washer motor
22	Direction indicator switch	69	Fog rearguard lamp switch
23	RH front direction indicator lamp	70	Fog rearguard warning lamp
24	LH front direction indicator lamp	71	Fog rearguard lamp(s)
25	RH rear direction indicator lamp	72	Fuel pump relay*
26	LH rear direction indicator lamp	73	Windscreen wiper delay
27	Heater motor switch	74	Ignition switch relay
28	Heater motor	75	Header console
29	Fuel level indicator tank unit	76	Brake pad wear sensor
30	Windscreen wiper motor	77	Speaker
31	Ignition/starter switch	78	Rear screen wiper switch
32	Ignition coil	79	Rear screen wash switch
33	Distributor	80	Door lock motor
34	Fuel pump*	81	Door lock control unit
35	Oil pressure switch	82	Electronic control unit*
36	Headlamp flash switch	83	Control valve solenoid*
37	Water temperature transducer	84	Load space lamp/switch
38	Reverse lamp switch	85	Carburettor vent valve*
39	Reverse lamp(s)	86	Window lift relay
40	Clock†	87	Column switch illumination
41	Cigar lighter	88	Footwell illumination
42	Radio or Radio/Cassette unit	89	Fusebox illumination
43	Automatic gearbox selector indicator lamp†	90	Auxiliary ignition relay
44	Windscreen washer motor	91	Fusible links
45	Switch illumination lamp(s)	92	Mechanical instruments
46	Direction indicator repeater lamps	93	Rear screen programmed wash/wipe unit
47	Heated rear screen switch	94	Fuel pump resistor*

† Non-Turbo models
* Turbo models

For colour code see key to Fig. 13.57

For symbols see Fig. 10.21 on page 144

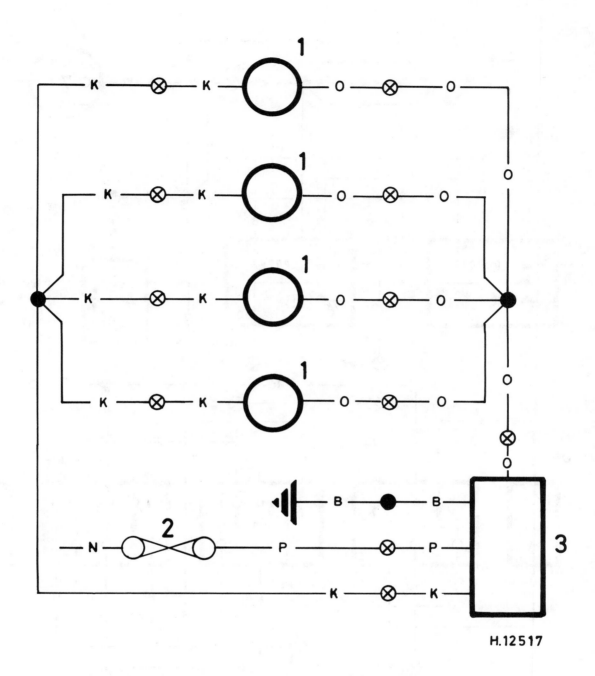

**Fig. 13.63 Wiring diagram for central locking system.
For symbols see Fig. 10.21 on page 144**

1   Door lock motor – tailgate and passenger doors
2   Fusebox
3   Door lock motor/control unit – driver's door

For colour code see key to Fig. 13.57

H.12517

240

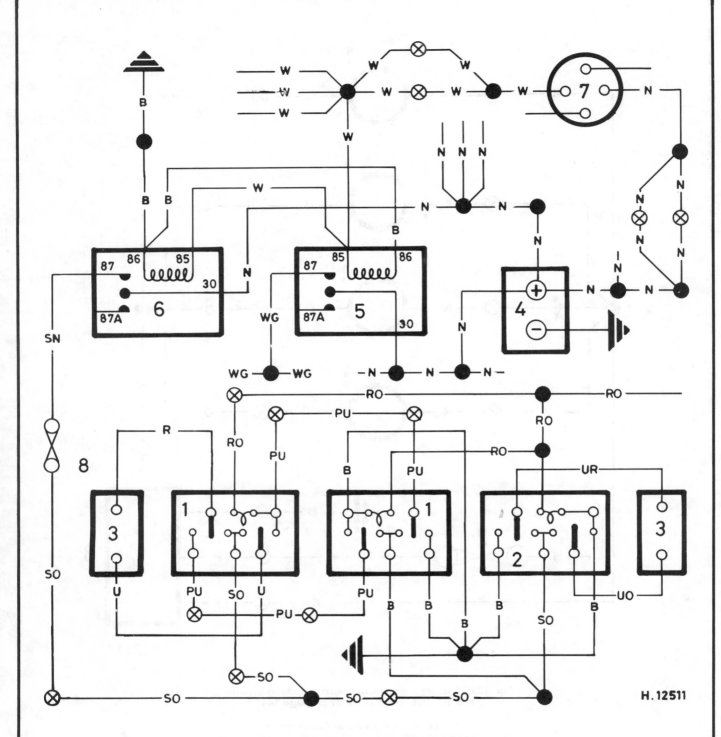

Fig. 13.64 Wiring diagram for electric window system.
For symbols see Fig. 10.21 on page 144

H.12511

1   Window lift switch front LH
2   Window lift switch front RH
3   Window lift motor
4   Battery
5   Ignition switch relay
6   Window lift relay
7   Ignition switch
8   Fusebox

For colour code see key to Fig. 13.57

14 Suspension and steering

General description

1   Few changes have been made to the systems and procedures described in Chapter 11. The MG Turbo model is fitted with a rear anti-roll bar, details of which ar given later in this Section.
2   Low rolling resistance tyres are fitted as standard equipment to 1983 HLE models. Denovo 'run-flat' tyres are no longer available. Tyre sizes and pressures for later models are given in the Specifications.
3   1985 and 1986-on models are fitted with modified steering columns, and a modified rack and pinion assembly. The only suspension modification consists of repositioning the front suspension bump stops on the subframe brackets (photo). From 1985, with the exception of MG Turbo models, front shock absorbers are no longer fitted.

Leaks from Hydragas units

4   Where a leak in a Hydragas unit is suspected, clean the area around the charging valve threads to determine whether the valve is the source of the leak. (Talcum powder dusted around the clean valve may be helpful in tracing a leak.)
5   If it is established that the leak is occurring round the valve threads, have the system depressurised by your BL dealer, then unscrew the valve.
6   Screw in a new valve, using a suitable sealant on the threads (Loctite 270 or equivalent). Tighten the valve to the specified torque. Have the system recharged by your BL dealer on completion, and check for leaks.

Front suspension spacers

7   The number and thickness of the spacer(s) fitted between the front Hydragas units and their knuckle joint varies according to model.
8   Incorrect fitting of spacers will make the suspension seem firmer on one side of the car than on the other. Correct applications are as follows:

Model	LH side	RH side	Thickness in (mm)
MG Turbo	1	3	0.09 (2.29)
MG and Vanden Plas (manual)	0	2	0.09 (2.29)
MG and Vanden Plas (manual) – alternative fitting	1	1	0.05 (1.27)
Automotive models	1	4	0.09 (2.29)
All other models except Van	0	2	0.09 (2.29)
Van	0	0	–

Front shock absorber rubber bush

9   The rubber bush in the front shock absorber lower mounting eye may be renewed separately to the shock absorber if necessary. First remove the shock absorber as described in Chapter 11, Section 5.
10   Drive the metal sleeve from the centre of the bush.

11   Using a metal tube, long bolt, thick washers and nut, pull the bush from the mounting eye. If necessary, cut the bush with a small hacksaw before removing it.
12   Dip the new bush in soapy water before pressing it into the eye, then refit the shock absorber.

Front anti-roll bar knock – rectification

13   If front anti-roll bar knock is diagnosed (see Section 11), it may be rectified as follows.
14   Check the anti-roll bar bushes for deterioration. Renew them if necessary. Lubricate the new bushes with Duckhams Keenol grease or equivalent.
15   Clean any grease from the anti-roll bar itself in the area next to the bushes.
16   If not already so equipped, fit clamps and U-bolts on the inboard side of each bush as shown (Fig. 13.65). The correct clamps are available from your BL dealer.
17   Tighten the U-bolt nuts evenly to the specified torque, making sure that the clamps are pulled down evenly and that the clamps are firmly up against the bushes, thus preventing sideways movement of the anti-roll bar (photo).

Rear suspension spacers

18   Spacers are now fitted between the rear struts and Hydragas units as given in the following table:

Model	LH side	RH side	Thickness in (mm)
MG Turbo	1	1	0.145 (3.68)
All other 3-door models (except Van)	1	1	0.05 (1.27)
Van and 5-door models	0	0	–

Rear Hydragas struts

19   When depressurising and pressurising the rear Hydragas units, care must be taken to ensure the struts are correctly located, otherwise irreparable damage will be caused to the Hydragas units.
20   The struts must be located in the centre hole within the units, and where helper springs are fitted, these must locate on the split collars welded to the subframe. If the split collars are loose, have them re-welded in position.

Rear anti-roll bar (MG Turbo) – removal and refitting

21   Chock the front wheels, slacken the rear wheel nuts and raise and support the rear of the vehicle. Remove the rear wheels.
22   Undo the nut and bolt on each side which hold the ends of the anti-roll bar to the suspension links.
23   Remove the mounting clamps from the central section of the anti-roll bar. The bar and mounting rubbers can now be removed.
24   Renew any mounting components which have deteriorated. Renew the anti-roll bar if it is distorted or damaged.

14.3 Front suspension bump stop (arrowed) on 1985-on models

14.17 U-bolt and clamp next to anti-roll bar bush

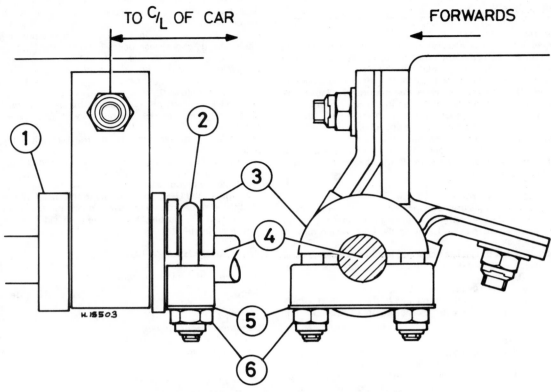

Fig. 13.65 Views of anti-roll bar clamps (Sec 14)

1	Bush	3	Clamp top half	5	Washer
2	U-Bolt	4	Anti-roll bar	6	Nut

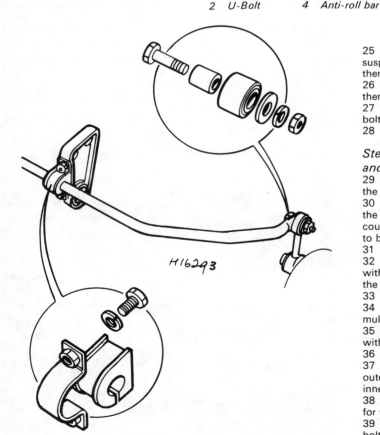

Fig. 13.66 Rear anti-roll bar mounting details (Sec 14)

25 Commence refitting by connecting the ends of the bar to the suspension links. Fit the nut and bolt on each side but do not tighten them yet.

26 Fit the mounting clamps over the mounting rubbers and secure them to their brackets.

27 Tighten the mounting clamp bolts and then the end link nuts and bolts.

28 Refit the roadwheels and lower the car to the ground.

Steering column (1985 models) – removal, overhaul and refitting

29 Remove the steering wheel as described in Chapter 11. Disconnect the battery negative lead.

30 Prise the circular grommet from the coupling cover at the bottom of the column and unscrew the nuts securing the steering rack pinion coupling to the flexible coupling. Turn the steering column as required to bring each nut into view by pivoting the front wheels by hand.

31 Lift the carpet and unbolt the coupling cover from the bulkhead.

32 Remove the screws from the steering column cowl lower half and withdraw the lower cowl, then remove the upper screw and withdraw the upper cowl. Disconnect the wiring multi-plugs.

33 Disconnect the bulbholder from the combination switch assembly.

34 Remove the fusebox cover and disconnect the ignition switch multi-plug.

35 Unbolt the steering column from the top mounting bracket and withdraw the assembly upwards from the pinion coupling.

36 Remove the combination switch assembly (1 screw).

37 Unbolt the upper column, withdraw the inner column from the outer column, then remove the upper column and top bush from the inner column.

38 Clean the components in paraffin and wipe dry. Examine the bush for wear and renew it, if necessary.

39 To reassemble, insert the inner column in the outer column then bolt the top bush and upper column to the outer column.

40 Fit the combination switch assembly and tighten the clamp screw.

41 Centralise the inner steering column and roadwheels, and engage the pinion coupling with the flexible coupling. Align the column and fit the top mounting bracket bolts finger tight.

42 Fully tighten the coupling nuts.

43 Position the coupling cover as shown in Fig. 13.68, centralise the inner column in the outer column, then insert and tighten the coupling cover bolts. Fit the circular grommet.

44 Fully tighten the top mounting bracket bolts.

45 Reconnect the ignition switch multi-plug and combination switch bulbholder, and refit the fusebox cover.

46 Reconnect the wiring multi-plugs.

47 Refit the steering column cowls and steering wheel (Chapter 11).

48 Reconnect the battery negative lead.

Steering rack and pinion (1985 models) – removal, overhaul and refitting

Note: *Overhaul is limited to removal and refitting of the tie-rods; full overhaul information is not currently available.*

49 Disconnect the battery negative lead.

50 Apply the handbrake, then jack up the front of the car and support it on stands. Remove both front wheels, and centralise the steering.

51 Prise the circular grommet from the coupling cover at the bottom of the column and unscrew the nuts securing the steering rack pinion coupling to the flexible coupling. Turn the steering as required to bring each nut into view.

52 Prise back the cover and loosen the coupling cover clamp bolt.

53 Remove the fusebox cover, then unscrew and remove the left-hand bolt from the column top mounting bracket. Loosen only the right-hand bolt.

54 Move the steering column upwards sufficiently to free the flexible coupling from the pinion coupling studs.

55 Unscrew the tie-rod and balljoint nuts and use a separator tool to detach the balljoints from the steering arms.

56 Unscrew the nuts and bolts and remove the U-bolt and mounting pad and clamp.

57 Rotate the rack assembly and withdraw it from the driver's side of the subframe.

58 Remove the tie-rod ends, locknuts, gaiters and clips, with reference to Chapter 11.

59 Mount the rack assembly in a soft-jawed vice, then unscrew the tie-rod ball housings. If available use BL tools 18G 1440 to grip the rack and housing (Fig. 13.69) otherwise make up wooden substitutes used with G-cramps, but take care not to damage the components.

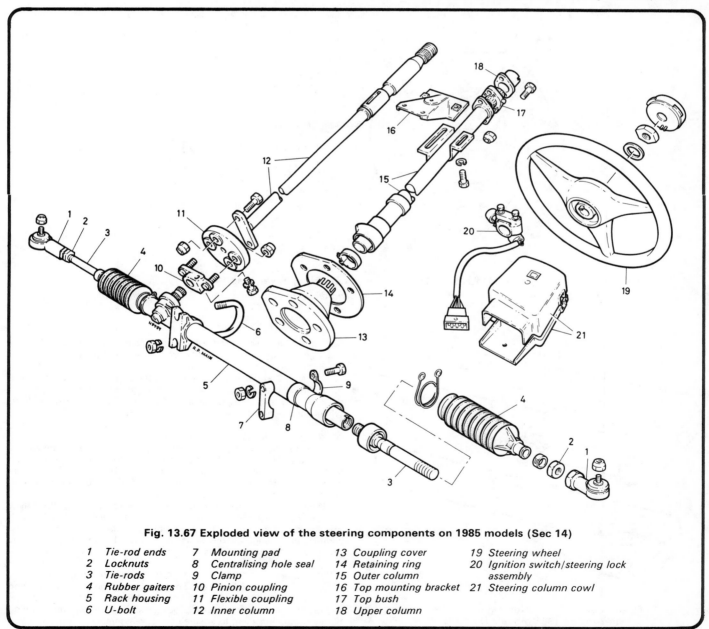

Fig. 13.67 Exploded view of the steering components on 1985 models (Sec 14)

1 Tie-rod ends	7 Mounting pad	13 Coupling cover	19 Steering wheel
2 Locknuts	8 Centralising hole seal	14 Retaining ring	20 Ignition switch/steering lock
3 Tie-rods	9 Clamp	15 Outer column	assembly
4 Rubber gaiters	10 Pinion coupling	16 Top mounting bracket	21 Steering column cowl
5 Rack housing	11 Flexible coupling	17 Top bush	
6 U-bolt	12 Inner column	18 Upper column	

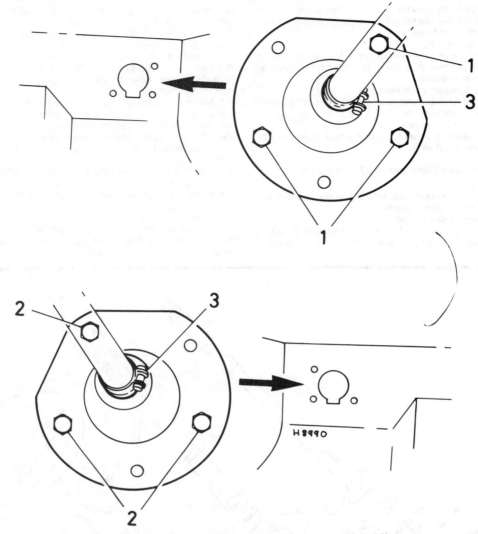

Fig. 13.68 Correct position of coupling cover (Sec 14)

1   *Right-hand drive coupling cover bolts*   2   *Left-hand drive coupling cover bolts*   3   *Clamp bolt*

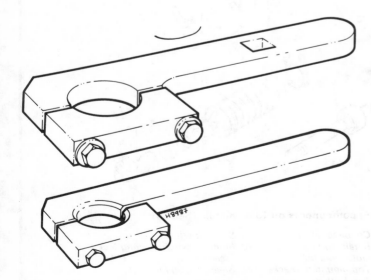

**Fig. 13.69 BL tools 18G 1440 for removing the steering
tie-rods on 1985 models (Sec 14)**

60 Tighten the new tie-rod ball housings to the rack and lock them by staking their edges into the slots on the ends of the rack.
61 Refit the gaiters and tie-rod ends with reference to Chapter 11, making sure that the assembly contains the correct quantity of grease.
62 Refitting is a reversal of removal, but tighten all nuts and bolts to the specified torque, as given in Chapter 11. Finally adjust the front wheel alignment, as described in Chapter 11.

Steering column (1986-on models)

63 The steering column components for 1986-on models are shown in Fig. 13.70. The top bush is a press fit in the top of the outer column, and should be coated with graphite grease before fitting. The flexible coupling incorporates a support plate which must contact the pinion coupling with the lugs located over the studs.
64 When refitting the steering column, make sure that there is a clearance between the bottom of the steering wheel and the cowls. If not, loosen the outer column mounting bolts, lower the column slightly, then retighten the bolts. Note that the adjustment is only possible on 1986-on models.

Steering rack and pinion – removal and refitting

65 Where difficulty is experienced in removing the steering rack and pinion assembly, the pinion coupling may be removed from the pinion splines after removing the clamp bolt. Mark the pinion and coupling before separating them to ensure correct reassembly.

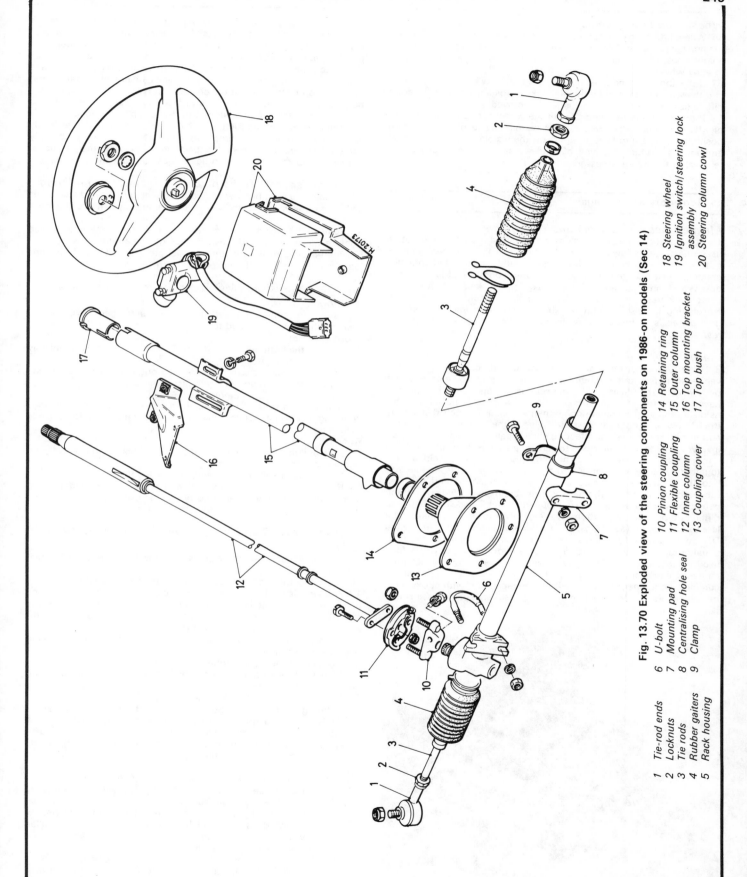

Fig. 13.70 Exploded view of the steering components on 1986-on models (Sec 14)

1 Tie-rod ends
2 Locknuts
3 Tie rods
4 Rubber gaiters
5 Rack housing

6 U-bolt
7 Mounting pad
8 Centralising hole seal
9 Clamp

10 Pinion coupling
11 Flexible coupling
12 Inner column
13 Coupling cover

14 Retaining ring
15 Outer column
16 Top mounting bracket
17 Top bush

18 Steering wheel
19 Ignition switch/steering lock
     assembly
20 Steering column cowl

Wheels and tyres – general

66 Where fitting a roadwheel for any reason, it is a good idea to grease the hub spigot (or the hole in the wheel into which the spigot fits) with a light smear of general purpose grease. This applies both to steel and to alloy wheels.

67 If the above procedure is not followed, there is a risk of the spigot and the wheel becoming firmly joined by corrosion, which will lead to difficulties next time the wheel is to be removed.

68 If problems are experienced with the wheel centre trim falling out of MG or Vanden Plas wheels, it is permissible to glue the trim in position. Take care to keep the glue off the visible parts of the wheel and trim, and choose a type of glue which will allow subsequent removal of the trim if necessary.

15 Bodywork and fittings

Maintenance – bodywork and underframe

1 The steam cleaning method described in Chapter 12 should not be used on vehicles with wax-based underbody protective coating or the coating will be removed. Such vehicles should be inspected annually, preferably just prior to winter, when the underbody should be washed down and any damage to the wax coating repaired. Ideally, a completely fresh coat should be applied. It would also be worth considering the use of such wax-based protection for injection into door panels, sills, box sections etc, as an additional safeguard against rust damage.

Plastic components

2 With the use of more and more plastic body components by the vehicle manufacturers (eg bumpers, spoilers, and in some cases major body panels), rectification of more serious damage to such items has become a matter of either entrusting repair work to a specialist in this field, or renewing complete components. Repair of such damage by the DIY owner is not really feasible owing to the cost of the equipment and materials required for effecting such repairs. The basic technique involves making a groove along the line of the crack in the plastic using a rotary burr in a power drill. The damaged part is then welded back together by using a hot air gun to heat up and fuse a plastic filler rod into the groove. Any excess plastic is then removed and the area rubbed down to a smooth finish. It is important that a filler rod of the correct plastic is used, as body components can be made of a variety of different types (eg polycarbonate, ABS, polypropylene). Damage of a less serious nature (abrasions, minor cracks etc) can be repaired by the DIY owner using a two-part epoxy filler repair material. Once mixed in equal proportions, this is used in similar fashion to the bodywork filler used on metal panels. The filler is usually cured in twenty to thirty minutes, ready for sanding and painting. If the owner is renewing a complete component himself, or if he has repaired it with epoxy filler, he will be left with the problem of finding a suitable paint for finishing

15.15 Rear spoiler screw cover plug

which is compatible with the type of plastic used. At one time the use of a universal paint was not possible owing to the complex range of plastics encountered in body component applications. Standard paints, generally speaking, will not bond to plastic or rubber satisfactorily. However, it is now possible to obtain a plastic body parts finishing kit which consists of a pre-primer treatment, a primer and coloured top coat. Full instructions are normally supplied with a kit, but basically the method of use is to first apply the pre-primer to the component concerned and allow it to dry for up to 30 minutes. Then the primer is applied and left to dry for about an hour before finally applying the special coloured top coat. The result is a correctly coloured component where the paint will flex with the plastic or rubber, a property that standard paint does not normally possess.

Front spoiler (MG Turbo models) – removal and refitting

3 Remove the front bumper end caps, and remove the end fastenings from the spoiler. On 1985-on models completely remove the front bumper.

4 Remove the screws which secure the top and bottom of the spoiler. Remove the spoiler and (if wished) take off the air ducts.

5 Refitting is a reversal of the removal procedure. Fit all fastenings loosely at first and check the spoiler alignment before tightening.

Wheel arch finishers (MG Turbo models) – removal and refitting

6 Raise and support the vehicle at the quarter being worked on. Remove the wheel if wished to improve access.

Front finisher

7 Remove the front bumper end cap. On 1985-on models completely remove the front bumper.

8 Remove the screws which secure the front and rear of the finisher.

9 Remove the securing nuts from inside the wheel arch.

10 The finisher can now be removed.

11 Refitting is a reversal of the removal procedure. Fit the fastenings finger-tight at first. Check the fit of the finisher before finally tightening.

Rear finisher

12 Drill out the rivets which secure the finisher to the wheel arch (where applicable).

13 Follow paragraphs 8 to 10 and remove the finisher.

14 Refit the finisher using the nuts and screws. When alignment is correct, either drill new rivet holes or use the existing ones to fit new pop-rivets.

Rear spoiler (MG and 1985-on models) – removal and refitting

15 Prise out the screw cover plugs from the top edge of the spoiler (photo).

16 Disconnect the tailgate support struts from the tailgate.

17 From inside the tailgate, remove the two long securing screws (one below the strut attachment, the other in the same position on the opposite side) and the two securing nuts (one above the strut attachment, and the corresponding position opposite).

18 From outside the tailgate, remove the four securing screws from the top edge of the spoiler.

19 Disconnect the washer tube from the washer jet.

20 Remove the spoiler from the tailgate. Some effort may be needed to free it from the sealer.

21 Remove the washer jet and the sealing washers.

22 Refitting is a reversal of the removal procedure. Make sure that the spoiler is correctly aligned before tightening the screws and nuts.

23 Note that replacement tailgates are not supplied ready drilled to accept a spoiler. Consult your BL dealer concerning the components and tools needed to prepare the tailgate for spoiler fitting.

Opening rear quarterlight – removal and refitting

24 Protect the vehicle's paintwork during the following operations by covering the area between the quarterlight hinges with masking tape.

25 Open the quarterlight. Have an assistant support the window whilst you remove the screws which secure the catch to the rear pillar.

26 Carefully open the quarterlight until the hinge tabs can be withdrawn from their grommets in the middle pillar.

27 Detach the catch from the clip by drilling out the hollow rivet.

28 Remove the frame and rubber surround by drilling out the rivet which secures the frame to the channel.

29 Refitting is a reversal of the removal procedure. Use new rivets

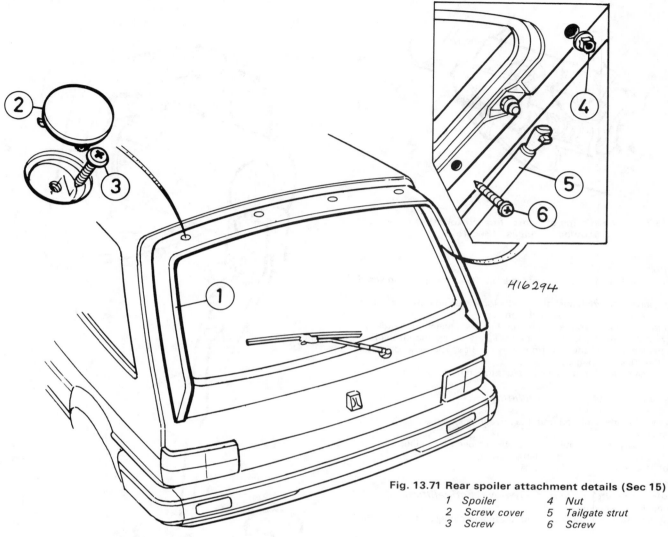

Fig. 13.71 Rear spoiler attachment details (Sec 15)

1	Spoiler	4	Nut
2	Screw cover	5	Tailgate strut
3	Screw	6	Screw

where these had to be removed. In the absence of a riveting tool for use with hollow rivets, it may be possible to use a small nut and bolt instead. Lubricate the hinge tabs with liquid soap or washing-up liquid before inserting them in the grommets.

Increasing front seat rearward adjustment

30 From mid-1981, front seat assemblies which allow increased rearward travel have been fitted.

31 To take advantage of the increased travel, the stops at the rear of the outer runners must be removed.

32 Note that if the front seats are then moved to their rearmost position, they will foul the rear seat if any attempt is made to fold it.

33 Protective plates are available from your BL dealer for preventing damage to the backs of the front seats caused by careless folding forward of the rear seat.

Seat belt lowering kit

34 For people who find the existing seat belt mountings too high for comfortable use of the belt, a lowering kit is available (Fig. 13.72).

35 Follow the fitting sequence shown in the illustration if no instructions are provided with the kit. More spacers may be provided than are actually needed. The original mounting bolt is used to secure the bracket to the body.

Rear bumper fixings (1983 models)

36 Starting with 1983 models, the lower fixing bolt on the rear bumper bracket on each side is no longer fitted.

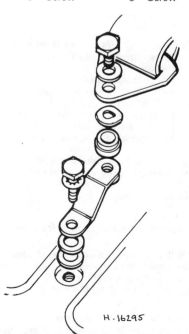

Fig. 13.72 Seat belt top mounting lowering kit (Sec 15)

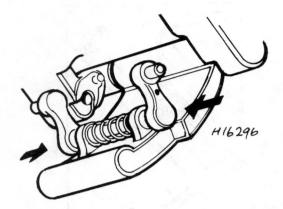

Fig. 13.73 Squeeze arms of sunroof catch together at points arrowed to release (Sec 15)

Sunroof – general
37 A removable panel type sunroof is available as an option on some models.
38 To open the sunroof, push the handle forwards and upwards until it locks. Close by reversing this operation.
39 To remove the sunroof, open it and then disconnect the handle by squeezing its arms together. Unhook the safety spring and lift the roof panel rearwards until the two front lugs are free. The wind deflector will automatically spring upwards.
40 Refit the sunroof in the reverse order to removal.

Tailgate lock – removal and refitting
41 Prise out the trim pad.
42 Unclip the operating rod from the private lock then unbolt the lock from the door.
43 If necessary, the private lock may be removed by pulling out the clip. Note the location of the sealing washer.
44 Refitting is a reversal of removal.

Remote control door mirror – removal and refitting
45 Remove the adjusting knob.
46 Remove the inner cover then unbolt the assembly and remove the seal.
47 Refitting is a reversal of removal.

Door trim pad (5-door models) – removal and refitting
48 Prise out the plastic cap, then remove the interior handle surround screw and withdraw the surround (photo).
49 Prise out the plastic cap, then remove the screw from the window regulator handle and withdraw the handle (photo).
50 Where a door pull is fitted, prise out the end covers and remove the screws (photo). Where an arm rest is fitted remove the screws.
51 On the front door, remove the screws from the door pocket and disconnect the wiring plugs to the speaker and electric window switch, as applicable.
52 With a wide-bladed screwdriver, release the trim pad retaining clips from the door inner panel, starting at the bottom rear corner, and withdraw the pad.
53 Refitting is a reversal of removal.

Front door lock (central locking models) – removal and refitting
54 The procedure is the same as that described in Chapter 12, but it is important to first disconnect the battery negative lead. Also unbolt the lock motor and disconnect the operating rod.
55 Reverse the procedure on refitting the lock.

Rear door lock – removal and refitting
56 The procedure is as given in Chapter 12, except that there is no private lock.

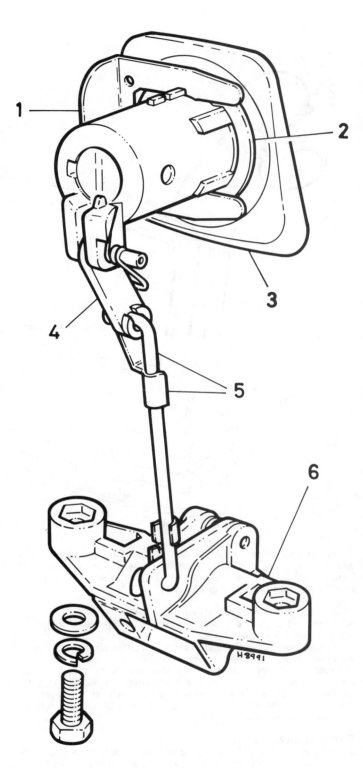

Fig. 13.74 Tailgate lock components (Sec 15)

1 Clip	4 Private lock lever
2 Sealing washer	5 Operating rod and clip
3 Retainer	6 Lock

15.48 Removing the plastic cap from the interior door handle surround

15.49 Removing the plastic cap from the window regulator handle

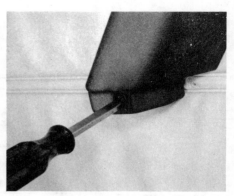

15.50 Removing the front door pull lower screw on 5-door models

Door glass (central locking models) – removal and refitting
57 The procedure is as given in Chapter 12, but the door lock motor must be removed.

Door (1985-on models) – removal and refitting
58 On the front door, remove the glovebox and body side trim, as applicable. Also disconnect the wiring multi-plugs, release the rubber gaiter and pull the wiring through the body.
59 On the rear door, remove the lower trim panel and seat belt reel from the centre post.

60 Using a pencil, mark the position of the hinges on the body.
61 Support the door.
62 On the front door, prise out the plug and remove the lower hinge nuts and bolt. Remove the top hinge bolts, withdraw the door and recover the lower hinge plate.
63 On the rear door, remove the lower hinge nuts and recover the hinge plate. Remove the top hinge bolts, withdraw the door and recover the upper hinge plate.
64 Refitting is a reversal of removal, but check that the door is correctly aligned with the surrounding bodywork before finally tightening the hinge nuts.

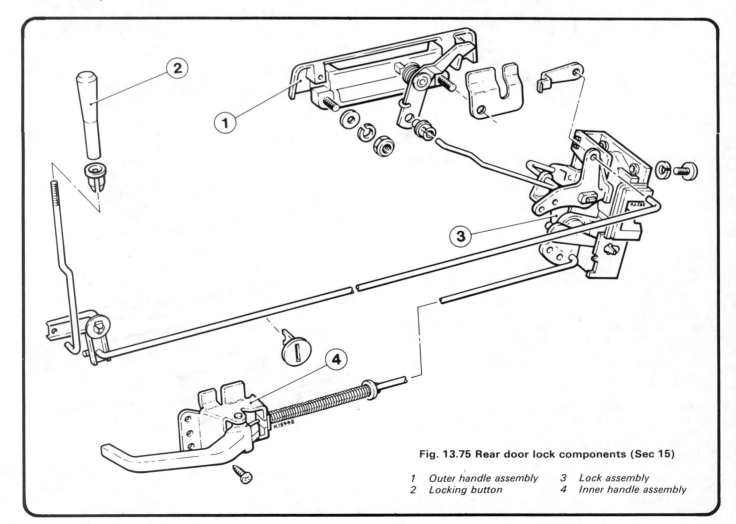

Fig. 13.75 Rear door lock components (Sec 15)

1	Outer handle assembly	3	Lock assembly
2	Locking button	4	Inner handle assembly

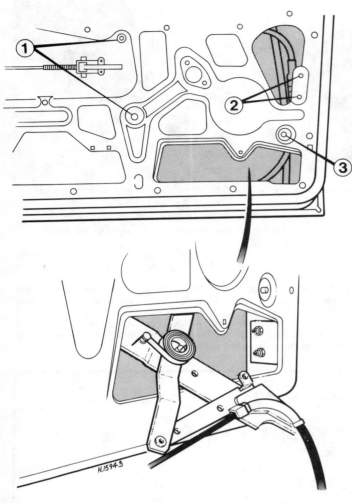

Fig. 13.76 Electric window motor components (Sec 15)

1   *Regulator mounting bolts*
2   *Electric motor mounting bolts*
3   *Window channel bolt*

Central locking door lock motor – removal and refitting
65 Disconnect the battery negative lead.
66 Remove the trim pad and, except for on the tailgate, peel off the polythene sheet.
67 Disconnect the wiring multi-plug(s) to the motor.
68 On the tailgate, remove the mounting bracket screws, unclip the mounting bracket from the private lock and unclip the operating rod from the lock lever. Remove the private lock then remove the mounting bracket and motor, and unbolt the motor.
69 On the front or rear door, unbolt the motor and disconnect the operating rod.
70 Refitting is a reversal of removal.

Electric window motor – removal and refitting
71 Fully close the window then disconnect the battery negative lead.
72 Remove the door trim panel and peel off the polythene sheet.
73 Wedge the window in the closed position.
74 Disconnect the wiring multi-plug to the motor.
75 Unscrew the window regulator bolts.
76 Remove the front window channel bolt, unclip the top of the channel, and withdraw it from the door.
77 Unbolt the motor and withdraw it from the door together with the regulator.

78 Refitting is a reversal of removal, but the window channel should be positioned so that the window movement is smooth.

Facia (1985-on models) – removal and refitting
79 Remove the instrument panel, as described in Section 13.
80 Remove the steering column, as described in Section 14.
81 Disconnect the choke cable from the carburettor and pull it through the bulkhead.
82 Disconnect the heater control rods from the flap levers.
83 Prise out the plastic covers and remove the upper screws. Also remove the screws securing the facia to the heater.
84 Remove the facia side mounting screws.
85 Withdraw the facia rearwards, disconnect the multi-plugs and aerial, and remove the facia from the car.
86 Refitting is a reversal of removal.

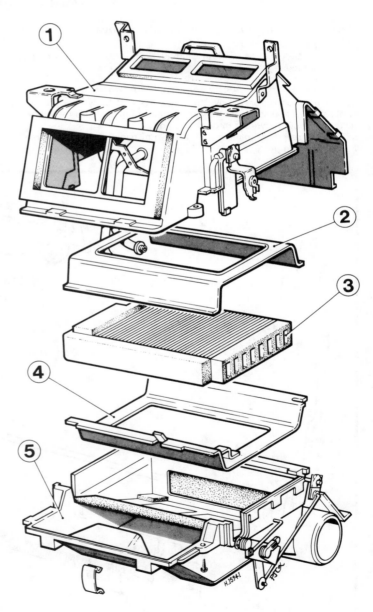

Fig. 13.77 Heater components for 1985-on models (Sec 15)

1 *Top case half*	4 *Bottom radiator retaining*
2 *Top radiator retaining plate*	*plate*
3 *Radiator*	5 *Bottom case half*

*Heater and heater radiator (1985-on models) – removal
and refitting*
87 Drain the cooling system (Chapter 2) and remove the air cleaner
(Chapter 3).
88 Identify the heater hoses on the engine side of the bulkhead, then
disconnect them from the heater.
89 Remove the facia, as described in paragraphs 79 to 85.
90 Remove the demister and vent ducts for the side window, and the
face level and windscreen vents.
91 Unscrew the nut securing the air inlet duct to the heater motor
mounting plate.
92 Unscrew the mounting bolts and withdraw the heater from the car.
93 Unbolt the air inlet duct and blanking plate and remove them by
breaking the seal.
94 Remove the radiator pipe seal and drill out the rivets from the pipe
flange.
95 Disconnect the air temperature control rod from the lever.
96 Remove the clips and screws, and lift off the top case half.
97 Remove the screws and lift off the top radiator retaining plate,
followed by the radiator, seals and bottom plate.
98 Refitting is a reversal of removal, but it will be necessary to use a
riveting tool to secure the pipe flange. Use sealing compound to seal
the inlet duct and blanking plate to the case halves. If necessary adjust
the controls, as described in paragraphs 99 to 103. Fill the cooling
system with reference to Chapter 2.

Heater (1985-on models) – adjustment
Note: *On some models the heater has preset cables which cannot be
adjusted.*
99 Remove the fusebox cover.
100 Adjustment of the air distribution and the air temperature controls
is identical. However, when adjusting the latter, the air distribution
control should be moved fully down.
101 Move the relevant control fully upwards and release the adjuster
clip from the control rod.
102 Turn the flap lever fully clockwise to close the flap then refit the
adjuster clip to the control rod.
103 Refit the fusebox cover.

*Front seat release lever cable (3-door models) – removal
and refitting*
104 Pull the plastic clip from the bottom of the front seat backrest. If
the cables on each side have been broken, reach through the rear of the
seat and release the pawls from each side so that the seat back may be
folded forward.
105 On 1985-on models, prise out the plug and unbolt the protection
plate from the lever.
106 Carefully roll the seat covering up the backrest sufficiently to
disconnect the cable from the lever and pawls.
107 Refitting is a reversal of removal.

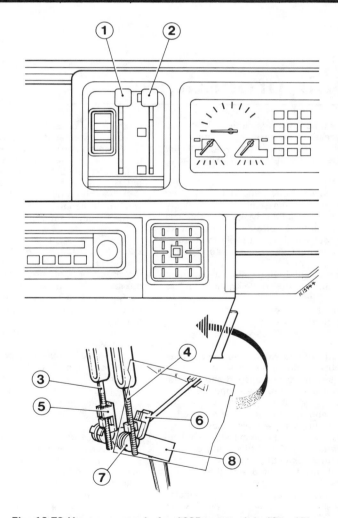

Fig. 13.78 Heater controls for 1985-on models (Sec 15)

1 Air temperature control	4 Air distribution control rod	7 Air temperature flap lever
2 Air distribution control	5 Adjuster clip (locked)	8 Air distribution flap lever
3 Air temperature control rod	6 Adjuster clip (unlocked)	

General repair procedures

Whenever servicing, repair or overhaul work is carried out on the car or its components, it is necessary to observe the following procedures and instructions. This will assist in carrying out the operation efficiently and to a professional standard of workmanship.

Joint mating faces and gaskets

Where a gasket is used between the mating faces of two components, ensure that it is renewed on reassembly, and fit it dry unless otherwise stated in the repair procedure. Make sure that the mating faces are clean and dry with all traces of old gasket removed. When cleaning a joint face, use a tool which is not likely to score or damage the face, and remove any burrs or nicks with an oilstone or fine file.

Make sure that tapped holes are cleaned with a pipe cleaner, and keep them free of jointing compound if this is being used unless specifically instructed otherwise.

Ensure that all orifices, channels or pipes are clear and blow through them, preferably using compressed air.

Oil seals

Whenever an oil seal is removed from its working location, either individually or as part of an assembly, it should be renewed.

The very fine sealing lip of the seal is easily damaged and will not seal if the surface it contacts is not completely clean and free from scratches, nicks or grooves. If the original sealing surface of the component cannot be restored, the component should be renewed.

Protect the lips of the seal from any surface which may damage them in the course of fitting. Use tape or a conical sleeve where possible. Lubricate the seal lips with oil before fitting and, on dual lipped seals, fill the space between the lips with grease.

Unless otherwise stated, oil seals must be fitted with their sealing lips toward the lubricant to be sealed.

Use a tubular drift or block of wood of the appropriate size to install the seal and, if the seal housing is shouldered, drive the seal down to the shoulder. If the seal housing is unshouldered, the seal should be fitted with its face flush with the housing top face.

Screw threads and fastenings

Always ensure that a blind tapped hole is completely free from oil, grease, water or other fluid before installing the bolt or stud. Failure to do this could cause the housing to crack due to the hydraulic action of the bolt or stud as it is screwed in.

When tightening a castellated nut to accept a split pin, tighten the nut to the specified torque, where applicable, and then tighten further to the next split pin hole. Never slacken the nut to align a split pin hole unless stated in the repair procedure.

When checking or retightening a nut or bolt to a specified torque setting, slacken the nut or bolt by a quarter of a turn, and then retighten to the specified setting.

Locknuts, locktabs and washers

Any fastening which will rotate against a component or housing in the course of tightening should always have a washer between it and the relevant component or housing.

Spring or split washers should always be renewed when they are used to lock a critical component such as a big-end bearing retaining nut or bolt.

Locktabs which are folded over to retain a nut or bolt should always be renewed.

Self-locking nuts can be reused in non-critical areas, providing resistance can be felt when the locking portion passes over the bolt or stud thread.

Split pins must always be replaced with new ones of the correct size for the hole.

Special tools

Some repair procedures in this manual entail the use of special tools such as a press, two or three-legged pullers, spring compressors etc. Wherever possible, suitable readily available alternatives to the manufacturer's special tools are described, and are shown in use. In some instances, where no alternative is possible, it has been necessary to resort to the use of a manufacturer's tool and this has been done for reasons of safety as well as the efficient completion of the repair operation. Unless you are highly skilled and have a thorough understanding of the procedure described, never attempt to bypass the use of any special tool when the procedure described specifies its use. Not only is there a very great risk of personal injury, but expensive damage could be caused to the components involved.

Conversion factors

Length (distance)

	X		=		X		=	
Inches (in)	X	25.4	=	Millimetres (mm)	X	0.0394	=	Inches (in)
Feet (ft)	X	0.305	=	Metres (m)	X	3.281	=	Feet (ft)
Miles	X	1.609	=	Kilometres (km)	X	0.621	=	Miles

Volume (capacity)

	X		=		X		=	
Cubic inches (cu in; in³)	X	16.387	=	Cubic centimetres (cc; cm³)	X	0.061	=	Cubic inches (cu in; in³)
Imperial pints (Imp pt)	X	0.568	=	Litres (l)	X	1.76	=	Imperial pints (Imp pt)
Imperial quarts (Imp qt)	X	1.137	=	Litres (l)	X	0.88	=	Imperial quarts (Imp qt)
Imperial quarts (Imp qt)	X	1.201	=	US quarts (US qt)	X	0.833	=	Imperial quarts (Imp qt)
US quarts (US qt)	X	0.946	=	Litres (l)	X	1.057	=	US quarts (US qt)
Imperial gallons (Imp gal)	X	4.546	=	Litres (l)	X	0.22	=	Imperial gallons (Imp gal)
Imperial gallons (Imp gal)	X	1.201	=	US gallons (US gal)	X	0.833	=	Imperial gallons (Imp gal)
US gallons (US gal)	X	3.785	=	Litres (l)	X	0.264	=	US gallons (US gal)

Mass (weight)

	X		=		X		=	
Ounces (oz)	X	28.35	=	Grams (g)	X	0.035	=	Ounces (oz)
Pounds (lb)	X	0.454	=	Kilograms (kg)	X	2.205	=	Pounds (lb)

Force

	X		=		X		=	
Ounces-force (ozf; oz)	X	0.278	=	Newtons (N)	X	3.6	=	Ounces-force (ozf; oz)
Pounds-force (lbf; lb)	X	4.448	=	Newtons (N)	X	0.225	=	Pounds-force (lbf; lb)
Newtons (N)	X	0.1	=	Kilograms-force (kgf; kg)	X	9.81	=	Newtons (N)

Pressure

	X		=		X		=	
Pounds-force per square inch (psi; lbf/in²; lb/in²)	X	0.070	=	Kilograms-force per square centimetre (kgf/cm²; kg/cm²)	X	14.223	=	Pounds-force per square inch (psi; lbf/in²; lb/in²)
Pounds-force per square inch (psi; lbf/in²; lb/in²)	X	0.068	=	Atmospheres (atm)	X	14.696	=	Pounds-force per square inch (psi; lbf/in²; lb/in²)
Pounds-force per square inch (psi; lbf/in²; lb/in²)	X	0.069	=	Bars	X	14.5	=	Pounds-force per square inch (psi; lbf/in²; lb/in²)
Pounds-force per square inch (psi; lbf/in²; lb/in²)	X	6.895	=	Kilopascals (kPa)	X	0.145	=	Pounds-force per square inch (psi; lbf/in²; lb/in²)
Kilopascals (kPa)	X	0.01	=	Kilograms-force per square centimetre (kgf/cm²; kg/cm²)	X	98.1	=	Kilopascals (kPa)
Millibar (mbar)	X	100	=	Pascals (Pa)	X	0.01	=	Millibar (mbar)
Millibar (mbar)	X	0.0145	=	Pounds-force per square inch (psi; lbf/in²; lb/in²)	X	68.947	=	Millibar (mbar)
Millibar (mbar)	X	0.75	=	Millimetres of mercury (mmHg)	X	1.333	=	Millibar (mbar)
Millibar (mbar)	X	1.40	=	Inches of water (inH₂O)	X	0.714	=	Millibar (mbar)
Millimetres of mercury (mmHg)	X	1.868	=	Inches of water (inH₂O)	X	0.535	=	Millimetres of mercury (mmHg)
Inches of water (inH₂O)	X	27.68	=	Pounds-force per square inch (psi, lbf/in², lb/in²)	X	0.036	=	Inches of water (inH₂O)

Torque (moment of force)

	X		=		X		=	
Pounds-force inches (lbf in; lb in)	X	1.152	=	Kilograms-force centimetre (kgf cm; kg cm)	X	0.868	=	Pounds-force inches (lbf in; lb in)
Pounds-force inches (lbf in; lb in)	X	0.113	=	Newton metres (Nm)	X	8.85	=	Pounds-force inches (lbf in; lb in)
Pounds-force inches (lbf in; lb in)	X	0.083	=	Pounds-force feet (lbf ft; lb ft)	X	12	=	Pounds-force inches (lbf in; lb in)
Pounds-force feet (lbf ft; lb ft)	X	0.138	=	Kilograms-force metres (kgf m; kg m)	X	7.233	=	Pounds-force feet (lbf ft; lb ft)
Pounds-force feet (lbf ft; lb ft)	X	1.356	=	Newton metres (Nm)	X	0.738	=	Pounds-force feet (lbf ft; lb ft)
Newton metres (Nm)	X	0.102	=	Kilograms-force metres (kgf m; kg m)	X	9.804	=	Newton metres (Nm)

Power

	X		=		X		=	
Horsepower (hp)	X	745.7	=	Watts (W)	X	0.0013	=	Horsepower (hp)

Velocity (speed)

	X		=		X		=	
Miles per hour (miles/hr; mph)	X	1.609	=	Kilometres per hour (km/hr; kph)	X	0.621	=	Miles per hour (miles/hr; mph)

Fuel consumption*

	X		=		X		=	
Miles per gallon, Imperial (mpg)	X	0.354	=	Kilometres per litre (km/l)	X	2.825	=	Miles per gallon, Imperial (mpg)
Miles per gallon, US (mpg)	X	0.425	=	Kilometres per litre (km/l)	X	2.352	=	Miles per gallon, US (mpg)

Temperature

Degrees Fahrenheit = (°C x 1.8) + 32

Degrees Celsius (Degrees Centigrade; °C) = (°F - 32) x 0.56

*It is common practice to convert from miles per gallon (mpg) to litres/100 kilometres (l/100km), where mpg (Imperial) x l/100 km = 282 and mpg (US) x l/100 km = 235

Index

A

About this manual – 2
Accelerator cable
    removal and refitting – 53
Accelerator pedal
    removal and refitting – 55
Air cleaner
    description and testing – 193
    removal and refitting – 50, 193
Alternator
    brushes – 126, 127
    fault finding and testing – 126
    maintenance and special precautions – 125
    removal and refitting – 125
    specifications – 123, 182
Ancillary components (engine)
    refitting – 41
    removal – 31
Antifreeze mixture – 44
Anti-roll bar
    knock – 241
    rear (MG Turbo) – 241
    removal and refitting – 149
Anti-run-on valve (MG 1300)
    removal and refitting – 194
Automatic transmission
    description – 96
    fault diagnosis – 100
    gear selection problems – 212
    loss of drive when cold – 212
    ratios – 79
    removal and refitting – 96
    specifications – 79, 182
    torque wrench settings – 79
Auxiliary circuits relay and circuit diode – 133

B

Balljoints (front suspension) – 151
Battery
    charging – 125
    electrolyte replenishment – 125
    maintenance – 124
    removal and refitting – 124
    type and capacity – 123
Bleeding the brakes – 118, 217
Bleeding the clutch – 73

Bodywork and fittings – 158 *et seq*, 246
Bodywork and fittings
    damage repair – 158 to 160
    description – 158
    maintenance – 158, 160, 246
    repair sequence (colour chart) – 166, 167
Bonnet
    removal, refitting and adjustment – 160
Bonnet lock
    adjustment – 162
Bonnet release cable
    removal and refitting – 162
Bore and stroke
    998 cc engine – 22
    1275 cc engine – 23
Brake judder – 216
Braking system – 111 *et seq*, 214
Braking system
    anti-squeal paste – 214
    bleeding – 118
    brake lines and hoses – 118
    description – 111
    fault diagnosis – 122
    hydraulic system – 118
    routine maintenance – 111
    specifications – 111, 182
    stone trapping – 214
    torque wrench settings – 111
Brake disc
    examination, removal and refitting – 115
    orientation – 214
    renewal – 214
Brake drum
    inspection and renovation – 116
Brake pedal
    removal and refitting – 120
Brake shoe linings
    inspection – 214
Brake squeal – 214
    rear fixings – 247
    removal and refitting – 165
Buying spare parts – 8

C

Camshaft
    refitting – 38
    removal – 33

Camshaft and tappets
  examination and renovation – 36
Camshaft/distributor driveshaft
  refitting – 191
Capacities – 7
Carburettor
  description – 55
  dismantling, overhaul and reassembly – 56, 194
  idle and fast idle adjustment – 55
  removal and refitting – 55
  specifications – 50, 177 to 180
  throttle damper adjustment – 55
Carburettor (MG Turbo)
  description and maintenance – 199
  removal and refitting – 199
Central locking motor – 250
Choke control cable
  removal and refitting – 53, 194
Cigar lighter
  removal and refitting – 132
Clock
  removal and refitting – 221, 222
Clutch – 71 *et seq*, 207
Clutch
  adjustment and maintenance – 71
  description – 71
  fault diagnosis – 77
  hydraulic system – 73
  inspection – 75
  refitting – 75
  release bearing – 77
  removal – 75, 207
  specifications – 71, 181
  torque wrench settings – 71, 182
  Verto clutch – 209
Clutch hydraulic damper
  description, removal and refitting – 207
Clutch judder
  causes and remedies – 209
Clutch linkage
  lubrication – 209
Clutch pedal
  removal and refitting – 73
Clutch release bearing
  removal and refitting – 77
Clutch (Verto)
  description – 209
  release bearing
    removal and refitting – 211
  removal, overhaul and refitting – 209
  throw-out stop adjustment – 211
Coil
  description and testing – 69
Combination switches
  removal and refitting – 131, 222
Compression ratios
  998 cc engines – 22, 175
  1275 cc engines – 23, 176
Condenser
  testing, removal and refitting – 65
Constant velocity joints
  removal and refitting
    inner – 109
    outer (and driveshaft) – 106
Contact breaker points
  checking and adjustment – 63
  renewal – 63
Conversion factors – 253
Cooling fan assembly
  removal, overhaul and refitting – 46, 192
Cooling fan thermostatic switch
  testing, removal and refitting – 48
Cooling system – 43 *et seq*, 191
Cooling system
  capacity – 43
  description – 43

  draining – 43
  fault diagnosis – 49
  filling – 44
  flushing – 43
  modifications – 192
  specifications – 43, 177
  torque wrench settings – 43, 177
Courtesy light switch
  removal and refitting – 132
Crankcase ventilation – 35, 189
Crankcase and main bearings
  examination and renovation – 35
  refitting – 37
  removal – 36
Crankshaft pulley bolt
  removal and refitting – 188
Cylinder block and crankcase
  examination and renovation – 35
Cylinder head
  decarbonising, valve grinding and renovation – 36
  dismantling – 31
  reassembly and refitting – 40
  removal – 31
Cylinder head (MG Turbo)
  removal and refitting – 188

D

Damage repair (body)
  major – 160
  minor – 158
  work sequence (colour chart) – 166, 167
Differential unit
  removal, overhaul and refitting – 101
  thrust block – 214
Dim/dip headlamps – 221
Dimensions – 7
Direction indicator and hazard flasher system – 131
Disc (brake)
  renewal – 214
  ventilated – 214
  wear – 214
Disc caliper
  removal, overhaul and refitting – 114
Disc pads
  inspection and renewal – 112
Distributor
  dismantling, overhaul and reassembly – 66
  removal and refitting – 65
Door
  removal and refitting – 163, 249
Door glass
  removal and refitting – 164, 249
Door lock
  removal, refitting and adjustment – 163, 248
Door lock motor (central locking)
  removal and refitting – 250
Door private lock
  removal and refitting – 164
Door rattles
  tracing and rectification – 160
Door trim pad
  removal and refitting – 163, 248
Drivebelt
  renewal and adjustment – 48
Driveshafts – 106 *et seq*, 214
Driveshafts
  description – 106
  driveshaft knock – 214
  fault diagnosis – 110
  inner CV joint – 109
  lubrication of CV joints – 214
  outer CV joint and driveshaft – 106
  specifications – 106, 182
  torque wrench settings – 106, 182

E

Electric window motor
  removal and refitting – 250
Electric window switch and relay
  removal and refitting – 222
Electrical system – 123 *et seq*, 217
Electrical system
  auxiliary circuits – 133
  description – 124
  fault diagnosis – 140
  specifications – 123, 182
  torque wrench settings – 124
Electronic ignition amplifier – 205, 207
Electronic ignition distributor
  dismantling and reassembly – 204, 205
  removal and refitting – 207
Electronic ignition system
  description – 202
  fault diagnosis – 207
  maintenance – 202
  static timing – 202
  test procedure – 201
Engine – 22 *et seq*, 187
Engine
  adjustment after major overhaul – 41
  ancillary components – 31
  decarbonising – 36
  description – 25
  dismantling – 31
  examination and renovation – 35
  fault diagnosis – 42
  operations possible with engine/gearbox in car – 25
  operations requiring engine/gearbox removal – 25
  reassembly – 37
  refitting to gearbox – 41
  removal method – 25
  separation from gearbox – 31
  specifications – 22 to 24, 175 to 177
  torque wrench settings – 24, 177
  valve clearances – 41, 176
  valve grinding – 36
Engine/gearbox assembly
  refitting – 41, 187
  removal – 25, 187
Engine mounting
  modifications – 187
Exhaust elbow gasket (MG Turbo)
  removal and refitting – 200
Exhaust system
  checking, removal and refitting – 59
  modifications – 200
Expansion tank
  leakage – 191

F

Facia
  removal and refitting – 165, 250
Fan (cooling) – 46
Fan switch – 48
Fault diagnosis – 18 *et seq*
Fault diagnosis
  braking system – 122
  clutch – 77
  cooling system – 49
  driveshafts – 110
  electrical system – 140
  electronic ignition – 207
  engine – 42
  final drive – 105
  fuel and exhaust systems – 61
  gearbox (manual and automatic) – 110
  ignition system – 69
  suspension and steering – 157

  turbocharger – 201
Final drive – 101 *et seq*, 214
Final drive
  description – 101
  fault diagnosis – 105
  specifications – 101, 182
  torque wrench settings – 101
Final drive pinion (manual gearbox)
  removal and refitting – 104
Firing order – 22
First motion shaft
  servicing – 86
Flywheel housing oil seal
  renewal – 95
Flywheel/torque converter
  examination and renovation – 36
Front anti-roll bar knock
  rectification – 241
Front hub assembly
  removal, overhaul and refitting – 11
Front seat release cable
  removal and refitting – 251
Front shock absorber
  removal and refitting – 149
Front shock absorber bush – 241
Front suspension arms
  removal, overhaul and refitting – 150
Front suspension balljoints
  renewal – 151
Front suspension spacer – 241
Front wing
  removal and refitting – 160
Fuel and exhaust systems – 50 *et seq*, 193
Fuel and exhaust systems
  description – 50
  fault diagnosis – 61, 201
  specifications – 50, 177
  torque wrench settings – 50, 180
Fuel filter (MG Turbo)
  renewal – 193
Fuel gauge sender unit
  removal and refitting – 51
Fuel pump
  testing, removal and refitting – 51, 194
Fuel pump knock
  rectification – 194
Fuel tank
  capacity – 50
  removal, servicing and refitting – 51, 194
Fuses
  general – 131, 218
  ratings – 123

G

Gearbox (manual)
  dismantling into major assemblies – 81 to 86
  reassembly – 91
  removal and refitting – 79
  specifications – 78, 182
Gearchange remote control
  removal, overhaul and refitting – 93
Gear ratios
  automatic – 79
  manual – 78, 182
General repair procedures – 252

H

Handbrake
  adjustment – 120, 217
Handbrake cable
  removal and refitting – 120
Handbrake lever and switch
  removal and refitting – 120

Headlamps
    alignment – 134
    dim-dip type – 221
Headlamps and bulbs
    removal and refitting – 133
Heater
    adjustment – 169, 251
Heater and heater radiator
    removal and refitting – 168, 251
Heater control illumination bulb
    removal and refitting – 223
Heater motor
    removal and refitting – 169
Horn
    removal and refitting – 138
HT leads – 69
Hub assembly
    front – 151
    rear – 153
Hydragas units
    leaks – 241
    removal and refitting
        front – 149
        rear – 152
    testing – 146
Hydragas struts (rear) – 241
Hydraulic brake lines and hoses
    inspection, removal and refitting – 118
Hydraulic system (brakes)
    bleeding – 118, 217
Hydraulic system (clutch)
    bleeding – 73

I

Idle speed
    adjustment – 50, 177 to 180, 199
    and idler gear noise – 194
Ignition switch/steering column lock
    removal and refitting – 131
Ignition system – 62 *et seq*, 202
Ignition system
    description – 62
    fault diagnosis – 69, 201
    specifications – 62, 180
    torque wrench settings – 62
Ignition warning light bulb – 218
Inertia/pressure regulating valve (vans)
    description, removal and refitting – 217
Inlet and exhaust manifolds
    description, removal and refitting – 59, 199
Inlet valve oil seals (998 cc) – 188
Instrument panel (pre-1985 MG Turbo)
    dismantling – 220
Instrument panel and instruments
    removal and refitting – 132, 220
Instrument panel printed circuit and voltage stabiliser
    removal and refitting – 133
Instrument panel surround switch
    removal and refitting – 222

J

Jacking and towing – 11
Joint mating faces and gaskets – 252

K

Kickdown linkage (automatic transmission)
    adjustment – 99

L

Laygear, reverse idler gear and shafts
    servicing – 86

Lamp bulbs – 123, 135, 218, 223
Lighting switch
    removal and refitting – 132
Locknuts, locktabs and washers – 252
Lubricants and fluids (recommended) – 13
Lubrication chart – 13

M

Main bearing shells (plain) – 188
Maintenance
    bodywork and underframe – 158, 246
    hinges and locks – 160
    routine – 15
    schedules – 15
    upholstery and carpets – 158
Manual gearbox and automatic transmission – 78 *et seq*, 212
Manual gearbox
    description – 79
    removal and refitting – 79
    specifications – 78, 182
Manifolds *see* **Inlet and exhaust manifolds**
Master cylinder (brakes)
    modification – 217
    removal, overhaul and refitting – 116
Master cylinder (clutch)
    removal, overhaul and refitting – 71
Mirrors
    remote control – 248

O

Oil coolers – 189, 190
Oil filter
    refitting – 38
    removal – 33
Oil pump
    examination and renovation – 35
    refitting – 38
    removal – 33
Oil seals – 252

P

Pedal (footbrake) – 120
Pistons and connecting rods
    examination and renovation – 36
    modifications (998 cc) – 189
    refitting – 38
    removal – 33
Plastic components – 246
Pressure compensating valve (brakes)
    removal, overhaul and refitting – 118
Pressure reducing valve (braking system)
    description, removal and refitting – 217

Q

Quarterlight glass
    removal and refitting – 162

R

Radiator
    bottom hose fitting – 191
    removal and refitting (1985 models on) – 192
    removal, inspection, cleaning and refitting – 45
Radio
    removal and refitting – 140
Radio/cassette player (electronic)
    removal and refitting – 226

Radio equipment (mobile)
  aerials
    selection and fitting – 226
  interference – 227
  loudspeakers – 227
  suppression methods – 228
  VHF/FM broadcasts – 228
Radius arm (rear) – 153
Rear anti-roll bar (MG Turbo)
  removal and refitting – 241
Rear brake adjuster
  removal and refitting – 116
Rear brake backplate
  removal and refitting – 116
Rear brakes
  adjustment – 112
Rear brake shoes
  inspection and renewal – 112, 214
  squeal – 214
Rear bumper fixings – 247
Rear hub assembly
  removal, overhaul and refitting – 153
Rear hydragas struts – 241
Rear suspension radius arm
  removal, overhaul and refitting – 153
Rear wheel cylinder
  removal, overhaul and refitting – 115
Remote control door mirror
  removal and refitting – 248
Reverse gear disengagement
  rectification – 212
Reversing light switch (automatic transmission)
  removal, refitting and adjustment – 100
Routine maintenance – 15 *et seq*, 111, 146

S

Safety first! – 14
Screw threads and fastenings – 252
Seat belt lowering kit – 247
Seats
  removal and refitting – 164
Seats (front)
  increasing rearward adjustment – 247
  release cable – 251
Selector components and gearbox housings – 91, 98, 212
Selector shaft oil seal
  general – 212
  renewal – 95
Shock absorber (front) – 149
Slave cylinder (clutch)
  removal, overhaul and refitting – 72
Spacer (suspension) – 241
Spanner jaw gap comparison table – 10
Spare parts buying – 8
Spares and toolkit – 19
Spark plugs
  and HT leads – 69
  condition (colour chart) – 67
  specifications – 62, 180, 181
Speedometer cable
  removal and refitting – 132, 221
Speedometer drivegear
  removal and refitting – 214
Speedometer pinion and drivegear (automatic transmission)
  removal and refitting – 100
Spoilers
  removal and refitting – 246
Starter inhibitor switch
  removal, refitting and adjustment – 100
Starter motor
  overhaul
    inertia type – 128
    pre-engaged type – 130
  removal and refitting – 128

  testing in car – 128
Starter relay – 218
Starter solenoid (inertia starters) – 218
Steering column
  1986-on models – 244
  removal, overhaul and refitting – 154, 242
Steering column lock/ignition switch
  removal and refitting – 154
Steering rack and pinion
  removal, overhaul and refitting – 156, 243, 244
Steering rack gaiter
  renewal – 154
Steering wheel
  removal and refitting – 154
Stone trapping (disc brakes)
  prevention – 214
Subframes
  removal and refitting – 170
Sunroof – 248
Supplement: revisions/information on later models – 174 *et seq*
  introduction – 175
  specifications – 175 to 183
Suspension and steering – 145 *et seq*, 241
Suspension and steering
  description – 146
  fault diagnosis – 157
  modifications – 241
  routine maintenance – 146
  specifications – 145, 183
  torque wrench settings – 146
Suspension arms (front) – 150
Switch panel switches
  removal and refitting – 132

T

Tailgate
  removal and refitting – 160
Tailgate glass
  removal and refitting – 162
Tailgate lock
  removal and refitting – 248
Tailgate support strut
  removal and refitting – 161
Tailgate wiper motor and gearbox
  removal, overhaul and refitting – 138
Tappets (998 cc engine)
  refitting – 39
  removal – 33
Temperature gauge transmitter
  removal and refitting – 49
Thermostat
  fitting – 192
  removal, testing and refitting – 45
Third motion shaft
  servicing – 87
Third motion shaft bearing – 212
Throttle damper selection – 194
Tie-rod end balljoint
  removal and refitting – 154
Timing cover
  removal and refitting (engine in car) – 188
Timing cover, chain and gears
  examination and renovation – 36
  refitting – 39
  removal – 33
Timing (ignition)
  adjustment – 65
  electronic – 202
  marks – 207
Tool kits
  maintenance and minor repair – 9
  repair and overhaul – 9
Tools
  buying – 10

care and maintenance – 10
special – 10, 252
Tools and working facilities – 9
Torque converter and oil seal
removal and refitting – 97
Torque converter housing and transfer gears
removal, servicing and refitting – 97
Towing – 11
Transfer gears
servicing – 90
Trip computer – 223
Turbocharger and components
cautions – 195
dump valve – 198
description – 195
electronic control unit – 198
fuel pressure regulator – 198
pressure reducing valve – 198
removal, inspection and refitting – 195
wastegate actuator – 198
Tyres
pressure – 146, 183
sizes and types – 145, 183

V

Vacuum servo unit (brakes)
description – 120
removal and refitting – 122
Valve clearances
adjustment – 41
specifications – 23, 176
Valve timing
998 cc engines – 23
1275 cc engines – 24
Vehicle identification numbers – 8

Voltage stabiliser – 133

W

Washer (headlamp) system – 223
Washer (screen) pumps (MG Turbo)
removal and refitting – 223
Washer (screen) tube (MG Turbo)
removal and refitting – 223
Water in brake drums
prevention – 216
Water pump
removal and refitting – 46
Weights – 7
Wheel alignment
angles – 145, 183
checking and adjusting – 156
Wheel arch finishers
removal and refitting – 246
Wheels and tyres
general – 246
types and sizes – 145, 183
Window regulator
removal and refitting – 164
Windscreen glass
removal and refitting – 161
Windscreen and tailgate window washers – 222
Windscreen wiper linkage
removal, overhaul and refitting – 138
Windscreen wiper motor
removal and refitting – 138
Wiper blades
renewal – 136
Wiring diagrams – 141 to 144, 228 to 40
Working facilities – 9

Printed by
J H Haynes & Co Ltd
Sparkford Nr Yeovil
Somerset BA22 7JJ England